GRIEF AND GENDER: 700–1700

GRIEF AND GENDER: 700–1700
EDITED BY JENNIFER C. VAUGHT

with Lynne Dickson Bruckner

GRIEF AND GENDER

First published 2003 by
PALGRAVE MACMILLAN™
175 Fifth Avenue, New York, N.Y. 10010 and
Houndmills, Basingstoke, Hampshire, England RG21 6XS.
Companies and representatives throughout the world.

PALGRAVE MACMILLAN is the global academic imprint of the Palgrave Macmillan division of St. Martin's Press, LLC and of Palgrave Macmillan Ltd. Macmillan® is a registered trademark in the United States, United Kingdom and other countries. Palgrave is a registered trademark in the European Union and other countries.

ISBN 0-312-29382-8 hardback 0-312-29381-x paperback

Library of Congress Cataloging-in-Publication Data
Grief and gender, 700–1700 / edited by Jennifer C. Vaught with Lynne
    Dickson Bruckner.
        p. cm.
    Includes bibliographical references and index.
    ISBN 0-312-29382-8 and 0-312-29381-X
1. Literature, Medieval–History and criticism. 2. Grief in literature. 3. Sex role in literature. I. Vaught, Jennifer C. II. Bruckner, Lynne Dickson. III. Title.

PN682.G74G75 2003
809'.93353–dc21   2003051704

A catalogue record for this book is available from the British Library.

Design by Kolam Information Services Pvt. Ltd, Pondicherry, India

First edition: October 2003
10 9 8 7 6 5 4 3 2 1

Printed in the United States of America

CONTENTS

ACKNOWLEDGEMENTS

The idea for this project developed out of the Special Session entitled "Men Who Weep and Wail: Innovative Constructions of Masculinity in the Middle Ages and Renaissance" that I organized for the International Congress on Medieval Studies in Kalamazoo, Michigan, in 1999. I am grateful to the audience who listened to this panel and confirmed the need for a volume on grief and gender from 700 to 1700. I would also like to thank the audiences who heard earlier versions of some of the essays included in this collection in a Special Session entitled "Grief and Gender in Early Modern England" that I chaired with Lynne Dickson Bruckner at the meeting of the Modern Language Association in Washington, D.C., in 2000, and at a Special Session entitled "Loss and Lamentation: The Recovery of Psyches and Texts" presented at the meeting of the Renaissance Society of America in Tempe, Arizona, in 2002. I am indebted to Lynne Dickson Bruckner at Chatham College for contributing to the original proposal for this project. I wish to thank Darrell Bourque, author of the dedicatory poem "Postcard from China" and my department chair at the University of Louisiana at Lafayette through the Spring of 2003, and A. David Barry, Dean of the College of Liberal Arts at the University of Louisiana, for their support of this volume. I am grateful to Lana Henry for assisting with the Index. Most of all, I am indebted to the contributors to this volume for their excellent work and particularly Judith Anderson, whose initial suggestions about whom to invite to contribute were invaluable.

I have dedicated this book to my father-in-law, William J. Emblom, a philosophy professor at Southern Illinois University at Edwardsville from 1966 to 1987. His death on September 10, 2001, the evening before the September 11 terrorist attack upon the World Trade Center in New York City, gave personal meaning to the themes addressed in this volume such as the relation of grief to creative activity; consolation through *memoria*; and the importance of family, friends, and a sense of community in the event of loss. The introduction for this volume was written with Bill Emblom very much in mind. Finally, I wish to thank my parents, Carl and Jane Vaught, for their love and encouragement since before I can remember, and my husband, Will, for his abiding patience, wit, and support. His unsurpassed willingness to listen and respond insightfully to matters related to this collection has sustained me from the beginning of this project through its completion.

Grateful acknowledgements are made to the following publishers for permission to quote from copyrighted works:

Harry Berger, Jr., "For Tommy: Commencement Address, 1976," in *Quarry West* (copyright 1983 by University of California at Santa Cruz).

Patricia Phillippy, " 'I might againe have been the Sepulcure': Paternal and Maternal Mourning in Early Modern England" in *Women, Death and Literature in Post-Reformation England* (copyright 2002 by Cambridge University Press).

LIST OF ILLUSTRATIONS

INTRODUCTION

JENNIFER C. VAUGHT

In the literature and the visual arts that appeared in England and Europe during the Middle Ages and Renaissance, representations of grief were profoundly shaped by gender. In this early modern context grief results most commonly from the death of another, but also from separation from a beloved or other kinds of loss. The following textual examples from Spenser's *Faerie Queene* and Shakespeare's *Richard II* and *The Winter's Tale* highlight the importance of examining grief from the perspective of gender. Likewise, the essays in this collection focus on a range of early modern writers and visual artists and explore the development—literary, historical, and theoretical—of the related concepts of grief and gender.

In Book III of *The Faerie Queene*, Spenser lends comedy to Scudamour's grieving over the abduction of his beloved, Amoret, on their wedding day. In the Legend of Chastity in which gender is central, Britomart, who is crossdressed as a man, administers "med'cine" to the chivalric knight's "grief" by venturing to rescue Amoret from the enchanter, Busirane. When Scudamour is unable to enter the House of Busirane with Britomart, his "grieuous" groans, sighs, and sobs become particularly comic. Out of frustration, he "wilfully" throws himself on the ground, where he "did beat and bounse his head and brest full sore."[1] Though knights often deliver laments or complaints over the unattainable affections of their ladies, Spenser surprises the reader with hyperbolic details such as Scudamour's banging his head and chest on the ground. The interlacing of issues of grief and gender intensifies the comedy of this episode. Ironically, Britomart keeps her cool, while Scudamour loses his head.

Shakespeare's *Richard II* further illustrates the importance of examining representations of grief in terms of gender, though in a tragic rather than comic context. In this play the word "grief" occurs more times than in any other work by Shakespeare.[2] King Richard grieves over the loss of his kingdom when he returns from Ireland to discover that his troops now support his political opponent, Bolingbroke. Realizing that he will be deposed and eventually murdered, Richard delivers his famous speech, "For God's sake let us sit upon the ground/And tell sad stories of the death of kings." In response to Richard's lament, the Bishop of Carlisle exclaims, "wise men ne're sit and wail their woes,/But presently prevent the ways to wail."[3] The Bishop views excessive expressions of grief as unmanly and characteristic of women, a view still held by many today. His stoic response to Richard highlights the distinct and even rigid grieving practices imposed upon men and women during the Middle Ages and Renaissance.

Early modern men and women in literature and the visual arts, however, often counter or transgress cultural limitations placed upon how they grieve or mourn. In Shakespeare's tragicomedy *The Winter's Tale*, for instance, Hermione states that she is "not prone to weeping, as [her] sex/Commonly are." Yet in response to Leontes' false claim that she is guilty of adultery, Hermione proclaims with dignity over the loss of her husband's faith that she has "that honourable grief lodg'd here which burns/Worse than tears drown." Leontes, by contrast, sheds "tears" beside the grave of Hermione and his young son, Mamillius, for sixteen years after he faces the tragic consequences of misjudging his wife.[4] Her self-restraint is as remarkable as the extent of his tears.

Like Hermione, Paulina defies convention by angrily venting her grief over the destruction of Hermione's family and falsely reporting to Leontes that his wife is dead. She does so out of fury at the King for triggering the death of his son and ordering the abandonment of his infant daughter, Perdita, on a foreign shore. As a result of the charade Paulina orchestrates, Leontes mourns his loss of Hermione until Perdita returns to Sicilia as a young woman and figuratively restores her mother back to life. His performance of mourning rites for someone he thinks is dead points to the vital role of the imagination in the grieving process. Even though grief resists language profoundly and is ultimately inexpressible, signifying loss through "sad stories," laments, and elegies or by the silent gesture of tears is often regenerative.

These textual examples from Spenser and Shakespeare showcase the extent to which gender shapes representations of grief. Gender tends to limit how men and women grieve or mourn in early modern literature and the visual arts. Men at this time often vent their grief through violent action or respond stoically to loss, whereas women frequently mourn by weeping and wailing. Nevertheless, early modern writers and visual artists also imagined those who redefine customary rhetoric about how men and women should grieve or mourn. Not surprisingly, mourning customs and perceptions of acceptable grieving practices for both sexes changed considerably from the Middle Ages through the Renaissance. The figure of Leontes in Shakespeare's *Winter's Tale* exemplifies the greater tolerance and compassion for bereaved men and women in seventeenth-century England.

Examining representations of grief in early modern England and Europe highlights the degree to which expressions of this emotion vary according to time and place. A common misperception about early modern people is that they "were not particularly conscious of emotions" and were "lacking a vocabulary to discuss emotional experience directly."[5] On the contrary, the various ways in which early modern writers used the words "grief" and "mourn" illustrate their subtle and complex understanding of these emotions. The word "mourn," for instance, was defined c. 888 as "to feel sorrow, grief, or regret," and "grief" was a term c. 1350 that referred to "mental pain, distress, or sorrow . . . caused by loss or trouble."[6] In other words, grief is an emotion akin to intense sorrow that commonly results from a concrete form of loss, such as a death or a separation from a loved one.[7] In this way "grief" differs from related terms expressing "sadness" or "melancholy." In his famous essay of 1917, "Mourning and Melancholia," Sigmund Freud defines melancholia as "a pathological fixation on an imaginary sense of loss" resulting from the subject's unconscious repression of a neurosis.[8] Antonio's statement at the beginning of Shakespeare's *Merchant of Venice*, "I know not why I am so sad," demonstrates the elusive, psychological origin of sadness or melancholy for English Renaissance subjects as well.[9]

This collection of essays on early modern representations of grief and gender aims to contribute to the larger field of the history and comparative study of emotion.[10] Interest in the emotions has blossomed in the last decade, in fields ranging from anthropology and sociology to philosophy and feminism. Nevertheless, relatively few literary or historical investigations of early modern emotions exist.[11] Recent scholars in the humanities and social sciences tend to agree that the expression of emotions, including "grief," "anger," "fear," or "happiness," varies across cultures. As Lila Abu-Lughod and Catherine Lutz state in relation to anthropology, "emotion . . . is a sociocultural construct."[12] Discussing the emotions in terms of philosophy and feminism, Alison Jaggar adds that these constructs "are historical products, bearing the marks of the society that constructed them."[13] The prevailing argument that expressions of emotions change historically suggests that figures in literature and the visual arts can contest and revise their culture's expectations about how men and women should grieve or mourn. Those who do so exhibit a degree of agency as a result.[14]

In medieval England and Europe, mourning practices varied widely. In the Anglo-Saxon period, women inherited the work of mourning the bodies of particular family members because they were closely associated with structures of kinship and physical decay. Nevertheless, Middle High German literature includes representations of men who often cried during public mourning rituals and sought consolation for grief through the promise of transcendence offered by the Christian Church. Those associated with the Church during the Middle Ages tended to view excessive grief as offensive to God because it exhibited a lack of faith by denying or overlooking salvation. The medieval code of courtly love, however, sanctioned the expression of melancholy in noblemen and led to wider acceptance of chivalric lovers delivering erotic complaints and venting their anguish over unfulfilled desire by weeping.[15]

Humanism played a defining role in the shaping of attitudes toward grief and the practices of mourning in Renaissance England and Europe. An increase of stoical attitudes toward emotions, ranging from passion to grief, resulted from the revival of classical culture by devout Italian and French humanists. From the classical period through the Renaissance, Stoics emphasized the perfection of the rational faculties of the mind and the cultivation of indifference toward bodily impulses and affections. Reflecting the patriarchal bias of classical culture, Renaissance humanists curtailed the emphasis on mutual, heterosexual relationships found in medieval, courtly love literature. They instead emphasized the value of asexuality between a poet lover and his lady. As a result, poets such as Petrarch tended to focus on their "narcissistic" experiences as unfulfilled lovers. Like Petrarch, who objected to public rituals of women's weeping and wailing in the streets, fifteenth-century Italian humanists reinforced the misogynistic notion that women should restrict their mourning to the private domain.[16] Despite Petrarch's humanistic influence on the composure of grieving women, his insistence on the possibility of triumphing over the loss of a beloved through writing transformed how later poets represented the relationship between mourning and creativity.

Representatives of the Augustinian branch of humanism reacted negatively to the stoical branch of humanism that took hold around 1550 in England and Europe. They objected to the rigorous view that men and women should moderate and contain excessive demonstrations of emotion, such as grief or sorrow. The French Protestant reformer John Calvin, for example, criticized "new Stoics who count it depraved not only to groan and weep but also to be sad and care-ridden." He claimed that those who follow the example of Christ's tears "have nothing to do with this iron-hearted philosophy." As illustrated by Calvin, the

Augustinian branch of humanism emphasized the importance of intense sorrow for sins in religious experience.[17] On the Continent, the Roman Catholic focus on the power of the iconographic tears of Jesus and Mary Magdalene to inspire devotion contributed to the increase of tolerance for weeping among Protestant, humanist writers in England. Discussing John Donne's tears of remorse in his Holy Sonnets, Louis Martz associates him "with Spain—with the vehement grief of its bleeding statues and the strenuous, anxious art of El Greco."[18]

In Renaissance England, mourning practices and attitudes toward grief began to change remarkably toward the end of the sixteenth and throughout the seventeenth century. Although men continued to respond anxiously to feminine tears of grief and channeled their impulses for weeping into masculine acts of violence, their tears were sometimes represented as a necessary sign of their humanity. The gradual shift from stoicism to greater compassion for those who grieve became particularly marked during the seventeenth century, when the Christian Church exerted a decreasing role in burial and mourning practices. The increasing recognition of the uniqueness of the individual led to the introduction of portraiture as a funeral memorial in the 1620s in England and the flourishing of introspective genres of writing such as the autobiography and diary.

Although medieval and Renaissance mourning practices continue to influence those of today, early modern people in England and Europe exhibited a vastly different understanding of male and female bodies and the influence of body chemistry on modes of grieving. Thomas Laqueur has recently discussed Galen's classical theory of the "one-sex body" in relation to Renaissance anatomists. According to this theory, males and females share analogous genitalia, with the vagina and ovaries corresponding to the penis and testicles, but possess a unique body chemistry consisting of four elements and "humours."[19] Unlike male bodies, which were thought to exhibit more of the higher elements of air and fire, female bodies were imagined as containing more of the lower elements of earth and water and were considered to be colder and moister as a result. From a premodern perspective the body chemistry of women explained why they possessed insufficient heat to push their genitals outside of the body at birth and were more prone to weeping than men. The openness of female bodies, which were commonly depicted as "leaky vessels," also led to the perception that women possess less innate ability to control their emotions.[20] As the Dutch physician Levinus Lemnius asserts in *The Secret Miracles of Nature*, "women are subject to all passions and perturbations . . . a woman enraged, is besides her selfe, and hath not power over her self, so that she cannot rule her passions, or bridle her disturbed affections, or stand against them with force of reason and judgment."[21]

Excessive bodily fluids were not limited to conceptions of women in the early modern period, however. According to Galen's theory of the four "humours," men who possessed an excess of black bile were vulnerable to melancholy, a word derived from Greek roots meaning "black bile" and epitomized by Hamlet. Throughout Shakespeare's play, Hamlet is afraid that his tears of grief and melancholia in response to his father's death are less manly than bloody deeds motivated by his choleric desire for revenge. Hamlet is sensitive to his culture's expectations about how men and women should mourn. His notion of grief is intimately tied to gender, a term referring to a social category imposed upon a sexed body.[22] Nevertheless, Hamlet resists and transforms the gender identity constructed for him by his historical moment and becomes a forerunner of men of sensibility in the eighteenth century.

Gender roles vary with respect to different historical periods because they are largely social constructions. According to Judith Butler, constructivism does not foreclose the possibility of agency. She argues that the "activity" of constructing this gender identity occurs over a lifetime and in relation to language. This process begins when the infant is designated as "he" or "she," rather than "it."[23] Early modern cultural rites for becoming a man or woman were multiple and varied. In Renaissance England males at the approximate age of five were "breeched," or dressed in breeches instead of coats worn by both sexes, to signify their transition from early effeminacy to boyhood.[24] A puberty rite for middle- and upper-class boys in England was to leave female caretakers to attend male grammar schools. There, they learned Latin and read classical literature and philosophy. Girls, by contrast, commonly learned what reading and writing they knew in the privacy of the home.[25] These cultural practices left the impression of masculinity or femininity upon the bodies and minds of early modern subjects.

As we might expect, the construction of gendered identities involves the psyche as well as the body. A number of contributors to this volume combine their understanding of the historical complexities of the early modern period with contemporary thinking about psychoanalysis. In *The Interpretation of Dreams*, published in Austria in 1900, Freud discusses his famous discovery of the importance of the Oedipal Complex in the development of the child, and particularly male children. According to Freud, the male child fears that his father will castrate him for desiring his mother and represses these unspoken feelings as a result. Freud's theory of the id, ego, and superego exposes the ways in which unconscious desires influence the construction of masculinity and femininity.

Subsequent psychoanalysts, such as Jacques Lacan, D. W. Winnicott, and Luce Irigarary, develop or challenge Freud's theories in pivotal ways. Building upon Freud, Lacan adds that the unconscious mind, so influential upon the formation of gender identities, is based upon language. This insight suggests that we can learn more about the unconscious mind by studying literature and vice versa. Object-relations psychoanalyst D. W. Winnicott revises Freud's discussion of the crucial, oedipal stage by focusing on the developmental importance of the space between the infant and mother in the first days of infancy. Similarly, Luce Irigaray nuances Freudian and Lacanian definitions of early life in terms of castration or lack of the phallus by emphasizing the importance of the mother in the development of the child and the joy that accompanies necessary separation from her with the first breath of life. This collection of essays on *Grief and Gender: 700–1700* acknowledges the continued importance of both parents in the construction of gendered identities. In doing so, it begins with an essay on mothers who mourn in Anglo-Saxon England and ends with a commencement address by a contemporary, American father.[26]

The following essays explore a number of major questions about grief and gender. What roles did men and women perform in mourning rituals in England and Europe during the Middle Ages and Renaissance? What cultural factors shaped representations of grief and mourning practices in Germany, Italy, France, and England during this period? To what extent did early modern men stoically restrain their grief? How did they attempt to control excessive grief in women? What's the relation between grief and creativity? In what ways did early modern men and women channel their grief into anger and acts of aggression or violence? How were the literary forms of the lament and elegy transformed by changing attitudes toward grief in relation to gender?

Collectively, these essays demonstrate that early modern representations of grief and mourning vary dramatically with respect to country and century. Grief, often expressed in the form of tears, provides individuals with a powerful source of agency instead of rendering them passive or helpless. Although the humoral theory of personality identifies women as the "moist sex," both sexes mourn in public and private spaces in early modern literature and the visual arts. Men in these works respond emotionally to loss in terms other than stoicism, melancholy, or anger and are as prone to hysteria as women. From approximately 700 to 1700 in England and Europe, public, communal mourning rituals gradually developed into increasingly private, individual expressions of grief that were felt as well as performed in written and visual mediums.[27]

The first section, "Anglo-Saxon and Middle High German Laments," opens with two essays that provide an anthropological basis for understanding grief in the early and later Middle Ages. These essays demonstrate that at this time in England and Germany, both sexes participated in the communal act of remembering the dead, though faith in the transcendence of the physical body tended to offer greater consolation for men than for women. From mothers who seek vengeance for the death of family members, to kings and husbands who risk disapproval by the Christian Church or loss of manhood for their pronounced mourning, the expression of grief can lead to culturally transgressive action.

In the first essay, Patricia Clare Ingham focuses on women who mourn the loss of kin in the Anglo-Saxon poems *Wulf and Eadwacer* and *The Wife's Lament* and the epic *Beowulf.* Rather than viewing their affective responses as passive, she argues that mourning provides the women in these poems with "important cultural power," or agency. Drawing on the work of anthropologist Maurice Bloch, who discusses "the cultural assignment of physical decay and fragmentation" to women, Ingham points out that assigning women the work of mourning particular bodies and families allows for the linking of heroic men such as Beowulf to "a transcendental community beyond the grave." The Anglo-Saxon elegies that Ingham discusses are culturally important as laments for the loss of "kin structures" that resulted from the shift to a "centralized medieval English sovereign"—the move from kinship to kingship.

Albrecht Classen examines men who mourn the loss of an entire army, a village, or a loved one in several Middle High German poems. He begins by noting that during the German Middle Ages, the Christian Church generally urged its people to control expressions of bereavement or joy and strive for salvation. Since the twelfth century, however, theologians and secular poets became increasingly interested in the psyche and on the effect of emotions on the individual. The Middle High German poem *The Lament* from the thirteenth century, for example, focuses on a king's bereavement over the slaughter of the Burgundian army and his family. Though a few of his subjects in the poem accuse him of acting "like some silly woman," Classen notes that medieval kings such as this one often cried or lamented in ritual performances of mourning. His lament develops into a communal activity during which he and several inconsolable women die of grief.

Part II, "Medieval Tears and Trauma," includes two essays on grief and gender in the later Middle Ages. Together, they expose the fragmenting effect of the chivalric codes of courtly love and violence on grieving men and explore the restrictive influence of humanism and Petrarchism on the gendering of mourning practices for both sexes.

Despite efforts to contain and even silence early modern women who dare to grieve in public, tears remain a powerful source of agency for them. In later medieval literature, chivalric knights sometimes grieve privately and turn to writing as a means of coping with unfulfilled desire.

M. C. Bodden argues in relation to Chaucer's *Franklin's Tale* and the *Clerk's Tale* that artificial, social codes lead to extreme representations of grief in both sexes. She demonstrates that men in the *Franklin's Tale* either suffer from melancholy, an eroticized form of grief often viewed as a noble affliction, or assume a stoic pose in response to loss. Whereas these forms of grief in men are generally viewed as socially acceptable, women who mourn excessively in public are seen as disorderly because of cultural hostility directed toward women who grieve outside the home. The fact that none of the men and women in these tales gains knowledge as a result of their grief suggests that the cultural codes determining how and where these literary figures express their grief are indeed unhealthy.

Bonnie Wheeler focuses on expressions of male grief in Malory's *Le Morte Darthur*, using especially Sir Palomydes, a Moor whom Malory exploits in the role of "Other," to interrogate the chivalric project and its ritual repetition of masculine violence. Although Sir Palomydes' masculine status is intact as a result of his crucial participation in martial projects, he undergoes psychic breaks as a result of his failure to win La Beall Isode, who is in love with his friend, Sir Tristram. The most emotionally expressive of Malory's knights, Sir Palomydes voices his anxieties and frustrations continually, weeps copiously, and shapes his grief by writing songs and poems about her. In contrast to much of late medieval literature in which grief in men is public, gestural, and communal, Palomydes' grief is largely private. Through this lone Saracen knight, Malory manages to fix various ideologies of chivalric violence—and inevitable grief—to the fragmented male subject as well as to the integral male community.

In Part III, "Male, Female, and Cross-Gendered Mourning Rituals in Renaissance Italy and France," all the essays build upon the Petrarchan notion that writing provides a degree of consolation for a sense of loss resulting from the death or unattainability of a beloved. They also illustrate how cultural restraints upon male and female expressions of grief lead to transgressive acts by both sexes. Though humanists such as Petrarch attempted to restrict public mourning rituals to elite men, women continued to commemorate the dead by writing poetry or collecting objects related to those who are gone.

Approaching the topic of grief and gender from the perspective of an art historian, Allison Levy focuses on representations of the life of St. Augustine and the burial of his mother, Monica, in Italian

Renaissance art from fifteenth-century Tuscany. She begins by suggesting that Augustine's public displays of composure and stoicism at her funeral counter his mother's loud and constant lamentation over his loss of faith throughout the *Confessions*. In effect, his "male composure" holds her "presumed female hysteria" in check. Nevertheless, other male expressions of grief, such as Augustine's protracted weeping over his mother's death in private in the *Confessions* and the dramatic grieving of one of his contemporaries in a fifteenth-century fresco of Augustine's funeral, illustrate that individuals continually resist and transgress cultural expectations for mourning.

After writing a pivotal work on melancholia and masculinity in early modern culture, Juliana Schiesari turns to how a number of famous, six-teenth-century women poets in Italy adopt but transform the Petrarchan lyric model of triumphing over loss through writing. In Petrarch's poem, *Rime sparse* 92, he ostensibly mourns a deceased poet, but focuses on his own melancholia, instead. Schiesari defines melencholia in Freudian terms as a "narcissistic reversal" in which "the libido invested in the lost object is drawn back into the ego." The female speaker in a poem by Gaspara Stampa (1523–1554) modeled on Petrarch's *Rime sparse* 92, by contrast, makes herself the object rather than the subject of grief by depending upon a community of female readers to keep her memory alive through mourning rituals once she dies of lovesickness. Schiesari demonstrates that Renaissance women poets not only rewrote Petrarch, but also built a lineage of female writers, or "sirens," by recalling Sappho and the Sapphic poets—crucial, yet less recognized literary models for them.

In her essay, Anne Lake Prescott examines how gender relates to grief in Marguerite de Navarre's long poem, *Les Prisons*. In this religious allegory, Marguerite grieves for lost beloveds: her mother, Louise de Savoie; her first husband, Charles d'Alençon; her husband's mother; and her brother François I, dead in 1547. Prescott demonstrates that Marguerite's adopting a male voice throughout *Les Prisons* grants her necessary distance from this "tableau of mourning." She concludes that Marguerite's cross-gendered poetry enables her to "relocate desire for her brother" by "in some sense *being* him" and to use the imaginary maleness she borrows from him to express anger and aggression at the dead for dying. Prescott relates such an ambivalent reaction to loss to Julia Kristeva's psychoanalytic discussion of depression and mourning in which the subject embeds the lost object in him or herself in order to avoid losing it.

In Part IV, "Elizabethan Loss and Regeneration," the essays examine the relation of grief and creativity from the perspectives of dialogic intertextuality, context-sensitive reading, and psychoanalysis. All the essays in this section discuss Gardens of Adonis in some way, a myth that affirms a natural form of transcendence of death through regeneration. These essays on Spenser's *Daphnaïda*, the Garden of Adonis in *The Faerie Queene*, and Shakespeare's *Venus and Adonis* illuminate the creative benefit of yielding to grief—even at the price of appearing unmanly to some—and the joy that can follow the work of mourning. Two of these essays focus on the active figure of Venus as lover and mourner and on the connection of the female body with the cycles of life and death. The figure of the mother is central in all three essays and even serves as an emblem for Spenser the poet.

Donald Cheney discusses Spenser's imitation of Chaucer's *Book of the Duchess* in his *Daphnaïda* on Arthur Gorges' bereavement. Gorges, portrayed as "Alcyon," seems to yield to his sorrow in a way that is both unmanly and un-Christian. In his essay, Cheney looks at the poem in relation to Spenser's other complaints, early and late, and at the way he adapts Chaucer's rhetoric and mythological allusions. He illustrates that Spenser's elegy, *Daphnaïda*, develops out of the Petrarchan notion of seeing the loss of friend or partner as a necessary condition of one's own creativity: as Marvell was to put it, "Apollo hunted Daphne so,/Only that she might Laurel grow." Like Alcyone, the wife of Ceyx in Ovid, the male speaker in Spenser's *Daphnaïda* becomes a motherly creative figure by surrendering utterly to his grief, and like the halcyon (or like Milton's God) propagates by brooding over the dark waters of midwinter. Although Spenser's readers have usually joined the poem's narrator in standing apart from this gesture of despair, Spenser himself has provided an anatomy of necessary lamenting that affirms its intimate relationship to poetic creativity.

Theresa Krier examines the Garden of Adonis canto in Book III of Spenser's *Faerie Queene* and focuses on the poet's paradoxical mourning of birth rather than death as the original moment of loss. She builds upon a key idea of Luce Irigarary, that the process of mourning birth leads to acknowledgment of separateness from the mother and culminates with the celebration of maternal powers. Spenser anticipates and supplements Irigaray's psychoanalytic theory by recognizing that both mother and child need to perform such mourning work. Krier emphasizes the interplay between mourning and creativity by citing Spenser's identification with the grieving mother Ceres in a poem written to Gabriel Harvey, in which he affirms his decision to write poetry. The poet playfully anticipates that "his not writing will *cause* grief in a Muse." Krier concludes by reading the boar in the uterine cave directly under the Mount of Venus in the Garden of Adonis not only as a figure of death, but also as a manifestation of "the paradox that for both mother and infant to be mortal is first to be natal."

Complementing Krier's essay, Judith Anderson reflects on the ways in which Shakespeare read Spenser in related contexts of passion and grief. In Shakespeare's poem *Venus and Adonis*, the shift in Venus from aggressive lover to pathetic mourner over the body of Adonis makes sense as "an obsessive fixation transferred from hunger to loss"—both forms of desire. Illustrating that Shakespeare's familiarity with *The Faerie Queene* was extensive, Anderson begins by focusing on his allusions to Spenser's Garden of Adonis in *Richard III*. These allusions, which occur in the context of Richard's outrageous request to marry Queen Elizabeth's daughter, respond to and overemphasize the "threats, darkness, chaos, and death" contained in Spenser's Garden. Extending her discussion of context-sensitive methods of close reading, she demonstrates that Shakespeare alludes both to Spenser's Garden and to the larger context of Book III of *The Faerie Queene*. In his seriocomic poem *Venus and Adonis* and his later play *Antony and Cleopatra*, he transforms Spenser's "multiple refractions" of desire represented by female, allegorical figures in Book III into more "materially, realized" characters that assume erotic agency.

In Part V, "Gendered Performances of Affect in Shakespeare," both essays demonstrate that men, as they are presented in the histories and tragedies, often express their grief through stoicism, anger, or the desire for revenge. Together, they suggest that there was considerable debate about what it meant for a man to cry in the Renaissance. The essays not only criticize the restriction of grief in men to bloody deeds, but also validate the redemptive power of tears for both sexes. Those actors and audience members who display affect during the performances of these plays further challenge the notion that violent action in a man was a more powerful response to grief than rhetoric and tears.

In Martha Kurtz's essay on Shakespeare's early history plays, *Henry VI, Parts I, II, and III*, she focuses on the ambiguity surrounding the tearful, grieving man in the Renaissance. In *Henry VI, Part I* soldiers consider tears to be an expression of feminine weakness, and grieve by desiring vengeance upon their enemy instead. The belief that big boys don't cry persists in *Henry VI, Part II*, when the youthful King is feminized for bursting into tears instead of taking heroic action in response to the death of his Uncle Gloucester. The alarming increase in brutality in *Parts II and III*, however, transforms the stoical lack of tears in response to death as the mark of a beast rather than a man. The myth of the strong, dry-eyed man is only possible when war is viewed as a noble enterprise, as it is in *Part I*. Throughout the remainder of *Henry VI* tears are sometimes considered a patriotic virtue and can cleanse and heal a country's wounds caused by the horrors of civil war.

Adopting a psychoanalytic, Lacanian approach, Marshall Grossman demonstrates that the figure of the chiasmus serves as the channel through which "anger, pity, madness, and grief" circulate among the characters and spectators of *Hamlet*. Anger in the play takes the form of rivalry between King Hamlet and Claudius and between Hamlet and Laertes as they grieve over Ophelia—a repetition of Hamlet's Freudian rivalry with his father over Gertrude. Such rhetorical schemes and word-plays allow for the "mobility of affect" in the reader or audience through the psychoanalytic mode of transference, which Grossman uses to revise the Aristotelian notion of the spectator's identification with the tragic hero and the catharsis of pity and fear. The reader or audience's tracing of Hamlet's rhetorical path from grief to violent action leads to a psy-choanalytic kind of catharsis and avoidance of his madness through recognition of the historically contingent identification of masculinity with bloody violence, which leads Hamlet to sacrifice the complexity of his own variously gendered responses to grief.

In Part VI, "The Family, Absence, and Memory in the Seventeenth Century," both essays deal with representations of losing children or parents. Although secularizing forces during the transition from the six-teenth to the seventeenth century resulted in greater liberties for griev-ing individuals, male and female mourning practices continued to be designated to the respective public or private domain. These essays also discuss the transgression of such gender roles and the resulting social agency of men and women. This section of the collection focuses on those who seek consolation for loss through means other than tran-scendence, such as portraiture and literary texts that memorialize the dead.

In Patricia Phillippy's discussion of parents who mourn the loss of children in sixteenth- and seventeenth-century England, she stresses the fact that paternal mourning usually dominated the public sphere, whereas maternal mourning was often consigned to the household. She bases her discussion of the gendering of the experience of child-loss on portraiture, diaries, autobiographies, and elegies from this period. Paternal mourning, which was "copious in private, stoic in public," was sometimes conflated with sorrow for a national event or with "the con-solatory message of salvation." Elegies by mothers who had lost their children, by contrast, focused on the Physical fact of death or on the transformation of the womb into a tomb-like marker of inconsolable loss. Though men often instructed women to moderate their grief as a sign of acceptance of God's will, writers of maternal elegies resisted or transgressed such prescriptions for acceptable mourning, resulting in rebellious expressions of private grief.

W. Scott Howard reads the English elegy in relation to secularizing forces in the seventeenth century. Though consolation usually resides in a sacred, atemporal realm in English elegies from the tenth through the sixteenth century, it becomes rooted in temporal, linguistic forms in the early seventeenth century and signals a modern movement in the genre as a result. Anticipating modernists such as Elizabeth Bishop in "One Art" (1976), who indicates that a linguistic vehicle can serve as a remedy for grief by stating, "(*Write* it!)," Jonson in "On My First Son" (1603) finds consolation for the death of his son through writing. In "Eupheme," Jonson illustrates the conflict between sacred and secular forces in his culture by praising Lady Digby's timeless features within a composition that enacts decomposition over time. He criticizes the impulse to "monumentalize the past" and in particular, the vainglorious erection of tombs as a display of rank in the late sixteenth and early seventeenth centuries. Jonson concludes that poetry is the best medium for commemorating live human action because it provides a linguistic dwelling for it.

Part VII, "Elegies and Rites of Passage—Then and Now," features "For Tommy" the commencement address that Harry Berger, Jr. delivered at Cowell College, University of California at Santa Cruz, in June 1976, and David Lee Miller's Afterword, entitled "Only a Rite." Meditating upon the death of his sixteen-year-old son in 1965, Berger emphasizes the importance of community for reestablishing a sense of kinship in the event of loss. Responding to Berger's elegiac address, Miller demonstrates that the grieving process of acknowledging separation and letting go allows for the possibility of celebration, the root of which Berger defines as "to go away and come back." Without risking change, discontinuity, or even the devastating experience of losing a loved one, we cannot participate fully in the celebration that occurs between self and other. In the wake of loss we rebuild ourselves and our collective identities through sad stories about grief and mourning, whether in literature or criticism. These living fictions enable us to revisit frequently, or celebrate, those memories that continually shape us.

PART I

ANGLO-SAXON AND MIDDLE HIGH GERMAN LAMENTS

CHAPTER 1

FROM KINSHIP TO KINGSHIP: MOURNING, GENDER, AND ANGLO-SAXON COMMUNITY

PATRICIA CLARE INGHAM

The collocation of gender and grief has been a crucial part of the scholarly tradition concerning the shorter Anglo-Saxon elegiac poems *Wulf and Eadwacer* and *The Wife's Lament*. These poems, among the most puzzling and ambiguous texts extant in the Anglo-Saxon corpus, relate traumatic loss in moving and poignant ways. Identified variously as female "authored" or female "voiced," the poems also raise crucial questions about women's agency, both literary and cultural, in Anglo-Saxon history.[1] Linked to other texts from the Old English elegiac tradition (texts such as *Wanderer, Deor, Seafarer, Ruin*, all found in *The Exeter Book*), these two poems suggest the pertinence of issues of gender and agency to the grief and loss of the larger elegy tradition.

Indeed *Wulf and Eadwacer* and *The Wife's Lament* pose questions of gender precisely through representations of grief. And yet critics have not analyzed as fully as they might what these texts might teach us about the cultural work performed by the gendering of loss in both Anglo-Saxon culture and in the scholarly traditions concerning it. In general, feminist scholars in Anglo-Saxon studies have been reluctant to conceive of grief and mourning as a site for important cultural work performed by women. Assuming acts of mourning to be "passive" acts, such scholars have tended (perhaps understandably) to criticize rather than to analyze the identification of women in these texts with a particularly hopeless kind of loss. Thus Alexandra Hennessey Olsen takes some feminist accounts to task for what she sees as their exaggeration of female passivity.[2] Olsen seeks to dismantle the long-standing, and overdetermined, association of early medieval women with victimization and powerlessness, demanding that we resist the, often unacknowledged, scholarly assumption that medieval females spent their lives in ignominious suffering. Yet when she assumes female mourning to be a passive act, Olsen unwittingly contributes to the very scholarly devaluation of female activity that she wishes to critique.

Like Olsen, Helen T. Bennett notes that "the exclusively male class structure of Anglo-Saxon heroic society . . . is partially the product of the modern academic tradition of literary interpretation."[3] Yet where Olsen emphasizes the public power (as opposed to private grief) of women in Anglo-Saxon culture, Bennett argues that "women in [a] warrior society have the non-roles of (failed) peaceweaver and mourner for the dead produced by feud."[4] In describing peaceweaver and mourner as "non-roles," Bennett seems to share with Olsen the assumption that mourning is the opposite of agency, of activity. Neither those feminists (like Olsen) who wish to emphasize women's agency in early English culture, nor those (like Bennett) who seek to analyze the differences of gender for an Anglo-Saxon semiotics of exile, suggest the ways that female mourning might be an activity with important cultural power.[5] Even Bennett's very interesting feminist analysis of grief thus leaves us no closer to understanding the work of women's grief *for* Anglo-Saxon culture, nor for the literary history that tells about it.[6]

In contrast to these approaches, I wish to suggest that *Wulf and Eadwacer* and *The Wife's Lament* offer evidence that Anglo-Saxon culture deployed representations of female grief as a public and cultural power with important (though not necessarily self-evident) consequences for the position of actual women. This power has largely gone unnoticed, or undervalued, because of the opposition of agency to loss that I have just described. This opposition is part of a larger, and longer, narrative about agency and power according to which a victim or mourner, particularly a female one, is never understood to be an agent.[7] Female agency and power tend to be imagined as the opposite of pain and loss, an opposition that makes it difficult to see that a subject's response to loss might constitute a set of significant activities, rather than an elaboration of passive victimhood. This opposition also precludes us from noting how grief and agency might be gendered, indeed gendered in relationship to one another.

The story of the agency of female mourning that I seek to tell, moreover, has gone unnoticed in Anglo-Saxon studies because of its unacknowledged service to another story, this one historiographic and national: the story of early England's apparently progressivist move "from kinship to kingship." This historiographic trajectory celebrates the consolidation of a central English monarchy following the Norman Conquest, and identifies the Anglo-Saxon period with the kin-based brotherhood of the *comitatus*. Such a history assumes a progressive teleology in which the apparently primitive cultural modes of tribe and family gradually give way to the putative progress of "national" unification and sovereign centrality. Rereading the gendering of loss for the politics of Anglo-Saxon sovereignty, I will suggest that the gendered voices of *Wulf and Eadwacer* and *The Wife's Lament* underwrite the cultural transition "from kinship to kingship," from the Anglo-Saxon *comitatus* as a kin-based brotherhood to an English sovereign community of exogamous foreign alliance. Viewed in this larger context, the cultural work performed by the assignment of a particularly hopeless kind of loss to women emerges strikingly. The gendering of the loss of family means that the fiction of a transcendental community beyond the grave, beyond the particularities of specific families, bodies, or lives can remain tied to men and to brotherhoods. This putatively more sophisticated view of sovereignty is thus founded upon a tradition of managing grief by way of gender, and dependent upon the important activity of female mourning.

The losses suffered by females in the epic poem *Beowulf* suggest a subtext to traditional narratives of Anglo-Saxon kinship and loss against which we might read the "female" elegies. I will thus be reading the elegies in the context of accounts of peaceweaving queenship as depicted in *Beowulf*. Taken together, these texts suggest that women's identification with family, her liminal position between cognate kin and exogamous alliance, marks women most intensely as the bearers of the ties to family, ties that must be mourned. Despite the peaceweaving bride's liminal status between cultures (and thus far from home), she is also, paradoxically, closely identified with the loyalties of kin. The image of the peaceweaver becomes crucial, I will argue, because of this simultaneity: positioned within and without kin-based relations, she sits at the center of a complicated cultural nexus consistently embued with loss.

PROBLEMS OF KIN

Scholars analyzing the politics of late Anglo-Saxon England stress the important power wielded by foreign, noble women whose marital alliances with rulers serve to unite disparate peoples within one royal (or at least noble) household.[8] Amid a field of historical queens, the Norman Emma (Ælgifu), consort first to the Anglo-Saxon Æthelred and later to the Dane Canute, suggests the complications to such a practice.[9] The delicate network of relationships forged by such histories remind us

both of the extraordinary power and the political risks involved in placing marital relations in the service of political expediency. Yet despite the
fact that the *power* of these domestic kin relations functions across the
lines of gender—ambitious marriage alliances, after all, advance the
political prestige of groom as much as bride—medieval chroniclers consistently connect the potential for domestic *loss and risk* with the relational power of the female partner.[10]

Such links are repeated in the Anglo-Saxon epic *Beowulf.* Females like
Wealtheow, Hildeburh, even Grendel's mother, suffer threats to and
losses of kin in an especially intense way. In an important and complex
scene that occurs after Beowulf's triumph against Grendel, Wealtheow,
Queen of the Scyldings and Hrothgar's "peace-weaving" wife, displays
the power and complexity of her position at court. Her two public
speeches to Hrothgar demonstrate that her power is linked to her position within and without kin. Upon presenting the ritual cup to her
spouse, Wealtheow says:

> "Onfoh þissum fulle, freodrihten min,
> sinces brytta! þu on saelum wes,
> goldwine gumena." (ll. 1169–1187)

> [Receive this cup, my Lord,/giver of treasure!
> Be you happy/goldfriend of men.][11]

The use of variation in Wealtheow's address emphasizes Hrothgar's
political and economic power, and here the poet's versification draws
attention to the first in the series of titles. Wealtheow's own relationship
to the king—"my liege lord"—positionally and rhythmically takes prece-
dence over variant modes of address—"giver of treasure" and "gold-
friend of men," and recalls her own appellation during her first
appearance in the narrative, where she is described as "freolic wif"
[noble woman] and "freolicu folccwen" [noble folk-queen]. These parallel constructions draw attention to a similarity and complementarity of
king and queen, suggesting to an audience at this important ritual
moment that this female has access to extraordinary court power, precisely through her kin-based relationship to the sovereign.

Yet if the poem has emphasized Wealtheow's power as complement to
Hrothgar's, it will soon link Wealtheow more intensely than it does
Hrothgar with the demands of kin loyalty. In one moment the text
underscores the relational bonds through which the Queen holds power;
in the next it contrasts Wealtheow's interest in maintaining those kin
bonds to her consort's willingness to forego them. Wealtheow remarks

on rumors of the King's intentions for adopting Beowulf as son and heir, and subtly questions the legitimacy of Hrothgar's rumored choice of succession:

> Me man sægde,   þæt þu ðe for sunu wolde
> hereri[n]c habban.   Heorot is gefælsod,
> beahsele beorhta;   bruc þenden þu mote
> manigra medo,   on þinum magum læf
> folc ond rice,   þonne þu forð scyle,
> metodsceaft seon.   Ic minne can
> glædne Hroþulf,   þæt he þa geogoðe wile
> arum healdan,   gyf þu ær þonne he,
> wine Scildinga,   worold oflætest.
> (ll.1176B-1183)

[It is said, that you wished to have this warrior for a son. Heorot is cleansed, bright mead-hall; enjoy many rewards as long as you may, leave to your blood kin (your) people and kingdom, when you must (go) forth to see the ruler of fate. I know my gracious Hrothulf (that he) wishes to hold the young retainers in favor if you, friend of the Scyldings, relinquish this world before he (does).]

In contrast to Hrothgar (whose willingness to adopt Beowulf as a son imagines a model of royal succession that sidesteps kinship altogether), Wealtheow is here represented as bearing the responsibility for the bonds of Hrothgar's kin, a responsibility implicitly linked to the Queen's maternal attachment to her sons. If Wealtheow operates as a "peace-weaver," Hrothgar's confidence in exogamous alliance seems flimsy enough, given the rumor that he will disrupt the alliance that produced his sons in favor of his homosocial bond with Beowulf. Hrothgar, in other words, imagines greater cultural stability through royal militarism, jettisoning the bonds of (even royal) kin in favor of Beowulf's heroism. Wealtheow, whose name literally means "foreign captive," paradoxically becomes the primary protector of kin-based inheritance and of the Scylding family line. She argues the case against Beowulf's succession and for patrilineal inheritance: herself a foreigner, she now protests the succession of another outsider, a foreign war hero with no family ties to Hrothgar's sons. Hrothgar conceives a military solution to court insta-bility; in protecting her sons, Wealtheow counters with a suggestion that would ensure the continuity of patrilineal domesticity.

Recent treatments of Hrothgar's interest in adopting Beowulf as his son read the interpretive play available in the ideology of masculinity represented by the differences between Hrothgar's weakness and Beowulf's strength. Those debates emphasize the heroic world of the poem as a masculinist (if also anxious) enterprise in which Hrothgar's putative weakness functions as a "warning to other masculine figures [in the poem] about the fragility of that masculinity."[12] As scholars make clear, anxieties of loss and weakness surround figures of male sovereignty throughout. The poem returns, again and again, to the problems that death poses to dynastic continuity and cultural survival. It repeatedly worries over the people left "fatherless" from the loss of their king.

At the crucial moment of Hrothgar's proposed adoption of Beowulf, however, the issue of loss and masculinity remains further complicated by Wealtheow's important critique of her consort's plan. This moment of critique has two important functions: in the first place, it identifies concerns about kin (and thus with, as I will make clearer in a moment, the loss of kin) with females; secondly, it grounds the text's identification of masculinity with concern for the military power, even warrior preeminence, of the (male) sovereign. Yet while the poem thus links the protection of kin interests with women and opposes kinship interests to military ones, it does not clearly identify military kingship as an advance upon rule by kin. If the poem favors Hrothgar's program for Beowulf's succession over his wife's plan to guard her son's interests, it does so in an extraordinarily tenuous and ambivalent way. There is a long tradition of medieval historiography by which queens are thought to claim power unjustly through the management of the interests of their sons. Instead of foregrounding Wealtheow's ambitions as excessive, the poem contextualizes the relational aspect of the Queen's power as a complement to Hrothgar's, emphasizing the similarity rather than the differences of their roles. Given this larger context, Wealtheow's concern for the bonds of kin emerges as an understandable caution vis-à-vis the militaristic enthusiasms of her spouse. From the long view, Wealtheow's concern for her sons may well be politically astute. Beowulf, we will later discover, will die without leaving an heir, and despite his long rule, the Geats will find themselves at the end of Beowulf's life in an unenviable position. This development, combined with persistence of the poem's focus upon the losses that accrue to all kings, signals the ambivalence of the text's position with regard to Hrothgar's militaristic proposition.

Furthermore, Wealtheow prods Hrothgar (and the poem's audience) to remember that kinship remains one means by which kings are (re)produced. In so doing, she dismantles the familiar opposition of "kingship" to "kinship." In Wealtheow and Hrothgar's disagreement, kinship and kingship emerge not as a progressive development toward greater sovereign stability (this is Hrothgar's view, a view not clearly endorsed by the poem), but as a contestation between the values of a masculinist military culture and the diplomacy of exogamous marital alliance, of war by other means. *Beowulf* does, however, suggest that in this cultural dispute responsibility for the protection of family—ties that obtain for both king and queen—fall to the female sovereign.[13] By positioning this contestation as a problem publicly raised by Wealtheow, the poem displays the process by which important women are assigned responsibility for the concerns of family and kin, concerns that are in fact important to king and queen alike.

Viewed in this way, Wealtheow's activity emerges as important not only (as it has usually been read) to her own interests but also to the larger interests of cultural survival. And her pointed reminder to Hrothgar of Hrothulf's willingness to defend her sons suggests the violent stakes in this cultural debate. Wealtheow's cautionary rhetoric is girded with references to Hrothgar's death—references that may well be more than the "worried mother's forlorn parting shot" that critic Michael Enright describes.[14] Within the space of five lines, she alludes to the Sovereign's death twice, reminding him of his nephew Hrothulf's value, as kin and protector, to her sons. The poet identifies this violent potential, moreover, not with the explicit actions of Hrothulf or Hrothgar, but with the foreign Queen's political acumen, and, perhaps most significantly, with the Queen's interest in protecting the kin-based structures of inheritance. Wealtheow's words, in this her most elaborate and detailed public speech in the entire poem, suggest that she has the means through Hrothulf to protect her sons' inheritance. To be sure, from one view, this assertion may be intended to reassure Hrothgar that his sons do not need Beowulf's extraordinary might. But Wealtheow's warning implies as well that she may have access to (violent) methods of protection should Hrothgar himself prove recalcitrant, or dangerous to their interests.

Wealtheow's subtle caution also implicitly shows us that kinship loyalties can, under certain circumstances, produce militarism. At key moments the poem seems to want to suggest that the protection of kin is no real alternative to war, but instead another means to produce it, a point to which I will return. To this extent, the poem remains interested in the problems of masculinist militarism. As a consequence, the poem's ambivalence about heroic culture remains tied to another of its central concerns: the elaboration of loss and death. And this suggests again that in contrast to historical accounts that render kingship a progressive advance upon kinship, *Beowulf* remains interested in the tragedies and dramas of family and cultural passings.

The Finn episode (which precedes Wealtheow's speech) suggests the potentiality of the peaceweaver as threshold for, if not agent of, the loss of kin with devastating consequences for an entire people. In that story, a ruler dies at the hand of his wife's brother's thane when the peaceweaving queen's cognate kin gain deadly access to her husband's body. Queen Hildeburh negotiates conflicts between kinship rights and blood-loyalties, apparently faring less well than Wealtheow:

> [Hildeburh]   unsynnum wearð
> beloren leofum   æt þam lindplegan
> bearnum and broðrum;   hie on gebyrd hruron
> gare wunde;   þæt wæs geomuru ides!
>   (ll. 1072B-1075)

[Hildeburh guiltlessly became/deprived of beloved at that shield-play/of sons and of brothers; they fell [to] fate wounded by the spear; that was a mournful woman!]

Hildeburh's work as silent mourner has often been read in contrast to Wealtheow's work as articulate political agent. The power of Wealtheow's textual construction (she speaks, Hildeburh does not) and political stance (she oversees her sons' interests, while Hildeburh oversees her sons' funeral pyre) on its face seems to emphasizes the astute power of one female sovereign in contrast with what some critics deem the "passivity" of the other. And yet why should Hildeburh's activity be understood as no activity at all? Hildeburh remains the affective center throughout the Finn episode. Descriptions of her mourning and keening drive the details of poetic treatment; she is the central focus of the alliance that results in the death of all those men to whom she is most closely related. Indeed if, as I have been arguing, peaceweaving women are required to protect a loyalty to kin bonds trivialized by their consorts, that very assignment suggests that, in mourning those losses, women do important work for an entire culture.

The contrast between active and passive is also troubled by the text's emphasis on guiltless (or guilty) activity. The emphasis on Hildeburh as "*unsynnum*" [guiltless] implies that other queens have not been so innocent, and thus alludes to questions of the virtue, rather than the lack, of queenly activity. Further, the fragmentary nature of the Finn episode effectively obscures any action Hildeburh may have taken before that tale opens, and underscores, again, an ambivalent association of "peaceweaver" with violence as much as loss. The death of Hnæf, Hildeburh's brother, killed in a midnight raid of the Frisians while visiting Hildeburh and Finn, raises questions about both the reason for Hnæf's visit and the relationship between Finn and the attacking Frisians and Jutes. It may well be that, her "guiltless" character notwithstanding, Hildeburh has invited her blood kin to her home in an attempt to protect her son and herself; she may have tried to make good on the kind of threat we find implied in Wealtheow's words to Hrothgar. If this is the case, the Frisian midnight marauders might be acting with Finn's knowledge.

But regardless of any possibilities for Hildeburh's political activity, *Beowulf's* representation of Hildeburh's mourning clearly suggests that her grief constitutes more than private passivity. She manages, indeed organizes, the funerals:

> Het ða Hildeburh   aet Hnæfes ade
> hire selfre sunu   sweoloðe befæstan,
> ban-fatu bærnan   ond on bæl don.
> eame on eaxle   ides gnornode,
> geomrode giddum.   Guðrinc astah.
> Wand to wolcnum   wælfyra mæst,
> Hlynode for hlawe;   hafelan multon,
> Bengeato burston,   ðonne blod ætspranc,
> laðbite lices.

(ll. 1114-1121A)

[Then Hildeburh commanded that her own son be placed at Hnaef's side, to burn the bodies. Uncle at the shoulder. The woman lamented, mourned in dirges. The warrior ascended. Wound with the clouds of the funeral fire, roared around the burial-mound; heads melted, wound-gashes burst, grievous wounds spurted blood from the body.]

Wailing in grief, Hildeburh commands the funeral pyre, presiding over cultural rituals of death. In the arrangement of bodies (maternal uncle with son, an extraordinarily close kinship bond in Anglo-Saxon culture), Hildeburh commands in death the kin bonds that were so violently ruptured in life. The passage emphasizes the Queen's maternal tie to her son at the very moment of her mournful keening, and in the midst of a gruesome description of burned flesh, of bodies exploding on the funeral pyre. The scene emphasizes death as bodily disintegration, the grisly image of melting skulls, bursting corpses from which blood springs.

Anthropologist Maurice Bloch has described the cultural assignment of physical decay and fragmentation to women in hierarchically structured "traditional societies." Analyzing funeral rituals, Bloch argues that such cultures cope with the threats that death and loss pose to belief in a community's survival by splitting the morbid aspects of physical decay from the notion of death as a spiritual union, a life beyond the grave.

Women's cultural relation to the particularity of individual birth, according to Bloch, means that women come to stand for the individuality of particular dying bodies and particular fragmented lives, an image of division that threatens the fiction of the transcendent, unified clan or community. In assigning the gruesome elements of bodily death to women, Bloch argues, a different kind of death, a transcendent death, remains linked to men and to brotherhoods. Triumph over "death (in its polluting and sad aspects)," Bloch argues, "is achieved by breaking through, vanquishing the world of women, of sorrow, of death and division" (217–18).[15]

Mourning the loss of son and brother, officiating at the pyre and over the grisly scene of bones bursting, Hildeburh seems precisely the bearer of death as physical morbidity. She suffers the pain and loss of particular individuals, beloved family members. The description of her keening provides the poignancy for the remainder of the tale. Her important cultural work registers too as a textual activity: she sings songs of mourning, an activity duplicated by the ritual activity of Hrothgar's scop as he relates the tale within the tale. In the next few lines, the story turns away from Hildeburh to Finn, offering a rather more matter-of-fact description of the military dénouement of the episode: unlike the description of the funerals of Hildeburh's son and brother, Finn's death is related with little detail. The description of Finn's winter journey to avenge his losses resonates with the male elegy tradition of texts like *The Wanderer* and *The Seafarer*. In contrast Hildeburh, like the female speakers of *The Wife's Lament* and *Wulf and Eadwacer*, remains at the pyre, embodying the desolation and hopelessness of family losses.

Thus, if the poem displays the extraordinary activity required by Hildeburh's responsibility for grief, it also insists upon locating Hildeburh in a trajectory of perpetual loss. There is, it seems, no consolation to be found for her. In the end, she is taken back to the Danes, losing both her power as foreign queen and that place "*þær heo ær mæste heold/worolde wynne*" (l.1079 B-1080 A) [where she previously held greatest/joys of the world]. Finn, at least, dies a hero; Hildeburh remains trapped in an endless life of misery. From the long view, *Beowulf* may well be arguing that Wealtheow, Hildeburh, and foreign queens like them who fail to realign their interests with the military interests of their sovereign are dangerous both to the stability of the tribe or nation, and to their own "happiness." But the poem also makes it possible to read this as a cultural *assignment* of a particularly hopeless kind of loss to important women. And this suggests another implication of the gendering of grief: women's position as the bearers of hopeless loss may in part underwrite the ideology of their exclusion from the *realpolitik* of statecraft. Thus assumptions that female activity at court (like Wealtheow's) is narrowly self-interested, or that keening and mourning (like Hildeburh's) remains a passive act, constitute gendered ideologies of loss by which women, no matter what they do, are identified most closely with victimization. I have argued elsewhere that this ideology assigns victimization to women, so as to protect men from having to recognize the ways in which they are victimized by military culture.[16]

Of course, *Beowulf* is also replete with images of another kind of death-bearing woman, a female who is anything but passive—a mother who kills. In the figure of Grendel's mother we find the most obvious ways in which this text positions warrior culture as "vanquishing the world of women," which is also the world "of death and division." I only have time here to suggest the interesting connections of these concerns to the text's most alien, and most intrusive, female figure. Wealtheow's position, while explicitly represented with sympathy, will be finally undercut by the implicit configuration of her political concerns (protection of her sons) with the horrific figure of the avenging mother *ellorgast*. Alien Wealtheow's veiled threat against Hrothgar may thus be read as similar to this other feminine threat to Hrothgar's court. The poem addresses the possibility for female violence through the apparently consoling (and conservative) story of Beowulf's triumph, also now a story of female victimhood. Yet even here the poem reminds its audience that militarism might be one way that warriors can cope with death. As the hero prepares to descend into the murky waters of Grendel's mother's lair, he reflects upon military prowess as a response to the problem of death: "*Ure æghwylc sceal ende gibidan/worolde lifes; wyrce se þe mote/domes ær deaþe.*" [We each must endure the end of life in this world. Let he who can perform valorous deeds before death.][17] Beowulf's words make clear that in vanquishing Grendel's mother, he hopes to contain the threat of death as such. Valorous deeds and heroic reputation can, or so Beowulf implies, transcend the tyranny of our biological finitude.

Hildeburh's songs of mourning, described but not reproduced in the narrative of the Finn episode, nonetheless suggest the cultural power of elegy voiced by a female. Yet if there is a long tradition by which the mourning of male poets seems, like Beowulf's valorous deeds, productive for future fame, female mourning has not been often imagined as culturally productive in this way. Given the gendering of loss in *Beowulf*, it is no surprise that the Anglo-Saxon elegies identified with female speakers are usually thought, unlike their "male" counterparts, to offer particularly hopeless scenes of desolation. Martin Green takes a representative position: "It is perhaps the failure of the speaker in *The Wife's*

Lament to transcend her present that underscores the poignancy of her sad song and defines the poem's difference from the other elegies."[18] I turn now to examine the question of this apparently missing consolation, suggesting what it might tell us about the cultural work of gender and grief.

ELEGIAC CONSOLATIONS

If little is settled about the actual circumstances depicted in *The Wife's Lament* (hereafter *WL*) and *Wulf and Eadwacer* (hereafter *WE*), scholars have generally agreed that both poems depict a subject's mourning over the loss of family and kin. *WL* offers a first-person account of a female subject's loss of lover and lord (*hlaford*), her imprisonment by the family of her beloved, and her longing for reunion with him. *WE* has similarly been read to express a mournful longing for family, although Marijane Osborne, in an important feminist intervention, has compellingly argued that the lost beloved in this case is a son rather than lover.[19]

As elegiac representations of the loss of family, the texts are, moreover, extraordinarily enigmatic, so brief and allusive as to frustrate a reader's attempt to master them. From its first lines the *WL* conceives of grief as an experience of compelling interiority, expressing an intimate history in complicated syntax:

Ic þis giedd wrece	bi me ful geomorre,
minre sylfre sið.	Ic þæt secgan mæg,
hwæt ic yrmþa begad,	siþþan ic up aweox,
niwes oþþe ealdes,	no ma þonne nu.[20]

[I utter this word, from myself full of sadness/(narrate) my own experience. I can describe my misery since I grew up, recently or long ago no more than now.]

The first three lines repeat a series of first-person pronouns. The speaker claims to speak from an interior depth, in language that circles a space of sorrow identical with, even subsuming, the speaker's self. Words uttered come from "me," "myself" full of sadness. The first half-line of the poem's second full line ["Minre sylfre sið," literally "[the] experience of mine of self," and according to Mitchell and Robinson "a strange pattern rare in Old English"][21] reiterates a depth and intimacy of this experience of loss. The unusual syntax, poetically beautiful, breathtakingly succinct, renders the mourner's absorption as an interior space of isolation. The speaker describes her mournful position as stretching from youth to age, a ceaseless horizon of sadness to which her words respond.

In their linguistic partiality these poems enact the insufficiencies of language before the experience of grief. This linguistic poverty has, however, been used to consign the speaker as, in the case of the *WL*, so deeply imbricated in loss as to be death itself, a female corpse who, in the words of critic William Johnson, "dwells in the world of the grave, and is perhaps dead herself."[22] Patricia Belanoff asks that we revisit the gendered "differentness" of this use of language, a difference that she reads in terms of both loss and relationship: "the very differentness of the language serves (ironically) to give force to the . . . need we all have to be linked to others and to the still overwhelming emotion and sense of loss we experience when we are not."[23] By virtue of the very elusiveness of their language, in other words, *WL* and *WE* position the reader in the midst of sadness. These texts are thought to offer little view of transcendence or consolation in part because the experience of reading them constitutes not only a representation of an experience of loss, but an object lesson into loss.

William Johnson constructs the mourning woman as the opposite of transcendence, as death itself. The lack of elegiac transcendence assigned to the speaker of the *WL* bothers many feminist readers, and even those interested in viewing the poems as a site of female agency seem apologetic about this kind of sadness. Again we find a repetitive insistence upon the "passivity" (read unproductivity) of the speakers' mourning. In her analysis of the *WL*, for example, Barrie Ruth Straus reads the poem itself as a speech-act, by which the speaker "takes advantage of a form of action available to women at her time."[24] Linking the Wife's cultural position to that of Wealtheow, Straus emphasizes the power of her words, a narrative recounting "the patriarchal order as a cause of the unhappy fate of women, and which ends with a curse heaping woe on the specific males who perpetuate that order."[25] Straus' important point is made, however, by contrasting the speaker's speech with the apparent passivity of the Wife's mourning, a "passivity" even Straus, following Alain Renoir's close reading, understands to be "surely there." Straus would, one feels, be happier if the speaker would remain empowered as a critic of patriarchy, and refrain from narrating her weeping. Similarly, in comparing the exilic images from the *WL* and *WE* with those from *The Wanderer*, Wendy Larson notes that, "The despair and sense of radical loss in *Wulf and Eadwacer* and *The Wife's Lament* arises from speakers who cannot envision the possibility of change," in texts that "reproduce the causes of [female] exile, without compensating the female speakers with the positive aspects of marginal experience the male speakers enjoy."[26]

These are important distinctions, and I do not wish to dismiss them. But I am interested in dismantling the notion that the kind of mourning enacted by the *WL* and *WE* is unproductive because it refuses, or avoids, transcendence. Larson is undoubtedly right when she reminds us that the female speakers are denied the compensations and consolations available to their male counterparts. Yet in my view such denials are part of what these poems (whether female "voiced" or female "authored") gain for the larger elegy tradition of which they are a part. Women's identification with loss as ignoble, with a hopelessness beyond consolation, with linguistic inexpressibility constitutes the "other" through which the male elegiac texts are understood to constitute "good," "Christian," even "healthy" mourning.[27] As such, these texts are part of the structure of Anglo-Saxon "traditional society," one that we have already witnessed in the epic *Beowulf*, where women such as Hildeburh are both responsible for the funerary rituals for their families and suspended on a horizon of perpetual and ceaseless loss.

Yet it is also crucial to elaborate the cultural history implied by these texts and the gendering of mourning within them. Throughout this chapter we have noted the collocation of female mourning with issues of kin. And I have argued, particularly with respect to *Beowulf*, that structures of kinship and kingship emerge as a cultural contestation between two ways of imagining the tribe or nation's future. Evidence from Tacitus suggests, as Helen Bennett has noted, women's more intense identification in Germanic society, with the rituals of mourning for particular losses and particular bodies. Given the issues of kinship emphasized in all the texts read in this chapter, given what we know about the history of settlement, of intercultural exchange (both violent and peaceful) at the time, we might reconsider the poignant longings and losses of *WE* and *WL* as a series of cultural laments, a mourning for place and family, for kin structures that are, at least ideologically, being repudiated in order to make way for the absolute personal loyalty required by the centralized medieval English sovereign.

In this case the gendering of loss in these texts means that women bear the grief for a culture in transition. Suspended in perpetual mourning, women such as the speakers in *WE* and *WL*, offer constant reminders of a past beloved *comitatus*. Structured thus as the ground on which historical change is constituted, these mourners become exiled even from history. Culturally required for, even constituted by loss, these subjects facilitate the very cultural future that they, as mourners, are understood to be refusing.[28]

CONCLUSION: THE POLITICS OF HISTORY

The consolations of the elegy tradition, from the long view, are all about the cessation of mourning, a willingness to accept loss and to imagine a future beyond it. The insufficiency of language in the face of loss is, of course, an issue that much of the elegy tradition describes by overcoming it. In a critical account of the gendered aspects of this tradition of elegy for an analysis of Chaucer's poetry, Louise Fradenburg notes the ways in which the literary histories of the elegy contribute to the process by which women are culturally required to bear a lack of transcendence and, not coincidentally, a lack of linguistic mastery.[29] We can link the extraordinary emphasis upon hopelessness in *The Wife's Lament*, with an account of the sad self folded in upon itself uttered by another medieval female figure whose position Fradenburg analyzes: "Thereto we wrecched wommen nothing konne," sighs Geoffrey Chaucer's Criseyde, "Whan us is wo, but wepe and sitte and thinke;/Our wrecche is this, oure owen wo to drynke."[30] Reading such mournful sighs within the larger identification of women with hopeless, as opposed to transcendent, loss, Fradenburg reminds us of the cultural stakes in such an association. She writes: "If, and when, woman is constructed as the site of loss—made responsible, in any way, for mortality—her capacity to participate in that form of tribal or cultural knowledge which we call history, will inevitably be in doubt or denied altogether."[31]

If women's identification with a certain kind of hopeless loss in Anglo-Saxon culture has rendered feminists despondent over the evidence of female power within its history, we gain much by reexamining the cultural work performed by female grief. Recognizing that female participation in history is disavowed precisely by assigning her responsibility for a certain kind of loss, we might insist instead that such grief at the very least be acknowledged as an activity of important historical consequence. Furthermore, analyses of the work of female mourning remind us that the demand that we achieve transcendence in the face of loss is a demand made of us by the Law of the Father. The assumption that the refusal of such transcendence constitutes passivity, or a "bad" kind of mourning, should thus be met with considerable skepticism. In that context, the poignant representations of female grief in *The Wife's Lament*, *Wulf and Eadwacer*, and *Beowulf* might offer a subversive potential, suggesting how the management of loss and mourning, even in Anglo-Saxon days, was tied to the construction of gender.

CHAPTER 2

DEATH RITUALS AND MANHOOD IN THE MIDDLE HIGH GERMAN POEMS *THE LAMENT*, JOHANNES VON TEPL'S *THE PLOWMAN*, AND HEINRICH WITTENWILER'S *RING*

ALBRECHT CLASSEN

Life is temporary, as we all know. We are born to spend some time here on earth, and pass away once this time has run out. Some people die very young; other people grow very old. Religion has always served as one of the major vehicles to comprehend what actually happens when a loved one passes away, but rational answers escape us, as death remains an incomprehensible fact of life. But neither the teachings of the Church nor philosophical discussions about human existence seem to be enough to cope with the pain the survivors experience. Written, oral, audio, and visual memory builds important bridges between yesterday and tomorrow, bridges that we all must cross one day.[1] This memory, this actual interaction with the deceased person and a passed life, has often been integrated into religious rituals of mourning, yet the actual and most important, because most lasting, medium of mourning seems to be the literary forum. The German Baroque poet Andreas Gryphius (1616–1664) once reflected upon the status of war torn Germany (Thirty Years War, 1618–1648), realizing that something like an Armageddon had struck his fatherland, forcing him to compose a poem as a powerful and deeply felt medium for his mourning not only about the loss of a beloved person, but about the loss of an entire nation. To do justice to this moving poem, only a straightforward prose translation can do:

Threnen des Vatterlandes/Anno 1636
Tears of the Fatherland/Year 1636

We are now completely destroyed, oh, even more than completely!/ The troops of outrageous peoples, the raging trombone/the sword heavy with blood, the thundering canon/has devoured all the sweat and industriousness and supplies./The towers are burning coal, the church is turned upside down/the city hall is in shambles, the strong ones are hacked to pieces./The virgins are raped, and wherever we look/we see fire, pestilence and death which permeates heart and spirit./Ever fresh blood runs through the rampart and the city./It has already been three times six years that our rivers/have been slowed in their flow by so many corpses./But I keep silent of what is even worse than death./What is more painful than the pestilence, and fire and famine,/is that many people have been forced to give up the treasure of their soul (translation my own).[2]

Such a devastating experience was not, however, unique to the Baroque period, whether a poet responded to the death of a close relative, friend, or beloved, or to the destruction of an entire country. From a cultural-historical perspective the reaction to the experience of death, leading to grief, mourning, and lamentation, mostly cast in some type of literary form, proves to be the most interesting, revealing anthropological constants and variants.[3]

To comprehend the meaning of bereavement in its cultural-historical context, that is, in the way Franz Boaz, early in the past century, had designed his ethnographic studies,[4] here I will examine three specific literary cases, i.e., two Middle High German lament poems and one didactic verse narrative to find out how medieval poets reflected upon death, what rituals they described, and how they viewed and described the actual mourning procedure. The focus will rest on these narratives as they provide important cultural information about death rituals, "Todesarbeit," and coming to terms with the profoundly disturbing experience of losing a beloved person to the forces of death from the perspective of late-medieval writers. However, even though it could be considered anachronistic to do so, I will first survey modern psychological approaches to bereavement and identify the relevant elements in this process. Subsequently, I will briefly discuss the mourning rituals included in some of the most important thirteenth- through fifteenth-century German courtly epics as a backdrop for our critical reading of the two bereavement poems, and then conclude with an attempt to cor-relate modern psychological insights in the bereavement process with medieval approaches to death.

Throughout times people have been afraid of death, as the experience with death in their own family or circle of friends has always brought about pain, disbelief, shock, fear, and even trauma, easily victimizing the survivors.[5] But what are grief and mourning as human reactions to death? According to Sigmund Freud ("Mourning and Melancholia"), "grief is a process by which the individual progressively withdraws the energy that ties him or her to the object of his or her love."[6] John Bowlby argues that grief represents an attempt by the surviving person to reattach with the deceased, to restore the lost personal closeness.[7] In C. Murray Parkes' view, grief is a process by which "internal awareness is brought in line with external events."[8] For some people grief can assume exorbitant dimensions and turn into symptoms requiring med-ical treatment, whereas for others grief comes in smaller doses and even-tually heals their wounds by itself.[9] Those who are willing to accept the grief will generally go through the bereavement process faster than those who experience an internal denial.[10] "Trauerarbeit," as Freud had sug-gested, is not only possible, but represents the determining factor in dealing with grief to avoid a physical and psychological breakdown lead-ing to morbid forms of mourning.[11] Fulton has termed these two extremes "high grief" and "low grief"—situations that must be dealt with quite differently.[12] Another form of differentiation has been sug-gested by Stephenson, who observes the two types of "existential grief" and "reactive grief," where the former represents an experience in which the death of a loved person triggers feelings of life having no longer any meaning and of death as imminently approaching the mourner. The lat-ter experience "is concerned with the loss that the death represents to the person" and promises avenues for the mourner to recover from the shock.[13]

Whereas grief and mourning have obviously received extensive and also contradictory attention by modern psychologists and anthropolo-gists, the question of how people grieved in the past, what cultural aspects were involved in bereavement during, let's say, the eighteenth or fifteenth century, has been addressed much less in scholarship. The sources from the past do not easily speak to us about those seemingly highly personal aspects, although, as we have recently learned to see, the *histoire de longue durée* connects our modern emotional household and behavioral patterns more or less directly with those from the past as they are grounded in that culture and evolved over the centuries without ever losing the direct link with their origin.[14]

As to mourning, however, one crucial factor has to be taken into account, which strongly differentiates our modern world from the Middle Ages.[15] The dominance of the Christian Church undermined the value and relevance of material objects and personal feelings, as the individual was supposed to strive for his or her soul's salvation. The death of a beloved person was to be seen "sub specie aeternitatis," forcing the spectator and mourner to consider the relevance of the "ars moriendi,"[16] whereas emotions such as *tristitia* (sadness) and *acedia* (sloth) were regarded as severe moral shortcomings (deadly sins). Many religious and didactic texts from that time, such as Heinrich von Melk's *Von des todes gehugde* (ca. 1170–80), strongly admonished their audiences and readers to view human life as irrelevant and to pay attention only to the afterlife.[17] Consequently, the early church struggled against public and private expressions both of bereavement and joy, and admonished its flock to control the affects and strive for the tranquility of the soul as a precondition for possible salvation.[18]

Since the twelfth century, this situation changed quite radically as suddenly both theologians and secular poets began to explore the human psyche, to examine the impact of feelings and emotions on the individual, and to attempt to write autobiographies. The tropes of consolation, for instance, proved to be highly influential in Latin sermon literature.[19] In Bernhard of Clairvaux's sermons, for example, intensively emotionally charged concepts of human life gained in importance, as he talked about *amor praeceps, vehemens, flagrans, impetuose* (precipitous, vehement, burning, impetuous love) and described in concrete terms the experience of ecstasy in the spiritual encounter with God (mysticism).[20]

Three literary texts from the German Middle Ages, above all, invite a critical analysis as they are primarily dedicated to the treatment of bereavement and sorrow and are, curiously, neither concerned with the "ars moriendi" nor with the pragmatic issues of burial, inheritance, and artistic remembrance of the dead person.[21] The first one is the anonymous *Klage* poem, or *The Lament*, composed sometime in the early thirteenth century as a response, commentary to, or interpretation of the heroic epic *Nibelungenlied*.[22] The other text is Johannes of Tepl's *Der Ackermann aus Böhmen* or *The Plowman from Bohemia*, written in the early years of the fifteenth century in response to the poet's wife's death. The third text, Heinrich Wittenwiler's *Ring* from ca. 1400, has been preserved in only one manuscript but is highly regarded by German medieval scholarship as a major literary work.[23] The effects of death and the subsequent bereavement assume existential dimensions in all three narratives.

The Lament takes off where the famous *Nibelungenlied* has suddenly broken off, that is, at the point where the entire Burgundian army and vast scores of Hunnish warriors have been killed. *The Lament* poet was obviously deeply concerned with the shortcomings of the *Nibelungenlied* and concentrates on the aspect of mourning only.[24] The audience is familiar with what has happened and only waits for the continuation to find out how the few survivors handled the extreme grief, hence are only given a very scant overview of the events at the court in Worms and then of those at the court of King Etzel: "The facts are quite well known" (v. 47). Indeed, they are well known, and yet the narrator refers back to them over and over because the degree of pain and the near impossibility to come to terms with the extraordinary grief over the death of all the Burgundian warriors and their friends do not find adequate expression, and hence need to be linked with the actual events.[25]

These are recounted throughout the epic, first when the three surviving heroes, Etzel, Dietrich, and Hildebrand go from one corpse to the other and reflect upon his accomplishments, then at the occasion when the messengers report to the rest of the world the enormous catastrophe, and finally during the court deliberations back in Worms where the left-behind Burgundian lords and counselors investigate the causes for this tragic development and deliberate on the future of their kingdom.[26]

The Lament constitutes such an extraordinary, literary text from the early thirteenth century because its focus rests exclusively on the lament and highlights nothing but the bereavement of the few survivors. Although contemporary, courtly romances and heroic epics reflect on many different human emotions and experiences, including death and suffering, pain and grief, no other author has ever dared to limit himself completely to the mourning ritual. The text is not a guidebook on how to stage proper bereavement, but it illustrates with startling images what effect such a catastrophe had on an entire people. Consequently, the *Lament* poem is not concerned with anything else but with the theme of bereavement and explores how to illustrate the individual and general rituals performed in public.

After an initial introduction to the past events, the narrator discusses the tragedy from a global perspective and expresses his deep sense of sorrow about the fact that so many worthy men had to die senselessly. As soon as these past events have been dealt with, the narrator turns to his actual subjects, the grieving King Etzel and the other few survivors. The poem's significant aesthetic achievement rests in its ability to describe in ever new terms and with an increasing pitch of desperation the bereavement procedures. Etzel could see nothing but "the many rivers of blood flowing from deep wounds which, in a matter of a few hours, had deprived him of all joy" (vv. 606–09). His personal destiny finds no parallel among all other kings in the world (vv. 614ff.), and the more and louder he expresses his mourning, the more does the narrator formulate his admiration: "It was as though one were listening to the bellowing of a bison. How the voice of this well-bred nobleman thundered from his mouth! He lamented so loudly that the towers and the palace itself began to shake" (vv. 625–31). His royal status is reflected in his ritual performance of bereavement, which receives full attention by the bystanders and the remaining members of the court: "Many a high-bred orphan joined him in his lamentations" (vv. 638f.). Especially the young noblewomen wring their hands so much that their bones are breaking (v. 649). Whatever Etzel does to express his sorrow and grief, all other women copy, and they even try to go beyond it: "However loudly the king cried out, the women screamed along with him" (v. 652f.). The narrator assures his audience that this is the customary way of bereavement among many peoples who all lose their joy when they see another person in pain because of the death of a loved one: "This is still the custom among people today: whenever a person is pained to the heart, the other abandons his joy" (v. 655f.). Other aspects relevant for the mourning are the tearing of hair and even embracing the corpses of the deceased warriors (vv. 709–13).

From another point of view, at the time of mourning the difference in social rank does no longer seem to play a significant role, as the country folk also join in the weeping, even though they are subsequently ordered to begin with the burial process and to dig the graves (vv. 663ff.). In face of death no noteworthy distinction can be made between the corpses: they are all bloody and hacked to pieces (vv. 714–17). Nevertheless, the highborn persons receive particular attention and are lamented in short speeches glorifying their deeds. Dietrich, for example, asks the assembly to interrupt their own lamentations to give him a chance to talk about Kriemhild, whose corpse he has stumbled upon. First he expresses his deep sorrow for her untimely death, then he pronounces his determination to grieve for her as well although "your scheming has robbed me of my best kin" (vv. 778f.). Subsequently, Dietrich mentions her unfailing support, which she always had provided him with and for which he now wants to repay her. He picks up her body and places it on a bier and is then joined by Hildebrand and Etzel, the latter once again being described as "the epitome of despair" (802). The King curses his destiny and then throws himself upon Kriemhild's chest and kisses her hands. Whatever the Queen might have done throughout her life, she is here cleared of all wrong-doings and praised for her life-long truthfulness (v. 810f.). In honor of the deceased lady, Dietrich retells the King all he knows about the horrible events leading to Kriemhild's death. The royal husband laments his destiny once again, bemoans the loss of his wife, of his only child, of all his warriors, and even of his in-laws, the Burgundians, "who enjoyed such high esteem as long as they were alive" (vv. 825–27), obviously paying attention to a specific social order among the dead, but also venting his profound emotions of anger, aggression, hostility, and perhaps also guilt for being still alive after such atrocities have been committed at his court.[27] Moreover, Etzel remembers all his kinfolk and the noble guests from many different countries whom he had invited to his court festival, concluding with a praise of his own men who have fallen in the battle, "were they Christians or heathens, through whom my honor was steadily increased" (vv. 848f.).

Curiously, though, when Etzel, after having concluded his speech, finally breaks down in pain, Dietrich criticizes him for his excessive behavior, reprimanding him to act "like a wise man. My advice is: do not concern yourself with those things that cannot be of any advantage [to] you" (vv. 855–57). Scholarship has often harped on the strange contrast between Etzel's role as ruler and his extreme lamentation, referring to this passage with Dietrich's comments.[28] It seems, however, that the aesthetic and ethical categories used for this negative criticism ignore the simple fact that the *Lament* poet solely focuses on the experience with death and on the few survivors' reactions. A calm, self-controlled, and resolute Etzel would be inappropriate in narrative terms here, as in fact no medieval ruler whose entire family and army of men had been slaughtered would have assumed the behavior that these modern critics have demanded.[29] Interestingly, as Gerd Althoff points out, quite often medieval kings cried and lamented in public for very specific purposes, and their ritual performance of bereavement reflected profound cultural expectations and behavioral patterns required for concrete situations.[30] The same can be claimed for Etzel as the one person in the Hunnish kingdom who has lost the most in personal terms and as the highest ranking person among all mourners. Significantly, each individual bereavement of the most outstanding warriors killed on the battlefield is accompanied by extensive commentary on their previous achievements and their reputation as heroes. For instance, when the men bring the corpse of Blödelin, who was the first to die, to Etzel, his brother, the King exclaims his sorrow and pain over the great loss, but then also clearly states Blödelin's fault of having incited the Burgundians and criticizes him for having started the fight on Kriemhild's behalf. At the same time, Etzel considers the Burgundian heroes whom his brother killed, and subsequently bemoans the fact that all these early events were kept hidden from him.

Moreover, Etzel's bereavement includes self-accusations as he had previously abandoned the Christian god and had returned to his old belief not trusting the Church's teachings. Although he knows that Christianity is the only true religion, he feels so ashamed of his own apostasy that he does not "dare [to] appear before the one whom I wished to serve" (vv. 1002f.). His mourning now transforms into despair and assumes a dangerous level forcing Dietrich and Hildebrand to intervene because—at least in modern psychological terms—Etzel's "bereavement is best considered as a psychosomatic disease with possibly catastrophic consequences."[31] They try to appeal to his manly virtues and warn him against acting "like some silly woman who is moping around pining for her friends. We are not at all accustomed to seeing you act in such an unmanly fashion" (1021–23).

Dietrich attempts to divert Etzel's attention from his own suffering and pain to the needs of other people, such as himself, and requests his help in regaining his own home country, as now all of his men have died and nobody is left to support him in his quest: "help Dietrich out of his plight" (v. 1045f.). The King, however, brushes aside this effort and bluntly states that never before has such a tragedy struck any person in this world. All he can do is prepare the funeral of his family and friends and so he continues to focus on his personal experience in all of its drastic consequences. Dietrich makes another attempt to help Etzel when they come across Gunther's corpse, stressing the Burgundians' own fault, arrogance, and hatred as responsible for the furious slaughter (vv. 1148ff.). Hildebrand even curses at Hagen as a "devil" who was ultimately responsible for the outcome of the bloody event because he had refused, even under the worst conditions, to negotiate with him or anybody else and had been bent on killing everybody in his fury to defend King Gunther, his brothers, and the other Burgundians. Moreover, he reminds Etzel that Hagen had murdered Siegfried and so "deserved the wrath of God for a long time now" (v. 1272).

Even though Hildebrand's psychological strategy does not work as intended, the bystanders follow his suggestions and curse at Hagen's corpse, "for it was because of him that they had been deprived of so much joy" (vv. 1298–1300). Bereavement quickly proves to be a communal activity requiring all members of the affected group to participate in the ritual: "[t]e women were weeping outside and many a young lady stood there in great sorrow over the terrible sight" (vv. 1587–90). Dietrich and Hildebrand also collapse and weep miserably when they find their dead friends on the field, and Etzel commiserates with them every time (vv. 1667ff.).

When the news of the disastrous outcome of the court festivals reach the survivors in Vienna, Pöchlarn, and Worms, they also join in the heart-rending grieving process with very similar gestures, expressions, and actions. Those who are affected most by the inexpressible pain mourn until they themselves succumb to death. Although the narrator does not tell us much about Etzel's destiny, the context indicates that he will die as well: "The king had sat down in the blood below the door, and the good man was grieving so much that no one could console him" (vv. 1780–84), or: "They tried to console him, but it was all to no avail, for he had lost too much" (vv. 2479–81). When the terrible news reach Rüedeger's widow, Gotelind, she experiences so much pain that she passes away (v. 4232), and in Worms the old queen mother Uote succumbs to the same destiny because "[n]o one was able to find a way to console her in her grief" (vv. 3956f.). Etzel, in turn, is abandoned by Dietrich and Hildebrand, who want to return to their home country, and Rüedeger's daughter Dietlinde is left behind as well, all alone and in charge of her duchy. As soon as this point has been reached, the narrator breaks off and concludes quite abruptly with some mysterious allusions to Etzel's possible destiny and with the indication that Bishop Pilgrim had all the events copied down by a scribe (vv. 4315f.). This then became the source for many adaptations all over the German lands as "[o]ld and young alike are familiar with it" (vv. 4318f.), which can be translated as: mourning is an experience familiar to everyone.

In short, *The Lament* is not a glorification of death, but instead serves as a literary vehicle to understand the essential elements of bereavement and also to warn against political and military actions that lead to war, murder, and slaughter.[32]

About two hundred years later, the Bohemian scribe and cleric Johannes of Tepl, also known as Johannes of Saaz, composed a famous dialogue poem involving Death and a mourning widower, the Plowman, or rather, in the true meaning of the word, Everyman. Although Johannes created his text for rhetorical purposes, as he later revealed in a letter to a friend, and although *The Plowman*, as a work of fiction, demonstrates many direct connections with the literary tradition, it nevertheless provides important insight into late-medieval attitudes toward death and outlines standard bereavement practices of that time.

On August 1, 1400, Johannes' wife Margaretha passed away, to her husband's great chagrin. In his dialogue with the personified Death he raises heavy charges against him, condemns and curses death, and heavily laments the loss of his wife. Both from a philosophical and from an ethical point of view, Johannes developed a remarkable dialogue poem that reflects not only late-medieval attitudes toward death and mourning, but also indicates the first responses of a German writer to Italian Renaissance thinking that consolation for the mourner is found in the ideas that human life in itself excels through its divine dignity and that the human body proves to be, despite its ephemeral character and weak constitution, the crown of God's creation.[33] Whereas German scholarship has hitherto mostly focused on rhetorical strategies, philological features, lexicological elements, and the literary-historical sources,[34] here we will examine how Johannes developed the bereavement ritual and what model of public mourning is presented in his text.[35]

Whereas in *The Lament* the survivors were entirely given to weeping and moaning and were involved in the funeral of the scores of dead heroes, in *The Plowman* an individual speaker rises and curses Death for being a "dreadful murderer of all good folk" (11). In keeping with his rhetorical strategy, Johannes has his Everyman utter a series of harsh condemnations of Death, culminating in the typically irrational outburst: "may all that lives and breathes turn from you, abominate you and curse you to all eternity!" (11).[36] Although Death stays very calm and scoffs at his human opponent for his useless and insubordinate accusations, the Plowman casts him as a vile creature that "most cruelly ripped out the twelfth letter of my alphabet, the treasure house of my joys" (15). Death has robbed him of all his joys and happiness and deprived him of any sense of direction for his life. The pain and suffering resulting from his wife's death make him yell out against the eternal forces of death: "Death, be accursed!" (17). At first, however, he does not succeed in breaching through the energetic defense set up by Death, who in his superior manners and bemused affability inquires further into the reasons for such unheard-of accusations (17f.). The Plowman begins with his "Trauerarbeit" by bringing back to memory the beauty, love, and tenderness of his late wife: "You have taken her, the dear delight of my eyes; she is gone, my sure shield against adversity, my true divining rod" (19). Full with bile, the mourner charges Death as the one who deserves to die himself and to "rot in Hell!" (21). His wife was his "greatest treasure" (29), meaning that sorrow will fill his heart to the end of his life (29). He appeals to God to give his blessings to her, as she was an outstanding wife, always displayed a modest "demeanor and had a care for every honor, and people blessed her kindly" (29). The Plowman presents a moving eulogy on his wife and bitterly characterizes Death as "wicked" and as an "enemy of all mankind" (31). Similarly, in a subsequent speech, the widower lauds the deceased once again as a mirror of all human virtues and begs God to guard her in the afterlife (35). The beauty and glory of the wife are always directly contrasted with the ugliness, meanness, and murderous nature of Death, whom he charges with having robbed him of his wife and his children of their mother: "Wretched, lonely and full of sorrow I remain, without amends from you" (41). Similarly as Kriemhild, the Plowman requests God to avenge him against "that arch-villain Death" (43), not yet understanding, of course, that death is as much a part of God's creation as he himself. At this point the widower is not even able to argue rationally against Death, who ridicules him and undermines the mourner's claims as he knows too well that death is inevitable and that a life that lasts too long proves to be miserable (45). Moreover, Death now points out that he is infinitely powerful and cannot be opposed; that is, death is part of nature. The Plowman therefore begins to reflect upon his own existence, begs God for consolation and—still—revenge against Death: "O God, consoler of the broken-hearted, console me and comfort me, poor, grieving, wretched lonely man that I am. And, Lord, send down torment and retribution upon cruel Death, Your enemy and the enemy of us all" (47).

In the subsequent debate Death quite successfully defends himself and his role in life, and so forces the Plowman to turn away from his immediate bereavement to an investigation of the meaning of death, whom the Plowman then accuses of being unfair in his treatment of people: "Where have they gone, all those of whom the chronicles tell so much, all the sages, the masters, the just, the brave? You have murdered them all and my dearest too. The base remain" (55). Subsequently, the Plowman develops a much more polite tone of voice, addresses Death in a more formal manner, and then even requests help from him: "show me how I can lift such heavy sorrow from my heart and how so virtuous a mother can be made good to my children" (67). In fact, after a while the Plowman begins to understand some of Death's arguments, yet still questions the justification for his existence and discusses the importance of remembering those who have passed away: "Though she is dead to me in the body, yet she still lives on in my memory" (77).

Most important, with chapters 24 and 25, the dialogue reaches a decisive turning point as the two combatants explore the meaning of life and love in general terms. Whereas Death outrightly rejects both aspects as not worth striving for and even decries the human body as a foul vessel "conceived in sin, nourished in his mother's body on unclean, indescribable filth, and born naked; he is a smeary beehive, a piece of loathsomeness" (77–79), the Plowman suddenly perceives his chance to turn the tables and forcefully counter-argues with a glorious defense of the human being as brilliantly conceived by God as his masterpiece. In particular, "[m]an alone possesses reason, that noble treasure. He alone is that dear clay which none but God can make" (83). This leaves Death almost speechless, and whereas before he had displayed a superior intelligence, calmness, and rationality, now, beginning with chapter 26, all these strengths are lost, and Death adduces rather emotional and

irrational countercharges that actually undermine his own early arguments against the Plowman. Whereas at the early stage of the debate the
mourner had displayed nothing but affects and externalized inner tur-
moil, it is now Death's turn to follow this path of fury, anger, and irri-
tation motivated only by the desire to defend his position and power
base. Insofar as he now even criticizes the seven liberal arts, and the
occult arts, jurisprudence, and scholasticism and claims that "[e]very man
must always be brought low by us" (87), and insofar as the Plowman
subsequently inquires about his own future course of life, whether he
should remarry or turn into a cleric, the actual bereavement process has
come to a conclusion and has been replaced with a political and ideological struggle over the value of women (*querelle des femmes*) and their
role in men's lives. Furthermore, the Plowman catches Death in making
contradictory statements and warns him that without life there would
also be no death: "What becomes of you then, Death?" (101). Whereas
the widower had been the spokesperson for all mourners in this world,
now he speaks up for the value of life, argues against Death's nihilistic
attitude, and solicits succor from God against his enemy.

   At the end God raises his voice as well and settles the debate by giving "honor to the plaintiff [Plowman] and victory to Death" (111), but
not without emphasizing the continuity of human life in spiritual terms.
Although all life is owed to Death and the body returns to the earth,
man's soul will rejoin with God (111). Johannes von Tepl breaks off at
this point, and was probably wise to do so, as no human argument has
any validity against death, "since every man is bound to give his life to
Death" (111). Insofar, however, as the starting point was the Plowman's
bereavement, a powerful message about how to cope with the pain associated with the passing away of a beloved person, is gradually conveyed.
The first stage proved to be the violent outpouring of grief, the lament
for the deceased. Especially because Death took such a radical stand in
opposition to all human life, the Plowman saw himself forced to turn his
attention away from his own pain toward general, rational deliberations
in which critical thinking, philosophical arguments, and rhetorical strategies play a major role. In other words, the Plowman carries out significant "Trauerarbeit" by coming to terms with his own individual case
through increasingly placing it in a general context that requires the
defense of life as such against the forces of Death.

   God, however, cannot but crown Death with victory because without
the passing away of the old life no new life could come into existence.
But the Plowman is awarded honor because he has proven to be a good
citizen in God's universe, as a powerful advocate of the *dignitas humani*,
as an outstanding defender of womanhood against ancient misogyny,

and also as someone who was able to go through the bereavement process in a constructive manner, realizing that *memoria* is the greatest accomplishment of the survivors in the face of their profound pain and suffering. As *The Plowman* indicates in the final analysis, memory guarantees that those who have died will continue to live in the minds of posterity, which is—in many senses—already indicative of Renaissance thinking.[37]

The Plowman's mourning, then, is not simply an instinctive response to his basic feelings, but emerges as a powerful tool to search one's own soul, to reflect upon one's station in life, to weigh human existence at large and evaluate it in terms of past and future events. In this regard the dialogue proves to be not really a dialogue between two sides, but rather the mourner's self-reflection and, so to speak, an internalized monologue,[38] dealing with the grief and realizing the need to live according to spiritual values. The death of his wife and his subsequent bereavement led him to examine in great detail how life and death can be viewed, how the various arguments for either side have to be evaluated, and how to place human existence within the divine creation. The poem represents masterful "Trauerarbeit," and as such it fulfilled a very specific, concrete purpose: to console those suffering from the enormous pain of the death of a loved one.[39] *Memoria*, that is, the detailed imaging and remembrance of the deceased person, the projection of her character and virtues, the argument with death over the justification of having taken her instead of any other person, and finally the defense of life as such, not only that of the dead wife, make up the key elements in the bereavement process and help the mourner to return to life, to his responsibilities, hopes, and tasks.[40]

Mourning and the lament about the death of beloved ones take a different twist in the highly idiosyncratic didactic epic *Der Ring* by the Constance lawyer Heinrich Wittenwiler (ca. 1400). The primary objective of this unusual verse narrative consists in ridiculing people's foolishness and ignorance even though they are given the relevant teachings. The author presents a peasant couple, Bertschi Triefnas and Mätzli Rüerenzumph—both names carry fairly obvious obscene meanings—who manage, after many struggles and oppositions, to get married. During the wedding celebrations a fight breaks out, which quickly erupts into a bitter war between the guests, who come from two different villages. Both sides call in help from all over the world, and subsequently the one side wins over the other and kills everybody, with the exception of the groom, who had hid in the attic of a barn and, when discovered, had pretended having lost his mind, scaring away his enemies. As soon as they have disappeared, he climbs down and surveys the battlefield. Immediately it dawns upon him that nobody has survived, that all human life has been wiped out in his village, Lappenhausen, as even all women and children have been killed (9661-66).[41] Quite similar to the Andreas Gryphius' poem, quoted at the beginning of this study, Bertschi realizes that there is nothing left for him in this world, not even any property or honor (9665). His first reaction in this devastating situation is to start crying (9668); next he faints—quite parallel to King Etzel in the epic *Lament*—and does not regain consciousness until half a day later, only to begin with the second stage of the bereavement process ("Trauerarbeit"), shouting, screaming, and lamenting: "Ein sendes gschrai derhuob er so" (9673; he began to cry miserably). During this mourning he also reflects upon the cause of his tragic destiny, and realizes that it was his own fault in the long run because he did not pay attention to the many wise instructions and ignored all advice. Apparently resonating Boethius' profound teachings about the impact of fortune on human life in his *De consolatione philosophiae* (Consolation of Philosophy, 524 or 525 C.E.), Bertschi concludes that human life is only temporary (9684), that all material goods are easily lost due to fortune's workings (985f.), and that man's effort to build his existence is easily brought to nought because of his weakness and ignorance (9698f.). Only fear of God and God's love for man remain stable factors in this world (9690f.). Consequently, the protagonist turns his back on his former life and disappears in the Black Forest, where he becomes a hermit and dedicates himself entirely to God's service. The narrator concludes with the comment that this was the only guarantee for Bertschi to gain eternal life (9696), offering us a religious perspective resulting from mourning.[42] Moreover, the death of his newly married wife, of his parents, friends, and all neighbors forces the young man to ponder the meaning of life and ways to achieve the salvation of his soul. Mourning thus serves as the major vehicle for religious philosophy, transforming the ignorant lad into a hermit. The peasant setting, however, and the global didactic teachings, which structure the huge verse epic, indicate the author's fundamental message, warning all his readers/listeners to pay close attention to serious advice, to develop meaningful, rational, and ethical goals, to pursue those in a devout and pious manner, and to bridle one's lust and cupidity. Even though the mourning scene in Wittenwiler's *Ring* occupies only a short segment of the entire epic, its cathartic function is of prime importance and provides the narrative with a fundamental corrective course out of the world of foolishness to a world dedicated to God (cf. Brant's *The Ship of Fools*[43]).

Undoubtedly, the literary forum proves to be a major vehicle for people of all ages and cultures to come to terms with the devastating

experience of the death of a beloved person. It is irrelevant whether
Andreas Gryphius or Heinrich Wittenwiler, the anonymous composer of
The Lament or Johannes von Tepl were individually impacted by the loss
and personally suffered from profound grief. What matters is that
mourning creates a community of people who share the same values and
emotions and gain support from the explicit treatment of grief by some
external means, and here in our case through the literary reflection.
Poets from all times have played a major role for their societies to formulate the rituals of mourning in literary form, allowing the outsiders to
gain insight into the painful experience of those who were directly
effected, and thus to join them in their bereavement. Moreover, the
poetic treatment of mourning also carries a powerful message against the
causes of the tragedy responsible for the death of the beloved person or
for the destruction of a whole country. In addition, these texts also provide the crucial means to begin with the constructive "Trauerarbeit,"
hence with the reconstruction of one's own life and to span a metaphoric
bridge over the gap left by the deceased. In this sense, perhaps, Johannes
von Tepl's *Plowman* might be the most impressive literary document,
insofar as, here, the mourner not only goes through the entire range of
emotions, but also begins to explore the meaning of life and at the end
successfully defends it against the vicious attacks by Death.

PART II

MEDIEVAL TEARS AND TRAUMA

CHAPTER 3

DISORDERED GRIEF AND FASHIONABLE AFFLICTIONS IN CHAUCER'S *FRANKLIN'S TALE* AND THE *CLERK'S TALE*

M. C. BODDEN

The *Franklin's Tale* and the *Clerk's Tale* are double tales—bound by stories of women who, beyond the marriage vow, plight a further vow to their husbands. Both women, subsequently, experience first their husbands' pressing that vow to the extreme, then near annihilation as complete women and wives, and, finally, through a twist of events at the end, a "rescue" from the tragic results of their ancillary or secondary vow. Both tales are fraught with those ideological tensions we've come to anticipate in Chaucer's work, including the nature of "trouthe," the issue of female agency in apparently powerless women, the concept of "gentilesse," the nature of freedom, etc. One other ideological tension—that of the signifying practices of grief and gender—is particularly striking, not so much because it cuts across genders but because it challenges gender itself, and, more specifically, gender roles, as a social construct. By exposing the way that prescribed roles of grieving subvert the natural expressions/feelings of both women and men, Chaucer intends (in my view) to radicalize the ambiguity or tension of these roles so as to—and this is the important point—lay bare their conflicting positions, revealing, thereby, the way that cultural contexts determine roles of grieving for women and men. In pushing these roles to the extreme—the women's forms of grief are conspicuously extreme, but so, too, in their seemingly acceptable, but more elaborate form of grief, are the men's—Chaucer exposes the damage done to both genders. (In some respects Chaucer's technique anticipates Pierre Macherey's theory of literary production, namely that in the process of becoming part of a text, ideology "undoes" the text by exposing its deficiencies and contradictions).[1] We are led not only to question the primacy of gender in the types of grief inscribed upon it, but also to recognize that the parameters of grief are circumscribed by the perimeters of unhealthy codes— such as, for example, the symbolically charged code of courtly love in the *Franklin's Tale*.[2] There, the lover's (Aurelius) fragmented self becomes glorified as the site of love, giving, as he does, his entire being over to excessive meditation upon the beloved; yet his meditation is disconnected from his social and public behavior because another code, *derne* love ("concealed" love), prevents him from disclosing that love to her. Or the cultural principle/code that underlies those ancillary pledges made by Arveragus and Dorigen, and by Griselda in the *Clerk's Tale:* there, the pledges presume a particular, flawed code, namely, the conviction that surviving a severe testing of that "trouthe" is evidence of the highest love. As a result of Dorigen's pledging her "trouthe . . . til that [her] herte brest" (759), her body becomes the site of men's negotiating sexual "rights." The same is true of Griselda. Keeping her pledge subjects her body and spirit to Walter's brutality. This chapter, then, examines how the prescribed roles of grieving undermine the natural expressions/feelings of both women and men, and how Chaucer leads us to question the primacy of gender in the types of grief inscribed upon it. It explores as a secondary concern the unhealthy codes that determine roles of grieving for women and men. Chiefly, I will focus upon the *Franklin's Tale*, with a glance at the way in which the second principle plays out in the *Clerk's Tale*.

In both the *Franklin's Tale* and the *Clerk's Tale*, grief expressed by women appears to be less a complex code than it is—perhaps designedly—a disordered construct, a possibility we shall consider, later. As expressed by the men in the *Franklin's Tale*, however, grief is deliberately an elaborate as well as a complex construct. Because both Arveragus and Aurelius are cast in the terms of courtly Romance, their grief assumes the ritualistic forms of that coded system, acted out as a fashionable affliction. "Love figured as illness is of course a commonplace of medieval literature," as Mary Wack notes.[3] Medieval medical handbooks and treatises abounded with discussions of classic cures for the grief and melancholy of lovesickness, its psychic forms (as well as its somatic forms). This aesthetic-medical discourse coincided with another event: the Petrarchan emphasis upon the poet's spiritualized passion for the unattainable beloved. Out of these cultural intersections emerged the perception that intense eroticized suffering was a mark of one's nobility, a testimony to one's patrician feelings. Indeed, Chaucer's Troilus "claims to prove the nobility of his love through his ability to suffer from it."[4]

Not content with melancholia simply being a mark of nobility, Marsilio Ficino (1433–1499) elevated it to the "'elite idleness' that afflicted men precisely as the sign of their exceptionality, as the inscription of genius within them"—a sign of spiritual greatness.[5] This may well have contributed to the longevity of eroticized grief as a socio-physical phenomenon. In his *Treatise on Lovesickness* [or *Erotic Melancholy*] (1623), Renaissance physician Jacques Ferrand, using historical and contemporary sources,[6] declared "the disease of love melancholy one of the most prominent of the age."[7] Ferrand's text, considered the "medical *summa* in the Renaissance on the diseases of erotic love,"[8] regarded the literary and social codes of courtly love as a chief cause behind the states of erotic despair, although the human condition was also to blame.[9] The "romantic fervor espoused as a mark of the gentleman, fostered by literary as well as by social models," promoted "a climate of psychological high risk in the fashions of love."[10] Ferrand is, of course, describing the early 1600s, when, presumably, the "disease" and its manifestations are cresting.[11] Except for the greater breadth of this "illness" among the aristocratic ranks of the Renaissance and the greater medical attention it received, Ferrand's conclusions equally describe the situation of the Middle Ages.[12]

With the *Franklin's Tale* (and the *Clerk's Tale*), Chaucer deliberately intervenes in the period's "conversation" about erotic suffering signifying a noble nature, and lays bare the terms at stake. In the *Franklin's Tale*, those terms are *fraunchise* and *fredom*, i.e., "nobility of character" or "generosity." All three characters, Arveragus, Aurelius, and the astrologer/magician, perform deeds inspired by or nurtured through an experienced loss. All three, consequently, view (and praise) the other as exemplary of *fraunchise* and *fredom*. However, what actually engenders this *fraunchise* and *fredom* is exposed through Chaucer's examination of two codes (with their implications). The first is the code that holds that chivalric exploits lead to superior character, thus enabling *fraunchise* and *fredom*. The second code maintains that erotic sorrow signals a depth of affection in the suitor's soul that is associated with a loss or unattainability of the beloved. In the *Franklin's Tale*, the first code is debunked when it becomes clear that chivalric exploits and daunting tasks get no one anywhere. It is solely erotic sorrow/melancholy that produces results for Arveragus' wooing of Dorigen (whether or not it signals profound affection in the suitor's soul, we will discover later). Despite the fact that for years Arveragus had wrought "many a labour" and "many a greet emprise" to win Dorigen's hand, her decision to "take hym for hir housbonde and hir lord" comes about not because of his exploits, but, rather, because of Arveragus' "penaunce" (distress)[13]—

> atte laste she, for his worthynesse,
> And namely for his meke obeysaunce,
> Hath swich a pittee caught of his penaunce
> That pryvely she fil of his accord.[14]

Already, then, early on in the tale we encounter the significance of suffering as an enabling ethos for a suitor—of more value to his courtship success, it seems, than were his worthiness and "obeysaunce." In fact, Chaucer uses Arveragus' literary grief to critique grief itself, or rather grief's socio-political benefits (giving us a glimpse of cultural connections intersecting a text at the time of its production—as the New Historicists would put it). Arveragus is keenly aware that he is Dorigen's social inferior. In a culture that promulgated suffering as a property of nobility, his distress may function as purely literary distress, a reflection of the courtly code; however, it may also reflect a competing cultural value: Arveragus may be using his distress to capitalize on the nobility inscribed within such grief to elevate his status in Dorigen's eyes.

The issue of grief is, in fact, more central to the tale's characterization and narrative movement than is the question asking which character is "mooste fre"—the subject of numerous articles. Grief not only opens the tale, it intrudes into the exchange of vows themselves, and initiates every subsequent major contract pledged between the characters. Immediately after the exchange of vows, themselves charged with the language of courtly love ("He swore hire as a knight" [745], she, thankful for his "gentillesse," offers, "Have heer my trouthe-til that myn herte breste"[759]), Arveragus is moved to rise above the traditional privileging of male domination through "maistrie." He will not, he pledges, exercise "maistrie" against Dorigen's will (747). But, he adds a proviso: since Dorigen is of higher lineage ("comen of so heigh kynrede" [735]), he would like to have at least the "name of soveraynetee" lest he be faced with "shame of his degree" (751–52). This prompts the Franklin to reflect aloud: granting mutual freedom, he says, carries a price, namely the need to have patience in love. "Lerneth to suffre," he crisply remarks (777). Learning to suffer, coupled with patience, prevents the consequences of doing or speaking amiss (780). His meaning is unmistakable: cultivation of suffering is desirable as a means of mediating freedom in a relationship; so, be open to experiencing melancholy. It seems to be good advice, and, oddly enough, it is the only advice on sustaining mutual happiness in marriage. As such, the phrase takes on exceptional weight. Is "lerneth to suffre" genuine advice or sardonic observation: will the cultivation of melancholy or suffering really prove to be valuable and acceptable for men and women, or will it lead to prescribed roles that subvert natural expressions/feelings of women and men? And, as it turns out, learning to suffer is precisely what each of them fails to do even as both engage in prescribed roles of suffering— roles that ultimately put their marriage at risk. During Arveragus' two-year absence, Dorigen had been importuned by Aurelius, a squire. Her grief over her fears of Arveragus' possible shipwreck leads her—in pley, as the Franklin notes—to give her "trouthe" to Aurileus if he removed the rocks "stoon by stoon" (993) from Brittany's shore (an "inpossible"). Unfortunately, she adds, "I seye, whan ye has maad the coost so clene/Of rookes that ther nys no stoon ysene" (995–996). That added line virtually changes her request from a material condition to a visual condition. And for an astrologer/magician this makes an "inpossible" possible; at Aurelius' request, he makes the rocks appear to disappear. Learning of the situation from Dorigen upon his return, Arveragus' initial response is intriguing: "with glad chiere, in freendly wyse/ Answerede . . . 'Is ther oght elles, Dorigen, but this?' " (1467–69). We are prompted to wonder, for a second, whether, remembering his pledge to share maistrie, he will turn over to her the problem of working out a solution, with his help, if she wishes.[15] Instead, he follows his question by immediately bursting into tears, and straightway threatening death for her if the promise is revealed to anyone. Further, he insists, their faces are never to reveal their difficulty. Here, then, in Arveragus' response, gender and grief come together, anchored within a wholly masculine ideology marked by a bracing, inflexible principle and by silent grief. Unilaterally exercising maistrie and prescribing the role of grief for both of them, Arveragus subverts the natural expression of feelings felt by both. Next, he privatizes the grief, silencing both her public countenance and her voice, and disempowering, therefore, Dorigen's access to any other person's help or advice. Finally, his command that she must keep her "trouthe" seems to violate his "trouthe" to her since he does not even seek to look into the "trouthe" of the situation.[16] After all, Dorigen's part of the bargain was to ask nothing less than that the entire Brittany "shoreline be cleaned of its boulders."[17] One would think that the fulfillment of this bizarre request bore looking into, especially if one's wife's body was implicated in the contract. Far from "nevere in al his lyfe" would he "take no maistrie Agayn hir wyl" but rather "folwe hir wyl in al" (747–49). Arveragus, instead, reverts to the traditional concern for male sovereignty and male honor. His actions likewise reinforce the two prevalent codes of grief, namely, the long-suffering lover and the stoic endurer. The extremity of the situation discloses the codes' inherent conflict: because he subscribes to the melancholy encoded in the courtly love system, he can grieve, but only within an artificial construct.

On the other hand as the abiding stoic, he denies himself any expression of grief at all—imposing the same denial upon Dorigen, as well. Neither code allows him to participate in natural mourning. The second code elevates his manhood, empowering his status; the first—abasing himself in mourning—risks his claim to sovereignty, undermining therefore the natural impulse to grieve. Yet, both cultural roles (the longsuffering lover and the stoic endurer) are sanctioned not only by the Franklin but also by early (and some later) Chaucer scholars. The Franklin and scholars, both, more than legitimate Arveragus' melancholy; they honor it by declaring it noble, "gentil," and "fre."[18]

Aurelius' grief is even more prescribed: it completely follows the classical formula of indulging in courtly love—with one critical exception: he performs no labors to win Dorigen. Indeed, the only labor he undertakes will prove to be an illusion wrought (significantly) by someone else. Rather, the whole of Aurelius' courtly love activity is non-stop grief-work, so to speak. His is textbook courtly love's grief, fashionably felt, and fashionably afflicted. Suffering his "penaunce" (942) for two years, he is constrained by the code of "derne" love never to speak of his love-sickness for Dorigen—"save in his songes" (944). There, he would "somwhat" reveal "his wo" (944–45). Of course, since Aurelius is a prolific songwriter, he composes copious layes, songs, complaints, roundels, and virelayes whose refrains repeatedly speak of how he cannot reveal his sorrow. Finally, he confesses to Dorigen his love for her. Her first response is direct and unambiguous: "By thilke God that yaf me soule and lyf,/Ne shal I nevere been untrewe wyf/In word ne work/. . . Taak this for fynal answere as of me" (983–87). Then, "in pley," Dorigen offers to give Aurelius her "trouthe" and to "love [him] best of any man" (997) provided he clear the entire coast of Britanny of rocks. Even Aurelius realizes the intended insurmountability of the task, declaring, "This were an inpossible" (1009). For the next two years, he gives himself up to suffering and immobilizing melancholy. This is what Juliana Schiesari regards as male melancholia "understood as an eroticized lack of the object that builds up the subject"[19]—much as Petrarch builds up his artistic self in the poetic idealizing of the loss of Laura. Aurelius' discourse of loss is mediated through cultural mythology: "Under his brest he baar it moore secree/Than evere dide Pamphilus for Galathee" and ". . . in his herte ay was the arwe kene./And wel ye knowe that of a sursanure[20]/In surgerye is perilous the cure,/But men myghte touche the arwe or come therby" (1109–1115). Mythological tragedies and medical metaphors hinting at the substantiality of his loss give cultural sanction to Aurelius' neurosis. In this climate of privileged suffering, the reader/audience will associate nobility of character with a grandness of melancholy. Things change only when Aurelius' brother takes the initiative, and with Aurelius, secures the services of an astrologer/magician from Orlean. The magician agrees to make the rocks seem to disappear, but, he says, the price is high: a thousand pounds of gold. Aurelius agrees to pay it, and the rocks appear to disappear. Commanded by Arveragus to keep her pledge to Aurelius, Dorigen heads toward the garden to find him. By his own arranged coincidence, Aurelius meets her on the way and asks her whither she was going. Her answer, "half as she were mad," stuns him: "Unto the gardyn, as myn housbonde bad,/My trouthe for to holde—allas, allas!" (1512–13). To his credit, Aurelius is moved at once by her "lamentacioun" and by compassion for Arveragus who virtually put his wife in jeopardy in order that she should not "breke hir trouthe" (1519). Unable to "doon so heigh a cherlyssh wrecchednesse/Agayns franchise and alle gentillesse" (1523–24), he releases Dorigen from her pledge. Nobility will out. But in his explanation to the magician (he has neither the "reward" of his contract, namely Dorigen, nor can he pay the second half of his debt; he needs time) we discover where the weight of his compassion seems to lie:

> He seide, "Arveragus, of gentillesse,
> Hadde levere dye in sorwe and in distresse
> Than that his wyf were of hir trouthe fals."
> The sorwe of Dorigen he tolde hym als;
> How looth hire was to been a wikked wyf,
> And that she levere had lost that day hir lyf,
> And that hir trouthe she swoor thurgh innocence,
> She nevere erst hadde herde speke of apparence.
> "That made me han of hire so greet pitee."
>
> (ll. 1595–1603)

It is, first, *Arveragus'* "sorwe" and "distresse" that evoke deep sympathy and admiration from Aurelius. Only then, four lines later, does he *also* ("als") tell of the sorrow of Dorigen. The conjunction "als" is telling.[21] *In addition* to his pity for Arveragus, he feels grief over Dorigen's suffering. Her naiveté about appearances and her sorrow, he says, caused him "greet pitee." The values in his confession are clear: Arveragus' grief is to be far more admired; Dorigen's is to be pitied. For Aurelius, Arveragus' grief is a sign of his nobility, his *fraunchise*.

In conspicuous contrast to Arveragus' and Aurelius' griefs, Dorigen's melancholy/grief is not at all glorified. In fact, her grief is presented largely as disorder. At the text's purely lexical level itself, disorder is already courted. Except for the two phrases at lines 734–35, "faireste

under sonne" and of "heigh kynrede," nearly all the remaining two
hundred and twenty - some lines devoted to Dorigen's character
describe a person given to excessive, and often inappropriate, melancholy. The effect of such *dyssymmetry in characterization is to produce
gender dyssymmetry*. Arveragus is at least credited with some valorous
deeds abroad before his crisis occurs, and Aurelius is allowed some few
lines of dancing before he drops into depression over Dorigen. We see,
then, broader and more balanced concerns assigned to the male characters. However, the majority of lines describing Dorigen are dedicated
to producing a single-dimension character. Dorigen's entire performance is grief-performance. Nor is her weeping mediated by mythological references or courtly love images. Rather, hers are endless sighs and
mournings and "plainings"—to the point that her friends eventually
object. To configure the character of Dorigen's grief-behavior—in contrast to the mens' grief-behavior—as wholly that of ceaseless sighs,
mourning, and weeping is to identify disordered weeping as female.
Mythological and biblical figures negotiate her grief once: when she
contemplates her choice after learning from Aurelius that he has fulfilled his part of their "pact." Significantly, those mythological and biblical characters—figures who committed suicide rather than lose their
chastity—are common exempla.[22] The effect is to make her grief, however extreme, conventionally extreme. In fact, the formulaic extrava-
gance of Dorigen's grief suggests an intended characterization of *types*
as distinct from complex characters.[23] Ultimately, there is no distinction
between Dorigen's "real" character and a *descriptio* of a female personification: she is grief personified. The Franklin's first four lines describing Dorigen richly support this:

> And speken I wole of Dorigen his wyf,
> That loveth hire housbonde as hire hertes lyf.
> For his absence wepeth she and siketh,
> As doon thise noble wyves whan hem liketh,
> She moorneth, waketh, wayleth, fasteth, pleyneth
> (ll. 815–19)

The Franklin's opening evaluation of her grief, "as doon thise noble
wyves," abruptly removes any individuality to her sorrow and consigns
her to a category of grief. Further, "whan hem liketh" merges Dorigen
with the *idea* of grief rather than with her distinctly personal feelings and
subjectivity. Moreover, hinting that her grief arises from choice as distinct from arising out of deep distress subverts the genuine and natural
quality of her grief. The effect is to inscribe within the character of

Dorigen a grief stance that wavers between the whim of mourning and non-stop pathos—in other words, a disordered grief.

Reinforcing that disorder is the fact that her display of grief is surrounded by a complex of antique beliefs, which control not simply her freedom to publicly express her sorrows, but control as well the community's attitude toward her grief conduct. Antique beliefs (those writings on grief aimed at women whose mourning was an expected behavior, namely widows)[24] were, fundamentally, patristic attitudes encoded with a sometimes repressive morality toward legitimate mourning—*mourning* referring, in this essay, to reactions not only to death but also to other kinds of loss.[25] When Dorigen's friends remonstrate with her about her public grieving, their remarks reflect that encryption. Leslie Abend Callahan examines the mixed signals contained in these beliefs regarding the mourners' image and the behaviors prescribed for them. Although Christian attitudes toward grieving questioned whether it was selfish or "unchristian" "to mourn for someone who has entered into eternal life,"[26] the general attitude of patristic writings on grief saw widows' tears as benefiting others. She cites Jerome's "Letter to Furia" as well as Ambrose of Milan's treatise "Concerning widows." There, Ambrose praises the widows' tears (insofar as these tears can be construed as redemptive), noting that "weeping of the eyes is fitted to the sadness of the mind, arouses pity,...preserves modesty," and are "proofs of pious memory."[27] On the other hand, John Chrysostom's objections and, later, Petrarch's hostile attempts to ban women's public mourning reflect an increasingly unstable and hostile attitude toward women's public expression of their grief.[28]

Whether or not the patristic commentaries against, or Petrarch's denunciation of, public mourning directly led to late medieval English attitudes toward grief,[29] it is clear, in any case, that when Dorigen "wepeth" and "siketh," and "moorneth, waketh, wayleth, fasteth" and "pleyneth," her friends view her grief as excessive (817, 819).[30] Indeed, they come close to accusing Dorigen of failing to live harmoniously in society: "Hir freendes...preyde hir on knees, for Goddes sake,/To come and romen hire in compaignye/Awey to dryve hire derke fantasye" (841–44). Admittedly, her extreme imaginings of dangers facing Arveragus are unhealthy. However, the cultural and religious beliefs surrounding the concept of women's public grief and her freedom to express it are themselves none too healthy—whether her grief is self-induced or legitimate. And legitimate grief is soon upon her. We have already considered the dilemma in which Dorigen finds herself with Aurelius (a dilemma, incidentally, that deserves future rethinking by critics attentive to Nina Manasan Greenberg's acute observation: "it is striking that the trickery used to fulfill Aurelius' half of the bargain is not an issue within the problematics of the text").[31] Faced with Aurelius' claim upon her, Dorigen intends to die as did women of the past who were faced with her choice. Although her crisis can be argued to be of her own doing, the choices ensuing from that crisis are not. The choice of either losing her chastity or committing suicide is based on the assumption that a woman's body is a commodity in a masculine economy, an assumption promulgated through a cultural (masculinist) discourse. In classic logocentric practice, that discourse provided models authenticating its own "trouthes" by furnishing lists of women whom patristic commentators saw as modeling this "trouthe" (i.e., who "correctly" chose suicide). The character of Dorigen's grief in her crisis is thus figured through a list of biblical and mythological women who grievously harmed themselves, with the approval of generations of men.

Moreover, because women's bodies were their identity, and the culture (its art, literature, and canon laws) viewed women's bodies as representations of their honor, the issue of honor comes down, again, to that of chastity. Insofar as chastity was the preservation of that body, chastity was also the preservation of her honor. The fact is that both in Dorigen's case and in Jerome's list of women, chastity was both dictated by men and threatened by men. I stress this point because women's grief, women's bodies, and women's description in Chaucer's tales are often of a piece. That fact ultimately devalues the cultural form of women's melancholy—from many a narrator's point of view (and frequently, in the past, from the readers' point of view). But is the same wholly true of Chaucer, himself? If Chaucer has shown how both genders are damaged in following their prescribed cultural roles—exposing the unhealthy context for those cultural roles—would he, in fact, sanction Jerome's protocols of self-murder as a meaningful cultural role for negotiating dishonor? Would he not be alert to the brutal choices imposed upon women in the name of negotiating such dishonor? And would he not be responsive to the effects of such choices? More to the point of this chapter's thesis, would he not be concerned with the patriarchal representation of those effects—as in Jerome's *Adversus Jovinianum*—exposing thereby the unwholesomeness of a dishonor-suicide code that legitimated men's grief[32] and the devaluation of women? In my view he shows more than a modicum of concern, inflected both in the self-analysis that Dorigen undertakes in her monologue, as well as in the incoherent nature of the discourse itself. Mary Bowman correctly insists that Dorigen's "reading of the *exempla* gives expression to her reading of her world."[33] There is in Dorigen's reflection a clear consciousness of self and otherness. That is, she is not merely repeating the historical perspective of the women who committed suicide; rather, she encounters these women in her restating their narratives, she comments on the condition of their choice itself, and she interrogates her own response.[34] In that respect, if Dorigen is interrogating the values of her world, both she and the audience are faced with the question of just how meaningful in terms of genuine grief-work it is to call upon lists of women who were given no choice.

Second, the incoherent nature of Dorigen's recitation of the exempla, complained of by countless critics,[35] prompts me to offer a twentieth-century socio-anthropological analogy, which, as a cross-cultural fact, offers an illuminating insight. In "Weeping as a Meta-signal in a Mexicano Woman's Narrative," Jane H. Hill, citing William Washabaugh, an anthropologist, comments that "not all discourse is, in fact, coherent; exemplary of incoherence are cases where the 'muting' of oppressed groups forces them to represent their condition in the discourse of a dominant group."[36] If we consider that in the patristic *exempla* women's subjectivities are refused their own voice and converted instead into a male expression of women trapped in a binary of dishonor or death, we have the classic "muting" of the oppressed group representing their condition in the discourse of the dominant group. Moreover, as a rhetorical tactic, Chaucer's technique is brilliant: incoherence is strategically mimetic of excessive distress.

Nevertheless, the Franklin's depiction of Dorigen's grief as excessive, the remonstration by her friend to leave off from her dark fantasies, the web of beliefs and hostility surrounding women's public display of grief, and Arveragus' threat against her revealing by her countenance any sign of her "hevynesse"—all reinforce the impression throughout the tale that Dorigen's registering of grief was either inappropriate or socially inexpedient.

Where, then, Arveragus' and Aurelius' griefs are represented as rooted in male honor and desire, respectively, Dorigen's is represented as rooted in inappropriate fears. Where theirs is a recuperation of high principles and imagined heroic tragedies, hers is a recuperation of patristic *exempla* of women faced with choosing suicide over dishonor. It is clear: fashionable and socially significant grief is gendered male, or, as it was phrased in this essay's opening lines, the primacy of gender is reflected in the types of grief inscribed upon it. It may be objected that the reasons for Arveragus' and Aurelius' grief being rooted in principles and desire, respectively, naturally called for a more ceremonial manifestation of their melancholy, whereas Dorigen's excessive envisionings of possible harms and death of her husband called for a conventional *descriptio* and gestures. However, the cause of grief expressed by Arveragus and

Aurelius seems scarcely to warrant ceremonial forms. Both exhibit a type of grieving that arises not out of themselves but rather out of a loss of power over their wives/woman. In a grief of that sort, arising as it does from their possessiveness of the other, they exhibit a disconnectedness from the self, a failure to reflect upon one's self and one's actions. Further, in a remarkable representation of male grief for another male— as distinct from grief for a female—all three men in the *Franklin's Tale,* Arveragus, Aurelius, and the astrologer, express their grief in terms of magnanimous acts toward each other, not toward Dorigen.

In the *Clerk's Tale,* on the other hand, Chaucer deliberately suppresses Walter's displays of grief found in his Petrarchan source.[37] Briefly, Walter, the Marquis of Saluces in Italy, urged by his people to marry, has consented. Nevertheless, he marries against social and political expectations, marrying Griselda, a peasant girl of "vertuous beautee," and described as "oon the faireste under sonne" (211–12). He adds a specific demand to the marriage contract: she must pledge never to say "ne" to his "ye," either by her face, behavior, or speech (351–56). For the first few years of their marriage he devises extreme situations to test her faithfulness to her pledge, among them, one in which he leads her to believe that he had their two children murdered. As a final test, he demands, after eighteen years of marriage, that she return home so that he can marry someone else. She is to take nothing with her. Sadistic as Walter is in Petrarch's version, Severs[38] remarks that Chaucer "makes [Walter] seem more obstinately wilful, more heartless, more cruel than he is made out to be in Petrarch's Tale." At one point, in fact, "in both the Latin and the French originals,[39] when Walter grants the single shift or garment in response to Griseldis' request that she not walk home in public without any garment on, he cannot restrain his tears, but weeps copiously."[40] No tears are shed in Chaucer's version. Emphasized, instead, is Walter's terrorizing of Griselda as the aim of his testings.[41] It suggests therefore that his (moderate) displays of grief, like that of Arveragus and Aurelius, arise from his possessiveness of Griselda.

The women, Dorigen and Griselda, on the other hand, grieve over a loss of power over the self. Like Dorigen, Griselda's anguish is expressed in extreme form, but in Griselda, grief is so suppressed that it is unnatural. In the first place, her grief has already been negotiated by Walter. He has literally built suffering into the marriage contract: compelling her to pledge never to say "ne" to his "ye," either by her face, behavior, or speech is an outright loss of power over her self. Second, such rigid formalization of emotional response can block feeling, and the unresolved grief can become pathological. And, third, because her grief is virtually incommunicable, subliminal anger is, as I have remarked elsewhere,[42] most certainly at work when, at last, she reproaches Walter about his future behavior to the new bride. Significantly, as to grief-work, since she is denied acknowledgment of her children's (phantom) death, she cannot ask for solace for her loss, either. Her expression of her loss, perforce, is extreme in its privateness. The reader recognizes the unhealthy nature of such privateness of grief by the almost pathological quality of Griselda's public suffering during her reunion with her children. She swoons and weeps and embraces them, and then weeps again; and then, after a poignant speech, she swoons again. Nevertheless, prior to the reunion scene, in nurturing Walter's public role, and executing her own duties before her banishment from the castle, Griselda's feelings of grief are unintegrated into these daily activities. If the men's grief is disconnected from the self, so, too, thus, is the women's. Through their grief both Dorigen and Griselda lament their powerlessness but, finally, they don't combat that powerlessness. Dorigen is on her knees to Aurelius, grateful to him for his reprieve of her rash promise,[43] and Griselda continues to live in obeisance to Walter.

In theory, grief-work ought to lead one to a reconstructive process, which itself is a kind of knowledge or truth.[44] Yet, no one, neither Dorigen nor Griselda nor Arveragus, Aurelius nor Walter, appears to acquire consoling insights much less appears to be transformed by the experience. When one attempts, as Chaucer does in these tales, to negotiate among competing discourses (the signifying practices of grief and gender, the principles of courtly love, the testing of "trouthe" by marriage partners, the figuring of love as an illness, erotic suffering as the mark of nobility, male discourse of loss mediated through mythology, and female discourse of loss represented in binaries of dishonor or death), the risk is that one will expose the fraudulence of those values that nearly every cultural institution attributes to grief and loss. The characters' failure to be transformed by their experiences is, I think, Chaucer's intervention in the discursive practices of that fraud.

CHAPTER 4

GRIEF IN AVALON: SIR PALOMYDES' PSYCHIC PAIN

BONNIE WHEELER

How does it come about, that out of the bitterness of life sweet fruit is picked by groaning and weeping and sighing and mourning?

—Augustine, *Confessions* Book 4

Literature is littered with iconic, gender-expressive explosions of grief.[1] In the "General Prologue" to the *Canterbury Tales,* Chaucer reminds us that the Horatian formula (literature pleases and instructs) contains also the notion of "solaas." We habitually turn to art in times of loss, hoping that it will give voice to our dumb, raw pain. By giving voice, it provides the possibility of solace, of comfort. Literature thus transforms grief. Of poetry Mark Strand says what is true of all art:

> Even when poetry celebrates something joyful, it bears the news that the particular joy is over. It is a long memorial, a valedictory to each discrete moment on earth. But its power is at variance with what it celebrates. For it is not just that we mourn the passage of time but that we are somehow isolated from the weight of time, and when we read poems, during those brief moments of absorption, the thought of death seems painless, even beautiful.[2]

Early vernacular literatures (I think especially of Welsh and Old English) bring us close to their cultures' bones in their searing, plangent laments for the dead. The poetics of grief is a crucial cultural tool, gender-expressive and imbricated in its cultural moment. Literary expressions of grief are universal, but their inflections are pointedly local. The hero Roland and his companions die at the pass of Roncevaux, and *La Chanson de Roland*'s emperor Charlemagne is emotionally devastated:

> 'Si grant doel ai que jo ne vuldreie estre!'
> Sa barbe blanche cumencet a detraire,
> Ad ambes mains les chevels de sa teste
> Cent milie Franc s'en pasment cuntre tere.

> ['I have such great anguish that I'd rather be dead!'
> He begins to tear his white beard
> And, with both hands, the hair from his head.
> A hundred thousand Franks fall to the ground in a swoon.][3]

Charlemagne tears the majestic beard that throughout the poem signals his masculine imperial power. Collectively, vast numbers of his soldiers swoon and swoon again. Charlemagne's grief then mobilizes his anger and propels his exacting revenge. Grief is almost but not entirely a male prerogative in the poem. When fair Alda—Roland's betrothed and sister to his boon companion Oliver—hears of Roland's death, her swoon is permanent:

> Pert la culor, chet as piez Carlemagne,
> Sempres est morte, Deus ait mercit de l'anme!
> Franceis barons en plurent e si la pleignent.
> Alde la bel est a sa fin alee.

> [She loses her color, she falls at Charlemagne's feet,
> She died on the spot, may God have mercy on her soul!
> The brave French knights weep over it and lament her.
> Fair Alda has met her end.][4]

Grief is thus written on the body, expressed in gendered signs that are older than the *Iliad*. When his companion Patroklos is killed by Hector, the "black cloud of sorrow closed on Achilleus," who laments and rolls in the soot with which he covers himself.[5] Anger and grief numb his hunger: "Food and drink mean nothing to my heart/but blood does, and slaughter, and the groaning of men in the hard work."[6] In Greek tragedies, choral women tear their hair, their faces, and their clothing to express grief. Grief often begins with a ritualized self-mutilation that culminates for men in revenge and for women in despair. Chaucer opens his *Canterbury Tales* with "The Knight's Tale," his version of the subjugation of Hippolyta and the Amazons—of the "regne of Femenye"—to the proud Duke Theseus (surely one of literature's most primal myths of patriarchal struggle). Fresh from this war, Theseus—a control freak if ever there was one—arrives home expecting a triumphal welcome. Instead, the women of Athens await him with their laments and mourning:

> He was war, as he caste his eye aside,
> Where that ther kneled in the heighe weye
> A compaignye of ladyes, tweye and tweye,
> Ech after oother clad in clothes blake;
> But swiche a cry and swich a wo they make
> That in this world nys creature lyvynge
> That herde swich another waymentynge.[7]

The women demand action from Theseus. He sympathetically participates in their grief by overcoming Creon, thus enabling the pitiful ladies to bury their dead husbands. The Knight who tells Chaucer's story recoils from emotional expressiveness, but he makes his point well. If men assert power over women, then they must also requite women's grief. Rarely do men (in literary fictions) salve their grief without pugnacity; rarely does womens' grief overflow the boundaries of their own bodies.

The evocative power of the medieval Arthurian story results in large measure from its various inflections of loss. Poignant death-mourning mounts in Malory's fifteenth-century *Le Morte Darthur* almost from its opening, but it moves to a relentless crescendo from the moment that King Arthur himself berates Sir Gawain for spurring Round Table knights to undertake the Grail Quest. " 'Alas,' seyde kynge Arthure unto Sir Gawayne, 'ye have nygh slayne me for the avow that ye have made, for thorow you ye have berauffte me the fayryst and the trewyst of knyghthode that ever was sene togydir in ony realme of the worlde.' "[8] The king mourns the vow that initiates the highest Arthurian success because he knows it will supercede the knights' oath to Arthurian chivalry. Pursuing the Grail will inevitably fragment the community. The word "alas" escalates in frequency, punctuating the rest of the romance to express the loss of wholeness in the Arthurian body politic as well as— one by one—the death of its prime movers. When these are all dead, the surviving male community is full of "wepyng and dolour out of mesure" (3.1259). In the face of their comrades' deaths, Malory's knights do not squelch their grief.

But death is not the only loss that evokes grief. In this chapter I am interested in Malory's most melancholy lover, Sir Palomydes, whose history emphasizes his status as an outsider—a Saracen—and as a chivalric failure. Few male characters in medieval romance vent their pain with the full subjectivity of Sir Palomydes. When he fails, and he fails frequently, he turns in upon himself. He fills a crucial but often unexplored role in chivalric society, that of the runner-up or, perhaps more accurately, the almost-best. The runner-up is never an utter loser like the comic Sir Dynadyn, who much to the amusement of the court pouts about his losses in tournaments as well as in love; nor like Sir Kay, who becomes the lowest common denominator of Round Table knights. Sir Palomydes does not scorn or successfully circumvent the winner-take-all rules of Arthurian chivalry; he simply cannot sustain himself in the games of love and war with his rival Sir Tristram. This lack causes him profound anguish, a form of self-castigating and specifically male grief required by the compulsory regimes of chivalry. Through the figure of Sir Palomydes, we are offered a lens into the "lack" at the heart of Malory's chivalric modes.

THE "SARAZEN UNCRYSTYNDE"

The "Tale of Sir Tristram" is a breathtaking aesthetic achievement in which Malory pinpoints fissures in the chivalric understanding of love, friendship, and the possibility of community. It contains some of medieval literature's most precisely realized scenes of individual battle as well as terrifying literary graphs of emotional pain and grief. In this tale (unlike its source, the Prose *Tristan*), there are conversations in which chivalric men and women express complex emotions fully. No character in Malory is more explicit in this fashion than Sir Tristram's foil, Sir Palomydes, "the Sarazen uncrystynde," who provides Malory with the structural trajectory of his narrative. This seemingly outsider Saracen is no more "Other" than the rest of the Arthurian orphanage. These lonely knights yearn for, and rarely find, relief from the anxiety and grief at the heart of the chivalric project.

Were we to believe the French Prose *Tristan,* we have the Emperor Charlemagne to thank for all we know about King Arthur and all his knights, including Palamédes. One hundred and thirty years after King Arthur's death, Charlemagne conquered Logres and discovered "true" stories, swords, and images of Arthurian heroes.[9] In one version of the story, Charlemagne was especially moved by the heroic deeds of Galahad, Tristan, Lancelot, and Palamédes, which he has recorded in a "great book."[10] As an old man, Charlemagne would recite the adventures of these four great knights before dinner. He "always wept about the death of peerless Tristan whom he thought better than Galahad, just as he preferred Palamédes to Lancelot."[11] Palamédes' sword, better than Tristan's and even Roland's, is so potent that Charlemagne claims it for himself. If Galahad's story is usually tied to Lancelot's, Palamédes' is inevitably tied to Tristan's. In their martial and amatory rivalry, in all versions of the story, Palamédes is always the runner-up.

Charlemagne, the great Moor-slayer, is unstinting in his praise of Palamédes. Charlemagne's hero worship is untainted in the Prose *Tristan* by any concern expressed about Palamédes' paganism, yet it is the sheer fact of Palamédes' *unchristened* state that defines and degrades him through most of Malory's Arthuriad, for which the Prose *Tristan*(s) serve as major source. Malory modulated his source to concentrate on the pattern of Sir Palomydes' adventures that culminate in baptism. Though Sir Palomydes is mentioned earlier and later, it is in Malory's "Tale of Sir Tristram," the centerpiece and pivot of the late-fifteenth-century *Le Morte Darthur*, that he figures most prominently.

Nominally bound by the biography of Sir Tristam, the "Tale of Sir Tristram" is a huge enterprise that recollects the full mature age of Arthurian culture before the taking of the Grail Quest. This tale—a full third of *Le Morte Darthur*—is as thick with adventures of "Arthur-land at large"[12] as is the opening tale of King Arthur's birth and ascendancy to kingship and adulthood. These two collective historiated romances bracket three brief, generically distinct tales: the epic story of King Arthur's ascent to Holy Roman Emperor, the untrammeled biographical romance of Sir Gareth's rise to success, and the complex anti-romance "Tale of Sir Lancelot." Sir Tristram is only one of the many characters who thread through his eponymous book;[13] of the others, his foil Sir Palamydes looms largest.

When he first appears in the text, Malory's Sir Palomydes functions as the typical worthy pagan antagonist known in the European heroic traditions from the twelfth century forward.[14] He gets "finalist" billing in martial excellence on often-cited lists of the "best knights in the world," although his Saracen status is then sufficient to explain his reflexive inferiority to Sir Lancelot and Sir Tristram. When he is most successful, however, Malory's Sir Palomydes *qua* Saracen provokes pity or anger from all the Christian knights with whom he shares fellowship and tests worship. When Sir Palomydes seems to be winning on the fourth day of the tournament of Surluse, for example, a furiously angry King Arthur yells, " 'A Jesu! . . . this is a grete dispite that such a Saryson shall smyte downe my blood!' " (2.663).

Few words are as good as the unstable term "Saracen" for meaning any strictly "Other."[15] In medieval discourse, Saracen is a useful signifier of what Foucault calls the "hollowed out void, this white space by which a culture isolates itself."[16] Though the term usually suggests any pagan outsider, it can simultaneously mean someone from Sarras, a numinous space variously located by Arthurian writers—eleven miles from Jerusalem, or in Wales, or Logres, or where the Saxons lived.[17] Yet Malory's Sarras is also the Grail city, where Galahad's earthly chores ended, and thus Sarras conjoins the exterior and interior as threats to Camelot's Christian secularity. If Camelot is home, Sarras is away.

Malory is as firmly inexplicit about the geography of Sarras as he is about the substance of Saracen belief.[18] The *Chanson de Roland* repeatedly asserts that "Christians are right and pagans are wrong," with the qualities of rightness and wrongness validated by winning and losing; the poem's Moors as warriors are otherwise interchangeable with Christians. Thus all Moors are potential Christians, aliens waiting to be appropriated into victorious Christian culture. The Moorish Queen Bramimonde in the *Chanson de Roland* becomes Juliana, and the process of her conversion to this new Christian identity is informed first by practical experience—her gods don't work—and then reinforced by ideological change and—*par amur*—spiritual conviction.[19] Arthurian romance explicitly requires the Other: knights must always prove themselves outside the court through encounters with "differences" (beasts, monsters, Saracens) and "likenesses" (other knights). One marker of Camelot is its power to absorb the Other.

Malory distributes his fictive Saracens among three basic literary types. First are the "worthy opponents" (wrong but not wicked), those Saracens who appear as allies of the Roman Emperor Lucius in the "Tale of Arthur and Lucius." Sir Lancelot himself is first mentioned in battle against Lucius; here Sir Lancelot kills the "full noble Saracen king Jacounde" (1.220), who is only the most notable of the more than 100,000 Romans and Saracens then slaughtered by a pitiless King Arthur and his troops. Next is the Saracen as "devilish heathen" (both wrong and wicked), as seen in Malory's "Tale of Sir Tristram," when the Saracen Sir Corsabryne, "a passing felownse knight" (2.666), practices an innovative mode of courtship. He attempts to woo the reluctant daughter of King Baudas by alienating her from other suitors, falsely claiming that she is insane. Interestingly, the maiden pleads for intervention to another Saracen, Sir Palomydes. In a formal battle in the lists before judges, he overwhelms Sir Corsabryne, who then refuses to be "recreant," to ask for mercy. Thus Sir Palomydes smote off his head, and "therewithall cam a stynke of his body, whan the soule departed, that there might nobody abyde the savour" (2.666). In Malory, then, Saracens except Sir Palomydes and his kin are always wrong, even disgusting, though they are also often noble by birth. So Saracens are usually on the wrong side and sometimes intrinsically evil, stinking as they die.

Sir Palomydes is the third type of Saracen, the insider-to-be, another common type of Saracen even in post-crusading literature: he is the

Saracen outsider who yearns for insider status. Saracens ordinarily don't visit: if they choose to enter Christian courts and cultures, they usually convert or die. Sir Palomydes' family ranges over the whole of *Le Morte Darthur*. Sir Palomydes stirs our interest when he is first mentioned in the "Tale of King Arthur" not as a Saracen but as the one who will succeed King Pellynor as pursuer of the Questing Beast.[20] Though he is next mentioned in the "Tale of Sir Gareth," our first close view of him comes early in "The Tale of Sir Tristram." Sir Tristram, disguised as Tramtryst, is recuperating at the Irish court where Sir Palomydes — "the Saracen ... well cherished by the King and Queen"—already admires La Beall Isode. He "drew unto La Beale Isode ... for he loved hir passyngly welle" (2.385). Malory highlights Sir Palomydes' noble lineage and family: he is son and heir of King Asclabor. Malory particularly stresses his brothers Sir Saphir and the notoriously cuckolded Sir Segwardes, both of whom are Christians and closely allied to the Arthurian court. In one of Malory's many averted fratricides, Sir Palomydes almost kills his brother Saphir when they are both disguised (2.773);[21] Sir Segwardes (along with Sir Gareth) is later killed by Sir Lancelot when Sir Lancelot furiously rescues Queen Guenevere from burning at the stake. What we know best about Sir Palomydes is his status as a lone Saracen knight on quest: for victory over Sir Tristram, for the love of La Beall Isode, for the Questing Beast, for seven great and formal jousts, and for baptism.

Yet Sir Palomydes is both the most accidental and deliberate of pagans. In all versions of the story, he is a postponed Christian who will remain unchristened only until he fulfills his (variously configured) quests. He is not—like Braimimonde/Juliana—a convert, since he enters the story as a Christian believer. Sir Palomydes is the saddest victim of crusading colonialism: he penetrates the chivalric world, adopts its strategies and shares its values. But he is forever doomed by his "almost" status: almost best, almost Christian, almost a Round Table insider. Sir Palomydes resists baptism as if it were a chivalric exercise: " 'I woll that ye all know that into this lande I cam to be christened, and in my harte I am christened, and christened woll be. But I have made such a vowe that I may not be christened tyll I have done seven true battles for Jesus' sake, and than woll I be christened. And I trust that God woll take mine entente, for I meane truly' " (2.666).

Malory achieves a certain kind of suspense in the "Tale of Sir Tristram" about whether Sir Palomydes will live long enough to be christened: "and now he be uncrystynde he shall never be crystynde" (2.717), say the villains who killed King Harmaunce of the Red City. Theologically the issue is strictly irrelevant, since Sir Palomydes is in effect already christened—not by water or by blood, but by desire. Before his final joust with Sir Tristram at the end of the tale, Sir Palomydes reflects that " 'I may not yet be christened for a vow that I have made many yeres agone. Howbehyt in my harte and in my soule I have had many a day belief in Jesus Christ and his mild mother Mary, but I have but one battle to do, and were that onys done I wold be baptyzed' " (2.842). Then he and Sir Tristram battle, with Sir Palomydes playing the leopard to Sir Tristram's lion, until Sir Palomydes has no "great lust to fight anymore." This exhaustion of desire, deadening of grief—the end of Sir Palomydes' great lust—is as radical as religious conversion, but it is not identical to it. Sir Palomydes asks Sir Tristram to take him to the next church to be "clene confessed and baptized" (2.844-45). Sir Tristam—the foe he loves, the antagonist he cannot subdue, the lover of the lady he cannot possess—acts as his godfather. Their intimate rivalry, configured by Malory into an unfulfilled oedipal struggle, merely stops with the end of the narrative.

Sir Palomydes' conversion is thus not propelled by mounting religious desire but by the frustration of desire. "Unchristened" in Malory is not a spiritual state, but a chivalric decoration to be eschewed after achieving (win or lose) seven formal fights in lists against Sir Tristram. Otherwise, Sir Palomydes achieves none of his goals: he does not capture the Questing Beast nor does he win La Beall Isode's heart. After his christening, he appears frequently in knightly adventure, but never again does he fight with Sir Tristram, never again does he mention La Beall Isode. Think of this contrast: in the Prose *Tristan,* soon after his humiliating defeat by Tristan, Palamédes submits to the plea of King Arthur's knights that he become both a Christian and a member of the Round Table, immediately after which he takes up the quest of the Grail. In Malory's "Tale of Sir Tristram," on the other hand, Sir Palomydes stops his final battle with Sir Tristram, is baptized just before the pivotal Pentecostal moment in which Galahad arrives and the Grail Quest begins. In lieu of the Grail Quest, Sir Palomydes once more goes off in search of the Questing Beast. Placing his pseudo-conversion narrative immediately prior to the Grail Quest and thus juxtaposing the two allows Malory to express its spiritual inauthenticity.

Sir Palomydes, never an authentic Saracen, was always a chivalric catechumen, whose markers of religious progress were fame and worship gained. Malory uses this postponement of christening to expose the competitive anxiety and spiritual lack in the chivalric enterprise. Sir Palomydes, Saracen-*manqué,* is just pretending to be the spiritual Other.[22] Malory exploits him in this role, using Sir Palomydes to interrogate the chivalric project, whose game of romance is played through postponement of closure and through the ritual repetition—battle by battle, tournament by tournament—of masculine violence.

ANXIETY AND GRIEF

Sir Palomydes is one of Malory's prime markers for male bonding and its anxieties in *Le Morte Darthur*. Even when unchristened, Malory's Sir Palomydes is not only a knight, but also a prominent one. He is a member of the Round Table, often cited as the fourth best fighter in the world,[23] a great friend to Sir Lamorak and Sir Gareth, loved by Sir Lancelot and especially by Sir Tristram.[24] Like his chivalric friends, most scholars are drawn to Sir Palomydes as The Knight Thwarted, the hopeless knight.[25] The promise of chivalry is that men who win through physical prowess on the battlefield will receive their chosen lady as booty, and chivalric literature celebrates the beauty of the male's romantic/martial quest. The chivalric story of Sir Palomydes as almost-best details the frustrating loss almost all men must experience so that the chosen few might succeed. Malory complicates our views of chivalric masculinity through Sir Palomydes, so this thwarted knight projects the blight as well as the glamour of chivalry.

Most critics agree that, for better or worse, Malory's "Tale of Sir Tristram" is not, like its source, primarily a dark exploration of *fin' amors,* but rather an investigation of models of chivalric homosociality, with many registers of male companionship.[26] What has not been noted is that Sir Palomydes himself is the center of this large network of knights seeking worship. He has a gift for friendship; his peer power is not diminished by his knightly losses. Though he ratifies the greater value of those who win worship from him, Sir Palomydes also retains intimacy with them, often acting as a conduit of news from knight to knight, especially in regard to his friend and peer in worship, Sir Lamerok. His network excludes Arthur's nephews (Sir Gawain and the other sons of Morgawse) with the exception of Sir Gareth. Sir Palomydes was listed as one of the best knights in the world as early as the "Tale of Sir Gareth" (1.316): he builds a special intimacy, new in Malory, with the golden boy Sir Gareth. They often disappear together on adventures in order to avoid Sir Gareth's brothers. In Malory, the friendship of Sir Gareth with Sir Palomydes reinforces their roles not only as alternatives to Sir Gareth's violent and troublesome brothers but also as special friends and allies of Sir Lancelot. This bond intensifies the shock of the pivotal later moment when Sir Gareth is accidentally killed at Sir Lancelot's hand. Malory's final mention of Sir Palomydes maintains his closeness with Sir Lancelot and provides him with a new role: when Sir Lancelot is exiled from England, he appoints Sir Palomydes as Duke of Provence. The now-Christian Palomydes enters the ranks of high French nobility.

Malory's knights perform extraordinary kindnesses for each other, just as they perform extraordinary acts of everyday betrayal. Infidelity to the marital and chivalric bond is rife in the "Tale of Sir Tristram." Knights lie. Sir Palomydes lies. Sir Lancelot lies. In the costumed world of this tale, identity is fractured, with disguise so commonplace that at one point Sir Palomydes ups the ante by borrowing his own identity when he disguises himself with the shield of the Questing Beast. Unlike his beloved and amusing friend Sir Dynadan, who is feminized by his martial and amatory failures, Sir Palomydes never challenges or rejects the reciprocity of reputational exchanges at the root of the chivalric enterprise. His humiliations are an ordinary consequence of knightly pursuits. In this respect, as a crucial participant in martial projects, his militant masculine status is intact. Yet in his own mind he dwells in the shadowland of failure, caught in the oscillations of triangulated desire for Sir Tristram and Queen Isode.[27] Losing the Castle of Maidens tournament, Sir Palomydes flees to the woodland well. He "wayled and wrange hys hondys, and at the laste, for pure sorow, he ran into that fountayne and sought aftire hys swerde" (2.528). Sir Tristram (unrecognized) interrupts his suicide attempt:

> "Alas," seyde sir Palomydes, "I may never wyn worship where sir Tristram ys, for ever where he ys and I be, there gete I no worshyp. And yf he be away, for the moste party I have the gre, onles that sir Lanucelot be there, othir ellis sir Lamerok." Than sir Palomydes sayde, "Onys in Irelonde syr Trystram put me to the wors, and anothir tyme in Cornwayle and in other placis in thys londe."
>
> "What wolde ye do," seyde sir Trystram, "and ye had sir Trystram?"
>
> "I wolde fyght with hym," seyde sir Palomydes, "and ease my harte uppon hym. And yet, to say the sothe, sir Trystram ys the jantyllste knyght in this worlde lyvynge." (2.529)

Oscillating between love and hate, Sir Palomydes cannot control his grief, nor can he escape its cause. Malory is succinct in his analysis during the Tournament of Lonezep; Sir Palomydes is winning until Sir Tristram arrives: "Than the noyse and the cry chonged fro syr Palomydes and turned unto sir Trystram. And than all the peple cryed, 'A, Trystram! A, Trystram!' And than was sir Palomydes clene forgotyn" (2.759). He persists in ritual reenactments of his major failures—he does not find the Questing Beast, nor win La Beall Isode in love, nor wrest warrior success from Sir Tristram. "The Tale of Sir Tristram" depends from beginning to end upon his incapacity to change quests, to dominate Sir Tristram, or to give up the pursuit of his lady. Miserable in this stalemate, Sir Palomydes suffers psychic breaks. He does not go conventionally mad, as Sir Lancelot and Sir Tristram do at various points when, chastened by their ladies, they lose their memories. He does not lose his identity as they do. Instead, he self-consciously sinks into himself physically and emotionally, collapsing into his self-inflicted though ideologically necessary pain. His psychic breaks are perhaps Malory's most subversive revelations about chivalric conditions.

As I suggested earlier, Malory's Sir Palomydes is distinguished by the degree of his subjectivity. His sense of his broken psyche and body is rendered by Malory with unusual precision. He began as a handsome man, "well made a clenely and bygly, and unmaimed of his limbs, and neither too yonge nother too olde" (2.717). In his grief when he fails to attain La Beall Isode, his fine body becomes a site of loss as his fragmentation is marked on his body: "But ever Sir Palomydes faded and mourned, that all men had merveyle wherefore he faded so away" (2.779). He grieves the physical ruination brought him by unrequited love when, narcissus-like, he looks into his well in the forest and sees himself "discolored and defaded": " 'Why arte thou thus defaced, and ever was wonte to be called one of the fayrest knights of [the] world? Forsooth I woll no more lyve this lyff, for I love that I may never gete nor recover' " (2.779).

The most emotionally expressive of Malory's knights, Sir Palomydes is torn between his desire for La Beall Isode and his desire to prove himself superior to Sir Tristram, whom he loves with equal intensity. Of all Malory's knights, Sir Palomydes projects the purest paradigm of *fin' amors*. His great prowess is amplified by his absorbing gaze on his beloved. He fights most fiercely when La Beall Isode is within view. Even so, he ultimately loses. Falling into envy and jealousy, he plots deviously and weeps copiously: "[he] wayled and wepte oute of mesure. And it was sene uppon his chekes that he had wepte full sore' "(2.758). He continually vents his anxieties and frustrations. The most artful and literate of Malory's knights, he writes songs and poems not only about La Beall Isode, but also about the beauty of Sir Tristram with La Beall Isode. His misery takes him compulsively to a well in the forest, where—like a Shakespearean lover, and equally often overheard—he rants and shapes his grief. Grief in medieval texts is usually public, often communal. Here we have the rare instance of a character who seeks privacy. Along with his privately expressed grief about his failures at prowess and passion, Sir Palomydes sometimes rants in public. On one pitiful occasion, after he decisively loses the Tournament of Lonezep to Sir Tristram, he is overwhelmed with the grief that accompanies envy and shame. Shame is the energizing source of his psychic anger and grief. This grief is not assuaged by wailing privately at his well, and his poignant impotence is given ironic force when he returns to the outskirts of Sir Tristram and Queen Isode's pavilions at the tournament site to shout, " 'fy on the[e], traitor' " (2.763). Out of control, flailing, he spews out his invective at Sir Tristram, who, inside his quarters with Queen Isode, is enjoying his supper, wondering all the while why his dear friend Sir Palomydes doesn't arrive to keep him company.

Proximity and distance are equal sources of emotional pain and disjunction for Sir Palomydes: he can't stand being with or without them. When he is with Sir Lancelot, Sir Tristram, and La Beall Isode, Malory says, "Than was there grete joy among them. And the ofter that Sir Palomydes saw La Beall Isode, the hevyar he waxed day be day'" (2.779). Yet when he is parted from Sir Tristram, Sir Palomydes makes "the grettyst dole that ony man cowde thynke, for he was nat all only so dolorous for the departynge frome La Beall Isode, but he was as sorrowful a parte to go frome the felyshyp of sir Tristram. For he was so kynde and so janytll that whan sir Palomydes remembyrd hym [thereof] he myght never be myrry" (2.763). With rare exceptions, Arthurian knights find loneliness when they search for each other. With persistent nostalgia, Sir Palomydes mourns the fellowship that rarely was, that might have been. Sir Palomydes' discontent and anxiety expose the inescapable hierarchy of the passion-prowess linkage that marks and mars the masculine chivalric project.

Thwarted desire always propels romance. The rapist Sir Epynogrys once asks Sir Palomydes: " '[S]yth that ye loved La Beall Isode, loved she ever you agayne by onythnge that ye cowde wyte, othir ellys ded ye ever *rejoyse her in ony plesure?*' 'Nay by my knighthood' " he responds (2.770; emphasis mine). Those who find Sir Palomydes sympathetic—in part because he is not a rapist—might nevertheless consider him for a moment from the perspective of La Beall Isode. " '[L]ove is fre for all men,' " says Sir Palomydes to Sir Tristram late in the game, " 'and thoughe I have loved your lady, she is my lady as well as yours. Howbehyt that *I* have wronge, if ony wrong be, for *ye* rejoyse her and *have your desire of her;* and so had I never, nore never am lyke to have, and yet I shall love her to the uttermost days of my life as well as ye' " (2.781; emphasis mine). Within this privileged masculine world, the lover is always free to pursue the beloved. Chivalric ideology perversely celebrates Sir Palomydes not as a Saracen convert, but (from La Beal Isolde's perspective) as a *stalker.*

Romance is a genre as suited to grief as it is to high celebration. Sir Palomydes' grief for his failure to achieve love and highest prestige, then, presages the larger loss and grief of the Round Table, but it also reminds us of the joys available to the (however temporary) winners—especially Sir Lancelot and Queen Guenevere, Sir Tristram and Queen Isode, and King Arthur himself. Like modern corporate life, medieval chivalry's ideology was a male game of hierarchical ranking. For someone to be on top, others must lose. But all others are not equally at the bottom: Sir Palomydes is no Sir Kay, Sir Aggravayne, or Sir Mordred. His grief comes from his shame at being un-best in forms of approved male violence, yet it is also the obverse of the honor he accords to those, like Sir Lancelot and Sir Tristram, who are judged best. His major quests are all fruitless. His quest for the Questing Beast is a paradigm of desire, since the aim and end of this adventure is infinitely postponed; his love for Sir Tristram illumines the constant struggle for superiority at the heart of chivalric friendship; and his love of the La Beall Isode is never reciprocated. Sir Palomydes embodies not only chivalric culture's compulsory male desire but aslso the grief inevitably found at the heart of this desire's lack.

PART III

MALE, FEMALE, AND CROSS-GENDERED MOURNING RITUALS IN RENAISSANCE ITALY AND FRANCE

Chapter 5

Augustine's Concessions and Other Failures: Mourning and Masculinity in Fifteenth-Century Tuscany

Allison Levy

> History is in mourning and eloquence is dumb...

Augustine, according to Botticelli, has writer's block (see figure 5.1).[1] That is to say, in the Uffizi panel dated to the 1490s, the delinquent-turned-Divine Doctor appears to be scholastically challenged: Cloistered and cramped, he struggles with rewrites and revisions; surrounding him, limp and broken quills and illegible scraps signal exhausted efforts, if not defeat. In striking contrast to this frustrated Augustine, Botticelli also painted a scripturally talented Augustine, this one of a decade earlier in the church of the Ognissanti in Florence (see figure 5.2).[2] Inspired and enlightened, this prolific Augustine demonstrates his productivity, the fruits of his calligraphic labor on display. Why two different characterizations of this Church father—the latter procreative, the former seemingly impotent? Further, why is the fourth-century Roman North African philosopher-saint twice repositioned by a fifteenth-century Florentine artist within a Renaissance studiolo? In other words, why so many conversions? A recent survey of Italian Renaissance art history recognizes these two conflicting characterizations of Augustine, though the comparison is employed mainly to call attention to the increasingly spiritual interests of the artist and the corresponding stylistic change evident in his work during the last decade of the fifteenth century.[3] Stylistic differences aside, split personalities and anachronisms point toward a double and divided subject, suggesting that there may be something covert about this Christian convert.

Figure 5.1   Botticelli, *Saint Augustine in his Cell*. Uffizi, Florence.

Figure 5.2 Botticelli, *Saint Augustine in his Study*. Chiesa di Ognissanti, Florence.

Within the context of grief and gender, I wish to examine episodes from the life of Augustine, specifically those surrounding the death, burial, and mourning of his mother, Saint Monica, both as recounted in his *Confessions*, written between 397 and 401, and as illustrated approximately one thousand years later in early modern Tuscany. Central to this discussion, I propose, is the rise of the Italian cult of Monica, the patron saint of widows at this time.[4] In particular, I read the early modern literary and visual texts of Augustine's mourning of Monica in conjunction with the early modern discourse on mourning: the socio-political re-orchestration of public grieving from Francesco Petrarch to Leonardo Bruni. But even beyond this, I examine the gender dichotomy implied there, suggesting that insofar as the popularity of Augustine's *Confessions* can be interpreted as contributing to a legitimization and perpetuation of gendered mourning patterns in early modern Tuscany, Augustine's *concessions* ultimately challenge and complicate those gender codes, specifically the cultural construction of masculinity.

By way of introduction, I cite Augustine's account of his mother's death and funeral, as described in Book IX, chapter xii of the *Confessions:*

> I closed her eyes and an overwhelming grief welled into my heart and was about to flow forth in floods of tears. But at the same time under a powerful act of mental control my eyes held back the flood and dried it up. The inward struggle put me in great agony. Then when she breathed her last, the boy Adeodatus cried out in sorrow and was pressed by all of us to be silent. In this way too something of the child in me, which had slipped towards weeping, was checked and silenced by the youthful voice, the voice of my heart. *We did not think it right to celebrate the funeral with tearful dirges and lamentations....* But in your ears where none of them heard me, I was reproaching the softness of my feelings and was holding back the torrent of sadness. It yielded a little to my efforts, but then again its attack swept over me—yet not so as to lead me to burst into tears or even to change the expression of my face.... When her body was carried out, we went and returned without a tear. Even during those prayers which we poured out to you when the sacrifice of our redemption was offered for her, when her corpse was placed beside the tomb prior to burial, as was the custom there, not even at those prayers did I weep.[5]

In contrast to Augustine's "inward struggle" to repress "an overwhelming grief," Monica "never ceased," by Augustine's account, *her* grieving for *him*, albeit her mourning is a loss of a different sort—Augustine's loss of faith. Book III, chapter xi of the *Confessions* reads as follows:

For my mother, your faithful servant, wept for me before you more than mothers weep when lamenting their dead children.... You heard her and did not despise her tears which poured forth to wet the ground under her eyes in every place where she prayed.... During this time this chaste, devout, and sober widow, one of the kind you love, already cheered by hope but no less constant in prayer and weeping, never ceased her hours of prayer to lament about me to you.[6]

Read in conjunction, these two passages call attention to a distinct dichotomy between male and female manners of mourning: Monica's loud and constant lamentation is countered by Augustine's stoicism and silence; presumed female hysteria is checked by male composure.

The Death of St. Monica and Return to Carthage, a fifteenth-century fresco in the choir of the church of Sant'Agostino in San Gimignano, illustrates the importance of Augustine's account one thousand years later (see figure 5.3). Painted by Benozzo Gozzoli and dated to 1465, the scene depicts Monica's burial at Ostia and Augustine's subsequent departure for Rome.[7] This representation of a melancholic Augustine

Figure 5.3   Benozzo Gozzoli, *The Death of Saint Monica*.
S. Agostino, San Gimignano, Italy.

follows the prescriptions and proscriptions of male mourning as self-imposed in the *Confessions*, including the physical and emotional separation implied there. The prototype, *The Burial of St. Monica and St. Augustine Departing for Africa*, a miniature in the Fitzwilliam Museum, Cambridge, also dated to the fifteenth century, is especially suggestive (see figure 5.4).[8] Just as the literary text presents the reader with a distinct dichotomy, there is a marked split—or cleavage—between the two realms of the miniature. Divided down the center, the left half depicts Monica's body enclosed in a sarcophagus, which is tightly framed by a ciborium; to the right, Augustine, depicted in a traditional melancholic pose with his head tilted and supported by one arm, sets sail, departing from the architectural structure that retains the boxed-in body of Monica.

Of particular curiosity, the Fitzwilliam miniature is cut from a choir book; thus, the words and music are hidden by the mount. What might

Figure 5.4   Master of the Osservanza, *The Burial of St. Monica and St. Augustine Departing for Africa*. Fitzwilliam Museum, Cambridge.

this obscurity, in turn, reveal? In other words, does the concealment of the score reflect the stoic silence of Augustine, or does it point toward a different sort of cover-up? Similarly, might the drawn curtain of the constricted studiolo in the Uffizi *Augustine* unveil more than just writer's block? That is to say, if Augustine's self-flattering discourse of control and composure can be interpreted as privileging a masculine manner of mourning, the early modern humanist critique of public grief and mourning offered from Petrarch onward, insofar as it can be generally characterized as discouraging, if not restricting altogether, female lamentation within public space, also reveals a gender politics at work.[9]

In a letter written in 1373 to Francesco da Carrara, Lord of Padua, and entitled, "How a Ruler Ought to Govern His State," Petrarch specifically argued for a reconceptualization of the role of women within the death ritual, advocating the banishment of women's vocal mourning practices, what he called "loud and uncontrolled shrieks," from the public streets:

> What then am I asking? I shall tell you. A coffin is carried out, a crowd of women bursts forth, filling the streets and square with loud and uncontrolled shrieks, so that if anyone does not know what is happening were to come on the scene, he could easily suspect either that they had gone mad or that the city had been captured by the enemy. Then when they have arrived at the church door, the horrible outburst doubles; and where hymns ought to be sung to Christ or devout prayers poured out for the soul of the departed in a subdued voice or in silence, their sad complaints echo and the sacred altars shake with the wailing of women, all because a mortal has died. This custom, because I consider it contrary to a decent, honorable society, and unworthy of your government, I not only advise you to reform, but if I may, I beg you. Order that no women should set foot outside her house on this account. If weeping is sweet for those in misery, let her weep at home to her heart's content, and not sadden the public spaces.[10]

A century earlier, Boncompagnus of Signa, in chapter 26 of *Antiqua Rhetorica*, offered the following description of the very "habits of mourning"—inarticulate utterances, wails, and ululations—Petrarch found so disturbing and uncivilized: "'In Tuscany there is [by women] lacerating of the face, rending of garments, and pulling of hair.'"[11]

The female voice, put simply, was problematic at this time, and a considerable amount of legislation was enacted to restrict such female lamentation within public space. For example, in Lombardy, in Milan and Como, as early as 1210, rulers tried to separate male citizens from what was deemed "the business of women."[12] More specific were the laws passed in 1255 in San Gimignano, whereby women were not only prohibited from directly following the funeral cortege but were also banned from using the church door through which it entered.[13] In Siena, according to extreme laws passed in 1262, all women were excluded entirely and at all times from the procession,[14] and, in Bologna, beginning in 1276, where legislation was only slightly less restrictive, women were prohibited from leaving the house until after the body had been buried.[15]

This attempt on the part of the new humanist elite to territorialize public space by suppressing women's mourning, calling for an end to dramatic ostentation and display, has been called "the defeminization of the public sphere."[16] Indeed, the desired result of this strategic revision of female lamentation was a masculinization of the death ritual and the spaces of that ritual. Thus, concerning the role of women within ritual, there is a notable shift from ritual sound to ritual silence, from incomprehensibility to inaudibility, and even, at times, from ephemerality to total absence. If the "domestication of female lament served to deprive women of a public voice of memorialization,"[17] and if women, traditionally, were considered memory specialists,[18] how, then, does the female mourner compensate for the fact that within the symbolic realm of language, to which she has been given limited access, she has no voice? In other words, having been muted and silenced, yet still required, how can the female mourner, seen and not heard, do her job? The censoring of the female mourner, though relatively successful, created a new set of challenges for the early modern humanist. In sum, ritual silence threatened masculine memory. The task of mourning—of marking memory—would have to be reassigned.

An exemplary (and, therefore, necessarily male) memory specialist soon emerged—the early modern humanist. In keeping with prescribed gender codes, the critic-turned-actor displayed outward decorum and control. For example, upon the death of his wife, Piera, Coluccio Salutati, echoing Augustine's mourning of Monica, prided himself on the sense of civic order conveyed by his composure at her funeral: "I dried my tears, I ended my weeping and, giving thanks to God, I composed myself with his assistance so that, feeling the loss, I was made absolutely insensible to the pain."[19] Of note, Salutati left the funeral early in order to attend to his professional duties. A new memorial form—the funeral oration—accompanied this newly scripted and choreographed manner of mourning.[20] Written and spoken by men and for men, the classicizing oration not only contributed to the socio-cultural construction of masculinity, insofar as it celebrated male rhetoric over female emotion, but it also helped to perpetuate masculine memory. For example, in addition to stressing political and civic accomplishments, the humanist oration also publicly praised the masculine ethos considered to be responsible for such achievements.

And yet, this new memorial form did not immediately take center stage. The political and rhetorical strategy of translating what had been women's inarticulate vocality into a more civilized, commemorative language developed gradually and coexisted with other memorial forms. Indeed, if rituals, as has been said, "speak with many voices,"[21] the various styles and practices of commemoration "meant that Florentines no longer enjoyed a standard set of death rites as their common cultural property."[22] Thus, the "many voices" of the death ritual were competing, if not literally screaming, for attention; I am precisely interested in this cacophony and what has been interpreted as a result of this early modern humanist re-orchestration—cleavages dividing women and men.[23]

Women in Florence, for example, were excluded from the particularly masculine convention of the funeral oration. Instead, if there was praise for Florentine women, it took the form of the private consolatory letter. Exchanged between close family and friends and meant to be read privately or at least semi-privately, these letters acknowledged women's accomplishments but only insofar as those accomplishments revolved around family matters. If Florentine women did demonstrate political or administrative acumen, recognition was only contingent upon the successful accomplishment of their domestic duties. Leonardo Bruni's letter to Nicola di Vieri de' Medici upon the death of Bice reads as follows:

> *Being detained by some necessary public business, I was unable to attend the sad funeral of that excellent woman and best of mothers; I can only try to fulfill my duty in this literary fashion....* The excellences of a woman's life are reckoned to be (unless I am mistaken) good family, a good appearance, modesty, fertility, children, riches, and above all virtue and a good name.... And married to a most fortunate man, the outstanding man of his day in our city for his wealth, resources, and celebrity of name, she bore a numerous progeny, and lived to see a multitude of grandchildren, nieces and nephews sprung from her.... The greatness of her prudence can be estimated from the way she governed a very large household, a large crowd of clients, [and] a vast and diversified business enterprise for more than thirty years after the death of her husband. So great were her powers of administration that no one felt the loss of her husband's advise and prudence, and there was no falling-off in the regulation of morals, or

the discipline and standards of integrity and honor ... let us not then, I pray, lament or weep for her good fortune. Finally, she herself, who was all benevolence, would surely bear it ill that we are overcome by grief, and would bid us cease and desist. Let us obey her even though she is dead, set aside our grief, and as far as nature allows, bear our loss with moderation.[24]

Despite Bruni's self-congratulatory beginning (he could not attend her funeral precisely because he was "detained by some necessary public business") and his purposeful privileging of mind over body ("I can only try to fulfill my duty in this literary fashion ... "), and despite the obvious limitations of what he considers to be the primary "excellences of a woman's life," Bruni does acknowledge her accomplishments during widowhood. Still, taking full advantage of this literary form, Bruni's rhetoric is self-complimentary.

Similarly, most women were praised only as a means of mourning, again, other men—fathers, husbands, or sons. For example, when Piccarda Bueri died in April 1433, Carlo Marsuppini wrote a consolatory letter for her sons, Cosimo and Lorenzo de' Medici; it was, precisely, for *them*. The letter, written on the occasion of Piccarda's death, addressed *their* achievements and, further, provided a strategic tool for reshaping and idealizing the public, political image of Cosimo.[25] By contrast, several distinguished women, residing north of Florence, did receive praise in the same or similar format as their male contemporaries—that is to say, in the form of a particular text, the humanist oration. For example, Elisabetta Malatesta and Caterina Visconti were eulogized anonymously in 1405 in Pesaro and in 1410 in Milan, respectively; Guarino da Verona eulogized Margherita Gonzaga in 1439; and Antonio Lollio praised Laudominia Piccolomini, the sister of Pius II, at mid-century.[26] Of particular note, some of these women, such as Elisabetta Malatesta, who, again, lived outside of Florence, were even praised for their eloquence.[27] Moreover, a eulogy read by Giannantonio Campano commended Battista Sforza, who, at the age of four, had herself delivered a Latin oration, a rhetorical skill frowned upon by humanists such as Bruni.[28]

To reiterate, one objective of the humanist oration was to praise the deceased in order to set an example for the community. Another was to reconfirm social placement and privilege. And yet, despite the rhetorical insistence upon stressing—and praising—difference, there was also a need to communicate across groups, and, in order to gain a large share of the listening audience, the orator had to compete against other memory specialists. Yet, "orators have always worked in the realm of probable truth. By approaching truth as probable, humanists could blur distinctions...."[29] Inadvertently, perhaps, in a desire to accumulate more mourners and, thus, to ensure masculine memory by securing ceremonial participants, the humanist and his oration inevitably blurred certain distinctions, which, according to his own personal and political agendas, should have remained cleavages or divisions.

A paradox soon becomes apparent: audiences were large and diverse. How, then, did the orator compensate for the fact that within the early modern community, his listening audience was deaf? In other words, how many members of his listening audience actually understood his Latin? If the audience turned a deaf ear to what seemed to be Bruni's babble, this caveat posed a particularly large challenge, especially if the goal was to reindoctrinate the community. According to Bruni, the early humanist orator, like the Roman orator, had to distinguish between the majority of listeners, who could understand the eulogy just as they did an average Latin mass, and the ruling class, whose comprehension skills would be more refined.[30] Thus, by directing oratory mainly toward fellow humanists, and rulers, bureaucrats, lawyers, doctors, and merchants—in short, toward men—Bruni's political campaign, to rewrite the codes of public mourning, fails to convert the masses; moreover, his personal agenda, to be mourned and remembered, poses even greater problems—for both himself and the larger humanist ideology concerning public mourning practice. As a short aside, we might look toward Bruni's tomb, made by Bernardo Rossellino in 1444, in the church of Santa Croce in Florence, as evidence of this failure. The inscription, written by Carlo Marsuppini, reads as follows: "History is in mourning and eloquence is dumb, and the Muses, Greek and Roman alike, cannot restrain their tears." Ironically, on the funerary monument of one of the strongest advocates of a reorchestration of the type and amount of mourning within the public death ritual, rhetoric is challenged and tears are unrestrained.[31]

And worse, for those for whom the humanist orator did not seem to be speaking in tongues, some of the most famous Florentine orations, those by Leonardo Bruni for Nanni Strozzi, and by Poggio Bracciolini for Niccolò Niccoli and for Lorenzo di Giovanni de' Medici, were never delivered.[32] That is to say, circulated only in written form, these texts were never read aloud. Thus, if the audience never heard, the deceased was never mourned, at least not according to the new humanist standard, whereby the reading of the Latin text during the requiem, which translated what had been women's inarticulate vocality into a more civilized language, was meant to commemorate the deceased and celebrate a specific community in a particularly ordered manner. Like the female mourner before him, whose "loud and indecent wailing," according to Petrarch, he sought to counter, the early modern humanist, ultimately, is silenced. His memorializing speech interrupted, might we consider these "widowed words?"[33] Fragmented, ruptured, incomplete—we might now even say feminized—how does the early modern humanist perform his text?

If incomprehensible and inaudible, how does the humanist orator negotiate this unsuccessful performance within his self-orchestrated mourning ritual? In other words, how does he compensate for the fact that, within the symbolic realm of language, the sights and sounds of which he now orchestrates, he has no voice? Recall that the sanctioned female mourner, muted and silenced, was similarly challenged, having to negotiate the necessity of her role as primary mourner within a newly censored ritual site. Possibly, the very ambiguity of these sites, visual images, and sounds guaranteed the female mourner prolonged access into the mourning ritual of the early modern humanist, who, in a struggle to maintain gender difference while competing against other mourners for control of the listening audience, had to continually redirect his own role as described above.

Social historians have pointed to an inherent ambiguity in the function and meaning of ritual.[34] I am suggesting, however, that what was deemed to be the very necessity of ritual performance points beyond an inherent ambiguity toward an inherent anxiety and, thus, toward an always already unstable subject. More specifically, death rites, which have been interpreted by some not as fixed, static models but as social and cultural moments, were constantly in a state of flux, pointing to a marked fluidity and multiplicity within ritual and society. Perhaps more importantly, though, this fluidity of the death ritual can be interpreted as being conditioned by the complexities of early modern gender roles.[35] As we have seen, these roles, too, could be reshaped or redirected to suit the particular needs and/or desires of an anxious and vulnerable community. And yet, what happens when too great a transgression occurs?

Returning to Augustine, having understood his *Confessions* as an early example of the strategic, rhetorical construction of masculinity evident in the humanist re-orchestration of the death ritual, we might now reexamine his performance, calling attention to and considering the implications of his ultimate *concession*. Augustine eventually confesses in Book IX, chapter xii:

Alone upon my bed... I was glad to weep before you about her and for her, about myself and for myself. Now I let flow the tears which I had held back so that they ran as freely as they wished. My heart rested upon them because it was your ears that were there, not those of some human critic who would put a proud interpretation on my weeping. And now, Lord, I make my confession to you in writing. Let anyone who wishes read and interpret as he pleases. If he finds fault that I wept for my mother for a fraction of an hour, the mother who had died before my eyes who had wept for me that I might live before your eyes, let him not mock me but rather, if a person of much charity, let him weep himself before you for my sins.... [36]

The implications of Augustine's gender transgression—his regressive, feminine performance of mourning—suggest repercussions not only for his own self-fashioning but also for that of the early modern humanist, who, recall, takes cues from the literary and visual texts of Augustine's mourning of Monica.

One last fresco by Benozzo Gozzoli in the choir of the church of Sant'Agostino in San Gimignano, *The Funeral of St. Augustine*, deserves special attention (see figure 5.5). This historical death scene, perhaps not surprisingly, is set within a well-ordered and organized urban landscape; for example, Augustine's funeral bier is centrally placed before a Brunelleschian arcade. And yet, in striking contrast to this rationally planned space, one of the contemporary characters, probably a portrait of one of the Augustinians at San Gimignano,[37] grieves dramatically, arms flailing and mouth agape, at the feet of Augustine, breaking all cultural and gendered codes of mourning, as prescribed from Augustine to Petrarch to Salutati to Bruni. Of note, two of these figures also appear in *The Death of St. Monica and Return to Carthage* (figure 5.3), although, there, they appropriately play the role of silent and stoic witness. Now, perhaps even as then, transgressions abound, leading us to reevaluate the desired outcome of gender and ceremonial performance for the sake of legitimizing and perpetuating masculinity and its memory. Thus, returning to the Uffizi *Augustine*, we might conclude the cause of the author's writer's block. If this confessant's masculinity is threatened by his ultimate concessions, his attempt to rescript—yet again—his role within ritual becomes urgent. And yet, discarded scraps, still illegible, and phallic instruments, always limp, cannot but suggest constant failure.

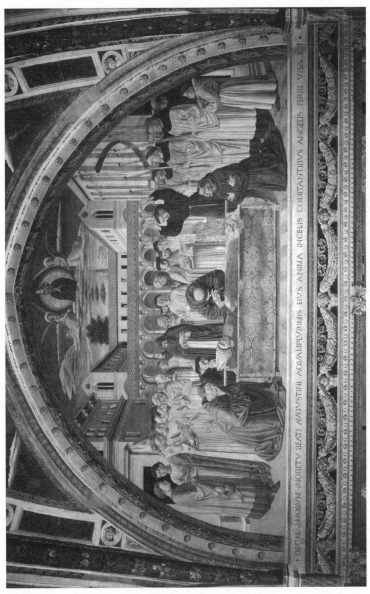

Figure 5.5   Benozzo Gozzoli, *The Funeral of Saint Augustine.*
S. Agostino, San Gimignano, Italy.

CHAPTER 6

PETRARCH'S "LADIES" AND SAPPHO'S "SIRENS": FETISHISM AND MOURNING IN RENAISSANCE WOMEN'S POETRY

JULIANA SCHIESARI

The articulation of loss and desire is integral to the Petrarchan lyric, and as such, often becomes a powerful theme in literary texts of the early modern period. A notion of self emerging from these early modern works can be said to *historicize* questions related to grief, mourning, and loss—tropes that enunciate psychoanalytic paradigms. Early modern lyric, in particular, because it often mourns a lost love, or grieves over an intangible Other, as in melancholia, is a rich source for the history of such emotions. Furthermore, the lyric, imbued as it often is with such a sense of loss, can also be said to describe the interior space of one's psychic life. It chronicles the upheaval of loss and gain figured by the poetic subject's relation to an unrequited, lost love.

A number of Renaissance women poets (Gaspara Stampa, Louise Labé, Veronica Franco, Isabella di Morra, among others) found a poetic model within the Petrarchan tropes of loss, anguish, and ambitious triumph over loss in the name of writing itself. Women poets gained notoriety by modeling their lyric on Petrarch's at the same time that they were able to elaborate a type of gendered difference in how they chose to mourn the beloved other. In so doing, they could construct a specifically feminine poetic identity that was grounded both in difference from and similarity with Petrarchan masculinity.

A case in point is Gaspara Stampa's sonnet "Piangete, Donne, e con voi pianga Amore" [Weep, Ladies, and let Love weep with you], whose opening line repeats that of Petrarch's famous *Rime sparse* 92. This deliberate repetition of the first line of Petrarch's poem immediately puts us in the Petrarchan context to which she may be indebted, but only up to a point, for in the following lines she deftly turns the whole Petrarchen metaphysics of loss into a much more specifically gendered form of grieving that in particular addresses a female readership. Petrarch's sonnet, it will be remembered, while ostensibly written in mournful tribute to the deceased poet, Cino da Pistoia, ends up foregrounding Petrarch as the real subject of the poem to the extent that he is presented as the melancholic subject of the mourning. In fact, the entire second quatrain is taken up representing the ostentatiousness of his own display of grief, one that overshadows not only all the conjoined "donne" of Pistoia but even the begrieved poet himself, whose own identity is not revealed till the following sestet:

> Piangete, Donne, et con voi pianga Amore,
> piangete, amanti, per ciascun paese.
> poi ch'è morto colui che tutto intese
> in farvi, mentre visse al mondo, onore.
>
> Io per me prego il mio acerbo dolore
> non sian da lui le lagrime comtese
> et mia sia di sospir tanto cortese
> quanto bisogna a disfogare il core.
> Piangan le rime ancor, piangano i versi,
> perché 'l nostro amoroso messer Cino
> novellamente s'è da noi partito.
>
> Pianga Pistoia e i cittadin perversi
> che perduto ànno sì dolce vicino,
> et rallegresi il cielo ov' ello è gito.

[Weep, Ladies, and let Love weep with you; weep, Lovers, in every land, since he is dead who was all intent to do you honor while he lived in the world.

For myself, I pray my cruel sorrow that it not prevent my tears and that it be so courteous as to let me sigh as much as is needful to unburden my heart.

Let rhymes weep also, let verses weep, for our loving Messer Cino has recently departed from us.

Let Pistoia weep and her wicked citizens, who have lost so sweet a neighbor; and let heaven be glad, where he has gone.]¹

Interestingly, the poem tells us virtually nothing about the object of mourning, Cino da Pistoia, while it positions that richly evoked *subject* of mourning, Petrarch, as the chorus leader for a whole world of mourners: ladies, Love, rhymes, verses, and the "cittadin perversi" of the poet's hometown. This narcissistic reversal whereby, as Freud described, the libido invested in the lost object is drawn back into the ego and cannot resurface is typical of melancholia rather than mourning. The excessive display of loss or mournful behavior without any apparent object of loss is typical of the narcissistic perversion of mourning that constitutes melancholia. At the same time, the melancholic turn in Petrarch is also what reveals a depth of subjectivity that is the hallmark not only of his lyric production but of his "modernity" as well, his humanism if you will.

For the same reasons, Petrarch's poetry became the dominant model for Renaissance lyric, the obvious standard to imitate, but by the same token the model from which to deviate, especially in the case of Renaissance women poets for whom Petrarch's emphasis on subjectivity opened up a field of poetic possibilities, while the narcissistic basis of his eros called for serious revision. Stampa's poem may begin with Petrarch's line, but reverses the entire Petrarchan dynamic by placing herself, not as the subject of grief, but as the object of mourning itself. Far from leading the world in a chorus of woe, she asks repeatedly and at multiple levels for *someone else* to take up her tale of sorrow:

> Piangete, donne, e con voi pianga Amore,
> poi che non piange lui, che m'ha ferita
> sí, che l'alma fará tosto partita
> da questo corpo tormentato fuore.
>   E, se mai da pietoso e gentil core
> l'estrema voce altrui fu essaudita.
> dapoi ch'io sarò morta e sepelita,
> scrivete la cagion del mio dolore:
>
> "Per amar molto ed esser poco amata
> visse e morí infelice, ed or qui giace
> la piú fidel amante che sia stata.
>
> Pregale, viator, riposo e pace,
> ed impara da lei, sí mal trattata,
> a non seguir un cor crudo e fugace."

[Weep, Ladies, and let Love join in your grief.
He does not weep, who wounded me so sore

That soon my soul will take its final leave
From this tormented and afflicted body.

If ever a compassionate, gentle heart
Should grant a loving woman's dying wish,
When, dead and cold, I in my grave shall lie,
Write down the reasons for my early death:

"Loving too much, loved little in return,
She lived and died unhappy, who now lies
Here, the most loyal lover of all times.
Pray for her soul's repose, good passer-by,
And learn from her, who was so badly used,
Never to love one cruel and untrue."][2]

Rather than the empowered projection of a voice that feels confident in calling forth many others to weep, Stampa offers the image of an unempowered voice, one not at all sure of being heard and dependent upon the community of other women to tell her story. She asks the "ladies and Love" to weep precisely because the one who wounds her in love does *not* weep, even as she is about to die from her broken heart. In particular, she asks that someone hear her dying gasp or final utterance (*ultima voce*) and writes down the "reasons for her death." The sestets then cite the epigraph that someone else will write down on her tombstone, which in turn asks those who wander by both to "pray" for her (in another act of verbal response) and to learn the lesson not to fall in love with someone incapable of reciprocating. This complex set of imbricated requests for a response to her plight both underscores repeatedly the highly determined fragility of her own voice as a woman in a patriarchal setting and her dependence upon the verbal response of others to keep her memory alive through the rituals of mourning: weeping, praying, and funereal inscriptions. Far from the individualized and transcendent subject of melancholia, Stampa's revision of Petrarch underscores the collectivity of women's mourning as a creative response whereby one woman's lesson in unhappy love is communicated *to* other women *by* other women, thereby engendering a community of women.

But in the contemporary rereading of the ways Renaissance women poets rewrote the Petrarchan metaphysics of loss and mourning to suit their own aims, a crucial source of both poetic inspiration and practical imitation needs to be rethought, namely Sappho and the Sapphic poets. The Greek poetesses were models for many women writers of the Renaissance, whose laments echo the poetry of these ancient sources.

The Sapphic writers already imbue their lyric with certain themes of loss due not to the aleatory mystic of amorous encounter, as in Petrarch, but to their gendered positioning within a patriarchal society, as do the women "imitators" of Petrarch. For Sapphic as well as Renaissance women's lyric, loss is less the result of an event (love at first sight) than the ongoing effect of an inequitable social structure. Moreover, the continuation of the Sapphic tradition in Renaissance women's poetry maintains that very feminine community that is repeatedly evoked by both ancient Greek and Renaissance women writers. At the same time, we see that Renaissance women poets are not simply engaged in the negative moment of rewriting key male poets like Petrarch, but also more positively in building upon a millennia-old but heterodox, deprecated, and sometimes persecuted lineage of women's writing.

The last half of Stampa's poem, for example, more than the evident reversal of its Petrarchan model also obliquely recalls the following poem from the Sapphic poet Erinna, readily available in Stampa's time from Planudes' *Antologia Graeca:*

> Stele and my sirens and mournful urn,
> which holds the meager ashes belonging to Hades,
> tell those passing by my tomb "farewell"
> (be they townsmen or from other places)
> and that this grave holds me, a bride. Say too,
> that my father called me Baukis and my family
> is from Tenos, so they may know, and that my friend
> Erinna on the tombstone engraved this epigram.[3]

Here, the whole poem is the epigraph written by the "other" woman, whose name appears only as a "signature" in the form of the deceased friend's acknowledgement of the writing she will do. The epigraph itself is addressed to the tomb in all its materiality—the sculpted sirens, column, and the very urn containing Baukis' ashes. Already evoked in its plurality, the tomb is further called upon to be the vocal entity that speaks for the dead Baukis by recalling her name and background. The lesson here, though, is not the grief of unhappy love but the expression of female "friendship" carved in stone upon the occasion of Baukis' passing and Erinna's mourning. Again, a complex verbal utterance takes place as Erinna writes the epigraph for Baukis, in which the latter asks the tomb to speak her "farewell" and states that Erinna wrote the epigraph. The stone "sirens" come to life to give Baukis a voice enabled by Erinna's writing. Fatal to men, perhaps, the sirens nonetheless serve as a powerful metaphor for the community of women's voices.

Stampa's sonnet thus takes us from one world to another. Petrarch's narcissistic homage to another male poet utterly subsumes the latter's identity into the depiction of Petrarch's own display of grief and his power over the chorus of other grieving voices. But whereas Cino da Pistoia disappears in all but name from Petrarch's poem, Erinna's eulogy to her friend absorbs *her* into Baukis' voice, wherein the poetess appears only as the scriptural signatory and guarantor of the truth of her friend's utterance, a kind of footnote if you will. By bridging the two, Stampa not only rewrites Petrarch but evokes a powerful alternative in the practice of women's grief, expressed through a collectivity (of at least two women) in which it is the lost object herself—the occasion for all the mourning—who becomes both subject *and* subject matter of the utterance.

Could it not be said, though, that a certain narcissism peeks through that poetic practice, insofar as it focuses so much attention on the self that is to be mourned? This is, of course, not the self-aggrandizing subjectivity of a Petrarch who speaks for everyone else (or commands them to speak), but a paradoxical narcissism of the object, to the extent that the mourned-for self represents a primary locus of emotional investment in the poem; yet the very fact of the mourning implies a self that no longer is. That loved but absent self (whether Stampa or Baukis) can no longer cathect anything at all—it is libidinally as well as pragmatically dead—and depends for its continued existence (as memory if nothing else) on the cathexes of others. This is not just a clever conceit to displace the poet's narcissism elsewhere (as in the melancholic's typically grandiose fantasy of imagining or even planning his funeral), but a desperate plea to forestall the poetic subject's possible oblivion. What subjectivity the woman poet can lay claim to is radically threatened by the nonresponsive behavior of some Other (callous lover or disinterested passerby). The pathos of this "object" narcissism, where the mourned self is cut off from the speaking subject, is underscored by the precarious state of feminine subjectivity in such classically phallocentric cultures as ancient Greece and Renaissance Europe, including the evanescence of her name under patrilinear rules—given by father, then husband, her name dies along with her, barring exceptional circumstances such as fame (or infamy). Finally, there is a peculiar pathos to the Sapphic tradition: its mere survival as a corpus of texts, being only a very few integral texts and dozens of tiny fragments, is both remarkable and frustrating. Vilified, neglected, even publicly burned (by Pope Gregory VII in 1073), it is amazing anything at all remains of the West's greatest woman poet and her many imitators/successors.

The "object" narcissism of Stampa and Erinna, among others, understands and underscores the dependency of the poet's expression not only upon the lover's attention but also the remembrance of other women. In her second and third elegies, Louise Labé splits these two dependencies apart. Her second elegy elegantly depicts her pains upon her lover's prolonged absence, ending once again with the citation of her own funerary epitaph, which he will find upon her tombstone if he returns too late. Without any news from him, she can only ponder the reasons: Is he ill? Has he taken another lover? Or has he simply forgotten her?:

> Cruel, Cruel, qui te faisoit promettre
> Ton brief retour en ta premiere lettre?
> As tu si peu de memoire de moy,
> Que de m'avoir si tot rompu la foy?
>
> [Heartless, heartless, why did you promise me,
> In your first letter, you would soon return?
> Have I so faded from your memory
> That you could break your faith with me so soon?][4]

She doubts his being sick, since she has so diligently prayed for his good health, though she worries she may have offended the Creator by adulating her lover in His place. Or has he found someone else? Here, the "object" narcissism requires her to list her attractive qualities, not as a boast but a plea:

> Si scay ie bien que t'amie nouvelle
> A peine aura le renom d'estre telle,
> Soit en beauté, vertu, grace & faconde,
> Comme plusieurs gens savans par le monde
> M'ont fait à tort, ce cróy ie, estre estimee.
> Mais qui pourra garder la renommee?
>
> [I know quite well that this new love of yours
> Could scarcely have the reputation yet
> Either in beauty, virtue, grace, or talents
> That many learned men throughout the world
> Have, wrongly I believe, accorded me,
> But who can keep a lofty reputation?]

Indeed, the poetess finds herself in the humiliating and objectifying position, despite her fame and success, of having to compete with someone else for his affections, like a choice between commodities:

Et croy qu'ailleurs n'en auras une telle.
Ie ne dy pas qu'elle ne soit plus belle:
Mais que iamais femme ne t'aymera,
Ne plus que moy d'honneur te portera.

[And know that elsewhere there's no one like me,
I don't say that she might not have more beauty,
But never will a woman love you more
Nor bring more fame to lay it at your door.]

Elegy Three (and the concluding Sonnet 24) develop the other side of
the pendant, namely the need for solidarity among women, for mistakes
in love can befall anyone (and perhaps even more so those who resist or
deny Love's power):

En ayant moins que moy d'occasion,
Et plus d'estrange & forte passion.

[And more than I you might love out of season
With stranger passion and for far less reason]
(Sonnet 24)

As in Stampa's poem, it is the force of women weeping together (and
not commanded to weep on someone else's behalf as in Petrarch's case)
that is affirming both of life in general and women's loves in particular.

Finally, the object narcissism—as I've been naming it—of these
women poets recalls the structure of fetishism, since the objectified self
is "scopulated," to use Freud's term, in its at least potential absence.
More to the point, the keeping of the self as object, and its maintenance
through an institution of memory (the collective voices of women, the
passerbys' response to the funerary injunctions, etc.) join up with the
retheorization of fetishism in a feminist register by Mary Kelly and Emily
Apter. In her crucial *Post-Partum Document*, Kelly revises the Freudian
male-centered theories of fetishism and maternal narcissism:

According to Freud, castration anxiety for the man is often expressed in
fantasy as the loss of arms, legs, hair, teeth, eyes, or the penis itself. When
he describes castration fears for the woman, this imaginary scenario takes
the form of losing her loved objects, especially her children; the child is
going to grow up, leave her, reject her, perhaps die. In order to delay, dis-
avow, that separation she has already in a way acknowledged, the woman
tends to fetishise the child: by dressing him up, by continuing to feed him
no matter how old he gets, or simply by having another "little one." So
perhaps in place of the more familiar notion of pornography, it is possible

to talk about the mother's memorabilia—the way she saves things—first shoes, photographs, locks of hair or school reports.[5]

Emily Apter, who quotes this entire passage in *Feminizing the Fetish*, notes that "Kelly hardly seeks to invalidate the proverbial equation of female fetishism with penis envy." On the contrary, continues Apter, Kelly's "aesthetic fabrication of a miniature museum of infantile detritus, however, privileges women in the role of (gender) constructors, preservationists, and caretakers" (114). Classic male fetishism, we can surmise, is predicated upon the sexualized anxiety of potential loss, whereas feminine fetishism acknowledges the *actuality of loss*. The little boy's castration fear is a threat in the future, but one rarely actualized. For the mother, the child's eventual departure is inscribed from the beginning, at its birth, a certitude of such magnitude as to make that future event already a virtual past. It is this "maternal reliquary" that Apter after Kelly understands as "a feminized poetics of mnemic traces," and even more, as "a feminist transposition of what might be called the 'discourse of the museum.' "[6]

To which it should be added that this "feminized poetics" is as much a *collective* as a collecting enterprise. It is the common bond of mothers, and the basis for Sapphic love as a *community of loss*, that of Stampa's women "weeping *together*" in memory of what each one has lost that is most precious.

If we return for a moment to Erinna's epitaph for Baukis, we can now ponder the significance of the poem's specific addresses: "Stele and my sirens and mournful urns," who are asked to speak to "those passing by my tomb." The concrete set of objects thus physically retains Erinna's love for Baukis even as the particular mention of the sirens sculpted on the tombstone evokes the communion of women giving voice together. The sirens are thus both a fetish and a means, both intra- and intersubjective, suggestive of a tradition that not only refuses to die despite all odds but flourishes again in the Renaissance and afterward. The legacy of Sappho and the Sapphic poets thus crucially enable early modern women poets to construct a female subjectivity that forms a kind of genealogy among the women who write love lyrics.

CHAPTER 7

FAMILY GRIEF: MOURNING AND GENDER IN MARGUERITE DE NAVARRE'S *LES PRISONS*

ANNE LAKE PRESCOTT

 W hy would a famous queen, grieved by the deaths of so many she had loved and aware that her own death could not be far away, write 4,928 lines of religious allegory in the person of a male lover? The queen is Marguerite de Navarre, the poem is *Les Prisons,* and her most recent sorrow is the death of her younger brother, François Ier, on March 31, 1547.[1] In this essay I will explore some of the possible contexts for her not unprecedented but nevertheless unusual decision to write in a male voice. At about this time Marguerite was composing her famous collection of stories, the *Heptaméron,* in which a variety of men speak with what evidently seemed to her a variety of male attitudes, from the suave to the cynical. But *Prisons* is her only long poem with a male speaker. It is impossible fully to understand the pressures and opportunities that guided her decision to narrate her poem's story as "Ami" and not "Amie," but to speculate about them is a useful exercise in imagining how poetic crossdressing, like any other kind, may be multidetermined. Nor can we long forget the narrator's sex, for in Romance languages grammatical gender renders any unisex speaker default-male.

In this essay I will speculate as to some of the reasons for and effects of Marguerite's decision. First, though, a summary of this long poem. Although its cleverly conceived primary narrative does not concern death or mourning, the poem moves toward four deathbed scenes that seem in turn to impel the narrator into rapturous religious comprehension and to at least the prospect of bliss and silence that are the best answer to loss.[2] Before we arrive at the deaths, we follow the narrator as he experiences his consecutive captivity in and release from three prisons, prisons that merely get bigger. If, as has been plausibly suggested, they form a triptych, it is a very lopsided one.[3] The poem is filled with Marguerite's Evangelical piety as well as with the irony at which she was also adept and to which she often joined a charity that comes, paradoxically, from thinking the entire world fetid with sin and pride. If we are *all* filthy, simple justice requires us to be as forgiving as we can.

In Book I of *Les Prisons* the narrator recounts to "Amie"—his female friend/beloved—how he was Love's captive. In Love's tower, darkness seems bright and the stones, chains, and bars seem pleasing: Amie's eyes and speech are his welcome bonds and his harmony. Thinking himself a king ("J'etais donc roy"), he finds that this tower is all his delight.[4] But Time does its work, and he finds that the tower has begun to collapse, so that despite his urgent efforts with mortar and tools, the tower's stones fall, its bars crack, and the lover's health decays. Eventually the tower burns, and the lover turns to blame Amie for the catastrophe until the Sun itself tells him that he is now free from a love that would have held him in the beloved's womb-like prison. God sends light, and the prisoner now can see how his tower had been built on sand, on piles of earth (ll. 411–42; the piles recall Adam ["earth"] and hence bondage to the law, to the letter, to the infected will). The lover rejoices in his new liberty, scorning his recent chains and the false pleasure he took in them when he lived with shadows. To God must go the praise: no father or mother or sister or brother or friend could have known the secret; nor was his escape his own doing. So farewell, tower, farewell abyss, fire, ice, and tremblings (he might as well add, "farewell Petrarch," now extending his power in France). He is free!

In Book II the liberated lover tells Amie of his life in the broad world of men, among creatures to whom alone God gave heads raised high (he has read Ovid's *Metamorphoses*). The lover sees trees, fields, flowers, animals, sailors and voyages, houses, wealth that leads to lawsuits, war, and politics (the progression recapitulates the myth of the Golden Age and its degeneration). He sees altars with rich images, hears organs, builds churches so as to be purged of his sins, buys masses to make up for his adulteries, jousts, drinks, dances, courts witty ladies, sleeps with women—but he has the nerve to assure Amie that she is the only one he ever actually loved, adding with something less than gallantry that thanks to *her* infidelity he will never marry. Ami now goes to court, where kings can kill with a single word, and men scramble for place and power (these pages are not bad anticourt satire, and by one who knew). At last an old man named "de science Amateur" (1555, "Learning's Lover") tells Ami that he is still a captive, bound in silk by "ambition,/Concupiscence et vayne affection" (1207–08). Read some history, he urges, and learn what happens to kings, emperors, and popes; learn to detect the cruelties sustaining splendor; scan the skies, not gold; find good *exempla;* study books, including the Bible. The sun shines and, citing Dante, the lover tells Amie to beware of the flesh, avarice, and pride.

So in Book III Ami turns to books, building for himself what turns out to be a new prison: piles of reading matter are its pillars, and the capital is laurel. He makes one pillar of philosophy; a gray and ashy one of canons and decretals; another of poetry that he loves so much he forgets to eat; another of law books he never reads for pleasure and is hard to keep upright; a thorny yet curiously addictive one of math books with geometric shapes on top; another of medicine, and so forth. Of course there is a theology pillar, not all of it sound; on its summit is a Bible, bound in bloodstained lambskin, closed by seven clasps, and locked to the uncomprehending. The lover is among these last—stuck in the letter and working by candlelight. Finally his eye falls on the passage in which Jesus thanks God that He has revealed his secrets to the humble and not to the wise. There is a burst of radiance as God's voice kills and remakes him with the Word that is both sword and lancet. Realizing that he is nothing and God is All, the lover sees his pillars collapse and the laurel burn; God has delivered his heart from books (2432, "mon cueur des livres delivra").

The story is effectively over, but the poem is not. Its second half includes, for example, a discussion of allegory.[5] Reading is still valuable; Ami learns that history, law, poetry, and all the other pillars are built upon truths found in Scripture. He now reads the work of a dead lady (in fact, Marguerite Porete, an unorthodox nun burned for her writings, something Marguerite may not have known) whose mystical view of God as "near" and "far" impresses him—although his creator subtly changes her source so as to retain some distinction between the human and the divine.[6] Now he is the commander of books, not their slave: his open books make a paved road to liberty. Many lines then explore the paradox that human nothingness gives us access to God's all (mortal zero, as Marguerite does not quite say, can join God's eternal circle). So why fear death? After describing the martyrdom of the French ambassador to the Sultan, the lover now recounts to Amie four important deaths. If the scenes make up a small percentage of *Les Prisons'* lines, they made up a large part of Marguerite's meditations during her stay at Tusson and cast a backward light on the poem's earlier narrative. Although their piety entails distaste for worldly illusion and distraction, there is nothing grisly or sadistic in this Evangelical version of a *contemptus mundi*. The scenes' specificity gives narrative vigor and interest, not monitory shudders, and makes them almost novelistic or dramaturgical. What can seem Marguerite's compulsion to recall even small details may be a desire to lend a convincing exemplarity to her theological arguments.[7] Such clarity of memory is also one way we have to work through grief: mourning as memory, as a family photo in the mind, a mental videotape to be played and replayed.

The first death is that of the pious Marguerite de Lorraine, mother of Marguerite's first husband, Charles d'Alençon. Born in 1463, widowed in 1492, she eventually took the veil and died in 1521. The account of her death, says Glasson (p. 364), accords well with other accounts except that Ami omits the dying lady's well-attested invocation of the Virgin and saints. As she goes to meet her divine "sweet husband" and "true sun," in other words, the nun sounds quite Evangelical. Marguerite's affection for her mother-in-law was doubtless genuine, but her resonant mixture of pity and admiration did not stop and probably encouraged her to revise the past. Nor does Marguerite claim for her devout mother-in-law any moral triumph; rather, she has the convent's wise abbess assure her that God will marry her despite her sins.[8]

The next death is that of Charles d'Alençon. Ami mentions the duke's wife, Marguerite, but as one present at the scene, not as one with any relation to the narrator himself. Marguerite's mourning was now long behind her, and in any case the degree of her marital happiness with Charles remains unclear, but the split between past self and current persona is especially curious here, as though such a narrator would enable her to remember as somebody else, to deploy gender difference to indicate or reinforce a temporal and perhaps an emotional gap. On Shrove Tuesday a sick Charles sits listening to his wife read the Bible. She playfully ("par jeu," l. 3976) reminds him to confess and take communion; he then retires, calls Marguerite, listens to her read the story of the Passion, and learnedly expounds upon it to five attendant theologians. To his mother-in-law, the regent Louise de Savoie, he laments the king's recent capture at Pavia, begs her pardon (we are not told why, but many thought that Charles had shown himself a coward during the battle), and praises his wife. Despite her mother's orders and unwilling to distress her husband (4043–44: "nonobstant maternelle deffence,/Ne voulu pas au mary faire offense"), Marguerite stays with Charles, who tells his doctor to keep her healthy, gives her final instructions he knows she will obey, and expresses a faith remarkably like Marguerite's own. A chariot arrives to bring the bride, Charles' soul, to her Creator.

And now, says the narrator to Amie, he will recount to her the death of Louise de Savoie. Louise, he says, had always followed virtue's path. Now, at fifty-five and after long sorrows and brief pleasures, she is dying.

A brief biography follows: children, widowhood, a refusal to remarry, and charity toward slanderous servants who tried to have her children removed. She was a prudent and powerful regent, so that François praises her for so well managing public affairs. Worn out, she asks God, speaking as a wife to a husband, why he delays; then, too weak to receive the Host, she asks Marguerite to take it for her. In many lines of quoted speech, Louise admits that she has sinned but relies on grace, not virtue, to save her (if hardly heretical, the stress is again Evangelical). She thus "showed herself to be God's spouse and daughter" (4325, "se monstrant de Dieu espouse et fille"; in her *Miroir,* Marguerite had also been His mother and sister). So long as she hears Scripture she is pain-free; when the reading pauses, the torment returns.

The king would not have been able to reach his mother in time, we read, but Louise reflects that the sorrow would have been unbearable on both sides. Their love had been too great, she adds, and she must think of it no longer. Indeed Louise sends Marguerite herself away, saying that while she is in the room her mother cannot rejoice at dying and would talk instead of being absorbed by divine love. This is, I think, a particularly interesting touch, granted Marguerite's conviction that silence is where language at its best is headed. Marguerite asks the company to leave, noting that Louise aimed at Heaven, considering power, wealth, children, and honors to be trash. In spite of her desire for silence, Louise praises Marguerite for these words, and, Ami reports, it was Marguerite alone who noticed the exact moment of her mother's passing. Louise dies, then, with praise for Marguerite on her lips and Marguerite's theology in her heart.

It is now the brother's turn to die, the address to Amie reminding us that the person speaking is still the poem's male narrator. Again there is some biography: the noble race, the wars, the captivity (which, says Marguerite implausibly, was nevertheless glorious), the fondness for letters, the learning, the handsome looks, the wisdom. True, those judging from outside would never take him to be another St. Louis in piety, but, says Ami, both he and Amie have heard him say at a feast that were God to call on him to die that dawn he would find the present delights nothing in comparison to Heaven. No one could say that he took his pleasures without the fear of God, and indeed he would weep at the mention of his Creator. His spirit loved God, then, even though his fragile flesh turned to sin. After all, says Ami, such sinning gave him humility. Had he not had such imperfection, so high-soaring a spirit would have been tempted by pride; had Satan not fixed his dart in François' flesh to lower his self-esteem, Pride would have raised him to the heights. (Well, yes. Maybe. A cynic might point out that royal gallivanting, also found, thinly disguised, in the *Heptaméron* and treated with possibly amused or possibly vexed tolerance, can result from rather than preclude arrogance; it's good to be the king—you get girls. Gary Ferguson, moreover, remarks that Marguerite's defense of her brother, whose sins Ferguson says she views with some humor, elides the traditional requirement that penitence entail amendment.[9] Yet Marguerite's defense is not wholly sophistical. She believed that because the world is fallen, has become wordy trash, and because our chief sin is the pride that separates us from God, only awareness of sin, of *naught*[i]*ness*, can save us. It can also make us charitable. The uncomfortable humor in the *Heptaméron* may come from disillusion, but a disillusion involving not so much moral indifference or misanthropy as a belief that pride, not love of justice, makes us relentlessly judgmental.[10])

The king, then, sinned in the flesh but preserved faith in his spirit, and it was that faith that blessed him in death. Amie witnessed this, Ami reminds her, although he himself was not so happy. (Nor was Marguerite present. Both male narrator and female author, that is, were missing from the book's final deathbed scene, but a lady—"Amye"—was there. Is she a surrogate for Marguerite? The speaker's soul [*âme*] with an added "y"?) Ami's absence does not stop him from reminding her what took place (Amie herself, as always, remains silent). We hear at length of the king's humility, receiving of the sacraments, farewell to his son, and recitation of his sins. With no regret for what he is leaving, François is joyful, saying—several times—that no sin is so mortal that Christ's blood cannot wash it, that he relies on divine mercy, and not on his own merit, to forgive his soiled and dirty life (4526: "vie salle et orde"). The king says farewell to those near him, evidently including Amye, for Ami knows that her heart still feels the pain. So the king passes through the gate of death, finding it sweet, and recovers life in the All because no sorrow or triumph had ever made him doubt God. If he had wandered into sin, repentance always drew him back to Jesus, fountain of penitence. So now he reigns with Christ, as he had reigned in this world. There is nothing about saints, Purgatory, or bequests. Her brother makes just the end Marguerite would wish.

What literary or psychological work does the maleness of Marguerite's narrator accomplish? First the obvious. To the extent that Marguerite wished to show that describing the traditional tower of love does not begin to exhaust the full story of our imprisonment in the Flesh she needs to take account of the more spacious jail, the World (the Flesh writ large, so to speak). In that world, whatever can be accomplished by kings' sisters, queens of tiny kingdoms, or even royal mistresses, for most women there can be little political power, large-scale capitalist enterprise, courtroom fame, or geographic discovery. To demonstrate that the great world is just another prison, then, requires a male visitor to this House of Lucifera, this Vanity Fair. Similarly, although many women in the Renaissance read a good deal, nearly all scholars were of course male. A female captive or two in the poem's third prison would not be inconceivable—Marguerite had read her way through more than one book-pillar—but the population of such captives would be vanishingly small, too small to make satire or exhortation worthwhile. If she wanted her main narrator for the deathbed scenes, she had to continue in the male voice.

Marguerite's family, moreover, offered her food for cross-gendered thought. The family was exceptional in any case because of its political power, wealth, and brilliance. It was also fatherless, with a mother who knew actual rule and a brother who had first the unmanning experience of being captured, then the less than patriarchal experience of being rescued by his sister and mother, then marriage to the sister of his captor and seeing all this sorted out by the so-called Peace of the Ladies. It was also a family much given to writing poems, including verse letters circulated among Marguerite, François, and their mother—a threesome that sometimes, risking at least a little blasphemy, called itself "la trinité."[11] Cross-gendering is not absent from this verse (nor, in more complex senses, from the trinity's political life). For a male poet to adopt the voice of a female is hardly unusual, of course. Indeed, to write a verse epistle in the person of an aggrieved woman was more likely to signal familiarity with Ovid's *Heroides* than a genuine and sympathetic curiosity about female subjectivity. Nevertheless, it is intriguing that François, flanked as he often was by powerful women (including some forceful mistresses), chose to experiment with a feminine voice. After all, he might have told himself, he was not unfamiliar with the sex. More surprising, though, is his imagination's pull toward the plight of betrayed or abandoned ones. Perhaps, some might say, what inspired him was a bad conscience. In any case, among the king's poems one finds an epistle in the voice of a lady to Claude Chappuys, her fickle lover ("Ami variable"), whose cruelty has ruined love and loyalty; now she lies beneath a marble monument with an epitaph expressing her innocence, her relief at being dead, and the lover's current discomfort. Other epigrams offer capsule versions of several poems in *Heroides*, verse nuggets of female misery. One finds Medea to Jason, Hero to Leander, and Briseis to Achilles. Most curious is the brief poem said by a suicidal Canace to Macaire, her brother and lover. Only her death, says Canace, can "declare her great passion." In Ovid's much longer poem Canace is less interested in the question of concealment than in the ghastly death her father, the wind-god Aeolus, devised for the siblings' newborn baby, and she kills herself not to reveal her incest but in obedience to her father's order.

François' poem is not evidence for the old ridiculous slander that he and Marguerite committed incest. Rather, as one might also say about Marguerite's tale of incest in the *Heptaméron*, somewhere in the royal mind family ties had particular resonance, perhaps as the result of those tensions that can attend a family's otherwise comforting and pleasurably tight emotional bonds.[12] Not that Marguerite would be startled to hear that those bonds had an erotic tinge. Love is Love—in God, *philia*, *eros*, and *agape* all have their function and discourse. By adopting a male voice, Marguerite can relocate desire for her brother (not sexual desire, I mean, but love with the erotic glow derived from power, prestige, and charm) by in some sense *being* him, or the him he should have been, the him who eventually—in her poem—gets things right. To be God's "ami" complicates the situation yet further, for to seek unity with God rather than with one's family is again to get around the impossibility and pathos of loving any "other" to the point of full union, to integrate the split self by giving it up in ways not even a vain royal brother would welcome.

The tightness of the siblings' bonds, erotic or not, shows in yet another poem by François, striking for its mixture of adroit charm, affection, and a certain egotism unsurprising in a monarch. The poem is a ballade to Marguerite written in early 1543, when the by now middle-aged queen was again pregnant. François thanks Christ for having given him "Conqueste, enfans, et defence et pouvoir" (conquest, children, protection, and power) and Christ replies with the reminder that His blood alone suffices to protect us.[13] Then the king turns to his pregnant sister: Come back, he says, so I may *see* and not just hear how much the glory of the "maison"—the "house"—has increased in "conquest, honor, and lineage," and we may together thank the One who gave us conquest, children, protection, and power. But what "house" does this mean? Valois? Navarre? Probably the former, for the poem seems to suggest that the baby will add to the king's already impressive list of blessings. The Valois dynasty as a family enterprise will have increased and prospered thanks to the birth of Marguerite's child (a futile hope, for it died); Marguerite's own pleasure, and doubtless her relief, were the baby to be a healthy son, is missing. A charitable reader might think that we are to take her joy for granted. To be sure, as the king's nephew or niece, the anticipated baby would in fact have been part of the larger "house" of Valois, but the siblings' familial self-absorption shows in the poem's indifference to the baby's possible future as a king of Navarre. Maybe Marguerite shared this view of her pregnancy; maybe she would have also welcomed a trace more happiness on her own behalf, or even on that of her husband's "house."

Whatever the possible trace of patriarchal tactlessness that accompanies this poem's sunny fraternal warmth, the fact remains that François could occasionally try to imagine a female subjectivity. A striking instance of the Valois family's interest in cross-gendered—or in this case bisexed—performance is a portrait of François combining the attributes of Mercury, Athena, Cupid, and Diana. Is it, as Edgar Wind says, an emblematic Platonic portrait of political and cosmic wholeness? Or is it, as Raymond Waddington says, a quasi-friendly mockery of François' taste and that of the Fontainebleau school of painting that sometimes exploited Greek mythology's interest in divine gender-ambiguity? Witness, Waddington notes, some remarkable paintings that show nymphs fondling each other (a sort of cross-gendering in early modern thinking about lesbianism), and one of Jove in the guise of Diana seducing a nymph. For Barbara Meyer, the portrait implies less a unified François than a merged François-Marguerite, dyadic remnant of the original "trinité." Even those who find Wind's reading plausible might agree with Waddington that the king's body and posture are remarkably effeminized even for a Platonic androgyne.[14]

The portrait, in other words, suggests yet another context for the Valois' interest in voicing poetry in the person of the "other," an interest that even if shared with many poets before and since may have had extra poignancy for so close a pair. This is all the more the case if, as has been recently argued, Marguerite was maneuvered by the "trinity"'s mythology into taking on the role of being "feminine"—soft, charitable, sexual, charming, maternal—so that Louise, regent from 1515 to 1516 and again from 1523 to 1527, could more readily take on the phallic role of hard-nosed ruler/adviser.[15] One can push this thought a bit further: freed not only by her mother's death but by her brother's, the surviving member of the "trinité" could shake off her soft feathers and adopt the masculinity of her phallic mother and the active maleness of her brother, a king with more than his share of "Amies."[16] Nor was Marguerite the only important sister of an even more important brother whose task, after the brother's death, was in significant ways to take on aspects of that brother's identity. Young Elizabeth Tudor, who was one day to have the heart and stomach of a king, had many reasons in 1553 to mourn her brother Edward's death, but she also could think, after she mounted the throne and new editions of her translation of Marguerite's *Miroir* saw print, that in a world of gender equality the older Valois sibling would have ruled France. An analogous mixture of love, replacement, and incorporation complicates the sibling relations of Mary "Philip's Phoenix" Sidney. Here too is sisterly devotion that eventuates in the ambiguities of post-mortem control: Mary edits and completes works by the defunct hero of Zutphen, and Marguerite makes her king her subject, if only the subject of verse.[17]

Such a family dynamic might also explain some of what we find in these death scenes, not least the tendency to give them all an Evangelical look—the sacraments are there, of course, but with the stress thrown on Scripture and salvific faith and the usual saints, masses, bequests, and Purgatory conspicuously absent, more utterly absent than is entirely cred-ible. These are deaths that Erasmus, author of the death bed dialogue *Funus,* would have applauded. In other words, Marguerite has, at least to some degree, taken the liberty, as the surviving person of the trinity, to remake her now helpless relatives, if not into out-and-out Lutherans, then into something more Erasmian, more Evangelical, more like Marguerite. By giving herself a male narrator she can, in some sense, throw the responsibility for this onto some other person, if only someone inside her own imagination, someone who is the more "other" for hav-ing a different sex. Perhaps the maleness of the narrator, then (although here I may be nearing the margin of legitimate speculation), enabled an increased aggression—and hence in our gender system a masculine atti-tude—toward those whom she also genuinely loved. Such maleness on the part of a female author certainly further enables a split in conscious-ness between the loving warm wife/daughter/sister and a narrator who although admiring is nevertheless willing to call a sin a sin.[18]

It might seem odd, granted Marguerite's love for the dead and her insistence on their piety and salvation, to hear aggression in *Les Prisons.*[19] Love, however, is seldom free from ambivalence, and mourning can include anger, if only anger at the dead for dying (blame is a common component of grief, and Marguerite had cause for resentment because her identity and value had for so long been bound to her brother's life and role). It cannot, that is, have been Evangelical theology alone that led the queen to comment so fully on her relatives' failures, from Charles' need for Louise's pardon to François' sins of the flesh. The ambivalence shows, I think, with some poignancy in Marguerite's lines on her mother. It is not to dishonor her grief, only to confess our species' complexity, to observe that after years of being third in the "trinité," a queen but never a ruler, well loved but not her mother's chief pride, and bearer of only one surviving child, Marguerite effectively erases the son/brother (loved, but absent) and records maternal praise for the wise daughter/sister. Marguerite and Louise, indeed, join in an intimacy so close that one may take the Host on behalf of the other: in a reversal of the ordinary course of things, the daughter eats that her mother may be nourished.[20]

The voice of the male narrator, on the other hand, also establishes *distance* between Marguerite and this tableau: a memorial narrative in her own voice would bring Marguerite too close to the scene, collapsing author and daughter. Ami gives her cover and perspective; Amye would do so less decisively. It is under such cover and with such perspective that Marguerite can endow her brother with the understanding she hoped he had finally achieved, or would have achieved had she been François. *Being* François may, in fact, be one of the fantasies haunting this poem. I doubt that Marguerite wanted to be a man, yet to adopt a male voice seems related somehow to her years of serving and advising her brother while also suffering his occasional disapproval and watching his sometimes murderous treatment of those whose religious views she shared. His death gives her the imaginary power, even as she loses influence in the real political world, to make her brother see things her way.

A complicated and ambivalent reaction to loss constitutes much psychoanalytic theory. Julia Kristeva's *Black Sun* may be particularly pertinent to Marguerite's imagination. Depression and mourning, says Kristeva, classically conceal "an aggressiveness toward the lost object, thus revealing the ambivalence of the depressed person with respect to the object of mourning. 'I love that object,' is what the person seems to say . . . 'but even more so I hate it because I love it, and in order not to lose it, I imbed it in myself but because I hate it, that other within myself is a bad self, I am bad, I am non-existent, I shall kill myself.' " Such logic, of course, assumes "a stern superego" and a "dialectic of idealization and devalorization of self and other, the aggregate of those activities being based on the mechanism of *identification*" (11). Sadness itself is nevertheless a way of maintaining a unity in the self, "an affective cohesion" in the face of loss (19). As for women and loss, narcissism will demand a large introjection of the ideal so as to satisfy both its negative side *and* a "longing to be present in the arena where the world's power is at stake" (30). The loss of an erotic object, says Kristeva, produces an inner void, but a void that creates separation can also enable further movement (82–83). Death, a "dramatic diachrony," creates a needed discontinuity, a hiatus or caesura that enables signification (132–34) and, in Christian terms, can both posit and offer an antidote to depression.[21]

Here is much of what happens in the *Prisons:* the willingness to acknowledge the sins of the dead even while praising them; the identification with the lost brother's gender; the insistence on being "nothing"; the condemnatory—and masculine—superego; the surge upward toward an idealized "All" in which the personal "nothing" can merge, especially after the hiatus of death, to find a new identity/identification; and even a certain *eros* in her feelings for François.[22] Kristeva's observations, moreover, might further explain why Marguerite takes so long to reach that silence in which *Rien* merges with *Tout*—it is hard work to get over death's hiatus, to stop talking and let the unspeakable miracle in the tomb proceed.[23] To apply such thinking to *Les Prisons* must ignore a great deal: the objective reality of her relatives' sins and what for Marguerite (and many others still) is the objective fact of God's judgment and mercy. It is also the case that Marguerite's absence from "the arena where worldly power is at stake" was historical fact. After her brother's death, her position in the French political theater had shifted from near center-stage to somewhere near the exit. This did not make her "nothing" in French eyes, but a transition from royal sister to royal aunt must have felt like an undoing. One way to respond to an undoing is to embrace it, to turn it into All, not as megalomania but as fulfilled desire.

The psychoanalytically inclined have other theories, of course, as witness Cottrell's Lacanian treatment of *Les Prisons* in *The Grammar of Silence*. For Cottrell, Lacan helps explain why Marguerite used a male speaker.[24] The difference between Ami and Amie marks that split that indicates "a progression away from the Imaginary" (Ami is growing up, in other words): the fire that burns his tower of love also scatters the self that is constructed in the Imaginary, freeing it (263). But the prisons of the world and of books simply trap Ami in the order of the Symbolic (269, 283). Final liberation is into the silence toward which this long poem strains. Cottrell does not say so, but perhaps leaving the Symbolic behind and unweaving the web of words required Marguerite to repeat to herself, to make even more real to herself, that her mother and brother were dead—behind her in time, if preceding her into eternity.[25]

Are there other reasons for mourning in the voice of a liberated male prisoner?

One, surely, is the gendered body and soul that traditionally find their hierarchal place on the Neoplatonic ladder leading upward to the divine.[26] Marguerite's decision to write as a male is not, however, readily mapped on the usual body/soul division. That division is trickier than sometimes thought in terms of gender, for although in much traditional thinking the material body—*mater, materia,* matrix—has seemed feminine (matter is female, form is male), both grammatically and conceptually the soul, *anima,* is, too. A male is made of matter (female in its labile frailty and ability to receive the imprint of form), but he has a female immortal part: "Ami" has an inner "Amie." Like all men, he has a body (material and thus in some sense "female" even if *corpus* and *corps* are grammatically masculine) that imprisons a lady-butterfly, or *psyche*, that when liberated can flutter its way back to God. The body/soul split is further complicated in much Christian and pagan tradition by the triad of body, soul, and *spirit*. If a man's body is male in shape and function but female in materiality, and if his soul, the part that can marry Christ, is traditionally imagined as female, his spirit (*spiritus*), the force that energizes him and mediates between the senses and the mind, is masculine, at least grammatically.

The problem is that in Renaissance usage "spirit" and "soul" are often confused. One writer's "anima" is another writer's "spiritus."[27] After all, our body is *animal,* is *animated* by its "soul" in a quite secular sense, just as to call teenagers "high-spirited" need not mean that their immortal parts are levitating, only that their vital "spirits" are strong. Even when the thinking is dualistic (soul/body, spirit/flesh), then, the availability of both masculine *spiritus* and feminine *anima* to represent—or not represent—what survives death and transcends the flesh can cause confusion. This in turn means that, in gendering the voice of the part of her that longed for God, Marguerite had more than one choice. We can, then, read Ami's love for Amie as the spirit's love for and initial entrapment by the (feminized) flesh. And yet Amie's role in *Les Prisons* seems ambiguous, if only because her name looks suspiciously like "Ame." Is it possible that Marguerite is simply uninterested in the spirit/soul's imprisonment in a material body and is instead exploring how spirit relates to soul? In her early poetry having been a sinful "âme," does she now want to be a temporarily foolish "esprit"? Or are Ami and Amie, finally, a team? Both find themselves in the flesh of love, world, and books. Not the world, the flesh, and the devil, but another anti-trinity: passion, world, and learning.

I do not wish further to snarl an already difficult and inconsistently used pair of terms, only to remember that the vocabulary and concepts available to Marguerite gave her room to play with gendered voices beyond the dyad of body/not-body. If loss and mourning can produce inner division and fragmentation, and if a switch of gender can seem to indicate that split, then it seems fitting that given a choice of terminology a woman poet might prefer the male voice to represent the spiritual part of herself, her *spiritus,* in a culture that could also imagine a man's immortal part as his *anima*. Marguerite can speak as *spiritus* and can love the *anima,* if we read Amie as that; or the flesh, if we prefer her in those terms. If I am right, and whatever Amie is or means, Marguerite's choice of speaker derives less from an identification with male theological or literary authority than from a desire to make an already cross-gendered psychological and religious tradition even more appropriate to her circumstance. In a strange set of reversals Marguerite, who in her early *Miroir de l'âme pécheresse* had been the "âme," is now a male speaker, perhaps the author's own *animus* or "esprit" addressing a female beloved. Her *animus* has an *anima*. And why not? We contain multitudes, and some of the persons in that multitude may well contain yet others.

The terms *animus* and *anima* of course suggest Jung, and indeed, a Jungian take on Marguerite's poem seems inviting.[28] G. Mallary Masters points to her mention of the Platonic Androgyne (3.921–22), a myth of psychic unity that he notes also sustains Jungian psychology. In this view, Marguerite's male voice represents what Jung calls the Animus, a woman's inner "other" in her unconscious, presenting itself to her as male precisely because "other" to a subjectively female psyche. Male mystics, longing to join themselves to Christ, notes Masters, sometimes speak from the perspective of the soul, the feminine *anima* (for Jung a male psyche's female "other" and for others the immortal part of ourselves). So it is only logical for a woman poet to speak as her Animus. Through this intuition, Masters adds, Marguerite finds yet another liberation, that of a feminist psychology that anticipates later psychoanalytic theories. Psychological development depends on a dialogue with the "other," much as spiritual progress engages the dynamic of Nothing and All. (To be sure, there is no dialogue in *Les Prisons* between Amye and Ami, but maybe Marguerite, a woman, thought that she already knew what Amye had to say.)

Whether or not Marguerite's male persona allegorizes some inner part of herself, and however we read her mourning the loss of her relatives in the voice of an "other," her writing as "Ami" does not in itself reverse the usual gender situation in her culture; indeed, she relies on it. But her decision to cross-gender her persona adds a further fold, a wrinkle, to her already multipleated familial circumstance and shifts the terms of her relationship with God. Marguerite's longing to be "rien," nothing, was by now likely to have been more real to her than ever. Yet, as she seems well aware, a zero can fit comfortably inside the circular God whose center is everywhere and circumference nowhere. To merge with, to *be*, that All can annihilate gender as well as death, collapse the distinctions between sister and brother, daughter and mother. The three persons of the Valois "trinité" can also be a "unité." Marguerite's impulse to be an Ami rather than an Amie, to be Spiritus rather than Anima was, as I hope I have shown, impelled by any number of motives—literary, religious, psychological, and philosophical. Merged with, identified with, the *Tout*, Marguerite's *Rien* is a very full "Nothing" indeed, quite as full as Thomas More's "Nowhere." It embraces love, family, prison, liberty, light, anger, envy, memory, resentment, charity, life, death, and, not least, Marguerite herself and God. Hers was not a simple grief. We can be moved by this intelligent and noble allegory even while sensing that in it Death loses its sting in large part because of the author's faith but also because the author has put some of that sting in her poetry.

PART IV

ELIZABETHAN LOSS AND REGENERATION

CHAPTER 8

GRIEF AND CREATIVITY IN SPENSER'S *DAPHNAÏDA*

DONALD CHENEY

> *Theseus . . .* "*The thrice three Muses mourning for the death*
> *Of Learning, late deceas'd in beggary.*"
> *That is some satire, keen and critical,*
> *Not sorting with a nuptial ceremony.*[1]

When Theseus reviews Philostrate's list of proposals for a wedding enter-
tainment designed to distract his Amazon bride from the violence with
which he wooed her, we are not surprised that he rejects something that
sounds suspiciously like *The Teares of the Muses* (1591): Spenser's complaints, along with other Elizabethan exercises in that mode, have
appealed to few modern readers. Shakespeare's audience may well have
recognized with amusement the tendency of contemporary poets to
whine about their own circumstances when they should be giving pleasure to their patrons. And on grounds of decorum alone, who can deny
that satire and complaint have no place in a nuptial ceremony?

Still, Theseus' more sweeping refusal, a few lines earlier, to put stock
in "antic fables" (V.i.3) could suggest to a more discriminating spectator or reader that he is not an entirely reliable critic; what he considers
an "aery nothing" may be something he is refusing to understand.
Similarly, since the other items on Philostrate's list are tales found in
Ovid's *Metamorphoses*, it may be that they not only allude to the contemporary fad for such fictions but suggest a pattern, to someone whose
Learning is not yet defunct, in which Theseus himself is implicated by
virtue of his project of marrying Hippolyta. The "battle with the
Centaurs, to be sung/By an Athenian eunuch to the harp" not only contrasts Theseus' own manliness (alongside his kinsman Hercules) at that

event with the status of the singer, it also reminds us of the dangers of exogamy. If Lapiths and Centaurs cannot drink together without a brawl ensuing, what will happen when an Athenian marries an Amazon queen? The "riot of the tipsy Bacchanals,/Tearing the Thracian singer in their rage" is another instance of Bacchic rage and poetic misfortune, but it is above all another story of love and loss: Orpheus' failure to bring Eurydice safely back from the underworld led him to spurn women and awaken their fury. Theseus may dismiss this as an old story he's heard before, but it too bears a warning—perhaps, at the very least, that it is equally dangerous to live with women or without them. And the "tragical mirth" of Pyramus and Thisbe is itself another cautionary tale of forbidden love, neutered to be sure by the incompetence of the actors so far as the ducal audience is concerned, but conveying its dramatic irony to those in Shakespeare's own audience who know their Ovid and remember that the unhappy Hippolytus will be the product of the wedding they are now applauding. Oberon may bless the marriage beds at the end of the play, but one of the couples is destined neither to remain "true in loving" nor to have a son fortunate in being born free of blemish.[2]

This episode from *A Midsummer Night's Dream* introduces several of the questions that I want to explore in this chapter. Shakespeare's comedy treats, lightly but exhaustively, the terrors as well as the joys of marriage: the capriciousness of desire and its urgency; the need to violate parental and social sanctions; and, ultimately, the return of the transgressed. It does so not merely in the interlace of its plot lines—lovers young and old, rude and sophisticated playwrights—but also in its dialogue with literary convention. Theseus and Hippolyta come from Chaucer's "Knight's Tale"; but here there are two women for the two men and the competition for a bride can be comically resolved where Chaucer's knight found tragedy.[3] At the same time, Ovidian allusions locate Theseus in an intricately interlaced fiction of mythical permutations. Finally, there is the question of genre, of finding an answerable style. The play opens with Theseus urging Philostrate to

> Stir up the Athenian youth to merriments,
> Awake the pert and nimble spirit of mirth,
> Turn melancholy forth to funerals:
> The pale companion is not for our pomp.
> (I.i.12–15)

Yet he has just told us that he must wait for a new moon while the old one lingers his desires, a pale companion whose influence will be repeatedly put in question throughout the play.[4] We must wonder, then, if melancholy can in fact be banished from this wedding. Puck may "sweep the dust behind the door" (V.i.390), but we cannot forget that it's there.

If we can plausibly find an intertextual dialogue enriching this lightest of comedies, reminding us of marriage's compact with mortality, we should not be surprised to look for something comparable in the complaints of a poet's poet like Spenser. His *Daphnaïda* of 1591, characterized by a recent editor as "one of his most experimental and least-loved works,"[5] is clearly related to the *Complaints* volume published the same year, but it differs most strikingly in being an adaptation of Chaucer's *Book of the Duchess*, where a narrator's unspecified sorrow is similarly projected and intensified in the figure of a Man in Black whose bereavement is both literal and factual, and where the Ovidian context is invoked with dramatic ironies not unlike those described above.[6] Closer attention to Spenser's negotiations with Chaucer, and to both poets' negotiations with Ovid and his post-Classical transmission, may help us to reconsider the vexed question of whether and how Spenser's poem criticizes or distances itself from a widower's excessive, unmanly grief.

Although Chaucer's negotiations with his French sources are both complex and essential to an adequate understanding of the *Book of the Duchess*,[7] my concern here is with a rather different question of Spenser's likely understanding of the poem's allusions.[8] Elizabethans considered Chaucer to be their principal vernacular ancestor, a source of undefiled English who had freed the native literary tradition from its French and Latin bondage and was thought to have dreamed as well of purging the native religion of its Romish impurities; in consequence, they tended to see him as engaged in projects much like their own. In the *Book of the Duchess*, the narrator's melancholy insomnia, for all its variations on the dream visions of his French predecessors,[9] shows a borrowing from Ovid that has a special resonance to Spenser's imagination.

Chaucer's poem opens with the narrator telling how his "sorwful ymagynacioun" has kept him sleepless for some eight years, and how on one recent sleepness night he happened to read the story of Ceyx and Alcyone (Ovid, *Metamorphoses* 11.410–748).[10] This is of course a tale of a wife's grief at the loss of her husband that will mirror the bereavement of John of Gaunt, the Man in Black in the main part of the poem; but for the naive narrator this is chiefly meaningful as the story of somebody as melancholy as himself to whom Juno grants the gift of sleep; the narrator promises Juno and Morpheus gifts of featherbeds if they will favor him similarly. His sleep, and the dream it contains, ensue.

Spenser borrowed from Chaucer's adaptation of Ovid his description of the house of Morpheus in *Faerie Queene* I.i.39ff; and it is instructive to note how he has made explicit what Chaucer leaves to his reader's sense of dramatic irony. Ovid describes the cavernous home of Sleep (*ignavi domus et penetralia Somni, Met.* 11.592); it is only when Father Sleep is charged with sending a dream to Alcyone that he rouses Morpheus, the most cunning of his thousand sons at imitating human shapes (as his name must have indicated to the author of the *Metamorphoses*). Chaucer's Juno simply dispatches Iris "to Morpheus— / Thou knowest hym wel, the god of slep" (136–37); and Spenser similarly suppresses Ovid's point about sleep generating dreams of varying sorts. But where Chaucer keeps a fragment of Ovid's sense of generation and variety—

> There these goddes lay and slepe,
> Morpheus and Eclympasteyr,
> That was the god of slepes heyr.
> (ll. 166–68)[11]

—Spenser's Morpheus is wholly in possession of, but possessed by, his troubled domain: like Redcrosse, who is similarly "drowned deepe/In drowsie fit," he seems unable to escape the waking world, even before Archimago's messenger, like Juno's, intervenes:

> And more, to lulle him in his slumber soft,
> > A trickling streame from high rock tumbling downe
> > And euer drizling raine vpon the loft,
> > Mixt with a murmuring winde, much like the sowne
> > Of swarming Bees, did cast him in a swowne:
> > No other noyse, nor peoples troublous cryes,
> > As still are wont t'annoy the walled towne,
> > Might there be heard: but careless Quiet lyes,
> Wrapt in eternall silence far from enimyes.
> (I.i.40–41)[12]

The trickling stream echoes Ovid's Lethe (*saxo tamen exit ab imo/rivus aquae Lethes, per quem cum murmure labens/invitat somnos,* 11.602–4), and both poets stress the effort to suppress care and exclude the troublesome noise of human society. Spenser's imitation of the Cave of Sleep is not only a bravura set piece showing his mastery of earlier masterpieces; it also invites the later reader to speculate on the truth and falsehood of dreams in the earlier texts as well. Redcrosse is given "A fit false dreame" of Una as sexual partner, and when he refuses to rise to that bait he is shown a squire who does. False as these "idle" dreams literally may be, they are true expressions of the knight's repressed fantasies and look forward to his enacting them with Duessa later in the Book.

When Ovid's Morpheus appears to Alcyone in the guise of her drowned husband Ceyx, she is given a fictive image of the truth, but it is a truth that echoes her fantasy, her "prophetic soul" much like Hamlet's vision of his murdered father.[13] Like the images that the poet shapes and informs, these dreams are true or false according as they are read by the viewer. As the poet of mutability, Spenser is peculiarly sensitive to the artist's involvement in an endless metamorphic process; like Morpheus he longs for rest but is driven to write of change.

The comedy in Ovid's portrayal of a god of sleep who is unable to rest without interruption is heightened by Chaucer's narrator (Juno's messenger blows a horn in the ear of Sleep's heirs, "That slep and dide noon other werk"), who conspicuously suppresses all of the story of Alcyone that does not bear directly on his own interest in sleep. Morpheus shows Alcyone the (actual) body of her husband in a dream; she wakes and dies "within the thridde morwe" (214). The rest of the story "were to longe for to dwelle" (217); but like Redcrosse, the narrator will later encounter what he has chosen to pass over, when his dream of the Man in Black forces him to confront, however uncomprehendingly, the grief of a bereft spouse.

The Book of the Duchess, whatever minor problems of interpretation it entails, is recognizably decorous in a way that Spenser's *Daphnaïda* is not. The poet-narrator's obtuseness serves as a foil to the dignity and depth of feeling of the aristocratic widower. Readers of the later Chaucer need no introduction to the figure of a self-mocking authorial persona, for the dreamer in this poem is not far removed from Geoffrey the Pilgrim in *The Canterbury Tales*. The actual grief of John of Gaunt is distanced by the structure of a dream-vision, so that this is not Gaunt himself speaking but a dream of him; and yet, the dreamer's ignorance of the story he is hearing makes the Man in Black seem the more authentic. The result is an elegy that balances joy and sorrow in an original but generically recognizable fashion. When the "hert-hunting" concludes at the end of the dream (1313), the term can refer to all the meanings it has in the courtly love tradition—the pursuit of the beloved, with a sense that the two forms of venery are both carried on with a view to a kill— and also to the narrator's search for the heart of the matter, which is again a matter of the heart.

Spenser's poem, by contrast, seems to imitate the overall shape of Chaucer's, but to do so with an infinite lack of tact. Alcyon is so unrelenting in his misery that narrator and reader alike despair of imposing any kind of closure:[14]

> But he no waie recomforted would be,
> Nor suffer solace to approach him nie,

> But casting vp a sdeinfull eie at me,
> That in his traunce I would not let him lie,
> Did rend his haire, and beat his blubbred face
> As one disposed wilfullie to die,
> That I sore grieu'd to see his wretched case.
>
>   (ll. 547–553)

In his wilfully "blubbered" state, Alcyon has largely forfeited the sympathy of modern readers, and William Oram's suggestion that Spenser is gently encouraging his friend to get over his unmanly grief has received a generally sympathetic hearing.[15]

It is highly likely that some of Spenser's choices of details in the poem were inspired if not dictated by the peculiar circumstances of his project. Sir Arthur Gorges was a friend and fellow poet, and his friendship with Ralegh, combined with the serious challenges to Gorges' marriage to Douglas Howard and to the estate of their daughter Ambrosia may well have led Spenser to present a highly colored celebration of the "noble and vertuous" heiress and to associate himself with yet another contested aristocratic union.[16] And the facts that the surviving daughter of this marriage was named Ambrosia (after her godfather Ambrose), and that Gorges referred to his wife as Daphne must have given Spenser a start on his intertextual project.

What seems most important to note about *Daphnaïda*, however, is its recognizability less as an elegy like *The Book of the Duchess* than as a Spenserian lament in the manner of the *Complaints* volume. Just as the naive narrator is recognizably Chaucerian and as such locates the poem in its poet's oeuvre, Alcyon's willful complaining is a distinct but characteristic voice in the chorus of meditations on mortality and the world's vanity that Spenser assembled for publication by Ponsonby in the same year. What sets him and his complaint apart, I believe, is an intertextuality that links him to Spenser's earlier project in *The Shepheardes Calender*. It is the Colin Clout of 1579, similarly "disposed wilfullie to die," who is closest to Alcyon in temperament; and when Colin comes home to the Spenserian corpus in 1595, he is still cultivating his loss of Rosalind to the continuing dismay of his fellow shepherds "which do see/And heare the languours of my too long dying" (*Colin Clouts Come Home Againe*, 947–48), for all his equally public joy in courting Elizabeth Boyle successfully.

Seen in the context of Spenser's other poems, therefore, *Daphnaïda* is at once a criticism and an endorsement of Alcyon's relentless grieving. The narrator, like Colin's friends, tries to bring Alcyon back into the sheltered pastoral world—the rustic cabin or "Cabinet" (558), which is a familiar trope for the community[17]—but he is intent on the solitary brooding that is essential to his art.[18] This is not only a lament for Douglas Howard but for "Daphne" as well, the name by which Gorges referred to his wife in his poems. Classical laments for Daphnis appear in Theocritus (*Idylls*, 1) and Virgil (*Eclogues*, 5); and since Daphne is the Greek name for laurel she recalls Petrarch's Laura and the tradition of poetic laureation. As Marvell was to remark, "Apollo hunted Daphne so,/Only that she might Laurell grow." That is to say (as with the "hert-hunting" mentioned earlier), the part of the love-object that remains unattainable, wild, or (in a Spenserian usage) "selfewild"[19] becomes "only" laurel; but at the same time (if Marvell's "that" is taken to introduce a clause of intent rather than of result) the poet has from the start been looking for poetic immortality rather than a single mortal beloved. The loss of one's friend or beloved is seen, in pastoral elegy, as a necessary condition of one's own creativity.

In the context of this allegory of poets, there is a nice irony to the fact that as she goes to her eternal rest, Daphne can leave a pledge

> Of the late loue, the which betwixt us past,
> My yong *Ambrosia*, in lieu of mee
> Loue her: so shall our loue for euer last.
>
> (ll. 289–291)

This is in contrast to the more traditional comfort seen in the "November" elegy:

> *Dido* is gone afore (whose turne shall be the next?)
> There liues shee with the blessed Gods in blisse,
> There drincks she *Nectar* with *Ambrosia* mixt,
> And ioyes enioyes, that mortall men doe misse.
>
> (ll. 193–96)

This is first and foremost, of course, a mother's exhortation to her surviving spouse to care for their daughter Ambrosia; but since ambrosia is food for the gods, the daughter is the parents' claim to immortality, and the poet's cherishing of her, perhaps, the means to his lasting glory as poet.[20]

In proposing to devote his life to a weary pilgrimage toward Daphne, Alcyon conflates two distinct but related myths:

> But as the mother of the Gods, that sought
> For faire *Eurydice* her daughter deere
> Throughout the world, with wofull heauie thought;
> So will I trauell whilest I tarrie heere . . .
>
> (ll. 463–66)

One might expect a bereaved husband to think of Orpheus' pursuit of his lost Eurydice, although such a comparison is ominous;[21] to overlay it with Ceres' search for Proserpina is to effect a change of sex and of relationship, possibly suggesting the transferred love for Ambrosia that Daphne has wished. But Alcyon seems to think only of the travel and the travail rather than the desired goal. The suggestion that he is mother to Daphne may make her more the product of his poetic creativity than the mortal Douglas Howard. In the next stanza he goes on (like Colin in his "August" sestina) to identify with Philomel in his sleeplessness: "But I will wake and sorrow all the night/With *Philumene*, my fortune to deplore,/With *Philumene*, the partner of my plight" (474–76). Although the mythological allusion makes this another transference of gender, it derives most likely from Petrarch 311, where the poet is accompanied all night by the (male) nightingale "who weeps so sweetly perhaps for his children or for his dear mate"[22]—once again with parental concern a part of the context.

Finally, then, we come to the implications of Spenser's choice to name Gorges after Ovid's (and Chaucer's) Alcyone, apparently without any basis in Gorges' own poetry for such an appellation. Like Chaucer, Spenser may have been attracted to the story of Ceyx and Alcyone because it was associated with the bravura description of the cave of Sleep with its potential for meditating on the ambiguities of dreams.[23] And for a friend whose marriage and its issue were under challenge, the story seemed well worth considering in view of the moral drawn at the end, when Ovid tells us an elderly spectator praises the couple for keeping their love intact to the end (*spectat et ad finem servatos laudat amores,* *Met.* 11.750). And as a poet who loved to complete what others had left unfinished, Spenser may have been challenged by the refusal of Chaucer's dreamer to tell the rest of Alcyone's story. That is a story, moreover, that combines a reunion in defiance of death and a transformation that enables peaceful procreation. Ovid tells us that after Alcyone received her dream vision of the drowned Ceyx, she ran to the shore, where she found her husband's body washed up against a breakwater. Rushing to him, she finds herself skimming the water's surface, a wretched bird. Bending down to kiss his body, he seems to respond. In a remarkable passage, Ovid tells us that people were uncertain whether Ceyx felt his wife's kiss, or whether the body simply rose to meet her with the movement of the water. But here the poet breaks in to affirm that Ceyx *did* feel the kiss:

> senserit hoc Ceyx, an vultum motibus undae
> tollere sit visus, populus dubitabat, at ille
> sensera . . .

> (*Met.* 11.739–741)

It seems plausible that a poet whose narrative voice was so heavily invested in affirming the survival of Adonis in Venus' bower (*F.Q.*, III.vi.46–47) would have responded to Ovid's moment of transcendence as he describes how the gods pitied the couple and changed them into birds[24] who continue to mate and propagate; for seven calm days in the winter season Alcyone broods over her nest floating on the water's surface. At that time the sea is calm, for Aeolus guards his winds and forbids their going out, calming the waves for the sake of his grandchildren.[25]

This legend of the Halcyon or kingfisher, and of the halcyon days that provide a brief respite to the winter's storms, bears an uncertain freight of suggestiveness in Ovid's poem and in later revisions and readings of it. Alcyone's triumph over mortality and seasonal death is a triumph of the conjugal bond (*foedus conjugale*), which produces a new generation that keeps the race "eterne in mutability," as Spenser understands the Gardens of Adonis. That she broods (*incubat*) on the waters reminds a reader in the Judaeo-Christian tradition of Genesis i.2, where the Spirit of God moved over the waters (Vulgate *ferebatur*; but in patristic authors *incubabat*, brooded). Thus, Milton will speak of the Spirit brooding, dove-like, on the vast abyss and making it pregnant. Myths of poetic creativity tend to invoke a female Muse to express the concept of artistic procreation. The same Milton whose early elegy for a drowned Edward King under the name of one of Sannazaro's fishermen, Lycidas, constitutes a vision of poetic survival and transmission, brings to a final culmination the image clusters we have been discussing here; but Spenser's Alcyon has already gone some considerable distance toward creating a figure of the poet as brooding mother.

CHAPTER 9

MOTHER'S SORROW, MOTHER'S JOY: MOURNING BIRTH IN EDMUND SPENSER'S GARDEN OF ADONIS

THERESA M. KRIER

To forget being is to forget the air, this first fluid given us gratis and free of interest in the mother's blood, given us again when we are born, like a natural profusion that raises a cry of pain: the pain of a being who comes into the world and is abandoned, forced henceforth to live with the immediate assistance of another body. Unmitigated mourning for the intrauterine nest, elemental homesickness that man will seek to assuage through his work as builder of worlds, and notably of the dwelling which seems to form the essence of his maleness: language.

—Luce Irigaray, *An Ethics of Sexual Difference*

These darkly riddling words about birth form part of Irigaray's unceasing call to acknowledge the mother and move beyond nostalgia for the maternal. As she suggests, the first step in this difficult work is to bring birth itself into the symbolic: to represent it, to take on the mourning of it as well as the celebrating of it, to make gold out of the straw of our experience of coming into the world and finding ourselves abandoned, dependent, exposed. For Irigaray, this mourning is a great work that we have failed to do again and again—in philosophy, in psychoanalysis, in popular culture, in law. In this chapter I read three moments from Edmund Spenser's great canto on the Garden of Adonis (*The Faerie Queene* III.vi), with its celebration of generativity, maternity, gestation, and filiation, in light of Irigaray's summons. For it might seem commonsensical that we could meet nostalgia or sentimentalization of the maternal in this major poem, if anywhere in Renaissance writing. I argue rather that Spenser does precisely a mourning work in the Garden of Adonis canto, and furthermore that he not only anticipates Irigaray's summons but supplements it as well, by recognizing the mourning work to be done by the mother as well as that to be done by the child. By the end it might be possible to venture a guess about what Irigaray could mean by her beautiful, riddling reference to "a natural profusion" that "raises a cry of pain."

Nostalgia for repletion or fusion with a maternal plenitude to which we can never return, and a concomitant fantasy of an archaic, mighty mother who evokes not only desire but also terror and loathing, saturate both Renaissance culture and psychoanalysis, as we have learned in recent years from feminist analysis done in the space between literature and psychoanalysis.[1] The loss of merger with a provident maternal body, whether this loss is understood as a fantasy or as a literal event, shadows us, fuels our actions, creates culture. It shadows boys in particular, who must negotiate a sharper separation from the mother than girls, and therefore repudiate the mother more rigorously. Such accounts are especially powerful in articulating how the masculine imagination can idealize the maternal-feminine, demonize it, abject it, split, dominate, confine, reify, murder—all those mechanisms for managing the first and always overwhelming relation with a woman. If we are subjects at all, we are made so through an ambivalent melancholy in relation to our first object, the body of the mother, which we cannot have.

Rather, Irigaray would say, we cannot or will not represent and claim or work through certain aspects of birth itself. Cultural nostalgia for the maternal and recoil from the maternal body are alike evasions of the difficult paradox that we were once entirely dependent on a mother for survival yet have always been separate from her, not merged or fused with her. Classical psychoanalysis often seems to replicate these evasions, in its elaborations of a pre-Oedipal condition of fusion or merger of infant and mother. As Hélène Rouch says in an interview conducted by Luce Irigaray, psychoanalysis

> justifies the imaginary fusion between a child and its mother by the undeveloped state of the child at birth and by its absolute need of the other, its mother.... The differentiation between the mother's self and the other of the child, and vice versa, is in place before it's given meaning in and by language, and the forms it takes don't necessarily accord with those our cultural imaginary relays: loss of paradise, traumatizing expulsion or exclusion, etc.[2]

Trapped in the melancholia of unperformed mourning for a fusion that we do not allow ourselves to know we have never exactly had, we consign ourselves to the pathos of nostalgia for an idealized first home. So goes one strand of an Irigarayan critique of psychoanalysis and of our Western cultures more generally.

The real work of mourning birth, which depends on symbolizing it adequately in the first place, would be a first step toward an unalienated jubilation for which Irigaray's recurrent topos is free movement in the air: "Once we have left the *waters* of the womb, we have to construct a space for ourselves in the *air* for the rest of our time on earth."[3] Irigaray has powerfully criticized philosophers for a disavowal or willful forgetfulness of the debt that we all owe to the mother, a disavowal evident not precisely in their using metaphor drawn from a realm of birth and generation that could be thought to belong to women alone, but in using such figuration *in order to* forget the debt to the mother and continue consuming her as resource, without acknowledging her as fellow creature. Thus in *Speculum of the Other Woman*, first published in 1974, Irigaray writes at length of Plato's cave myth:

> So men have lived in this cave since their childhood. Since time began. They have never left this space, or place, or topography, or topology, of the cave. . . . The cave is the representation of something always already there, of the original matrix/womb which these men cannot represent since they are held down by chains. . . . This project, or process, by which the *hystera* is displaced, transposed, transferred, metaphorized, always already holds them captive. The trans-position . . . is never susceptible to representation, but produces, facilitates, permits all representations. . . . But what has been forgotten . . . and with good reason, is how to pass through the passage, how to negotiate it—the forgotten transition. The corridor, the narrow pass, the neck.[4]

Later, in *The Forgetting of Air in Martin Heidegger*, Irigaray argues that Heidegger's privileging of earth in his figures of world, rift, dwelling, path, clearing, and so on are also refusals of air as the first gift of the mother; more, she says that such refusals occur as a way to evade the *mourning* of birth—an odd thing to say, hence worth some attention.

> The first call is an aspiration of air; it is indistinguishable from a cry. . . . Air remains—that which restores life, but it does so first in the form of an absence: there, nothing is merely that which it is, if it does not appear. This provenance of life, this mediation and medium of life, offers itself without appearing as these. The first time, these are experienced as pain. Free air represents the possibility for life, but it is also the sign of the loss of that which— of she who—at no remove, with no expectations, and with no difficulty, used

to provide everything. In air, life is, in the beginning, the boundless immensity of a mourning. In it the whole is lost. . . . It replaces that absence: that which has some properties of the absence takes its place and lets itself be forgotten as much as, if not more thoroughly than, the absence does. Not being perceived, air can serve as the base for mourning.

Air is, first, the being of the open expanse whose measure would be that of the yet-to-come of (the) mourning: of she who will never come back.[5]

To represent air as a gift of the mother, not only *in utero* but later, in the unalterable space between mother and infant that opens in birth, is painful because it would entail acknowledgment of our one-way temporality: we cannot go back, and we do not anticipate any joy on the far side of the abyss of this loss: "What unfolds in the womb unfolds in function of an interval, a cord, that is never done away with. Whence perhaps the infinite nostalgia for that first home? The interval cannot be done away with."[6] Better not to perceive this matrical "base," to defer or deter the necessary work of mourning the loss of the mother's provident body. This is so, for Irigaray, not in any simple sense because we just continue to want complete provision and encompassing; it is more that the neonate cannot give back but only receive, and the burden of gratitude for the man (here in the person of Heidegger) would be too great to be borne. The mother's giving is a relentless gift:

She gives first. She gives the possibility of that beginning from the whole of man will be constituted. This gift is received with no possibility of a return. He cannot pay her back in kind. . . . But what does this unpaid debt yield in him? A certain forgetting?

A certain void? . . .

This place of the first gift—or of the *from which*—will be closed up—folded up in an unthinkable beginning of Being. It is unthinkable . . . for its advent prior to all saying. . . . The Being of man will be constituted on the basis of a forgetting: of the gift of this *from which* of which he is. (*Forgetting of Air* 28–30)

The claiming of air, and of space (which is, in the first instance, the new distance from the mother, no longer within her) challenges the neonate; later, after language acquisition, the becoming subject cannot be exultant in air, or rather exultant as an ethical being, unless he first mourns the increase of separation from the mother that is birth, then celebrates that distance by acknowledging *her* separateness. This is arduous because remembering, symbolizing, and sustaining gratitude all entail a willingness for hard and transformative thinking toward unconscious and mostly disavowed matters; one of the pleasures of imagining intrauterine life is the pleasure of being in a literally unthinkable circumstance, lapped and sustained in an incubation that requires—not *no thinking*, exactly, but no burdensome thinking subject. Irigaray says:

> In psychoanalytic categories, this path has not been thought through. Not even imagined? Except in its pathological symptoms. It is left in the shadow of the *pre-object*, and in the suffering and abandonment of the fusional state which fails to emerge as a subject. No space-time is available for experiencing it. (*Ethics* 70)

Instead the "fusional state" leads psychoanalysis to fantasize both the insatiable infant and the devouring mother. Both of these specious stock character types cause damage by deflecting thought, allowing the processes and mechanisms by which they enter representation to remain in the shadow of what Freud called "those dim Minoan regions" of the maternal.[7]

Nonetheless, if cultures and philosophers fail to mourn birth, poets may occasionally do so. Edmund Spenser mourns it, for instance, in his Garden, which unquestionably celebrates generation yet also weaves a tone of sadness through its episodes, as readers have long recognized. How does he mourn birth? In part he does so by creating hopeful fantasies of life before birth or outside the requirement that we be born, in order to show what gets lost when we *are* born. For instance, it has been observed by Kenneth Gross, taking the Garden of Adonis as a model of the mind thinking, that here "thoughts circulate without a clear thinker."[8] I think this *generality* of circulation is part of the fantasy of life before birth; Spenser wants to impart the generosity of thought and terrestrial ease to his readers, both as part of a fantasy of living before or outside of birth—like the souls growing in garden beds—and as a means of making the hard process thinking of acknowledging and mourning birth into something pleasurable, granting it a sense of ease and fluency. To show how Spenser achieves and elicits from us this thinking/mourning work of birth through the representation of maternal experience, through the strangely botanical cast of the canto and its imparting of plant-like features to his characters, and through his troping of ancient mythology and philosophy, is the aim of the rest of this chapter.

The Garden is, among other things, "the first seminarie/Of all things, that are born to liue and die" (III.vi.30). Adonis is named "the Father of all formes" (III.vi.47); the porter Genius ushers infant souls out into the world of generation and welcomes them back again after their mortal life. Souls and forms or species grow in garden beds: "infinite shapes" and "euery sort" of creatures are bred in beds (III.vi.35), like those of fish, which "In endlesse rancks along enraunged were,/That seem'd the *Ocean* could not containe them there" (III.vi.35). Parent figures tend many of the young: Genius fosters "a thousand thousand naked babes" who attend him (III.vi.32); Venus has a recently improved relationship with her daughter-in-law Psyche; Cupid and Psyche beget a daughter, Pleasure; Venus brings the infant Amoret, whom she had found while seeking her own truant son Cupid, to the Garden for her rearing, and she and Pleasure become companions; when Time mows down the growing things of the Garden, its "endlesse progenie" (III.vi.30), "their great mother *Venus*" laments "the losse of her deare brood, her deare delight" (III.vi.40).

As I have said, my suggestion is that in the Garden canto Spenser creates narrative resources within which we can mourn birth, in the sense that Irigaray calls for, and that he recognizes that only in this way might mothers and children come to celebrate maternal powers while recognizing the mother's otherness, and that this recognition, call it respect, *releases* the poet to celebrate generation and gestation. The canto often treats of loss; these are the losses implicit less in mortality (though Spenser acknowledges this in a bow to devouring Time) than in the creaturely condition of *natality*.[9] The canto boldly represents the enclosed paradise of female genital structure, a feminine realm of reproductive power, infant forms. Multiplications of gestation, maternity, and filiation abound, as we've seen. Even before the narrator leads us to the Garden, the twins Amoret and Belphoebe have been born to a nymph impregnated by the Sun; one of the twins, Belphoebe, has graces poured on her by the fostering gods and a psalmic allusion bestowed on her by the narrator, who links her to the infant of the Christian Nativity story, another precious child born in perilous circumstances; Diana and Venus have become foster-mothers to the twins, Venus adopting and naming Amoret, "little love," as a substitute for the missing Cupid ("in her litle loues stead, which was strayd," III.vi.28).[10]

The Garden is also an erotic paradise (stanzas 43–48), home to Venus and site of a famous Mount of Venus at once topographical and anatomical. As in other earthly paradises there are many pairs of happy couples, here dwelling "Without fell rancor, or fond gealosie," with "goodly meriment, and gay felicitie" (III.vi.41); there are boughs and blooms and songbirds, continual spring and continual harvest.[11] In this paradisal garden, Venus makes love eternally with the revived Adonis:

> Right in the middest of that Paradise,
>   There stood a stately Mount, on whose round top
>   A gloomy groue of mirtle trees did rise,
>   Whose shadie boughes sharpe steele did neuer lop,
>   But like a girlond compassed the hight,
>   And from their fruitfull sides sweet gum did drop,

That all the ground with precious deaw bedight,
Threw forth most dainty odours, and most sweet delight.
                              . . .
There wont faire *Venus* often to enioy
Her deare *Adonis* ioyous company,
And reape sweet pleasure of the wanton boy;
There yet, some say, in secret he does ly,
Lapped in flowres and pretious spycery,
By her hid from the world, and from the skill
Of *Stygian* Gods, which doe her loue enuy;
But she her selfe, when euer that she will,
Possesseth him, and of his sweetnesse takes her fill.
                              (III.vi.43, 46)

Do stanzas like these, with their frank and voluptuous anatomical elaborations of women's sexual bodies and abounding forms of generation, make Spenser's Garden a representation that is a forgetting of the first home, a disavowal of birth and the independent existence of the mother? Does the Garden rely on conventions of a maternalized earth without acknowledgment of air, that is to say without a claiming of mother's and child's distinctness from each other? Does it succumb to nostalgia about a lost paradise of the mother's body? Readers have long noted the dominance of feminine-maternal energies in this Garden; in 1976 Isabel MacCaffrey remarked of the stanzas leading us up the Mount and into the bower, "The sense of coming into a small, protected, intimately enclosed space probably satisfies an atavistic urge in all of us."[12] Her appeal to infantine experience seems to me entirely well-founded, and phrased with a canny elusiveness that perfectly matches Spenser's own subtlety. Why, then, does the canto not lend itself to any easy reading about nostalgia for the first home? It does not, for example, simply identify Venus with the Garden or even with the Mount, though she presides over both as sponsoring divinity. Or again, the narrative separates Genius and the garden beds of generation from the eternal pleasures of Venus and Adonis' lovemaking, which itself is not valued for any literal reproductive capacity. Spenser clearly celebrates Venus as great genetrix in Lucretian vein, but the exact relationship between goddess and garden, character and place, in this allegorical-cosmological fiction remains inexplicit, or withdraws itself from analytical scrutiny, even while summoning the reader onto a path of thinking about birth. The path leads us into the work of mourning birth. That symbolic work, for Spenser if not so much for Irigaray, includes bringing to awareness not only the (male) child's combined desire and dread of maternal forces, but also maternal ambivalence.

Early in canto vi, Spenser brings birth startlingly and disturbingly into the poem, in the first of three episodes I read here. The nymph Chrysogonee (golden-born or gold-producing) bathes, falls asleep naked in the woods, is impregnated by the Sun, and gives birth to twin girls. The act that results in conception is not only nonconsensual; for the nymph it is not even conscious:

> It was vpon a Sommers shynie day,
> When *Titan* faire his beames did display,
> In a fresh fountaine, farre from all mens vew,
> She bath'd her brest, the boyling heat t'allay;
> She bath'd with roses red, and violets blew,
> And all the sweetest flowres, that in the forrest grew.
>
> Till faint through irkesome wearinesse, adowne
> Vpon the grassie ground her selfe she layd
> To sleepe, the whiles a gentle slombring swowne
> Vpon her fell all naked bare displayd;
> The sunne-beames bright vpon her body playd,
> Being through former bathing mollifide,
> And pierst into her wombe, where they embayd
> With so sweet sence and secret power vnspide,
> That in her pregnant flesh they shortly fructifide.
>
> (III.vi.6–7)

Moreover, the poem does not exactly represent a birth but rather represents the cost, to the mother especially but also to her daughters, of *not* being able to represent or symbolize birth:

> So sprong these twinnes in wombe of *Chrysogone*,
> Yet wist she nought thereof, but sore affright,
> Wondred to see her belly so vpblone,
> Which still increast, till she her terme had full outgone.
>
> Whereof conceiuing shame and foule disgrace,
> Albe her guiltlesse conscience her cleard,
> She fled into the wildernesse a space,
> Till that vnweeldy burden she had reard,
> And shund dishonor, which as death she feard:
> Where wearie of long trauell, downe to rest

> Her selfe she set, and comfortably cheard;
> There a sad cloud of sleepe her ouerkest,
> And seized euery sense with sorrow sore opprest.
>
> (III.vi.9–10)

Not even readers are given means to represent the birth, for the narrative conspicuously leaps over it. Chrysogonee, alienated from society and estranged from her own body, sleeps again in the woods and gives birth in her sleep:[13]

> Vnwares she them conceiu'd, vnwares she bore:
> She bore withouten paine, that she conceiued
> Withouten pleasure; ne her need implore
> *Lucinaes* aide ...
>
> (III.vi.27)

The goddesses Venus and Diana, coming upon this moment, take the infants for themselves, and their biological mother slips out of the poem.

I used to think this fate of Chrysogonee a failure on Spenser's part, a strange conclusion to his brilliant, moving, complex account of her.[14] Now I think rather that he freights birth by heightening the normal separation of mother and child with pathos in order to demonstrate the urgency of a general need to symbolize that separation. It would not be excessive to say that the massive representations of birth and generation in the Garden spring from this episode, in response to a need awakened by it: narrator and reader alike need to do the work of representing or thinking birth *because* Chrysogonee could not do it herself—a signature Spenserian form of displacement. Spenserian allegory often opens up for readers an arena for psychic work that cannot be performed by non-novelistic characters, whose circumstances and adventures nonetheless call for thought and feeling.[15] In this instance, Spenser turns an epistemological feature of his inherited forms into an apt instrument for examining the *problem* of representing birth—why it is so hard to acknowledge and mourn birth, thus why it is so hard to grant the mother her separateness. Throughout this canto, Spenser further relieves his characters of conscious, purposive thinking and control by conducting a kind of thought experiment, testing what happens when he gives to persons with a human form a plant-like nature as well. Chrysogonee is of course a very Ovidian nymph. In Ovid, nymphs undergo many transformations into trees and flowers; Chrysogonee metamorphoses from a condition enviably like a plant's—conscious but not in need of hard thinking; placid and grounded in intimacy and belonging with other natural objects like the fountain, the grass, the "roses red and violets blew;" "fructified" by the sun—to a self-alienated condition of uncanny and undesired pregnancy. To imagine a pregnancy this way, as a change from self-presence and poise to Ovidian self-estrangement, is to suggest that birth needs to be mourned by the one who gives birth as well as by those who are born. The Garden canto allows not only for readers' identification with a child's mourning of birth, but also for readers' identification with a *mother's* mourning of birth. If this is so, then the later representations of the *mons Veneris*, of gestation, and of Venus' sorrows do not *occlude* the mother while celebrating the faceless power of generation; rather the narrative surrounds instances of birth with the actions and emotions of maternal characters, or with mothers whose fates summon the reader to acknowledge the circumstances of mothers.

The Chrysogonee episode thus opens up in the poem a space in which birth, in its attendant losses as well as its evident joys, *needs* to be represented, and draws the reader into the Garden itself, which compounds recognition of maternal loss even as it celebrates generation. The nymph has lost two daughters whom she never knows that she had; Venus has come across them because she too has lost her child Cupid; as we will soon read, Venus has also lost (then regained) Adonis, and regularly mourns her other progeny, the creatures who are born and die; she enjoys Adonis but seems never to wander very far from a sense of the fragility of his connection to her, in part because of Adonis' share in plant nature. And the figure of Adonis offers the second moment of the canto I consider here.

When Venus fends off the threat of death from Adonis, who has already died many times in myth and religious cult, by keeping him to herself, he lies in secret, "Lapped in flowres and pretious spycery." Some readers have taken this imagery as Venus' consigning Adonis effectually to death, and this is true enough.[16] But I would rather say first that Spenser deploys Adonis' flowers and spices, which pervaded his cult in antiquity, hopefully, in order to assimilate him to the plant world, as in the cases of Chrysogonee and the souls in garden beds. This canto refers to a condition of not having been born—which may be read as a kind of death, or like death—because not vulnerable to the onslaughts and exposures of living. Adonis is, after all, born from the tree form of his mother Myrrha, and is immediately hidden away, laid in another enclosed, protected space.[17] Furthermore, where Adonis goes in literature, so go elegiac verses filled with floral catalogues representing other beloved youths who died young, leaving their older lovers bereft. So in Spenser's canto: having seen Venus grieve generally over the creatures who die, we next meet those elegiac flowers, on the very height of the Mount of Venus. About the arbor where Venus and Adonis make love, a metrically imperfect stanza falls oddly into the conventions of lyric elegy:

> And all about grew euery sort of flowre,
> To which sad louers were transformd of yore;
> Fresh *Hyacinthus, Phœbus* paramoure,
> And dearest loue,
> Foolish *Narcisse,* that likes the watry shore,
> Sad *Amaranthus,* made a flowre but late,
> Sad *Amaranthus,* in whose purple gore
> Me seemes I see *Amintas* wretched fate,
> To whom sweet Poets verse hath giuen endlesse date.
> (III.vi.45)

Readers have long speculated on this stanza, for instance in the suggestion that Amintas figures Sir Philip Sidney, who died young in 1586. Jon Quitslund, in the best argument to date, encompasses the likely topical reference to Sidney's death within Spenser's larger meditation on mortality and value: "Mourning is incorporated in Spenser's understanding of the world's order and vitality, right at its source; sadness is part of the human capacity for love"; the kind of love represented by Venus as great mother begins with "loss and a recognition that death plays a huge part in making the things of this world valuable" (25).[18] But why, exactly, would this be so, and how is the mourning work performed? What thinking or mourning is made possible by the flowers to which Adonis is assimilated?

Venus seems to want to preserve Adonis and herself from birth, even as she revels in his male adulthood and presides over the generation of the world. To represent a wish that Adonis could be protected, like a plant, or as if unborn, is to create for the reader a space in which to acknowledge more generally the maternal mourning of birth, a condition of ambivalence and paradox.[19] Adonis, once upon a time metamorphosed into a flower, would be the right figure to carry this ambivalence, oscillating in the mythic tradition between cherished infant and beautiful youth. These are categories that often collapse into each other or inspire thoughts of each other in Spenser's time; one way to mourn birth and then to move into adulthood, for the late sixteenth century, is to entertain the temptation to idealize and identify with the fair youth, youth's homosocial bonding, its dread of and desire for what Irigaray calls the feminine-maternal; then to let go of such adolescence in an intentional, conscious turn to dwelling in a world shared by women. Shakespeare's Benedick, for instance, finds himself challenged to this maturity in *Much Ado about Nothing*, and takes a step into it at the end of the play, when he crosses an open space to join Beatrice while his old friends, from whom he moves away, taunt him about it. Sidney's young princes in *The Countesse of Pembrokes Arcadia*, indeed the narrator himself, show a defensive resistance to and cruelty toward the maternal. In *The Faerie Queene* Spenser examines the relationship of the adolescent male of his period to the mother in the person of Marinell, whom Elizabeth Bellamy calls perhaps "the epic's greatest threat to genealogical continuity, rejecting, as he does, the split from the (m)other."[20]

Spenser's career provides a much earlier instance of a late-adolescent youth negotiating his relationship to the mother: a reference to Ceres, a mother who's lost her young adolescent daughter and who mourns their enforced separation. This reference occurs in his Latin epistolary poem "Ad Ornatissimum virum," addressed to Gabriel Harvey, who has been uneasy about Spenser's impending marriage (probably to Machabyas Childe, in 1579), a poem written when Spenser was anticipating or imagining a trip to the Continent in the service of Leicester.[21] (The trip does not seem to have materialized.) Spenser and Harvey's friendship took shape in the markedly male world of Pembroke College, Cambridge. Now, as career and marriage pull him away from his college comradeship with Harvey, he uses the poem to put some affective distance between himself and Harvey, while owning his attachment to him. The trip would provide a safe and unthreatening means to answer the need made urgent throughout the poem, "the poet's need," as Jon Quitslund puts it, "to separate his life from Harvey's," and to join it to his new wife's.[22] The marriage occasions a struggle between the writer's pull toward a unifiedly masculine world and an ardent identification with Harvey, on the one hand, and a pull toward erotic attachment and marriage, on the other. Allusion and sphere of imagery build a tension between the masculine world of philosophical scholarship and travel, on the one hand, and a feminized world of marriage, settling in, a little embarrassed about his wish to marry and stay at home, on the other. How will the writer choose his form of adult life?

He chooses by identifying with a goddess mourning her separation from her child, in the most moving and mysterious lines of the poem. The writer is imagining his hard journey:

> Then with tired feet we will accompany the grieving goddess,
> From whose searching the earth withheld the renowned theft.
> For one feels ashamed, as a youth not without talents,

To be wasting the green years uselessly,
At home with unworthy duties in the shameful shade,
Picking empty ears out of the hoped-for crops.
We will go, then, at once—who calls for blessings on my departure? –
And trek with tired feet across the steep Alps.
Meanwhile, who will send you little letters
Steeped in Britain's dew? or a poem impudent with love?
Out of practice, in the shadow of Mount Oebalius the Muse
Will bewail her long reticence with an endless complaint.

(ll. 93–104)

Literally, the lines about Ceres designate Sicily as a point on the itinerary of the journey, and Mt. Oebalius marks the site of Apollo's love for the youth Hyacinthus, whom he killed accidentally, a love to which Spenser returns in the Garden canto. But the allusion to Ceres presents us with an intricate knot of implications about the role of poetry in Spenser's emergent adult life, about the choices of gender identity among which he stands. The appearance of the grieving Ceres is a sudden, unexpected upsurge of the writer's willingness to identify with the feminine—but also, less obviously, Ceres allows him to formulate his need for manly action in the world of state affairs. Ceres presides over poetry and achieved wedded love and the world of generation. But she also represents arduous, wide-ranging travel and diplomacy, experiences she has gained in her mourning for her daughter. She condenses the two worlds that have been at odds in the poem, and opens the way for Spenser's playful, confident anticipation that his not writing will *cause* grief in a Muse. Through the Ceres allusion, living with a wife and writing poetry have become noble choices; the writer can loosen his hold on identification with a world of male adolescence by starting to identify with a divine grieving mother.

The proposal that Adonis' functions *for Venus* create a space for maternal mourning of birth allows us to entertain a new sense of the boar confined in a cave under the mount; the boar comprises the canto's third locus for the mourning of birth:

> There now he [Adonis] liueth in eternal blis,
>   Ioying his goddesse, and of her enioyd:
> Ne feareth he henceforth that foe of his,
>   Which with his cruell tuske him deadly cloyd:
> For that wilde Bore, the which him once annoyd,
>   She firmely hath emprisoned for ay,

That her sweet loue his malice mote auoyd,
In a strong rocky Caue, which is they say,
Hewen vnderneath that Mount, that none him losen may.
(III.vi.48)

This boar creates another narrative oddity. The boar was the agent of
Adonis' death, hence enemy to Venus, but why does Spenser place it
here at all? Couldn't Venus have done better simply to dispatch it? Is the
boar a figure of winter, as Renaissance mythographers said in their expli-
cations of the myth? Is it Privation, as Upton thought? Is it phallic, a figure of lust, or at least sexual appetite, a recognition of the aggression
within eros? But then whose? Is it a figure of death?[23]

The boar, overdetermined like so many features of cosmological fictions, clearly lends itself to multiple significances, most often taken to be
significances about Adonis. But, dwelling as it does in a uterine cave
directly under the *mons Veneris*, and that within the "first seminary of the
world," the boar may well embody *for Venus*, and for readers willing to
symbolize birth as it exists for the mother, the strong, not to say violent,
forces and risks of birthing. If the boar can be phallic, then that phallus
within the cave can certainly be metonymic for a hypothetical future
infant; by keeping it contained Venus would simultaneously separate her
own lovemaking with Adonis from the making of babies, and represent
women's suffering of birth pangs. The boar would figure natality as
much as mortality, or better, the boar manifests the paradox that for
both mother and infant to be mortal is first to be natal, to undergo the
birth process, to find oneself exposed, to claim a suddenly enlarged
space between mother and infant. To a sixteenth-century mother even
in the best medical circumstances, this is cause for sorrow as well as
joy, and an ambivalent relief, of the kind so often found in women's
documents of the period.[24]

I started thinking out the matter of this essay after reading Irigaray on
Plato's cave myth, and finding her logic about the disavowal of birth and
maternity persuasive. After writing at length here on the mourning of
birth, I don't think it a stretch to entertain the possibility that Spenser,
who often tropes Plato and neoplatonism, is creating in the Garden of
Adonis a wittily feminized reversal of Plato's cave. Lauren Silberman has
argued persuasively that "the eroticism of the garden functions both as
a corrective to Platonic dualism of body and spirit and as pretext for
questioning Aristotelian gendering of dualism as male form and female
matter" (44); surely the poet who can create the Garden of Adonis as a
reversal of Plato's trivializing of ancient Greek gardens of Adonis in the
Phaedrus would be capable of troping the cave myth in this way. It is not

literal men who are in chains but a boar whose figurative resonance, expanding to encompass the pains of birth, would remind us that valuing generation and profusion as we do has its costs. In the epigraph to this essay, Irigaray refers to the "natural profusion that raises a cry of pain." Profusion is by many poetic standards a good thing: we think of it as Shakespearean, Spenserian, Keatsian. It is salutary to remind ourselves that profusion first comes to us, *in utero*, as an excessive gift that we cannot recompense, and next comes to us as an assault of air, a forceful taking in of air; those who become biological mothers contribute to profusion of the family, the species, with a cry of pain. If we think about how humans enter into subjectivity, Irigaray argues, we need to think about early life events not only in terms of lack, castration, and so on, but also in terms of an excess that seems to be too much to bear. In spite of these excesses that we might wish to evade in a celebration of profusion, and generativity, Spenser dissolves our possible resistances to the labor of mourning birth; mourning birth through figure and narrative, we are *released* to think, and celebrate, generally and generously.

CHAPTER 10

VENUS AND ADONIS: SPENSER, SHAKESPEARE, AND THE FORMS OF DESIRE

JUDITH H. ANDERSON

In Shakespeare's *Venus and Adonis*, the switch from Venus as manhandler to Venus as the pathetic—some would say tragic—mourner over the body of dead Adonis has always been problematical. Although passion and grief are twinned conditions of want(ing), the shift in this poem from an aggressive, comic mode to a helpless, pathetic one proves larger than life and challenges credible mimesis or, otherwise put, human credibility. Or perhaps I should say balanced human credibility, since Venus' behavior makes sense as an obsessive fixation transferred from hunger to loss. Yes, Venus is a goddess and a figure of myth for whom excess is appropriate, yet her passion also verges too close to human passion and sexual realities to make such a rationalization convincing. Fixation, after all, is the basic given of personification allegory and, correlatively, of the demonic.

In what follows, I would suggest that, instead of a mythic rationalization, *Venus and Adonis* is a seriocomic meditation on the landscape of desire, or wanting—on passion and grief—and on the kinds of figures desire generates in the third book of Spenser's *Faerie Queene*. Shakespeare's poem explores the effects of folding into characters Spenser's multiple refractions of desire that are expressed in numerous allegorical figures and thus the effects of folding the multiple refractions of Book III into more fully and materially realized constructs. These effects and indeed this process bear on the gendered depiction of wanting, of passion and grief, over time.

*

The consensus of modern editors is that Shakespeare's *Venus and Adonis* was written in 1592–93, precisely the period in which Shakespeare is thought to have written *Richard III*, a play full of memories of the 1590 *Faerie Queene*. Harold Brooks has persuasively identified recollections of Spenser's Books II and III in the terror and riches of Clarence's dream of drowning—the Cave of Mammon (II.vii), the Bower of Bliss (II.xii), and Marinell's Rich Strand (III.iv)—and elsewhere I have noted allusions to the Garden of Adonis (III.vi) in Richard's words to Queen Elizabeth when he seeks her daughter's hand in marriage. I have suggested as well the plausibility of a further memory in the same scene of passages in Book III concerning an unavoidable destiny (*Richard III;* IV.iv.216 and *Faerie Queene;* III.i.37, vs. 9; iv.27, vs. 1).[1] The first of these passages occurs in Spenser's tale of Venus and Adonis in Malecasta's tapestry, and the second, equally relevant to this chapter, comes in the story of Marinell's downfall for being, like Shakespeare's Adonis, "loues enimy" (III.iv.26); the latter is also the story that furnished one of the Spenserian recollections demonstrated by Brooks. All these associations and allusions indicate that Spenser's poem was much in Shakespeare's mind at this time and that his familiarity with it was extensive.

Since *Venus and Adonis* is the subject at hand, Shakespeare's allusion in *Richard III* to Spenser's Garden of Adonis, the earthly paradise where Adonis becomes "eterne in mutability," is of special interest (III.vi.47). Beyond the obvious purpose of increasing the likelihood of a relation between Shakespeare's erotic epyllion and Spenser's mythic Garden, it indicates something of Shakespeare's response to this complexly nuanced site and to the 1590 *Faerie Queene* more generally. In the fourth act of the play, Richard replies to Queen Elizabeth's bitter rehearsal of the fates of her murdered sons that when he marries her daughter, "the liquid drops of tears that you have shed/Shall come again, transform'd to orient pearl" (iv.321–22). Suggestively close to a description of Shakespeare's hopeful but apprehensive Venus, whose tears are "prison'd in her eye like pearls in glass,/Yet sometimes falls an orient tear beside," Richard's promise of a regenerative metamorphosis fails at this stage to persuade the Queen (980–81). Before long she again reminds Richard, "Yet thou didst kill my children," and he quickly counters,

> But in thy daughter's womb I bury them;
> Where in that nest of spicery they will breed
> Selves of themselves, to your recomforture.
>   (iv.423–25).

Here the memory of Spenser's Garden of Adonis is striking: the boar, Richard's heraldic device and thus metonymically Richard, would root in its fertile soil.

In the Renaissance, a Garden of Adonis, from ancient times the term for a forcing bed or place of heightened fertility, became by etymological confusion of Adonis with Eden a "ioyous Paradize," as Spenser calls it, and the seminary of all created things.[2] At the center of Spenser's Garden is a *mons veneris*, and directly beneath it the deadly boar is imprisoned in a cave. The recycling babes returning through a gate of death "in that Garden *planted* be againe;/And grow afresh, as they had neuer seene/Fleshly corruption, nor mortall paine" (III.vi.33: my emphasis). On the Mount itself, Venus "takes her fill" of Adonis' "sweetnesse," and

> There yet, some say, in secret he does ly,
> Lapped in flowres and pretious *spycery* [my emphasis]
> By her hid from the world, and from the skill
> Of *Stygian* Gods. . . .
>
> (III.vi.46)

Similarity of situation, explicit verbal echoes, and Richard's otherwise unmotivated rhetorical flourish leave little question that Shakespeare alludes to "that nest of spicery" in Spenser's Garden.

An earlier passage in the same Shakespearean courtship scene had already played on the association of womb and tomb so noticeable in the allusion to Spenser's Garden. In it, Richard objects to the resistant Queen, "Your reasons are too shallow and too quick," and she delivers the punning rejoinder, "O no, my reasons are too deep and dead—/Too deep and dead, poor infants, in their graves" (363–63). Like Richard, Elizabeth refers to her reasons for resisting his suit, but her reasons come between the two explicit linkings of womb and tomb in the scene and evoke this link as well. Her reasons ironically recall the Renaissance commonplace of the *rationes seminales* (seminal reasons), "the germs of those things which were to develop in the course of time"—the potentialities implanted by God in the creation to develop by temporal unfolding.[3] In this way, they suggest a further associative link with that seminary of created forms in Spenser's Garden of Adonis, to which withered things return to be planted anew.

In the Richardian context, of course, such references to the seminary of life are heavy with negation. The point I would stress, however, is that their irony is directed not at the Garden as such but at Richard's outrageous hypocrisy and his presumption of the ultimate gullibility of the Queen.

This irony is chilling precisely because it invokes, by contrast, the safety, pleasure, and renewal of Spenser's mythic site of fertility and regeneration. Yet metaphorically (or metadramatically, which amounts to the same thing), it could be said also to mock a naive reading of the Garden. It responds to— if it also overemphasizes—the threats, darkness, chaos, and death that are in both senses *contained* in and by the Garden, not to mention the rest of Book III, without which an approach to the Garden violates its very nature. In question here is not merely the relation of Shakespeare's *Venus and Adonis* to Spenser's focal use of this myth but also the way Shakespeare might have read antecedent texts and in particular allegorical ones.

One method of reading—perhaps, more accurately, of utilizing—texts in this period that has lately received renewed attention involves the culling of textual nuggets, whether based on a moral, rhetorical, topical, or other principle of selection. This method, evident in the ubiquitous commonplace book and in other forms of anthologizing, can be highly insensitive to textual or historical context. But another important way of reading texts that is based on biblical interpretation and its controverted (hence publicized) methods is acutely aware of context, nuance, and detail. Here, rather than exclusively in the rhetoric books, is the parallel to modern close reading, whose popular dissemination religious training and sermons furthered. There is, then, no necessary reason to assume that Shakespeare would have played *Venus and Adonis* off against a single episode of *The Faerie Queene* while ignoring a conspicuously relevant larger context with which we have reason to suppose he was familiar. Within that context, the episodes to which *Venus and Adonis* is usually linked look different from the way they do in isolation, and the relation of the epyllion to the epic looks rather less like parody and critique and more like dialogue and complement.

The critical tradition has too often assumed rivalry or anxiety as the only possible relation between poets and precursors, whereas in a historical setting in which the mentality of a lingering manuscript culture coexisted with an incipient culture of print capitalism, there were other, more mixed and interesting possibilities. Shakespeare, after all, did not even bother to prepare his plays for publication, and his relation to his sources and analogues often looks less competitive than culturally assimilative or even comfortably dependent. At times this relation looks like the one Gerald Bruns ascribes to a manuscript culture, in which the appropriation and "embellishment" of another text "is an art of disclosure, as well as of amplification. Or rather, amplification is not merely supplementation but also interpretation: the act of . . . eliciting from it [the earlier text] that which remains unspoken."[4] Put otherwise, it is an act of reading and (in)habitation.

The relation of *Venus and Adonis* to the 1590 *Faerie Queene* has certainly been documented and explored these many years. A glance at the Shakespeare *Variorum* shows that the first canto of Book III has been the primary candidate for an analogue or occasionally for a source ("a certain resistance on the part of Adonis") simply on account of its subject matter, namely, the Ovidian rendering of Venus' love of Adonis depicted in Malecasta's tapestry.[5] Ellen Aprill Harwood also calls our attention to the 1590 ending of *The Faerie Queene* in which Scudamore and Amoret are described as if merging in a hermaphroditic union similar to that of Shakespeare's Venus and Adonis. Embracing, "lips together glued," Shakespeare's pair seems "incorporate [;] . . . face grows to face" (540, 546). As thirsty as Shakespeare's Venus, Spenser's Scudamour embraces Amoret, who "in sweete rauishment pourd out her spright:/No word they spake, nor earthly thing they felt,/but like two senceles stocks in long embracement dwelt." Arguably, Spenser's "senceles stocks" share with Shakespeare's images of gluing and facelessness a rejection of such amoebic blending for human beings; significantly at least, Britomart, Spenser's most fully realized figure, is never allowed it.

Aside from such peripheral analogies between Shakespeare's and Spenser's poems, the fullest, most provocative essay on their relation, Harwood's, argues that Spenser actually rejects an Ovidian rendering of the sort Shakespeare was to write simply by situating his in Malecasta's lustful domain, where, I would object, Britomart, the heroine of Book III, is wounded and thus touched by and vulnerable to what this domain represents. But Harwood concentrates instead on the Garden of Adonis, asserting that "much of *Venus and Adonis* can be read as a repudiation [and parody] of the erotic philosophy expounded" there.[6] Considering Shakespeare the exception, Harwood notes in this essay published in 1977 that "all the critics have praised the union of Venus and Adonis in the garden as an ideal, the very image of nature"; then she marvels, "that there the 'great mother Venus' 'possesseth' and 'takes her fill' of a 'boy' produces neither the least discomfort nor the smallest giggle," responses, I hasten to add, it has produced since Harwood wrote, notably from the pen of Harry Berger (53).[7] For Harwood, however, it originally took Shakespeare to appreciate the possibilities of humor and paradox unrealized in Spenser's myth of regeneration and to combine not merely a generative Venus with a heavenly one (Venus Pandemos with Venus Urania), as Spenser does, but a generative Venus with one both passionate and sexual (Venus Vulgaris). In contrast to Spenser's, Shakespeare's Venus, she observes, would be equally at home in Acrasia's lusty Bower of Bliss or in the fertile Garden of Adonis, although she also acknowledges that his chaste Adonis would decline the pleasure of either place (59–60).

More recently, Gordon Williams' highly suggestive reading of the death of Shakespeare's Adonis as a "violent sexual awakening" in which sex is collocated with death—indeed, just as the familiar pun on dying would have it—conversely would signal the later poet's approval of both sites and pointedly of Spenser's Garden, where grows "euery sort of flowre/To which sad louers were transformed of yore" and where, "in euerlasting ioy," Adonis finds the continuity of dying with the perpetuation of life (III.vi.45–47, 49).[8] Here indeed is "a life in death," though in quite a different sense from the meaningless, immediate alternation of laughter with weeping, the living death, that Shakespeare's Adonis has in mind (413–14). In Spenser's pleasure Garden, even more clearly than in Malecasta's tapestry, the poet of romance epic revises Ovid's story of Venus and Adonis to feature the explicit sexuality of consummation.[9]

Although Harwood ranges outside the Garden to glance at the Bower of Bliss and the figure of Mutability (not published until 1609), as well as at Malecasta's tapestry, her reading of Book III remains too selective. While offering evidence of the bearing of the Garden on Shakespeare's poem, it neglects not only the Garden's dark shadings but also the implication of the Garden in the rest of the 1590 poem, including the rest of the canto in which it exists. Spenser's is a poem that conspicuously and often uses a kind of refraction to relate largely disparate figures to a single type, such as Venus; as Peter Hawkins has observed, in such figures we recognize less the presence of the original type than the "degrees" of its presence.[10] Whereas an older criticism at ease with oppositions and clean boundaries between them confidently saw such refractions as invitations to read *in malo* or *in bono*, more recent ones have instead seen in them complex mixtures, receding depths, and indefinition. Spenser, like his "father" Chaucer and unlike the neoplatonizing philosophers with whom some readers of *Venus and Adonis* would group him, does not keep a "good" Venus and a "bad" one sharply and safely distinct. Instead he insists on their connection, even while insisting on a difference between them. If briefly I might invoke a perspective beyond the publication of Shakespeare's epyllion, much of Spenser's 1609 *Faerie Queene* is set between Acrasia's Bower and Nature's arbor, and thus between two Venerian figures, both veiled. Books III and IV, the pivotal books in the epic as we have it, most fully explore what lies beneath the veil, what relates and what differentiates these figures, which is actually the same question.

Characteristically, Spenser's cantos are units, and what is within them is in some way related. Within a single canto, the Garden of Adonis is preceded and introduced by a story that comes in two stages: the first concerns the birth of the twins Belphoebe and Amoret, and the second, which dovetails with the first, the search of Venus for a wayward Cupid, or desire. The second allots Belphoebe, or chastity, to Diana and allots Amoret, or love, to Venus, thus separating the twins, and Venus then takes Amoret, "in her little loues [Cupid's] stead" to the Garden of Adonis, "Where most she [Venus] wonnes, when she on earth does dwel" (III.vi.28–29). The birth of the twins is described in such a way as to ensure the continuity of heavenly influence with physical process— of a conception "Pure and unspotted from all loathly crime,/That is ingenerate in fleshly slime" with a very physically pregnant "belly so vpblone" (3, 9).[11] The second stage traces a Venus seamlessly and successively transforming herself from a heavenly manifestation to a more generalized social one, with more than a trace of Venus Vulgaris evident, and in the process managing to mollify Diana, whom Actaeon-like she has surprised in disarray. The first half of the canto thus shows the relatedness of higher and lower, ideal and physical, although the subsequent separation of the twins pulls against the apparently temporary rapprochement of Venus and Diana to suggest future problems for both of them. Nonetheless, this entrée to the Garden emphatically figures relation—the desirability and actuality of relation—rather than an otherworldly flight from the physical. And it remains Amoret's seemingly fortunate fate to be taken to the Garden, Venus' "ioyous Paradize."

The Garden itself, while dominantly benign, is a place that includes time and death, containing them mythically, impersonally, and cyclically. It also draws out of "the hateful darkenesse and . . . deepe horrore,/[of] An huge eternall *Chaos.* . . . The substances of natures fruitful progenyes" (36). Albeit in one aspect a Garden of forms, the Garden is very much a material and physical place and therefore not one that respects individual subjects or gendered egos; it is, in short, a myth of generation, situated, when once the relatively more individuated figures of Venus and Adonis are reached, clearly within the female body:

> Right in the middest of that Paradise
> There stood a stately Mount, on whose round top
> A gloomy groue of mirtle trees did rise,
> Whose shadie boughes sharpe steele did neuer lop,
> Nor wicked beasts their tender buds did crop,
> But like a girlond compassed the hight,

And from their fruitfull sides sweet gum did drop,
That all the ground with precious deaw bedight,
Threw forth most dainty odours, and most sweet delight.
                                          (III.vi.43)

For several stanzas, the description of this landscape of Venerian desire
affords a topos analogous to that of Shakespeare's Venus, who offers
to be a deer park for Adonis, where he might feed at will, "on moun-
tain, or in dale" and "Graze on . . . [her] lips, and if those hills be
dry,/Stray lower, where the pleasant fountains lie" (231–34). She
continues,

"Within this limit is relief enough,
Sweet bottom grass and high delightful plain
Round rising hillocks, brakes obscure and rough,
To shelter thee from tempest and from rain;
Then be my deer, since I am such a park,
No dog shall rouse thee, though a thousand bark."
                                          (235–40)

Shakespeare's deployment of the topos is, of course, quite different
from, as well as analogous to, Spenser's: the trace of mystery, secrecy,
shade, or darkness—Berger calls it gynephobia—that the Spenserian
description incorporates into the landscape with such words as
"gloomy" Shakespeare embodies here, both in an allusion to Scylla's
barking dogs and, as elsewhere, especially in the disdainful Adonis.[12] But
where Spenser's landscape belongs mainly to myth, Shakespeare's
belongs mainly to the social world. What the Spenserian landscape inti-
mates, Shakespeare makes explicit, comic, and more troubling. His wily,
resourceful Venus attempts to seduce Adonis with the kind of anatomical topos that many a poet has fantasied, but this youthful representative
of manhood responds to her plea of " 'Pity . . . some favor, some
remorse' " by springing away in fearful disgust and hastening, ironically,
to his sexually aroused horse (257–58).

Aside from the association of dying with life and of female desire with
generation, the Garden also impinges on the rest of Book III and on
Shakespeare's *Venus and Adonis* in the figure of a female bending over a
recumbent male. This silhouetted pietà is present in *The Faerie Queene*
from the Bower of Bliss at the end of Book II through nearly the end of
Book III: Acrasia, Cymoent, Belphoebe, Venus (twice), Argante, and
Britomart (twice) are all found in such a memorably refractive, relational, Venereal posture. In a conspicuous allusion to the Bower of Bliss

that is inescapable in the first canto to follow it, Venus leans over the sleeping Adonis in Malecasta's tapestry just as Acrasia leaned over the sleeping Verdant in the Bower, and as Venus will lean over Adonis' recumbent form in the Garden. While the lustful Acrasia and Venus, similarly lustful, voyeuristic, and motherly in the tapestry and dominant, contented, and contenting in the Garden, have immediate thematic relevance to *Venus and Adonis*, three of the other refractive figures, Cymoent, Belphoebe, and Argante, may be even of greater interest.

Like Shakespeare's Venus in one of her aspects and the Venus of Spenser's Garden, the sea nymph Cymoent figures motherhood. When she learns of her son Marinell's wounding, she rushes to his side, where her lament over his fallen body begins, "Deare image of myself," and suggests her possessive narcissism, which is also evident in her earlier warning to her son to avoid the love of women (III.iv.36). She subsequently takes the helpless Marinell to her own home in the sea, a state of primal flux, where he remains virtually captive until the 1596 edition, in which he is reborn in his love for a woman and reemerges from the sea of birth. Cymoent's well-meant but engulfing, infantilizing possession bears a suggestive relevance to the Shakespearean Venus' relation to Adonis, her "froward infant" and "fondling," who is "smother[ed]," "hemm'd" in, and manipulated both psychologically and physically by her (18, 229, 562). As I have earlier noted, the source of two allusions in *Richard III* to Spenser's Book III is the story of Marinell, in which "loues enimy" Marinell is felled by Britomart, the heroine of a quest for love.

Spenser's beautiful Belphoebe likewise assumes the aspect of motherhood, among other aspects, in a refraction of the death of Adonis in Book III. The double nature of Amoret's twin, who is also the poem's chief symbol of virginity, becomes evident when the young squire Timias, who has been wounded by a lustful forester, wakens from his swoon and, as Belphoebe bends over him, addresses her in words that align her at once with Spenser's lustful Acrasia and with Venus herself disguised as Diana in the *Aeneid*. "Mercy deare Lord," Timias asks, "what grace is this,... To send thine Angell from her bowre of blis," and then, echoing Aeneas, he continues, "Angell, or Goddesse do I call thee right?" (III.v.35). A strange, not fully realized amalgam of mother, lover, and virgin Queen, Belphoebe ministers to a youth who has been attacked by lustful villains armed with a boar-spear and arrows and, Adonis-like, has been badly wounded in the thigh. So wounded, he seems about to turn into a flower, thus participating in a major motif in Book III:

> His locks [of hair], like faded leaues fallen to grownd,
> Knotted with bloud, in bounches rudely ran,

> And his sweete lips, on which before that stownd
> The bud of youth to blossome faire began,
> Spoild of their rosie red, were woxen pale and wan.
>
> (III.v.29)

Throughout this book, beginning with the story of Venus and Adonis in Malecasta's tapestry, characters and episodes have variously and destructively been identified with one or another bipolar term, even as the fading flower of Timias (from Greek *time:* honor) is here: sensuouness and brutality, withdrawal or attack, passive loveliness or hostile aggression, the Venerian flower or the boar. It is Britomart's quest as a *Venus Armata* to seek their tempering and accord, not simply their suppression or separation, and in the House of Busirane, where she stands wounded but with sword erect between the captive Amoret and her felled captor Busirane, she is at once a figure of concord and yet another refraction of Venus.

The most outrageously provocative Venerian figure in Book III with respect to Shakespeare's poem is the monstrous Giantess Argante. Like her incestuous twin brother Ollyphant (destructive phantasy), Argante shares with Shakespeare's Venus a taste for boys, ranging over the countryside to find them, and

> Whom so she fittest finds to serue her lust,
> Through her maine strength, in which she most doth trust,
> She with her brings into a secret Ile,
> Where in eternall bondage dye he must,
> Or be the vassall of her pleasures vile,
> And all in shamefull sort him selfe with her defile.
>
> (III.vii.50)

When first sighted in Book III, Argante has athwart her horse and "before her lap a doefull Squire"—a perverse pietà if ever there was one (vii.37). Argante is an incestuous predator like the Venus of one facet of Shakespeare's imagination, who resembles a vulture or "an empty eagle" that tears "with her beak on feathers, flesh, and bone,/Shaking her wings, devouring all in haste" (555–57, 551). Argante, also compared to an eagle, is forced in mid-swoop to abandon her "quarrey" to ward off the attack of a mature knight who would rescue the subjected squire (III.vii.39). But she soon stuns the would-be rescuer, "And on his collar laying puissant hand,/Out of his wauering seat him pluckt perforse ... and laying thwart her horse, ... She bore him fast away" (43). Argante's manhandling is a rare match for Shakespeare's Venus, who,

Being so enrag'd, desire doth lend her force
Courageously to pluck him [the hapless Adonis] from his horse.

Over one arm the lusty courser's rein,
Under her other was the tender boy.

(29–32)

For those critics who suspect that Shakespeare's poem might have a satirical relation to courtship, especially under a Queen who affected a Petrarchan role, Argante's name affords further tantalizing connections with Spenser's poem: in Arthurian legend, this is the name of the Faerie Queen to whose island the mortally wounded Arthur is taken. Etymologically, the name of this legendary precursor of Spenser's Faerie figure of his own Queen could also be read as an allusion to the idle/idyll, unproductive life at court of an aspiring courtier: Greek *argos*.[13]

While the cast of Venerian refractions in Book III has not quite been exhausted, their range and relatedness should be evident by now. Evident as well, perhaps, is the relevance to Spenser's third book of Catherine Belsey's description of the burden of *Venus and Adonis*, namely, "an understanding of sexual desire as precisely sensual, irrational, anarchic, dangerous but also at the same time delicate, fragile, and precious."[14] Yet it would be misguided to see in Shakespeare's Venus, the major vehicle of Belsey's perception, an achieved equilibrium between life-enhancing and anarchic sex, as Harwood does, or, in Spenser's symbolic terms, to see such an equilibrium between the flower and the boar; and it would be equally misguided to see in Shakespeare's Venus merely the one or the other of these extremes. Describing *Venus and Adonis* as both polyphonic and indeterminate, Belsey is again on target, although a case with somewhat differing implications might as readily be made for over-as for in-determinacy.

Where Spenser typically channels his polyphony into separate, if also related, figures in Book III, however, Shakespeare gathers most of his into the single character of Venus. As Heather Dubrow has noted, Shakespeare's Venus speaks 537 of the poem's 1,194 lines, with the petulant Adonis speaking only 87 in my count and the narrator another 570.[15] In view of the dominance of Venus' role as a dramatized speaker, which is further augmented by the active and affective roles the narrator assigns her, it is not surprising that readers tend to concentrate on her figure and to conceive of it in theatrical terms: this epyllion, after all, has even been acted, and Philip Kolin's collection of essays on it assigns a whole section to "Venus and Adonis in Production."

Just such a lingering conviction of Shakespeare's theatrical "realism," however, has led us to downplay or misjudge the relation of his poem to Spenser's. Rather than a "repudiation" of Spenser's "erotic philosophy," as Harwood would have it, *Venus and Adonis* looks like a reveling in Spenserian eros. Shakespeare's recreative poem explores the effect of transforming a number of Spenser's allegorical figures into a *relatively* more realized character—what would result from the folding of its unfolded refractions into a more fully fleshed-out version. At the same time, however, Spenser's interlaced refractions represent a variety that actually exceeds and challenges such a concentration, defying containment by it, at least until Shakespeare's creation of the infinitely various Cleopatra, in whose figure I would discern a memory of his Venus, albeit further modified in both a testimony to the poet-dramatist's own development and to that of the taste of his age.

Formally, Shakespeare's *Venus and Adonis* has a mixed genealogy that conspicuously includes both drama and allegory, and instead of suppressing the opposite impulses this genealogy implies, it flaunts them. Not surprisingly in this tale of a goddess' infatuation with the son of a tree and great grandson of a statue, efforts to interpret intermittently symbolic characters realistically have faltered: a goddess who goes from burlesque to pathos is incongruously taken as "tragic," though taken she has been. Efforts to read the poem allegorically have similarly faltered, although in this instance in the face of its realism. But the poem makes a good deal of sense as a seriocomic meditation on the landscape of desire and the kinds of figures it generates in Book III of *The Faerie Queene*. Correlatively, to read *Venus and Adonis* beside this Spenserian book is to realize the nuances it highlights and the potencies it heightens within Spenser's allegory, even while appreciating the interpretive license, indeed the creativity, of such a "Shakespearean" reading. Where Shakespeare's Venus truly embodies gynephobia, as does Spenser's Argante, and Argante has a refractive relation with Spenser's Venus in the Garden, there is also a profound difference between the first two figures and the last. What is *in potentia*—barely a hint, a shadow, a memory, a refraction within the mythic Garden—is fulfilled in them, and it makes all the difference in the world.

PART V

GENDERED PERFORMANCES OF
AFFECT IN SHAKESPEARE

CHAPTER 11

TEARS AND MASCULINITY IN THE HISTORY PLAY: SHAKESPEARE'S *HENRY VI*

MARTHA A. KURTZ

The Elizabethan history play has often been regarded as a quintessentially masculine genre, one that enacted in its plots and characters a "masculine" ethos that glorified war and encouraged its audiences to emulate the virtues that would lead to success in war. Thomas Heywood, the author of several histories, spoke of the plays as having "power to new mold the harts of the spectators and fashion them to the shape of any noble and notable attempt," inspiring pride in the patriotic and shame in the cowardly, while Thomas Nashe described history plays as a celebration of "our forefathers valiant acts," and a "reproofe to these degenerate effeminate dayes of ours."[1] More recent critics tend to agree. Linda Bamber describes the history play as based on an "ethos of power and aggression" that excludes the feminine, while Jean Howard and Phyllis Rackin conclude that the plays, by "[c]ommemorating the valiant deeds of heroic forefathers and celebrating the masculine virtues of courage, honor, and patriotism . . . could actually help to reclaim the endangered masculinity of the men in the theatre audience."[2]

Central to this definition of the history play is the assumption that history, unlike tragedy, did not inspire its audience to weep. That tears were feminine—and, consequently, a sign of weakness, both physical and mental—was a commonplace in Shakespeare's time, as it often is today. "If you will share my fortunes, comfort then:/An hundred smiles for one sigh; what, we are men," Sir Thomas More exclaims to his grieving son-in-law shortly before More's execution in a play about the martyr's life; indicating his weeping daughters and wife, he urges the other man to "[r]esign wet passion to these weaker eyes,/Which proves their sex, but grants [them] ne'er more wise."[3] Among the many reasons that Elizabethan masculinity might have been thought to be endangered was the popularity of theatrical productions that moved their audiences to tears. According to one contemporary critic, "The beholding of troubles and miserable slaughters that are in Tragedies, drive us to immoderate sorrow, heavines, womanish weeping and mourning, whereby we become lovers of dumpes, and lamentation, both enemies to fortitude."[4] While Howard and Rackin acknowledge that "the distinction between history and tragedy was by no means clear in the period," they maintain that "contemporary descriptions of the ways they affected their audiences were gendered in strikingly different terms," with tragedy encouraging feminizing tears from its spectators, and history "reclaim[ing] . . . endangered masculinity" by emphasizing masculine virtues—including, it is implied, the ability to suppress emotion and its outward signs, such as tears.[5]

Yet the relationship between tears and masculinity in the history play is actually much more complex than such definitions allow. Howard and Rackin speak as though contemporary commentators were in agreement over history's redeeming qualities.[6] In fact, detractors of the theater, like Gosson, make no exceptions, while praise of the history play's ability to inspire heroic action comes from writers who clearly have an axe to grind in defending theatrical performances against such attacks. The history play, like so many other aspects of Elizabethan theater, was a site of cultural tension and debate. Far from offering clear and simple models of heroic masculine behavior that conform to generally recognized standards of the time, the plays often present complicated and troubling views of what it meant to be a man—and of what it meant to cry. The intersection of these two aspects is of particular importance to three of Shakespeare's early histories, the plays now known as *Henry VI, Parts I, II,* and *III,* in which we can see a definite progression—Gosson would say regression—in the ways in which warfare, tears, and manliness are presented. In these changing views of grief and gender we can see some of the most striking cultural tensions of Shakespeare's time acted out.

The conventional view of tears as feminine is deeply embedded in the first play of the series.[7] *Henry VI, Part I* opens with a scene of mourning. Henry V, the great hero who reconquered France for England, has died, leaving only an infant son to take his place. "We mourn in black, why mourn we not in blood?" one noble asks, but the group of men gathered on the stage are dispirited and hopeless without their leader:

> Posterity, await for wretched years
> When at their mothers' moistened eyes babes shall suck,

> Our isle be made a nourish of salt tears,
> And none but women left to wail the dead.
> 			(*Part I* 1.1.17, 48–51).[8]

Henry's death seems to have destroyed all hope of masculine action, and to have left an England feminized and infantalized by its unbearable grief.

Despite this beginning, the play soon makes it clear that tears are a weakness that English soldiers will not permit themselves. The mourners at Henry's funeral are besieged by messenger after messenger bringing reports of English losses and defeats in France. Yet the disastrous news seems to shake its hearers out of their paralyzing sorrow: "Give me my steeled coat. I'll fight for France," Bedford declares. "Away with these disgraceful wailing robes/Wounds will I lend the French, instead of eyes,/To weep their intermissive miseries" (*Part I* 1.1.85–88). Tears are a "disgrace" to manhood now, something to be inflicted on the enemy as a sign of England's masculine domination, not something in which English men will indulge.

In the scenes that follow, loss after devastating loss is met with dry eyes. The Duke of Bedford's death is accepted with stoic resignation, since "kings and mightiest potentates must die,/For that's the end of human misery" (*Part I* 3.2.134–35). When the great Talbot himself is fatally injured, together with his only son, he claims, like Thomas More, that death moves both of them only to "smile":

> Triumphant death, smeared with captivity,
> Young Talbot's valour makes me smile at thee.
>
> .   .   .   .
>
> Poor boy, he smiles, methinks, as who should say,
> "Had death been French, then death had died today."
> 			(*Part I* 4.115–16, 139–40)

The English are bitterly grieved by the loss of their hero, but, of course, they greet the news without tears. "O, were mine eyeballs into bullets turned," one Englishman exclaims when the French Joan tells him of Talbot's death, "[t]hat I in rage might shoot them at your faces" (*Part I* 4.4.191–92). However strange these words might sound today, they epitomize the "masculine" approach to grief in this play: instead of being softened with tears, eyes are imagined as hardening into bullets, weapons with which a man can vent his rage against his enemies. Implicit in this image is another: the enemies' faces, battered and bloodied by the bullet-eyeballs—softened, opened, feminized.[9]

"I am a soldier, and unapt to weep," a minor character says late in the play; the line might be taken as *Part I*'s motto (*Part I* 5.2.154). Yet at the beginning of *Henry VI, Part II,* one valiant soldier does weep. The scene is the king's wedding, and the cause is the articles of marriage that Henry has agreed to, in which important territories have been ceded to the French. Reading the articles aloud, the king's uncle, Gloucester, is so troubled he lets the paper fall— "Some sudden qualm hath struck me at the heart/And dimmed mine eyes, that I can read no further" (*Part II* 1.1.52–53)—while Warwick, whose soldiering will later earn him the nickname "Kingmaker," weeps openly "[f]or grief that [the territories] are past recovery."[10] "For were there hope to conquer them again," he adds, "My sword should shed hot blood, mine eyes no tears" (*Part II* 1.1.113–15). Only the irrecoverable loss of England's territory can move this brave soldier to tears. His open acknowledgement of his tears suggests that he is not ashamed of them; they are the reasonable response of an honorable man to his country's dishonor. The scene seems to say that there are times when even strong men must weep: to do so is a sign of the strength of a man's love for his country, even while it is also a result of helplessness and frustration.

Nothing in the scene suggests that we are meant to blame Warwick for weeping. That such a man should be driven to tears is a measure of the weakness, not of Warwick himself, but of the man responsible for the losses Warwick weeps for—the king. Henry's folly in surrendering important territory is only one of a long series of bad choices that mark the king as weak in reason and will, hopelessly inadequate to the task of governing a nation. Impulsive in choosing a wife and unable to keep her affections once he has her, Henry is equally inadequate in the domestic sphere, while on the battlefield he is so useless that his wife takes over, the soldiers all agreeing that "[t]hey prosper best of all when I am thence" (*Part III* 2.5.18).[11] We should hardly be surprised that such an unmanly character is also a prolific weeper.

In the first play, Henry's tears may seem excusable. Only a baby when he inherits the crown, he is a child through much of *Part I.* Caught between fractious and jealous nobles, he often has no other way to influence them than by appealing to their pity.[12] As a young man on the verge of marriage, however, his tearful passions are more ominous; ignoring his most trusted advisors, he persists in his foolish plan to trade England's French possessions for a beautiful but politically useless bride, asking his uncles to leave him alone to "revolve and ruminate my grief" (*Part I* 5.4.101). Later, when Gloucester has been accused of treason, Henry is certain of his uncle's innocence, yet he hands Gloucester over to his accusers, tells them to do "what to your wisdoms seemeth best," and leaves, bursting into tears (*Part II* 3.1.195, 198–200).

Such a response at such a crucial moment is maddening. Even the conspirators are astounded by it.[13] Convinced of Gloucester's innocence, aware of who his enemies are and what their goal is—Gloucester's death—the one man who might be able to save him abdicates all responsibility and takes refuge in tears. Comparing his uncle to a calf being led away to slaughter, Henry thinks of himself as its distressed "dam":

> And as the dam runs lowing up and down,
>
> . . . .
>
> And can do naught but wail her darling's loss,
> Even so myself bewails good Gloucester's case
> With sad unhelpful tears, and with dimmed eyes
> Look after him, and cannot do him good.
> (*Part II* 3.1.214–19)

Anything further from the heroism of Henry V or Talbot would be hard to imagine.

The England depicted in this play is not the England Shakespeare's audience knew; the feudal barons of Henry's time had more power, the monarch less, than was the case a century later under Tudor rule. Henry was also a young and inexperienced king, who might well have felt intimidated by the power of his nobility. But historical accuracy is surely not the only point here; Henry's weakness is. His portrayal of himself as a cow weeping for its calf suggests how problematic the king's image has become at this point in the plays. Both the cow—being female—and the tears imply a feminized Henry, weak and helpless. But the images also suggest something dehumanized, grotesque. The behavior of the weeping cow is perhaps greater than what we would normally consider animal, but less—being a cow—than fully human. A more natural image might have been a sheep; the equation of men with sheep was so common in the religious imagery of the time that such a pairing would not have seemed jarring, although some members of the audience might have wondered why their shepherd, the highest representative on earth of the Great Shepherd, was allowing himself to act like one of his flock. But there was no similar tradition of representing people as cows. Clumsy and lumbering (even in its smaller, early modern form), the cow is a ludicrous image for a king, one that negates a good deal of the pathos that is otherwise conveyed by this speech. While the plays have made it clear that soldiers are "unapt to weep," they have never before made it so difficult to sympathize with weeping. It would not be surprising if some members of even the play's earliest audiences found themselves wanting to laugh at the sobbing cow-king. And yet, if they did, they must also have felt acute discomfort and dismay: kings were not supposed to be either pathetic or absurd.

Margaret, who needs to preserve the nobles' respect for her husband if she is to maintain her own standing, tries to pass Henry's behavior off as a result of Gloucester's deceptive performance of innocence: "Gloucester's show/Beguiles him, as the mournful crocodile/With sorrow snares relenting passengers" (*Part II* 3.1.225–27). The weeping crocodile was a more familiar image to Elizabethans than Henry's weeping cow. The crocodile was thought to use its tears to entice its victims into taking pity on it, and so coming close enough to be caught.[14] In political thought the crocodile suggested the wily Machiavel, able to use shows of emotion to win an unsuspecting audience's trust. The image clearly fits Margaret herself better than Gloucester. Both her hatred of Gloucester and her role in the conspiracy against him have been well established in the play, yet after his death, she weeps copiously in an effort to convince the king of her innocence:

> Might liquid tears, or heart-offending groans,
> Or blood-consuming sighs recall his life,
> I would be blind with weeping, sick with groans,
> Look pale as primrose with blood-drinking sighs,
> And all to have the noble Duke alive.
> (*Part II* 3.2.60–64)

When Henry is not impressed, she weeps some more, this time in an attempt to prove that it is she, not Gloucester, who should be pitied: "Be woe for me, more wretched than he is," she begs, and draws an elaborate picture of her voyage across tempestuous seas to become Henry's bride, escaping shipwreck and drowning only to be "drowned on shore/With tears as salt as sea through thy unkindness." Her speech ends dramatically with the exclamation, "Die, Margaret,/For Henry weeps that thou dost live so long," at which point she presumably falls sobbing on the stage (*Part II* 3.2.73, 95–96, 120–21). Whatever effect she is hoping to obtain here, she fails; the speech, one of the longest and most emotional in the play, meets with no response at all from her on-stage audience. Margaret's crocodile tears, and her discomfiture— ignored by the man to whom she has been addressing all this emotion, at some point she must dry her face and get to her feet—are at least as ridiculous as Henry's bovine weeping; however feeble, Henry is, at least, sincere. Margaret's insincerity is so apparent that it is impossible to take either her words or her tears at face value. They are "feminine" in the worst sense that Elizabethans could construe that word: not merely weak or helpless, but devious, manipulative, and—if not recognized for what they are—deeply dangerous.

Yet the crocodile dangers are not all that Margaret has to show us about tears. However overwrought and false her performance in front of Henry may be, we see her a few scenes later weeping in earnest: first, as she bids farewell to her banished lover, Suffolk, and then as she holds his severed head after his brutal execution. The scene in which she parts from Suffolk, "dew[ing]" his hand with "mournful tears," and praying that no "rain of heaven wet this place/To wash away my mournful monuments," is conventional enough: two lovers forced to part, the woman weeping—a staple of the Elizabethan stage (*Part II* 3.2.340–42). Her tears are exactly what we would expect, although, after her scene with Henry, we might wonder how real this emotion is. That question is answered in the later scene. Cradling her lover's bloody head against her body, Margaret weeps now for no audience but herself. Her distracted words conjure up the horror of the moment:

> Oft have I heard that grief softens the mind
> And makes it fearful and degenerate;
> Think therefore on revenge and cease to weep.
> But who can cease to weep and look on this?
> Here may his head lie on my throbbing breast;
> But where's the body that I should embrace?
> (*Part II* 4.4.1–6)

Whatever Margaret has done, and however much an audience might dislike her, the scene compels us to enter into her emotions here, to feel her genuine shock, horror, and grief at the gruesome death of the man she loved.

This passage both sums up the conventional, "masculine" view of tears as we have seen it thus far in the *Henry VI* plays, and, at the same time, alters it radically. That grief would "soften" the mind, making it "fearful" and "degenerate,"[15] is the view of tears as feminizing and dangerous that we have encountered many times before. But Margaret's question adds something new: "But who can cease to weep and look on this?" As a woman, Margaret might be expected to weep, yet her language here seems to reach beyond the confines of her own sex to demand a more universal application. She does not mean, "What woman could cease to weep and look on this," but "What person could?" The question will resonate throughout the rest of this play and the next, as one horrible action succeeds another, and the way in which a character responds to pitiable sights becomes central to how he, or she, is judged.

An audience might well remember Margaret's question during the scenes that show Jack Cade's uprising. A peasant schooled in the brutal Irish wars, Jack Cade demonstrates his cruelty in many ways, one of the most memorable of which is the scene in which he refuses to be moved by an old man's pleas for his life. Lord Saye speaks eloquently of the innocent life he has led and the good he has done for others: "Justice with favour have I always done;/Prayers and tears have moved me, gifts could never," he cries, as he begs for mercy (*Part II* 4.7.62–63). Cade confesses himself affected by Saye's speech, but nevertheless orders his death: "I feel remorse in myself with his words, but I'll bridle it. He shall die, an it be but for pleading so well for his life" (*Part II* 4.7.98–100). The old man is led off to his death, and Cade rejoices when Saye's head is brought back, along with that of his son-in-law, on poles: "Let them kiss one another, for they loved well when they were alive," he orders, in sniggering mockery of all ordinary affection (*Part II* 4.7.122–23). Saye, we are told, had been moved by others' tears and had responded to them with pity and mercy; Cade feels the urge to respond, but suppresses it. The ability to control an emotional response, once an attribute of a hero like Talbot, is now the mark of a butcher like Jack Cade.[16]

Cade is a peasant, but dry-eyed butchery is not relegated to the lower classes in these plays. We see it carried out by lords and nobles again and again, but it is articulated most clearly near the end of *Part II,* when Lord Clifford finds his father dead on the battlefield and takes a terrible vow. Invoking all the chaos of the world's last day ("O, let the vile world end,/And the premised flames of the last day/Knit earth and heaven together!"), he declares his intention to harden his heart to all human sympathy, to be pitiless in his pursuit of vengeance:

> My heart is turned to stone, and while 'tis mine
> It shall be stony. York not our old men spares;
> No more will I their babes; tears virginal
> Shall be to me even as the dew to fire,
> And beauty, that the tyrant oft reclaims,
> Shall to my flaming wrath be oil and flax.
> Henceforth I will not have to do with pity.
> Meet I an infant of the house of York,
> Into as many gobbets will I cut it
> As wild Medea young Absyrtus did.
> In cruelty will I seek out my fame.
>   (*Part II* 5.2.50–60)

In *Part I*, the loss of fathers and aged father-figures is met with hardened eyes but not with hardened hearts. It is something to be expected, even celebrated. But for Clifford, the loss of his father is at once the cause of much greater emotion, and the death of all emotion except anger and the thirst for revenge. He grieves, but without tears; his stony heart will be hard and dry. He will look on every kind of horror, unmoved; the tears of petitioners will not inspire his pity and mercy, as they did in Lord Saye, but will be burned up in the flames of his wrath, and even the young and the beautiful will feel the full force of his rage. The vengeance Clifford describes here has abandoned all pretense of reason; it is not an eye for an eye, but an uninhibited passion to go farther and do more. Where once men measured their honor by what they could win from other fighting men—what battles won, what French towns taken—now, Clifford says, he will measure it by the horrors he can inflict on women and children. "In cruelty will I seek out my fame." If there is any difference between Young Clifford and Jack Cade, it is only in the narrowness of his focus and the intensity of his tearless determination to kill.

What Clifford promises, he delivers. If in *Part II* we have seen an alarming increase in brutality—the beheading of Suffolk, the rampages of Cade's rebels—in *Part III* we are thrust headlong into the full horrors of civil war. The play opens with the sight of York's three sons, each smeared in the blood of the Englishman he has wounded or slain; one of them, Richard, throws down his prize, Lord Somerset's gory head. A few minutes later Clifford carries out his promised revenge on another of York's sons, a boy too young to fight in battle, who is pulled away from his tutor to face his executioner. In a scene echoing Saye's plea to Jack Cade for his life, Young Rutland pleads for his; the result is no different, and the boy's tears and prayers meet only "[s]uch pity as my rapier's point affords" (*Part III* 1.3.36).

Rutland's death is horrifying, not simply because a child dies, but because a man is able to be so pitiless as to kill him; the child's tears are appalling, but the man's lack of tears are more appalling still. Yet this scene is succeeded by something even worse: the tormenting of the boy's father with the news of his child's death, and their enemies' brutal mockery of the father's desperate grief. In the most dreadful scene of the three plays, Queen Margaret and her men find York alone, overpower him, and, ignoring all the traditional courtesies to an enemy, mock, torture, and finally kill him. Pushing him onto a small hill, they thrust a paper crown on his temples, bow mockingly to him—and hand him a handkerchief soaked in his youngest son's blood, urging him to use it to wipe his tears away. "Look, York," cries Margaret,

> I stain'd this napkin with the blood
> That valiant Clifford with his rapier's point
> Made issue from the bosom of the boy;
> And if thine eyes can water for his death,
> I give thee this to dry thy cheeks withal.
> . . . .
> I prithee grieve, to make me merry, York.
>
> (*Part III* 1.4.79–86)

York at first remains silent and dry-eyed—out of shock, stoicism, or the refusal to give his enemy the satisfaction she begs him for. But then his feelings break loose, all the more powerful for having been withheld:

> Bid'st thou me rage? Why, now thou hast thy wish.
> Would'st have me weep? Why, now thou hast thy will.
> For raging wind blows up incessant showers,
> And when the rage allays, the rain begins.
> These tears are my sweet Rutland's obsequies,
> And every drop cries vengeance for his death.
> . . . .
> That face of his the hungry cannibals
> Would not have touch'd, would not have stain'd with blood;
> But you are more inhuman, more inexorable –
> O, ten times more—than tigers of Hyrcania.
> See, ruthless queen, a hapless father's tears.
> This cloth thou dipp'd'st in blood of my sweet boy,
> And I with tears do wash the blood away.
> Keep thou the napkin, and go boast of this;
> And if thou tell the heavy story right,
> Upon my soul, the hearers will shed tears;
> Yea, even my foes will shed fast-falling tears,
> And say "Alas! it was a piteous deed."
>
> (*Part III* 1.4.143–63)

And, in fact, one of his enemies does find himself moved to tears: "Beshrew me, but his passion moves me so/As hardly can I check my eyes from tears," Northumberland comments, and then, a little later, "Had he been slaughter-man to all my kin/I should not for my life but weep with him" (*Part III* 1.4.150–51, 169–70). But Margaret and Clifford are unmoved: "What, weeping-ripe, my lord Northumberland?" the Queen exclaims, "Think but upon the wrong he did us all,/And that will quickly dry thy melting tears" (*Part III*

1.4.172–74). Together, she and Clifford stab York and cut off his head.

No one would describe either York or Northumberland as weak or effeminate. Northumberland is "rough Northumberland," as sturdy a soldier as any, yet this torment of his enemy moves him to tears. York has been ruthless in battle and out of it, pressing his claim to the throne hard enough literally to wrest the crown from Henry for a while; when hopelessly outnumbered by his enemies, he remains staunchly defiant: "Come, bloody Clifford, rough Northumberland,/I dare your quenchless fury to more rage:/I am your butt, and I abide your shot" (*Part III* 1.4.27–29). And yet this man weeps, bitterly, copiously, unabashedly. His tears move another strong man to tears. Only the most hardened of his enemies remain dry-eyed.

Clearly something has happened to the status of tears in these plays. They have been, as Elizabethan culture generally regarded them, woman's work, an emblem of weakness and effeminacy. Now they are neither. Now women kill, and men weep for it. Margaret's savagery has been one of the most frequently commented-on developments of *Part III*; York's and Northumberland's response is just as striking.

"Oft have I heard that grief softens the mind/And makes it fearful and degenerate;/ . . . /But who can cease to weep and look on this?" (*Part II* 4.4.1–4). Margaret's words point to the two views of tears that inform these plays: on the one hand, they are weakening and effeminate; on the other hand, something essentially, unavoidably human. When she asked this question, Margaret was a different woman from the one who taunts York with his child's blood; an adulteress, a murderer, she nevertheless was capable of genuine tears. When she learns to steel herself so that she can "look on" something like this without tears, she loses her claim to full humanity, becoming instead the "tiger's heart wrapp'd in a woman's hide" that York calls her (*Part III* 1.4.137). She is joined by a host of others in these plays: Jack Cade, Clifford, and ultimately, of course, the most hardened and dehumanized murderer of them all, Richard III.[17]

In *Part I* war is a noble enterprise, seen through the misty glass of time and distance—something sad but splendid that was performed in a distant country by men who seem, at least some of the time, larger than life. That sense of nobility is undercut by the jeerings of a French peasant like Joan, and by England's own inability to be true to itself. But for all the ironies, there is still the fortitude and stoicism of Salisbury, Bedford, Warwick, Talbot, and Talbot's young son. When war is seen in this way, a mythic view of manhood as strong and dry-eyed is also possible.

But Shakespeare was clearly uncomfortable with that view. Even in *Part I* there are moments in which his dissatisfaction shows, as when

Joan urges Burgundy to defect from his allegiance with England and
return to the French fold, telling him that his country needs, not his dry-
eyed manhood, but his tears:

> Look on thy country, look on fertile France,
> And see the cities and the towns defaced
> By wasting ruin of the cruel foe
>
> .   .   .   .
>
> One drop of blood drawn from thy country's bosom
> Should grieve thee more than streams of foreign gore.
> Return thee therefore with a flood of tears
> And wash away thy country's stained spots.
>
> > (*Part I*, 3.3.44–57)

Grief is seen as something positive here, tears as cleansing and redemptive. In spite of the ironies that surround the speaker—the French peasant witch who will betray everything she has claimed to stand for—the
greater irony persists that the horrors of civil war that are described here
for France will be suffered more graphically, violently, and horribly by
England itself in the later plays. Yet none of the English lords will prove,
like Burgundy, willing to "[r]eturn" to a larger, more disinterested sense
of his duty to his countrymen; none will choose to try to wash his
nation's wounds with healing tears.

   None, that is, but one: the king. As the battles rage in *Part III*, Henry
retreats by himself to sit on the ground and wish, pathetically, that he
were dead (*Part III* 2.5.19). Hopeless and helpless, overmastered by his
wife, utterly lacking in any masculine ability or ambition, Henry should
seem an absurd parody of a king. And yet he does one thing well—so
well, that it is hard to see him as foolish. He weeps.

   In the earlier plays, his tears have indicated his weakness: juvenile, in
Part I; damningly feckless in *Part II*. But at this stage in the plays' depiction of war, they seem simply necessary. He does not weep alone, or for
himself alone, but at a scene that unfolds before him, a tableau that
emblemizes all that is wrong in the bloody struggle raging around him.
As Henry sits on a small hill, sighing, two men enter: a "Son that hath
kill'd his Father," and "a Father that hath kill'd his Son" (*Part III* 2.5.53
s.d.; 2.5.78 s.d.). Both men carry the bodies of their loved ones in their
arms, and weep. Henry weeps with them:

> Weep, wretched man; I'll aid thee tear for tear;
> And let our hearts and eyes, like civil war,
> Be blind with tears, and break o'ercharg'd with grief.

> . . . .
> Woe above woe! grief more than common grief!
> O that my death would stay these ruthful deeds!
>
> . . . .
> Sad-hearted men, much overgone with care,
> Here sits a king more woeful than you are.
> (*Part III* 2.5.76–78; 94–95; 123–24)

There is something salutary in his sorrow; in the midst of so much self-ishness and brutality, one man, at least, is still capable of responding with unselfish pity.

While the *Henry VI* plays begin with a conventional view of weeping as antithetical to manhood, they end by showing us something quite different. As the plays' vision of warfare changes from an honourable enterprise carried out on foreign soil to the horrifying butchery of civil strife, so too their view of what constitutes manly behavior changes. In *Part I* the most admirable character is a man who knows how to suppress his tears. In *Part III*, it is a man who weeps.

I would argue, too, that by *Part III*, questions of gender have become largely irrelevant to the way we view tears. We are no longer asked to categorize characters as manly or unmanly, masculine or feminine, depending on whether or not they cry; instead, the plays divide characters into those who cannot help weeping at pitiable sights, and those who can. Clifford and Margaret strike York together, as if Shakespeare wanted us to see this, the most memorable horror in the play, as something of which both men and women were capable. York's and Northumberland's tears are no longer a shameful badge of weakness, but a sign of humanity; the ability to suppress emotion no longer the mark of the hero, but the mark of the beast.

It is also the mark of a bad audience. In one of the few records we have of an original audience's response to one of Shakespeare's plays, Thomas Nashe described the death of Talbot in *Part I* in these terms:

> How would it have joyed brave *Talbot* (the terror of the French) to thinke that after he had lyne two hundred yeares in his Tombe, hee should triumphe againe on the Stage, and have his bones newe embalmed with the teares of ten thousand spectators at least (at severall times), who, in the Tragedian that represents his person, imagine they behold him fresh bleeding.[18]

To Nashe, tears in this context were nothing to be ashamed of. He has just spoken of the history play as offering a "reproofe to these degenerate effeminate dayes of ours," yet he presents the audience's tears as

proof of the history play's value. Men like Gosson would have been
appalled, but Nashe obviously expected his readers to agree with him.
Weeping is no longer a sign of feminine weakness but a patriotic virtue,
an appropriate tribute to the heroism of a Talbot—even, the passage
suggests, a kind of substitute, in modern times, for that heroism.[19]

We will, of course, never know what the real John Talbot would actually have thought of the audience's tears, but we can be certain that the
actor who took his place on stage would have been just as pleased as
Nashe imagines the "terror of the French" to be. The tears are what any
actor would hope for. To have thousands of men and women weep in
response to one's acting is an obvious gratification for an actor, a form
of psychological power that should not be ignored. The power to move
people in the theater also had social and economic implications. If, as
seems likely, Talbot's part was taken by Edward Alleyn, it was one in a
series of tragic roles that made him famous—and rich.[20] Alleyn was a
superstar in his own time; he made enough money from the theater to
be able to endow a college and a hospital. There was real social and economic power to be gained from acting in popular roles, and it was parts
that moved the audience that were most popular. Each of the plays in
the *Henry VI* trilogy features at least one hugely emotional scene: the
death of Talbot, the murder of Gloucester, the death of Suffolk, the torture and death of York. Actors clearly wanted these parts, and writers like
Shakespeare wanted to provide them. When we think about the gendering of tears in the history play, we need to remember this: in the theater,
weeping and causing others to weep was never actually a weakness, but
a very real way of exercising strength.

CHAPTER 12

HAMLET AND THE GENDERS OF GRIEF

MARSHALL GROSSMAN

Ham. . . . Farewell, dear mother.
King. Thy loving father, Hamlet.
Ham. My mother. Father and mother is man and wife, man and
wife is one flesh; so my mother. Come, for England.[1]

"No! I am not Prince Hamlet, nor was meant to be;
Am an attendant lord, one that will do
To swell a progress, start a scene or two,
Advise the prince; no doubt an easy tool.
. . .
Almost, at times, the fool."[2]

"From one end of Hamlet to the other, all anyone talks about is
mourning."[3]

1

In the first passage quoted as epigraph above, Hamlet either experiences or, more likely, feigns some gender confusion. But, as is usually the case with Hamlet, the "either" and the "or" are not exclusive: his antic madness has method in it, but the method has a touch of madness to it. The method is simple; Hamlet speaks the accusation of incest and at the same time disowns his speech by passing it off as delirious. He says something outrageous and then invites the King to forego outrage in favor of pity. As the recently deceased Polonius put it, using "no art at all": "That he is mad 'tis true; 'tis true 'tis pity;/And pity 'tis 'tis true. A foolish figure –" (II.ii.97–98). If we admit that Hamlet's *madness* connotes anger as well as unreason, Polonius' foolish figure is a chiasmus that cross-couples truth to madness, but also, to anger and pity: the same two emotions that Hamlet manipulates when he evokes the royal incest by taking literally the assimilation of husband and wife to one flesh.[4] Doubled as it is, the chiasmus defines a range that includes pitiful madness, pitiful truth, true pity, true madness, and mad truth. Holding "as t'were, the mirror up to nature" (III.ii.22), Polonius' foolish figure joins *truth*—the truth of the figure—to madness and to pity: in truth, to look at Hamlet's madness is to pity him, and it joins anger to grief. The pitiful madness ascribed to Hamlet, reflected back into him, corresponds to the anger and grief he feels; these affects are the *truth* of his foolish figure. Equally true, when reflected back into Polonius, the foolish figure—without art—is the figure of a fool. But the truth of the figure is still further complicated. Hamlet's madness, to the extent that it is "antic" is, itself, a figure, a representation or performance of madness, which Claudius, who is no fool, attributes not to true madness but to "something in his soul/O'er which his melancholy sits on brood" (III.i.166–67).

In looking for the truth of the figure of Hamlet's grief, I propose to track the foolish figure of chiasmus as the channel in which anger, pity, madness, and grief circulate among the characters and spectators of the play and transmute from one emotion to another within them. I aim to explore the peculiar ability of chiasmus in general, and this chiasmus in particular, to mediate rhetorically—through its schematic coupling of doubled and reversed attributes—the unmediable impasse between representation and affect: between "actions that a man might play"—as the performance of an antic madness, for example—and "that within which passes show"—that "something in [the] soul" on which melancholy broods (I.ii.84–85). Finally, I want to explore the extension of this coupling and reversing rhetoric across the mirroring (chiasmic) boundary between stage and audience to work upon the consciences of "guilty creatures sitting at a play" and "by the very cunning of the scene" strike "so to the soul that presently/They have proclaim'd their malefactions" (II.ii.585–88). Following the peregrinations of this figure in the text and out of the text will take us along a trail in which gender is mapped by navigating alternative paths from grief to anger, madness, action, and performance.

To begin, and at the risk of being tedious, I want to unpack further Polonius' foolish figure, arguing that beyond this smearing out of madness and anger, pity and grief, of foolish truths and true fools, the chiasmic structures of *Hamlet* extend also into gender, smearing the categories of male and female across its couplings of conflicted feelings. A certain fluidity of gender is immediately in play in Hamlet's reaction to his mother's marriage, even before the revenge plot takes shape. If husband and wife are one flesh, then, strictly speaking, the incest of Gertrude and Claudius is not that of brother and sister, but that of fratricidal brothers.[5] It is not Gertrude and Claudius who are related too closely, but King Hamlet, now of Gertrude's flesh, and the younger brother who has assumed his bed and his throne: "A little more than kin and less than kind" (I.ii.65). There is, then, even in the incest prohibitions of Leviticus a shadow of homoerotic competition. One ought not to go where his brother has been, for he will meet his brother there and see what he should not see. But Hamlet's taunt at once asserts the implicit assimilation of the wife to the brother in Leviticus and inverts it; in his version, if husband and wife are one flesh, the flesh is that of the wife. Because Claudius has succeeded to the throne only by his marriage to Gertrude, he has, in a sense, become king by taking on his brother's position as mediated to him by the flesh of the Queen. Gertrude is thus the cross-coupler in a chiasmic exchange: King Hamlet: Gertrude:: Gertrude: King Claudius. The homoerotic rivalry of the brothers is thus a peculiarly heterosexual homoerotic rivalry—acted out through the female body on which it is sited.[6] The ghost identifies itself to Hamlet as "thy father's spirit" (I.v.9), but it is in Gertrude and her new husband that we may now find his flesh. This would seem more far-fetched, if fratricidal rivalry were not a pervasive theme in Shakespeare's plays. But Hamlet and Claudius, Edgar and Edmund, Prospero and Antonio, Orlando and Oliver come readily to mind, as well as symbolic though not genetic brothers, like the "twinned lambs" Leontes and Polixenes and Hostspur and Hal, the two stars that "keep not their motion in one sphere."[7]

The criss-crossings of incest and intrafamial rivalry in *Hamlet* easily overflow the boundaries of the play. For example, Bruce Boehrer explores the uncanny resonance of the play's incest theme and Elizabeth's complicated succession to the throne.

> If Claudius is to Gertrude as Henry was to Catherine—an affined relation and an inappropriate marriage partner—we must also recognize that Gertrude is to Hamlet as Henry was to Elizabeth—the legitimate biological parent who has married improperly and thus made problematical the royal succession. . . . Gertrude plays Catherine to Claudius' Henry, yet she equally plays Henry to Hamlet's Elizabeth. . . . Thus we return to the scholarly consensus that *Hamlet's* affective component is centered . . . on the figure of the woman. For it is onto this figure that Shakespeare's story displaces the cumulative anxieties of the Tudor order: the threat of incest, the danger of feminine misrule, the instability implied by legal revisions of the line of succession. . . . Thus we may possibly consider Hamlet's uncenteredness of character—his simultaneous and confusing preoccupation with the uncle and the mother, the murder and the incest—as reflecting the contradictory concerns of an Elizabethan political unconscious: the

desire to prove oneself a man against men, and the prior necessity to overcome the sovereign influence of the female. (64–65)

I am less interested in the putative politics of this transgendered cross-coupling of Henry, Gertrude, Claudius, and Hamlet to Catherine, Henry, and
Elizabeth than in the relentless energy in the play of the cross-coupling
figure itself. We may, for example, note that its coupling of Gertrude and
Henry includes also a curious temporal inversion: Henry's incest precedes
the birth of Elizabeth; Gertrude's occurs when Hamlet is an adult.
Whatever else it does, Hamlet's temporal priority erases the claim of the
rival child, Mary, whose role would seem, in the play, to be displaced onto
Laertes. Hamlet's marked preoccupation with female sexual desire and its
effect on men is one side of a coin, the obverse of which is the familiar
Shakespearean theme of homoerotic rivalry. By way of example, we may
note that, reflected back again into Hamlet, the motive of the play-within-
the-play will have been precisely to expiate *his* guilt and proclaim his *male*
factions—through the chiasmic coupling of himself and his uncle in his
strange editorial introduction of the play's murderer, "one Lucianus,"
with the epithet: "nephew to the King" (III.ii.239).

The symbolic brotherhood and rivalry of Hamlet and Laertes is reinforced when Laertes begins his angry confrontation with Claudius with
the demand, "O thou vile king,/Give me my father" (IV.v.115–16), but
ends it by accepting, as a communion of grief, Claudius' protection and
complicity in the plot against Hamlet (IV.v.198–216):

> Laertes, I must commune with your grief,
> Or you deny me right. Go but apart,
> Make choice of whom your wisest friends you will,
> And they shall hear and judge 'twixt you and me.
> If by direct or by collateral hand
> They find us touch'd, we will our kingdom give,
> Our crown, our life, and all that we call ours
> To you in satisfaction; but if not,
> Be you content to lend your patience to us,
> And we shall jointly labour with your soul
> To give it due content.
>   (IV.vi.199–208)

What I am trying to get at here is not the political allegory of *Hamlet*, much
less the politics of superposing Laertes and Mary Tudor, but rather the pro-
liferating force the cross-coupling rhetoric has to shape one's experience of
the play and to extend an iterative structure of connections beyond it.

Perhaps the succession crisis at the beginning of Elizabeth's reign and the one impending at the end of it cast a shadow over Shakespeare's adaptation of an old plot, but that literary adaptation overwhelms the political by shaping a response to it. From whence does that response come?

Hamlet addresses Claudius as mother immediately after telling him where "the dead body [of Polonius] is bestow'd" (IV.iii.13)—the answer to a question that, put to him by Rosencrantz in the previous scene, elicited yet another chiasmic response: "The body is with the King, but the King is not with the body. The King is a thing—" (IV.ii.26). These associations exemplify the way in which rhetoric and language facilitate the mobility of emotion in *Hamlet* and in Hamlet. In this instance, Hamlet's chiasmus is something of a double-negative, a cross-decoupler. The familiar notion that when the King's body dies his divine mandate passes immediately to his successor—"The king is dead; long live the king"—is collapsed back on itself. King Hamlet is dead and the body is with the King, though the King is not with the body [of Claudius]. Suspended between the dead king's son, who does not quite own his father's spirit, and his "incestuous" and "adulterate" (I.v.42) brother, the Kingdom of Denmark is not embodied in its monarch; not an actor but a thing, until Hamlet replays, with Laertes, the rivalry of the brothers as a strange competition of griefs over the corpse of Ophelia:

> What is he whose grief
> Bears such an emphasis, whose phrase of sorrow
> Conjures the wand'ring stars and makes them stand
> Like wonder-wounded hearers? This is I,
> Hamlet, the Dane.
>
> (V.i.248–51)

That Hamlet's belated claim to his father's name and title is facilitated by the chiasmus that structures these lines—"What is he . . . This is I,/Hamlet the Dane"—makes for an uncanny structural similarity between the way in which Claudius becomes king and husband by slaying his brother and Hamlet assumes his father's name by exchanging places with his symbolic brother, Laertes, in a contest of grief:

> 'Swounds, show me what thou't do.
> Woo't weep, woo't fight, woo't fast, woo't tear thyself,
> Woo't drink up eisel, eat a crocodile?
> I'll do't. Dost come here to whine,
> To outface me with leaping in her grave?
> Be buried quick with her, and so will I.

And if thou prate of mountains, let them throw
Millions of acres on us, till our ground,
Singeing his pate against the burning zone,
Make Ossa like a wart. Nay, and thou'lt mouth,
I'll rant as well as thou.

(V.1.269–79)

It is at least curious that these lines should reprise Hamlet's first extended speech to his mother in act 1, scene 2, in which he despairs of expressing his inward grief in something other than "actions that a man might play."

The oddly quantitative precision of Hamlet's hyperbolic claim in the preceding lines to have loved Ophelia more than "forty thousand brothers" (V.1.264–65) invites attention. Claudius, we recall, won Laertes' loyalty by communing with his grief over the death of his father. In this strange line Hamlet proposes to overgo Laertes' grief for Ophelia by invoking a direct proportionality of grief and love and asserting, by an outlandish factor, the primacy over Laertes' familial love of the erotic love that Hamlet denied to Ophelia before her derangement and death. Immediately after Hamlet's outburst, the Queen comments in language that reasserts the relationship of gender and grief:

This is mere madness,
And thus a while the fit will work on him.
Anon, as patient as the female dove
When that her golden couplets are disclos'd,
His silence will sit drooping.

(V.i.279–82)

The language of exculpation by reason of temporary insanity is very dense, reaching back to Hamlet's conclusion in II.ii. that he must be "pigeon-liver'd and lack gall/To make oppression bitter" to be so "unpregnant of [his] cause" (573–74, 563). We will return to it later, but, for now, it suffices to observe that Gertrude depicts Hamlet, returned to his mind, not only as female, but as a mother nurturing her fledgling chicks. What has Hamlet's madness, which is, at this point, hardly "antic," disclosed? In baldest summary: Claudius kills Hamlet's father to get the love of Gertrude and the throne. Hamlet, perhaps taking Polonius for Claudius, kills him, which triggers grief that kills Ophelia and enrages Laertes. Hamlet then superposes Ophelia, who died of grief—as he thinks he and Gertrude should have—on Gertrude, and replaces Laertes in incestuous affection. But the body is not with Ophelia (mother, nun, breeder of sinners). The body is with Yorick in "my lady's chamber" (V.i.187), and the quantitative competition of grief is a competition for who feels more keenly her absence. Hamlet is to Laertes as Claudius is to Hamlet, the slayer of his father and lover of his flesh and blood—in Leviticus' terms, the uncoverer of his nakedness. Gender is sorted out (partly) by female self-murder and murderous male rage, except that Hamlet, in Gertrude's discourse, will pass again from rage to feminine patience. Are brother and sister one-flesh? Hamlet's rivalry with Laertes over the body of Ophelia repeats—even works through—his rivalry with his father and facilitates his identification with Claudius, his uncle-brother, in seeking the desire of Gertrude, and, as it were for emphasis, the whole thing is replayed yet again in the fencing match, with its exchange of swords, wounds, and apologies.

The remainder of this chapter will focus on the rhetorical schemes and word-plays that choreograph this intricate dance of gender, grief, and rage in the play and will explore the possibility that these effects are transitive; that is, that they act not only mimetically to create the characters in the play, but also transferentially, to fashion and facilitate a corresponding mobility of affect in the reader or audience. In effect, I will be revisiting Aristotle's claim, contra Plato, that theater is good for its audience, but attempting to revise the Aristotelian model of identification and catharsis with a somewhat more detailed model drawn from the psychoanalytic understanding of transference. Pace Fineman, my argument is not that the psychological underlies or makes possible the literary, but exactly the contrary, that the literary makes possible the psychological.[8]

2

A simplified schematic of what appears to be the normative relation of grief and anger may be found in *Macbeth*. When Macduff hears of the murder of his family and laments the loss of "all [his] pretty chickens and their dam/At one fell swoop," that other son of a murdered father, Malcolm, admonishes him to "make us medicines of our great revenge/To cure this deadly grief," and let sorrow be "the whetstone of your sword. Let grief/Convert to anger: blunt not the heart, enrage it."[9] Accepting this advice with a negative and gendered comparison, Macduff says he will not "play the woman with mine eyes/And braggart with my tongue!" Rather, he will "front" Macbeth "Within my sword's length" and take revenge. Malcolm's approving response, "This tune goes manly," affirms the explicit gendering of grief already implicit in the imagery of blunted heart and sharpened sword: women grieve with tears, but men transmute grief to rage and rage to vengeance.[10] Poised between the female and the manly is the braggart, a performer for whom emotion takes a detour through words. In *Hamlet*, these three signs of grief—tears, words, and violence—and their associated gender positions, form an intricate fabric woven in the pattern of Polonius' foolish figure.

For example, in *Hamlet* 1.2, Claudius responds to Hamlet's impolitic mourning by asserting gendered constraints on grief similar to those advanced by Malcolm. Conceding that a son is bound by "filial obligation" "for some term/To do obsequious sorrow" for a lost father, he warns Hamlet that "to persever/In obstinate condolement" is "unmanly grief" (91–94). The same gender expectations are also adopted by Hamlet, in his second soliloquy, when he chastises himself for his inability to act according to his just "cue for passion":

> Yet I,
> A dull and muddy-mettled rascal, peak
> Like John-a-dreams, unpregnant of my cause,
> And can say nothing—no, not for a king,
> Upon whose property and most dear life
> A damn'd defeat was made. Am I coward?
> . . . .
> Why, what an ass am I! This is most brave,
> That I, the son of a dear father murder'd,
> Prompted to my revenge by heaven and hell,
> Must like a whore unpack my heart with words
> And fall a cursing like a very drab,
> A [stallyon]! Fie upon't! Foh!
>   (II.ii.561–66; 578–83)[11]

If Hamlet's failure to turn grief into violence is unmanly, Gertrude's apparent failure to grieve longer for her late husband is, in Hamlet's view, inhuman: though Gertrude followed her husband's casket—"like Niobe, all tears"—"A beast that wants discourse of reason/Would have mourn'd longer" (I.ii.144–51). Gertrude's tears are first too many, too demonstrative. That they are perhaps actions that a woman might play is suggested by the alacrity with which they too soon disappear. In contrast, the Queen in Hamlet's version of the *Murder of Gonzago*—no doubt protesting too much—represents verbally a female grief that may be expressed in outward shows but is confirmed by a vow of sexual abstinence:

> Such love must needs be treason in my breast.
> In second husband let me be accurst;
> None wed the second but who kill'd the first.

.   .   .   .

The instances that second marriage move
Are base respects of thrift, but none of love.
A second time I kill my husband dead,
When second husband kisses me in bed.

(III.ii.174–80)

It would seem that in Hamlet's view the presence of female grief cannot
be confirmed by the presence of tears unless the tears are supplemented
by an absence of sexual desire. Hamlet's expectation that female grief
extinguish female desire is challenged, however, not only by the Queen's
presumed sexual activity with Claudius, but, in a more puzzling way,
when the banter of the more or less suicidal prince is oddly refracted in
Ophelia's grief after the death of her father, which manifests in some
distinctly bawdy raving, followed by suicide.

The gendering of grief in *Hamlet* works through the mirroring relations of Hamlet's suicidal soliloquies, Ophelia's achieved suicide, and
Laertes' rage. We can follow in these examples the specific distribution
of grief among sons and daughters in the play and the correlation of filial mourning with the counterplot of sacrifice implicit in the ghost's
demand to be avenged at his son's expense and the politic manipulation
of Ophelia that Hamlet associates with the story of Jephthah and his
daughter.

3

A brief detour through the psychoanalytic theory of transference will set
out the warrants for the transitive effects of this peculiar rhetoric of grief.
Psychoanalysis invites us to think of Hamlet's position as a problem in
the transference and binding of affect and of our engagement with
Hamlet as similar to analytic transference. Transference in Freud's work
takes three distinct forms, so some explanation is in order.[12] Early on,
Freud argues that the emotions attendant on a repressed trauma,
although they are never consciously experienced, remain mobile in the
unconscious. This "unbound affect" can be transferred to something in
consciousness that lends itself to representing—though not disclosing—
the repressed material. Freud first notices this transference of affect in
dreams, where targets of opportunity in what Freud calls, elegantly, "the
remains of the day" may be seized on to represent something in the
latent dream thoughts.[13] While the traumatic cause of these emotions
remains unconscious, the emotions themselves may gain access to consciousness by a transference that ascribes them—at least in part—to

some conscious cause. Every Freudian reading of *Hamlet* begins with the assumption that—were Hamlet a living analytic subject—his grief would be overdetermined. The distress attendant on his father's death and his mother's marriage could then be understood to revive and represent some earlier, disabling trauma whose melancholy affect attaches to and intensifies his present circumstances. In other words, the situation in which Hamlet finds himself would serve to represent an earlier, repressed episode so that the unexperienced emotions persisting in the unconscious could be released, while their archaic cause remains locked away. Because Hamlet is a fictional character, who is always thirty years old, and whose youthful experience could only be a speculative extension of the plot, I am not interested in identifying this earlier trauma.[14] The contents of the repressed trauma are, in any case, irrelevant to the psychic performance of the play, *Hamlet*, and the details of rhetoric that enable the transference of affects in and through it. The transference effects I am looking for are structures—rhetorical patterns—rather than contents. Rhetoric facilitates the mobility of emotion by articulating disparate chains of signifiers in ways that allow associated feelings to jump from one chain to another, the links of which are similarly configured. What psychoanalysts call "repetition automaton" may be understood as the circulation of emotion between two linked chains, in which the rhetorical scheme of an earlier chain unconsciously configures succeeding engagements according to its pattern. Freud called these preemptive configurations, "complexes." As we shall see, becoming aware of the configurations on which stray emotions map is independent of constructing a narrative memory of some originary trauma.

Therefore, I propose instead to put in play Freud's later elaborations of transference specific to analysis. Transfer of affect is a general mechanism of the mobility of emotion, a way to explain, for example, why neurotics invest certain seemingly trivial objects, events, or performances with apparently disproportionate importance. Specific to the "talking cure" itself, analytic transference occurs during the course of analysis, when the analysand comes to identify the analyst with a significant figure in the repressed drama from which his or her archaic emotions derive. This identification allows the analysand to *project* onto the analyst emotions originally evoked by the figure he or she has come to represent. Freud at first thought this phenomenon, which he experienced as illusory love or hate directed toward him by his patients, presented an obstacle to the analysis, in fact the most difficult to overcome of the resistances.[15] Later, however, he came to see the transference as an essential element of the analytic process. Identification of the analyst with a key figure from the past enabled the analysand not simply to recall what had been repressed but to "work through" or experience the free-floating emotions attached to it. "Remembering" and "working through" in this way binds these emotions and allows them to be discharged into conscious memory, thus freeing the neurotic, for example, from repetition compulsion in which the emotion is bound by endlessly repeating the configuration of the unremembered scene in various opaque representations—as in Lady Macbeth's nocturnal reenactment of the washing off of Duncan's blood.[16] It is important to note, however, that identification *with* a figure from the past does not require identification *of* a figure from the past. For transference to occur, Hamlet does not need to remember an event (which may or may not have occurred in the past); rather he must become aware of the structure of repetition that invests his present actions with some otherwise mysterious affect, and for this transference to extend to us—readers and spectators—we identify with Hamlet (or some other character) to the extent that we extrapolate from his repetitions to our own. Remembering may be understood, then, as a disruption of the complex of associations that allows its elements to be reassembled in a different way. The ability to restructure the flow of affect is more independent of and more powerful than *knowing* its cause. So we come by this circuitous route to something that shares the general shape of Aristotle's melioristic view of tragedy in which by identifying with the tragic hero, the spectator is able to purge himself of pity and fear, to achieve, as Milton put it, "calm of mind, all passion spent."[17]

It is my hope that understanding the rhetorical transference of affect within the play will also help us consider the possibilities of transference onto and through the play. Thus the aim of my analysis is to engage what Hamlet might call "the purpose of playing," the dynamic engagement of the reader or spectator with the play, and to suggest that this engagement might follow a course that resembles Freud's model of analytic transference. I want to know why we care about *Hamlet* after all these years, and how the play does whatever it is that it does to demand continued attention. But first it will be necessary to extend the model of transference one more step, to include what came to be called the counter transference. Counter transference is the reciprocating effect of analysis on the analyst, his or her projection of emotions in response to those of the transference. An analyst, like a reader, must recognize that his or her unconscious is submitted to modification by its engagement with that of another. In the analytic work of Jacques Lacan the reciprocal transactions of transference are understood to involve fantasies of knowing. Lacan argues that in the transference, the analysand, wishing to engage the desire of the analyst, may produce associations of which (he or she thinks) the analyst will approve. The analysand seeks, that is, to persuade the analyst that the analysis is going somewhere, or, in literary terms, that it is heading toward narrative closure. If the desire of the analyst is for the truth and the analysand wishes, therefore, to produce the truth to satisfy this desire, he or she first constructs the analyst as the one who knows the truth and so can distinguish progress from resistance, analytic work from evasion. Similarly, in counter transference, an analyst, whose desire is, indeed, the patient's truth might presume that the patient knows the truth and produces or withholds it so as to express pleasure or displeasure with the analyst. It is the task of the analyst to refuse both positions. The analyst must neither allow himself to believe that the analysand knows the truth—knows, that is, the true path of desire—nor allow the analysand to believe that the analyst knows the truth. For Lacan not knowing the truth of desire is precisely the ethical position of psychoanalysis.[18] In a lucid study entitled *Truth and Eros: Foucault, Lacan and the Question of Ethics*, John Rajchman spells out the ethical import of Lacan's view of transference:

> In Lacan's eyes, analysis would be the form of love which never supposes that it knows what is good for someone else. . . . In this way, it would be distinguished from *philia* and *caritas*. For *philia* is a love that brings men together in the knowledge of the good that is the same in each of us, and *caritas* supposes a knowledge of salvation or grace. . . . Psychoanalysis is a form of love that is not based in those ideal parts of ourselves that would allow us to master our fate or to obtain salvation. On the contrary, it would open up even our first love, our love of ourselves, to a traumatic and fateful cause.[19]

This cause is inherent to the traumatic stitching of our desire to ourselves, the result, at once historical, radically contingent and unrepresentable, of our coming to represent ourselves to ourselves at the cost of interposing a symbolic representation between ourselves and the unmediated self-presence we never had.

The process has more than a passing resemblance to metaphor.[20] As Julia Reinhard Lupton and Kenneth Reinhard have noted, "If *Hamlet* is the 'translation' of *Oedipus*, it is also a *translatio* in the sense of metaphor" and "a translation" in the sense of psychoanalytic transference." Insofar as its "repetition of childhood conflicts" is the posterior construction of analysis and analysand, . . . its very figurative distortion, points back to a structure only retroactively 'prior,' rather than being the secondary meaning of its archetype."[21] Through what Freud calls a transfer of affect, the trauma Hamlet can remember—his father's death and his mother's marriage—serves as the vehicle for the emotional affect of the trauma that he cannot remember to become manifest. Transference, like metaphor, lives in the tension between pertinent and impertinent predication. For example, Hamlet pretends to take Polonius for a fishmonger, and he implies that, like Jephtha, Polonius will sacrifice his daughter without being totally conscious of the bargain he has struck. *Polonius is a fishmonger* is metaphoric only to the extent that we recognize it as a semantic impertinence or inappropriate attribution, yet presume that the locution makes sense. To make sense of it, we compare Polonius to a fishmonger and look for pertinent resemblances. Perhaps Polonius *hawks* his daughter as a fishmonger might hawk his fish. On the one hand, if it were to turn out that the Polonius to whom we refer is not Polonius, the medieval Danish courtier, but Polonius, the fishmonger, who sells fresh blues off his boat in the local bay, there would be no semantic impertinence and no metaphor. On the other hand, confronted with something like, say, "Polonius is bubble gum," we might not be able to find any useful points of comparison. There is no semantic pertinence, thus no metaphor, only nonsense or gibberish. Like the tenor of a metaphor, when a transferred affect surfaces, the repressed trauma to which the feelings once belonged remains implicit in the disproportion between the explicit trauma and the emotional experience it releases. It is, in fact, this manifest disproportion that led T. S. Eliot to declare *Hamlet* an artistic failure because its action is not an "objective correlative" adequate to the emotion Hamlet displays.[22] Analysis, on the contrary, sees this disproportion as a group of symptoms—in Hamlet's case, melancholy, inability to act on his resolves, frustration, and hostility, particularly, as Eliot noted, hostility directed toward his mother. It is the work of analysis to find in the symptom the comparison that establishes its semantic pertinence so as to make sense.

Now, when posing (or borrowing from Hamlet) the example of Polonius and the fishmonger and wanting to establish pertinence by suggesting that Polonius sells Ophelia the way a fishmonger sells fish, I felt that the verb *to sell* would not do. Polonius does not really sell his daughter so much as he displays her as bait (fishing again)—offers the use of her for his and the King's benefit, while still retaining control over her.[23] Unable to come up with the verb that would *literally* say what I thought I meant, I resorted to another metaphor, *hawks*. This metaphor is barely breathing for me, because I really do not know exactly what it is about hawks or falconers that resembles glib or overaggressive salespeople, but I do know that *hawks* seems to work in the sentence, perhaps because the hawk returns to the hawker and surrenders its catch. It is characteristic of metaphors and of transference effects that, like Claudius' sorrows, they "come not single spies,/But in battalions" (IV.v.78–79). The attempt to elucidate *Polonius is a fishmonger*, elicits Polonius the *hawker*. *Fishmonger* and *hawker* each put into play a different network of associations. These are arbitrary examples, but it happens that Hamlet neglects neither in his larger discourse. Moments before Polonius "looses" his daughter to him, Hamlet explains his own desire for and fear of death as a case in which:

> the native hue of resolution
> Is sicklied o'er with the pale cast of thought,
> And enterprises of great *pitch* and *moment*
> With this regard their currents turn awry
> And lose the name of action.
> > (III.i.84–88; my emphasis)[24]

Perhaps it is Hamlet's description of enterprises soaring like falcons and his claim to know a "hawk from a handsaw" (II.ii.368) that helped me to find the verb *to hawk* as a supplementary metaphor with which to unpack *Polonius is a fishmonger*. Certainly Hamlet's description of himself as "pigeon liver'd" and Gertrude's reassurance that when the fit is passed he will be "patient as the female dove" create an inviting context in which to think of Hamlet's vacillations in terms of hawks and doves. But perhaps Hamlet's hawks and mine are utterly unrelated.[25] They share little semantic ground, and that is precisely the point I want to make both about metaphor and about transference. Both procedures engage representations that engage other representations to generate a network or web of *more* and *less* motivated associations and both engage in a reader or an analyst associations not easily extricated from that individual's history. In psychoanalysis, the transference proper to analysis (as opposed to the simple transference of affect, which is an everyday occurrence) occurs when the analysand unconsciously (if impertinently) identifies the analyst with a figure from the past that is significant in the etiology of his or her symptoms. A reciprocal effect, or counter transference, mobilizes the analyst's emotions in response to the transference. It is this transitive aspect of analytic discourse that suggests to me an ethical relationship of reader and text, audience and play, reminiscent of Aristotle's melioristic *catharsis*.[26]

Returning to terms contemporaneous with the play: we have seen that to be manly, Hamlet needs to transmute grief over his father's death and his mother's marriage to anger toward Claudius and to purge this anger through violent action. As the story unfolds, however, he is able to transmute grief to anger and hostility, but unable to direct it at the desired object. This is because the grief is peculiarly gendered. Hamlet's anger is directed toward his mother, and, through a metonymy of genus for species (the trope of common and particular introduced in Hamlet's testy exchange with his mother in I.ii and put in play in his first soliloquy)—"Frailty, thy name is woman" (I.ii.146)—he is able to transfer it to women and thus to Ophelia—but lacking a corresponding category for the male (lacking the phallus, Lacan might say)—he constitutes maleness either under the genus *father* or through invidious comparison (I to Hercules: Hyperion to a satyr [I.ii.140, 153])—he can go no further. Only when Gertrude dies by Claudius' cup can Hamlet transfer his anger onto Claudius and vent it violently. He has desired the desire of his mother; he has desired to extinguish her desire; and he has desired death. With her death, he attains his heart's desire and dies.

In the silence that is the rest, Claudius' prescient diagnosis echoes:

> Love? His affections do not that way tend,
> Nor what he spake, though it lack'd form a little,
> Was not like madness. There's something in his soul
> O'er which his melancholy sits on brood,
> And I do doubt the hatch and the disclose
> Will be some danger.
>
> (III.i.164–69)

In a brilliant discussion of mourning and masculinity in Renaissance literature, Lynn Enterline finds that "[t]he story of loss that Renaissance writers and some psychoanalytic authors would call melancholic is a name given to any of a series of poetic or rhetorical problems destabilizing enough to undermine the identity of the self presumed to be the subject of such suffering."[27]

I have sought to understand Hamlet in precisely these terms. Hamlet had momentarily become "I, Hamlet, the Dane" when he repeated a displaced version of his uncle's act by attempting to take his "brother's" place in the grave of Ophelia, Gertrude's metonymic substitute. With Gertrude's death and his own, "the something in his soul" over which his "melancholy sits on brood" is hatched. Beginning with his first soliloquy, Hamlet names this something *incest*, a naming affirmed in the play only by the ghost's reference to Claudius as an "incestuous and adulterate beast" (I.v.42). But what matters to (and for) the reader/spectator is not the precise content of the notion of incest that so disrupts the conflicted and traumatic kernel of Hamlet's identity, but rather the structural homology between incest and chiasmus: the rhetorical cross-coupling of antonymous accidents of lineage and gender, already implicit in the prohibitions of Leviticus. "My mother. Father and

mother is man and wife, man and wife is one flesh; so my mother"
(IV.iii.54–55).

Grammatically, "Man and wife" is a single element, a singularity that
the text emphasizes by using the compound subject with a singular verb.
Thus, the chiasmic coupling diagrams as: A [mother] . . . is B [man and
wife] X B [man and wife] . . . is A [mother]. How does this facilitate
transference and what story about grief and gender does it preview—as
in dumb show? It cross-couples the two embedded clauses: "*Father* and
Mother is *man and wife*" but "*man and wife* is one flesh [and] *so
my mother*." Thus the category Father [or, if you will, the phallus]
disappears into *man and wife*, but only mother emerges from the other
side. What mediates this disappearance? *Flesh: The paternal phallus
has disappeared into the mother's flesh.* And that, after all, is how little
princes are made.

Why then is Hamlet "unpregnant of his cause"? Gertrude's remar-
riage, her failure to certify her tears with sexual aphanisis disrupts the
grammar of his mourning, with its gendered division of labor between
rage and tears. If vindictive rage is the concrete signifier of masculine
grief, Gertrude's *incestuous* refusal to relinquish the body of the king
from the stronghold of her flesh, leaves Hamlet unable to locate the
grammatical object of his mourning and so unable to express his grief as
vengeance. The bodies of his father and his uncle—now mediated in
Gertrude's flesh—are insufficiently distinct. Only when he sees Laertes
mourning Ophelia, whom he is linguistically unable to separate from
Gertrude, does Hamlet become enraged and momentarily articulate his
succession with the infolding of the subject and object implicit in the
predicate nominative: "This is I, Hamlet, the Dane." This first movement, however, is doubly turned. He will fight not his father's brother,
but Ophelia's, and their fencing match will be but the simulacrum of a
fight—until he learns that Laertes foil is unbuttoned and envenomed.
The exchange of foils follows, and with the question of identity resolved
by imminent death, Hamlet's inhibited transformation of grief to violence finally completes its culturally appointed masculine path.

What then does Hamlet's melancholy hatch? Choosing an ideal ego
closest to the ego ideal he has constructed of his spectral father, Hamlet
settles the election on Fortinbras.[28] His one and only royal act is to
bequeath his kingdom to the man who comes to Denmark to avenge a
father who has died by the hand of Hamlet's father. What does Hamlet
see in this man who had earlier been easily diverted from his revenge to
a Polish adventure, when Claudius pressured him through his uncle?
Fortinbras is, to Hamlet, a "delicate and tender prince" who, under the
name of *strong arms*, exposes "what is mortal and unsure/To all that for-

tune, death, and danger dare,/Even for an *eggshell*" (IV.iv.48, 52–53; emphasis mine). It is as though Hamlet has chosen the anti-Hamlet in this precise negation of his own relentless self-examination, and, in so doing, has imagined a resolution of the contradiction between the delicacy of a Renaissance prince and the strong-armed politics on which his masculinity rests.

The course of this transfer, in which Hamlet briefly becomes the "father" of a new and far less complicated prince, has traced its way along a bumpy rhetoric of chiasmic couplings: hawks, doves, handsaws, fishmongers, and eggs: "'tis true; 'tis true 'tis pity;/And pity 'tis 'tis true." What transfers and transforms along this rhetorical path is not the content of desire but its structure. And yet, Hamlet has a choice. "My mother. Father and mother is man and wife, man and wife is one flesh; so my mother." The chiasmus is itself embedded in an anaphora. [*My mother*] Father and Mother is man and wife; man and wife is one flesh, [*so my mother*]. Nothing in the rhetorical structure compels Hamlet's elision of the Father and re-assertion of the mother. The fact that the two appositive assertions of "*my mother*" can be added without disturbing the chiasmic form facilitates Hamlet's reading, but it does not demand it. Rhetorically enfolding the phallus in the maternal body is rather his choice and his responsibility. This decisive moment cannot be evaded as "a special providence." "The readiness is all," is supplemented by a choice at the rhetorical crossroad.

As these associations extend into the structure of *my* own desire, they disclose not *its* content, but its rhetoric. Because I love *Hamlet* I survive him, pity him, and, having traced his rhetorical path to "My thoughts be bloody or be nothing worth," I avoid his madness. Reading continues and interpretation is forestalled. *Hamlet* tells us a good deal about how grief was gendered at the beginning of the seventeenth century and the dynamics that might follow from it. But its most enduring "truth" is to dramatize, perhaps to transfer, the rhetorical structure of a certain, violent connection among the demands of masculine identification and the bloodiness of thought. To the extent that we are conscious of this structure and its historical contingence, we may be relieved of its necessity.

PART VI

THE FAMILY, ABSENCE, AND MEMORY IN THE SEVENTEENTH CENTURY

Chapter 13

"I might againe have been the Sepulcure": Paternal and Maternal Mourning in Early Modern England

Patricia Phillippy

Writing on Lavinia Fontana's *Portrait of a Newborn in a Cradle*, dated ca. 1583 (see figure 13.1), Vera Fortunati states that the painting may "depict a deceased newborn." She explains, "At a time when European infant mortality was high, the artist may have sought to retain the memory of a young child for the family's history, which otherwise would inevitably have been lost."[1] Within the elaborately inlaid cradle, the infant's eyes calmly fix upon viewers with a surprising maturity. While the rich adornments of the cradle, the delicate lace of the bedding and garments, and the pearls that encircle the child's neck assert his or her aristocratic status, the form of the canopied cradle itself recalls funerary sculpture of the period whose English examples borrow from Continental models the living-dead postures of their reclining inhabitants.[2] For instance, the tomb of Princess Mary Stuart in Westminster Abbey (see figure 13.2), similarly offers a portrait of the toddler-princess *en vivant*, while the tomb of John Russell (see figure 13.3), also in Westminster, covers its dead with a canopy below which the effigy of the infant Francis Russell rests (see figure 13.4). Fontana's newborn is thus displayed in a cradle that is also a tomb.[3] Beyond the cradle in a domestic scene, dimly lit and barely discernible, a female figure gestures with both arms toward a closed chest. Although this dark figure is almost inscrutable, her outstretched arms recall a standard gesture of mourning in the period[4] while the grim enclosure of the small chest, which may figure the child's coffin, stands in sharp contrast to the open, well-lit,

Figure 13.1   Lavinia Fontana, *Portrait of a Newborn in a Cradle*. Pinacoteca Nazionale, Bologna.

and opulent cradle in the foreground. Buried in the dark background of the portrait's memorial function is its recollection of maternal mourning—an obscure, but still visible figure whose violent reaction to loss, only partially contained within the domestic space, belies the calm surface of the portrait's public face.

Fontana's painting suggests that the experience of child-loss in the early modern period was gendered in ways that figure the public sphere as that of paternal mourning, where moderate sorrow and living memory record the socio-cultural loss exacted by the child's death, while consigning maternal lament to the dimly lit reaches of the household. This essay explores this suggestion further in maternal elegies by Anne de Vere and Mary Carey and in Philippe de Mornay's work of paternal mourning, *Teares for the Death of his Sonne*. Within these works, I briefly

Figure 13.2   Maximilian Colt, Tomb of Mary Stuart. Westminster Abbey.
Author's photograph.

trace an early modern gendering of grief that constructs maternity as a
site of affective license useful in different ways to male and female
authors as they posit rival styles of mourning in intimate association with
the sexes. Setting the features of maternal mourning in relation to
Mornay's tears indicates the gendering of parental grief and the degree
to which women manipulate, transgress, or resist male-authored prescriptions for acceptable mourning. Women elegists, I argue, employ the
culturally charged discourse of lamentation to empower and authorize
their textual performances by rooting them within the resistant form of
the maternal mourner herself.

One goal of this discussion is to challenge the assumption that the
authority of these female-authored texts rests exclusively on their
authors' sex (with maternity as its prominent feature and emblem) and,
alternatively, to wonder whether an essentialist notion of sex is deployed
or performed in the construction of the woman's voice in these works.
My reading of "maternal affection"—"the first cause of writing" according to Dorothy Leigh's *The Mother's Blessing* —[5] sees this emotion, and
the maternal body to which it refers, "as an effect or consequence of a
system of sexuality in which the female body is required to assume
maternity as the essence of its self and the law of its desire."[6] I ask, in
other words, What cultural work is done by the performative concept of

Figure 13.3   Cornelius Cure and William Cure II, Tomb of John Russell.
Westminster Abbey. Author's photograph.

maternity as it is deployed by men and women in the period? This question both informs and involves those attending the publication of works of maternal mourning—particularly vexing questions since female-authored works often ground their notion of authorial presence on absence (that is, on their authors' assertions of privacy rather than pub-

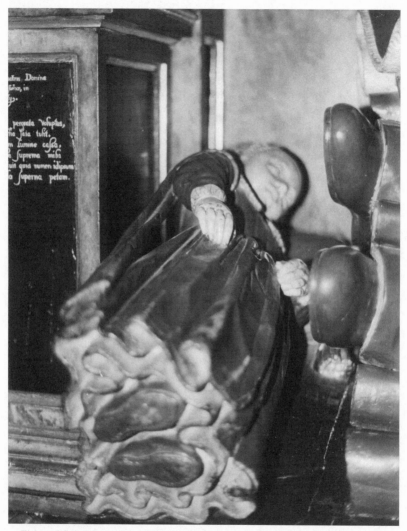

Figure 13.4   Cornelius Cure and William Cure II, Tomb of John Russell.
Westminster Abbey (detail). Author's photograph.

lic performance).[7] Works of maternal mourning are particularly valuable
in this respect, however, since they suggest that assertions of privacy
may, in fact, take part in *constructing* the view of mothers as domestic,
even as it seems to *describe* them as such. Moreover, these works underscore the degree to which the performance of gender is always in play,

even in moments of self-representation intended only for one's most intimate audience—and even, ultimately, for oneself alone. Unrestrained by male authors' ventriloquism, maternal mourning becomes "melancholic mourning,"[8] which seeks to encrypt the corpse within the maternal body itself; in Anne de Vere's words, within the living "Sepulcure,/ Of him that I bare in mee, so long ago."[9]

*

In his seventeenth-century life of Martin Luther, Samuel Clarke describes a father's grief at the death of his daughter:

> When he saw his daughter Magdalen ready to dye, he read to her Isay 26:19. Thy dead men shall live; together with my dead body shall they arise, &c. Adding, My daughter enter thou into thy chamber in peace: I shall ere long be with thee. For God will not permit me to see the punishment which hangs over the head of Germany, whereupon he wept plentifully; but when he followed the Corps, he so restrained his affection that he shed not a tear.[10]

The image of Luther's plentiful tears shed in private, while in public "he shed not a tear," implies the participation of men as well as women in the culture of grief, which mandated that public demonstrations of sorrow be suitably stoic while immoderation, if permitted at all, was confined to the privacy of the household. The narrative recalls the early humanist complaint that women's excessive mourning constituted a public nuisance: "If some lamentation is necessary to the grieved," Petrarch writes in a letter of 1373, "let them do it at home" and "do not let them disturb the public thoroughfares."[11] While Clarke's hagiography uses Luther's copious private tears to illustrate that "[h]e was full of affections toward his children"[12] and posits paternal affection as a Christian virtue, the episode not only asserts the decorum governing public mourning but also interjects into the moment of private child-loss the memory of civic government: thus Magdalen's death is an occasion for Luther to predict "the punishment that hangs over Germany." Luther's mourning for his lost daughter is painfully conflated with his sorrow for the nation. Moreover, Clarke's dissemination of this portrait of private paternal grief further appropriates the moment within the politico-religious project advanced by his text. Paternal mourning—copious in private, stoic in public—is, in the end, neither fully private nor solely commemorative of the lost child, but also grieves the political and social losses figured in or attendant upon her death.

Early modern diaries and autobiographies written by men leave no doubt that, generally speaking, fathers' affections for their children were as heartfelt as were mothers' in the period and that men were subject to grief as profound as their wives' at child-loss.[13] Ralph Josselin, for instance, writes affectively of the death of his adult son in 1673, "about one a clocke in the morning my eldest sonne Thomas and my most deare child ascended early hence to keepe his everlasting Sabbath with his heavenly father, and Saviour with the church above. . . . [A] wett morning, the heavens for some time have mourned over us."[14] Josselin's emphasis on his son's spiritual transcendence despite his own grief is typical of paternal mourning as expressed in men's diaries and autobiographies. As vicar of Earls Colne, Essex, from 1641 until his death in 1683, Josselin's personal losses are occasions to reiterate privately the consolatory message of salvation whose public affirmation was his duty. On the death of his infant son, Ralph, Josselin writes, "god hath taken away a sonne: I hope the lord will keepe my feete in uprightness . . . and also that I should bee more carefull of my family to instruct them in the theory of god, that they may live in his sight and bee servicable to his glory."[15] Meditation upon the loss results, finally, in a turn toward domestic government: as the spiritual head of his household, Josselin sees his son's death as a call to diligence in the religious instruction of his family.

The commencement of Josselin's diary with that of his religious career suggests,[16] as do his responses to child-loss, that his private sorrow reaffirms his public role: that is, throughout his undeniable experiences of grief, the orthodox, consolatory message of mourning in measure casts the private subject as an extension of his public role. For mothers, whose cultural identity was intimately related to their reproductive functions and whose spiritual salvation depended upon the bearing and nurturing of children— as the anonymous *Preparacyon to Death* restates the familiar dictum, "The woman shal be saved throughe bearynge of chyldren, yf she contynue in faythe, love, and sanctificacyon, wyth sobernes"[17]—expressions of grief at child-loss are less measured and more prone to resistance, anger, and transgression. Based on the physical bond between mother and child, naturalized in early modern culture as essentially feminine, the maternal mourner contemplates the complete dissolution of identity in inconsolable grief.[18]

This figure of self-dissolution informs the period's most coherent and programmatic work of *paternal* mourning, Philippe de Mornay's *Teares for the Death of his Sonne*, translated into English by John Healey in 1609.[19] Addressed to his grieving wife, Charlotte d'Arbaleste, Mornay's treatise publicizes and exploits the voice of maternal mourning to embody excessive sorrow and to subdue it within stoic measure. In doing so, it illustrates the passage from private tears to public restraint that marks the cultural performance of mourning as it moves from the household into the commonwealth.

Mourning his son, who died in 1605 at the age of twenty-six, Mornay begins his treatise by expressing the mutuality of his own and his wife's "aboundant sorrow" (A4) at their loss. By associating his tears with his wife's, Mornay participates in the excesses of mourning commonly figured as maternal in the early modern period: thus he complains that neither speech nor silence is adequate to express the depth of his sorrow (A7v). He voices his own wish for death, since child-loss signals the loss of oneself (B3), and figures his excessive mourning as an empathetic disfigurement: "Nay thou hast shot me thorow, & that through the sides of mine onely sonne: striking Father and child starke dead both at one stroke" (B5v).

Mornay's engagement in immoderate mourning for his son is not undertaken innocently within his tears. On the contrary, these excesses are presented, we discover, to instruct Mornay's wife (and, incidentally, the reader) in their appropriate restraint. Throughout the text, the speaker continually returns to the question of whether he ought to give voice to his sorrow: "What," he asks, "shall I speake out my woes, or shall I entombe them in silence?" (A6). Repeatedly, he displays his awareness that his expression of immoderate grief constitutes a rebellion against God's will, and self-consciously records his dangerous swerves into blasphemous immoderation ("I am full of dolorous matter: my spirit swells within me, and compells mee!" B4v) and, at moments of most "outragious murmure" (A8v), his prayers for forgiveness and self-restraint: "But thou (LORD) keepe a bridle within my mouth" (B4). Mornay invokes the gendering of grief to censure his immoderation as a token of effeminacy: "Therefore thou talkest like a foolish Woman: go and learne better language of the wise" (B8).

This wavering between the venting of excessive sorrow and its attempted restraint continues until the speaker is able definitively to bridle his blasphemous speech: "Why so then, I am satisfied: give mee leave, I will now take the bitte out of my mouth my selfe, and plead the case of the all-sufficient Creator, even against mine owne soule" (C3). At this moment, he turns once again to his wife, no longer a feminized co-mourner but a stoic male governor, encouraging her to "Wipe away those tears once more that gush out in such aboundance (seeming as if hee wer [*sic*] not dead already, to drowne him in his grave)" (C7v). "Rebellious affects," he assures her, "flye beyond the pitche of our obedience to our maker" (D2v-D3). The treatise ends by translating "plaints to praiers and . . . sorrowes into speciall songs" (D7) and by offering the text as a school of sorrow, teaching Mornay's wife and the reader how to weep lawful tears of penance, obedience, and acceptance:

"In these teares (beloved wife) and in this manner of sorrow, it is no
sinne to take our orders and proceed graduates" (E2v).

Mornay's tears illustrate the translation of maternal excess into paternal moderation, enacted by appropriating the maternal mourner's voice
within the law of the father. The treatise gains affective and rhetorical
power by exploiting the excesses of maternal mourning and by staging a
definitive turn toward masculine moderation in the voice of the father,
which, as Mornay makes clear, substitutes for and articulates the will of
God the Father. The overt, self-conscious concern of the treatise with the
problematics of speech are figured in its opening image, in which Mornay
compares "aboundant sorrow" to a "deepe wound" and seeks a mean
between extremes in its treatment: "stoppe it too soone," he claims, "it
spoiles us: stay it too long, it kills us" (A4). At the treatise's close, the
image returns, when Mornay quotes Psalm 147 to affirm that God "*mak-
est the wounde, and . . . bindest it up . . .* [H]e annointeth all their sores
with his precious Balsam" (D8v). Mornay's imagery of the wound of
child-loss conflates grief and its articulation, opposing the potentially
toxic language of excessive mourning to the restorative embalming of
submissive tears. Certainly the orthodox language of paternal measure is
the balm offered by Mornay's text to cure the wound of child-loss, but it
is a cure enacted through the exercise and exorcism of maternal excess.

Charlotte d'Arbaleste de Mornay is given no voice in her husband's text,
where her silence may as easily denote her submission to her husband's lessons as her refusal of them. Elsewhere, in fact, both she and her biographers provide evidence of her inconsolable grief.[20] Unable to conquer her
sorrow, she died only three weeks after her son's funeral. Following her
death, her biographers report, "La cause de sa mort au Rapport des
Medecins qui en firent l'ouverture fut; Que l'humeur melancholique se
respandant dans les Intestins y avoit fair erosion, mesme au Colon, cause
des insupportable tranches qui la tourmentoient" ["The cause of her death
according to the doctors who opened her was that the melancholic humor
spreading in the intestines eroded the colon, causing the insupportable
colic that tormented her"].[21] Madame de Mornay, in effect, dies of grief.

In the elegies of mourning mothers, to which we now turn, Philippe
de Mornay's consolatory conflation of the wound and the mouth
bespeaks an injury as difficult to cure as the fatal melancholy of his wife.
In these poems, "the complex of melancholia behaves like an open
wound,"[22] and the transgressive language of maternal mourning—more
a "rebellious affect" than a "precious Balsam"—seeks words to articulate
its unspeakable loss.

*

In 1584, John Soowthern included in his collection of poems, *Pandora*, a series of sonnets attributed to Anne de Vere, Countess of Oxford, on the death of her infant son the year before. Vere's clear disappointment at the child's death, the dynastic aspects of which are subsumed within the personal discourse of maternal lament, resonates throughout the four complete sonnets and two fragments printed by Soowthern. In brutal and complex imagery completely devoid of allusions to Christian consolation, the poems reveal their author's engagement in, as Ellen Moody puts it, "an impious, rebellious violence against her fate and that of her child."[23]

The depth of maternal despair can be gauged by the poems' images of self-consuming grief and their melancholic gestures toward self-cancellation, dissolution, and death. In expressing their speaker's desire to join the lost child in death, the sonnets are characteristic of female-authored elegies, which tend to concentrate on the physical fact of death and on the corruption, rather than the resurrection, of the beloved body.[24] Vere, for example, complains in her third sonnet:

> The heavens, death, and life: have conjured my yll:
> For death hath take away the breath of my sonne:
> The hevens receve, and consent, that he hath donne:
> And my life dooth keep mee heere against my will.
> (C4v; ll. 1–4)

Again in the fragmentary sixth poem, she laments, "My sonne is gone: and with it, death end my sorrow," and displays her empathetic self-cancellation in mourning for the lost child as Death informs the speaker, "that [body] of yours, is no more now, but a shadow" (C4v; l. 4). Rather than devoting themselves to consolatory considerations of the child's resurrection in the afterlife, Vere's poems are filled with images of burial and entombment: "the Marble, of my Childe" (C3v; sonnet 1, l. 8) and the inarticulate "stone . . . that doth it inclose" (C3v; sonnet 2, l. 8) merge with the sequence's final image of the maternal body as tomb in Vere's identification with Niobe:[25]

> Amphion's wife was turned to a rocke. O
> How well I had been, had I had such adventure,
> For then I might againe have been the Sepulcure,
> Of him that I bare in mee, so long ago.
> (C4v; sonnet 6, 1–4)

This emphasis on the physical body of mourning and on the material connection between the living-dead body of the maternal mourner and the

corpse of her offspring poses an overt challenge to the consolatory poetics of transcendence. In the fourth poem, for instance, Vere stages a
parodic resurrection enacted by the mourning mother, in which the physical reincorporation of the lost child within the regenerative body of
maternal mourning revises the patriarchal notion of spiritual rebirth in
the afterlife:

> But if our life be caus'de with moisture and heate,
>   I care neither for the death, the life, nor skyes:
> For I'll sigh him warmth, and weat him with my eies:
>   (And thus I shall be thought a second Promet).
>
> (C4, ll. 5–8)

Vere engages the period's humoral idea of reproduction, which understands the female body as primarily moist and cold and the male as warm
and dry,[26] to locate reproductive power exclusively in the female body
of maternal mourning. Like a second, female Prometheus, she will res-
urrect the dead child through the recreative sighs and tears of maternal
lament.[27] Vere's self-casting as Prometheus figures the recreation of the
lost child within the offspring poems themselves, enacting not so much
his immortality within the text as his perpetual entombment.
Permanently encrypted in the poems—which are simultaneously the
womb and the tomb constructed of the living-dead maternal body—the
infant resides forever as an indelible marker of irreplaceable loss.

Elsewhere in the sequence, Vere reflects the material practices of the
early modern female culture of mourning. In both the first and fourth
sonnets of the sequence, for instance, she energizes the tradition of
women's communal mourning by calling upon Venus as co-mourner for
her lost son. In the first poem, the tears of Venus merge with those of
the speaker, offering an affective, monumental portrait of the maternal
mourner petrified in inconsolable grief:

> Whose brest Venus, with a face dolefull and milde,
>   Doth washe with golden teares, inveying the skies:
>   And when the water of the Goddesses eyes,
> Makes almost alive, the Marble, of my Childe,
>   One byds her leave styll, her dollor so extreme,
>   Telling her it is not, her young sonne Papheme,
>   To which she make aunswer with a voice inflamed,
>   (Feeling therewith her venime, to be more bitter)
> As I was of Cupid, even so of it mother:
> And a womans last chylde, is the most beloved.
>
> (C3v; ll. 5–12)

By granting to Venus the tokens of immoderate mourning ("dollor so extreme," "a voice inflamed," "venime"), Vere, of course, also claims these extremes for herself. Her revision of the communal mourning of the Three Maries, where the Virgin gives way to the grief-stricken Venus, remarkably imports into the sequence the affective power of the Christian tradition but without its consolatory implications. This classicized Virgin is free to indulge in passionate excess. Thus she reappears in the fourth sonnet as well, where the Virgin's empathetic passion—the traditional subject matter of the *planctus Mariae*—reflects the speaker's own desire for death:[28]

> At the brute of it, the Aphroditan Queene,
>   Caused more silver to distyll fro her eyes:
>   Then when the droppes of her cheekes raysed Daisyes:
> And to die with him, mortall, she would have beene.
>
> (C4; ll. 5–8)

Vere's imagery of consumption and self-consumption shares Mornay's merger of the wound of child-loss and its articulation, but, in doing so, clears a discursive space for a transgressive language of maternal mourning. The first sonnet complains of her son's arbitrary and meaningless death, employing, as Kim Walker notes, negative syntax and rough metrics to underscore the jarring, rebellious tone of the lament:[29]

> Had with moorning the Gods, left their willes undon,
>   They had not so soone herited such a soule:
> Or if the mouth, tyme dyd not glooton up all.
>   Nor I, nor the world, were depriv'd of my Sonne.
>
> (C3v; ll. 1–4)

The image of Time as a gluttonous mouth suggests the emptying of meaning that Freud describes as the experience of the melancholic: "In mourning it is the world which has become poor and empty; in melancholia it is the ego itself."[30] The wound of child-loss—that is, the empty womb—is figured as the empty mouth, and Vere's maternal laments are the effusions of that difficult rupture, attempting to fill the void left by the child's death with language that reincorporates the lost object into the maternal body.[31] The maternal mourner's fantasy of incorporation not only provokes Vere's imagery of the gluttonous mouth of Time, but also prompts her own transgressive language of maternal lamentation. Her second sonnet turns to the image of the eaten heart to represent her own perpetual self-consumption: "In dolefull wayes I spend the wealth of my time:/Feeding on my heart, that ever comes agen" (C3v, ll. 1–2).[32] The merger of the bodies of mother and child constructs empathetic mourning as a self-consumption that simultaneously devours the lost child and gives voice to this unprofitable feeding. In its insistence upon the literal, material conditions of childbirth and child-loss as authorizing the metaphor of consumption, Vere's maternal mourning values excess as a symptom of the unfilled and irreparable void left by the empty womb.

As a symptom of her own wounded womb, Mary Carey's poem, "Upon the Sight of my abortive Birth the 31th: of December 1657," illustrates not only the poet's difficult acceptance of the masculine call to moderate sorrow but also, as Jonathan Sawday points out, the degree to which the view of flawed femininity grounded on scriptural texts "acted as a means of fashioning an internalized system of suppression and domination."[33] Certainly Carey's poem, unlike the sonnets of Anne de Vere, is thoroughly rooted in scriptural authority, as her copious marginal citations of Old and New Testament loci (thirty of them in a poem of ninety-two lines) reveal. Much of the poem recites not only conventional metaphors for female fertility but also commonplaces of Christian consolation. Thus we hear that despite the deaths of five infant children prior to this miscarriage, God still loans two surviving offspring to Carey: "My living pretty payre; Nat: & Bethia;/the Childrene deare, (God yett lends to Maria)."[34] She prays, "Lett not my hart, (as doth my wombe) miscarrie" (l. 74), echoing the language with which Josselin's diary records his wife's near-miscarriage a year before Carey's: "This morning my wife thought shee miscarried, lord a miscarrying womb is a sad affliction, keepe us from a miscarrying heart."[35] While Carey's unpublished poem and Josselin's diary share the allegory of miscarriage as symptomatic of spiritual health, only Carey, as a female, can fully experience the sad affliction of the miscarrying womb. As such, her deployment of the scriptural metaphors of reproduction, or more correctly, her representation of birth as a matter of the soul rather than the body, cannot forget the physical womb and bears the imprint of the material female body throughout.[36] In the mouth of a female speaker, whether literally or only figuratively connected to a female body, the issue of the womb is not *only* metaphoric. Rather, the female voice insists upon the material facts of the body and its issue, particularly as it mourns the loss of that issue. This naturalization of maternity as a matter of the womb, then, enables Carey's poem to negotiate doctrinal calls to moderate sorrow in order to transvalue the faulty womb and its all-too-perishable fruit. Carey's struggle to assert the experience of the female body as a grounds on which to validate maternal mourning constitutes female subjectivity in the poem.

This insistence on the material facts of birth and child-loss begins in the poem's title, where the *sight* of the abortive birth and its date both serve to underscore the physicality of the miscarriage as a real event—a death—to which the speaker reacts and that she seeks to memorialize.[37] The physical presence of the corpse in women's lamentation reflects the feminine culture of early modern mourning, which placed women in a unique intimacy with bodies in death: thus Gertrude Thimelby's elegy for her father, "Upon a Command to Write on my Father," positions the speaker before the body itself en route to burial: "Teares I could soone have brought unto this hearse,/And thoughts, and sighs, but you command a verse."[38] Grace, Lady Mildmay's "Meditation upon her [that is, her husband's] Corpse," similarly, takes place in the presence of the departed: "Let me behold my corpse which lieth folden in cerecloths, leaded and coffined here before me yet unburied, and consider: he was a man, and as he is, I shall be."[39] Carey's gesture toward presence continues in the poem's opening lines, where the speaker imagines herself to be in the physical presence of the lost fetus, looking upon its material reality as she begins the meditative process of allegorizing and spiritualizing the loss: "What birth is this; a poore despissed creature?/A little Embrio; voyd of life, and feature" (ll. 1–2). Carey's description of the fetus as a "poore despissed creature" implicitly questions the benevolence of a God who would despise his own (innocent) creation and suggests her struggle with the idea of original sin as an orthodox explanation of the death of newborns. Thomas Tuke's *A Discourse of Death* (1613), for instance, reveals the resistance of some of his parishioners to this doctrine as he reiterates the rationale that "death is not the condition of Nature, but the Daughter and desert of sinne." He explains, "But you will say, How is it that Infants of a day olde doe dye, seeing that they commit no sinne? I answere, Sinne is either the corruption of nature, or any evill which proceedes as the fruits thereof; or thus, sinne is either originall, or actuall: the former is in Infants, though not the latter."[40] While Carey's poem opens in the transgressive realm of material experience, it quickly turns toward restraint in a review of Carey's maternal history and her assertion of her acceptance of God's will in the outcomes of her deliveries:

> Seven tymes I went my tyme; when mercy giving
>   deliverance unto me: & mine all living:
> Stronge, right-proportioned, lovely Girles, & boyes
>   There father; Mother's present hope't for Joyes:

That was greate wisedome, goodnesse, power love praise
to my deare lord; lovely in all his wayes:

This is no lesse; ye same God hath it donne;
submits my hart, thats better than a sonne.

(ll. 4–11)

Moreover, Carey asserts a Calvinist faith in the predestination of her
unborn child, which converts the fetus from a "poore despissed creature" to a soule in bliss: "And that this babe (as well as all the
rest,)/since 't had a soule, shalbe for ever blest" (ll. 18–19). She thus
enacts her momentary challenge to God's will and enables it by staging
her return to orthodoxy.[41]

If Carey's expressions of moderate mourning emerge from her resistance to it, however, that resistance reasserts itself throughout the poem
in her relentless use of the imagery of female reproduction, already
tainted by the indelible imprint of the poem's opening sight. When she
turns to God to discover "the reason why he tooke in hand his rodd"
(l. 35), God himself enters the poem as a speaker who adjusts his
language to the level and experience of the maternal mourner:

Methinkes I heare Gods voyce, this is thy sinne;
    And Conscience justifies ye same within:

Thou often dost present me with dead frute;
    Why should not my returns, thy presents sute:
Dead dutys; prayers; praises thou doest bring,
    affections dead; dead hart in every thinge:
. . . .
Whose taught or better'd by ye no Relation;
    thou'rt Cause of Mourning, not of Immitation
                                    (ll. 38–43, 46–7)

Carey's God attributes to the female mourner the "dead frute" literalized in the aborted embryo, thereby suggesting not only the retributive
nature of the affliction ("Why should not my returns, thy presents sute")
but also the spiritual lesson to be taken from this graphic embodiment
of her sin: "Mend now, my Child," God advises her, "& lively frute
bring me" (l. 50). The episode is characteristic of Carey's meditative
stance toward God in her other poems of maternal mourning, where her
deal-making and claims of "equivalent parenthood" with God in her
children's creation illustrate that, as Helen Wilcox states, "the ability to

hold her own with God is Mary Carey's outstanding quality."[42] In her poem "On the death of my 4th & only Child, Robert Payler," for instance, Carey proposes an exchange of her son for God's with the audacious statement, "Change with me; doe, as I have done/give me thy all; Even thy deare sonne."[43] In a revision of Mornay's consolatory reminder that, "[God] hath spared our sonne, that spared not his owne onely begotten for us" (A5), Carey reverses the relationship between believer and God by suggesting that the model of maternal sacrifice—*her* willingness to surrender all in the sacrifice of her child—ought to prompt God to offer his son in recompense for her loss.[44] Her interjection of the language of physical reproduction into the spiritual discourses of salvation, based on her willing surrender of the child—"a lovely bonne"—to God, continues as the poem concludes with a prayer for the speaker's "quikning":

> In my whole Life; lively doe thou make me:
>   for thy praise. And name's sake, O quicken mee:
>
> Lord I begg quickning grace; that grace aford;
>   quicken me lord according to they word.
>
> It is a lovely bonne I make to thee.
>   after thy loving Kindnesse quicken mee:
>
> Thy quickning Spirit unto me convey;
>   And thereby Quicken me; in thine owne way:
>
> And lett the Presence of thy spirit deare,
>   be witnessd by his fruts; lett them appeare.
>   (ll. 76–87)

As a prayer not only for spiritual quickening but also for a pregnancy that will result in the delivery of "lively frute," the poem concludes on the material grounds on which it began, rooting its reciprocal vision of what is due to the obedient speaker firmly in the physical body of maternal mourning.

*

Bringing Elizabeth Jocelin's *The Mothers Legacie to her Unborne Childe* (1624) to press following the author's death, Thomas Goad inserts an "Approbation," which briefly describes her life and death and commends the book to the reader on the basis of its author's "piety and humility."[45] As simultaneously a confirmation or sanction, and a trial, the approbation elaborates the figure of the text as the author's will, describing Jocelin, first and foremost, as a subject before the law: "Our lawes disable those that are under *Covert-baron*, from disposing by Will and Testament any temporall estate. But no law prohibiteth any professor of morall and spiritual riches, to impart them unto others, either in life or in death by bequeathing."[46] While Jocelin, like any *femme covert* in the period, was prohibited from owning or disposing of property without the consent of her husband, Goad puts forth a second, more compelling law to justify the publication of her legacy. Under this moral law, Jocelin's sex (while, admittedly a "debility") actually recommends this exceptional work for publication, since it is "the rather worthy, because proceeding from the weaker sex."[47] Thus Goad explains, "I willingly not only subscribed my *Approbat* for the registering of this *Will*, among the most publike Monuments . . . but also, as bound to doe right unto knowne vertue, undertooke the care of the publication thereof my selfe."[48] While Goad's intervention renders Jocelin's text a "most publike Monument," her own dedicatory epistle to her husband predicates the work on its self-avowed and intended privacy. In fear of "the danger that might prevent me from executing that care I so exceedingly desired, I mean in the religious training of our child," Jocelin explains, "I send it [the treatise] only to the eyes of a most loving husband, and a child exceedingly beloved, to whom I hope it will not be altogether unprofitable."[49]

For Jocelin, privacy guarantees her self-representation as a dutiful mother and obedient wife. It is only after her death that the private document can become a "publike Monument," a translation enabled by the maternal corpse itself. The dissolution and self-consumption figured by maternal mourners as their appropriate, if unorthodox, responses to child-loss are literalized as the condition upon which the mother's legacy can be printed. The public monument of this text, in effect, memorializes the private work of mourning performed in the household by a woman whose pregnancy had been "as then travelling with death itself."[50] Like a Rachel who mourns the loss of her child even in the afterlife, Jocelin's work—written during her pregnancy, her child literally incorporated within her flesh—interrogates and troubles the boundaries between self and other, public and private, in terms that echo maternal elegies' preoccupations with the body of death. Goad's report that Jocelin, in a prophetic moment early in her pregnancy, "secretly tooke order for the buying of a new winding sheet" and, following the birth of her daughter, "instantly called for her winding-sheet to bee brought forth and laid upon her,"[51] illustrates the translation from private fear to public performance implicit in the narrative of maternal death in child-bearing. The winding sheet, secretly procured, becomes the main prop with which Jocelin stages her memorable good death. Significantly, Goad locates the unfolding of this drama in a strangely crowded privacy where Jocelin communes with God, with the inscrutable "bowels" of the maternal mourner herself, and ultimately (in Goad's quotation of the text's opening sentence), with the reader:

> And about that time undauntedly looking death in the face, privately in her Closet between God and her, she wrote these pious Meditations: whereof her selfe strangely speaketh to her own bowels in this manner, *It may seeme strange to thee to receive these lines from a Mother, that dyed when thou wert borne.*[52]

Jocelin's Closet—at once public and private, self-enclosed and repro-ductive, singular and plural, living and dead—is an apt figure for the period's complex representations of the body of maternal mourning.[53]

Celeste Schenck has argued that the "coherence of a female funeral aesthetic across centuries suggests that women poets have clearly enjoyed an elegiac mode of their own, an intertextually verifiable tradi-tion of mourning their dead in a poetic form that calls the genre, as patriarchally codified, into question."[54] While maternal mourners clearly employ similar strategies for establishing feminine subjectivity as a func-tion of maternity and its proper grief, it is important to stress that the transgressive discourse of maternal mourning is not purely or simply a matter of the body: that is, the early modern gendering of grief enables women—as well as men, as we have seen—to posit an affective bond between mother and child that, in turn, underwrites the construction of femininity by means of gestures that describe and attend mothers' tears. If maternity is naturalized in the early modern period insofar as it masks the origins that produce it, maternal mourners make use of this essen-tialized notion to enable and energize their textual performances of grief as uniquely feminine. The case of maternal mourning illustrates vividly the essentialist interpretation of women's grief more generally in the early modern period, which sees emotional excess as a natural function of women's weak, immoderate bodies. *Represented* as a matter of the body, maternal lament remains a resistant, self-conscious, constructed voice that interrogates the gendering of mourning from which it evolves by exposing the cultural desires and demands that insist upon feminine immoderation as the exiled but necessary means of creating the social body of mourning and its stable, unarguable sex. It is an index of the gendering of grief in the early modern period and an example of one of the strategies available to women to express a female subjectivity that might otherwise have remained forever entombed in silence.

CHAPTER 14

"MINE OWN BREAKING": RESISTANCE, GENDER, AND TEMPORALITY IN SEVENTEENTH-CENTURY ENGLISH ELEGIES AND JONSON'S "EUPHEME"

W. SCOTT HOWARD

—Even losing you (the joking voice, a gesture
I love) I shan't have lied. It's evident
the art of losing's not too hard to master
though it may look like (Write it!) like disaster.
                    —Elizabeth Bishop, "One Art," 1976

Rest in soft peace, and, asked, say here doth lie
Ben Jonson his best piece of poetry.
For whose sake, henceforth, all his vows be such,
As what he loves may never like too much.
                    —Ben Jonson, "On My First Son," 1603

Although modernist poets, such as Elizabeth Bishop, may strive against the poetic elegy's conventional rhetorical movement from lamentation to praise to consolation, their attempted repudiations of the genre's tradition in fact recapitulate one of elegy's most central topoi: the representation of a loss that exceeds signification. Indeed, one of the genre's oldest concerns is the resistance to consolation, which nonetheless furnishes a diminished solace by way of rhetorical negation. Jahan Ramazani distinguishes the "traditional" from the "modern" elegy, claiming that the former—epitomized by John Milton's "Lycidas" (1645)—performs an "art of saving" through which the poet achieves

positive consolation; the latter—exemplified by Bishop's elegiac villanelle, "One Art" (1976)—an "art of losing" within and against which
the poet resists consolation, thereby performing oppositional cultural
work through the elegy's critique of the social conventions that govern
private grief expression and public mourning practice.[1]

However, that paradigm, while useful for Ramazani's study's scope of
modern Anglo-American poetry from Hardy and Owen to Stevens and
Plath, proves to be grounded upon a tenuous dichotomy when it is
noted, as Ramazani reluctantly admits (9, 361), that elegiac resistance to
consolation significantly inflects virtually all of the genre's earliest and
more recent avatars—from, for example, Bion's "Lament for Adonis"
(c. 100 BCE) to Lyn Hejinian's "*Elegy, for K. B.*" (1992).[2] While the
resistance to consolation does persist across elegy's transhistorical spec-
trum, specific articulations of and consequences from that counter-
discourse in the Western poetics of loss change significantly for the
poetic elegy during the early modern and modern eras, just as those factors also shift in important and altogether different ways for the Greek
lament between the sixth and fifth centuries BCE and for psychoanalytic
theories of grief and mourning from Freud to Klein.[3]

This chapter concerns a particular kind of resistance within and transgression against the English elegy's modal characteristics that emerges
during the seventeenth century and thereby signals, I wish to argue, a
truly modern development in the genre's historical and discursive realities that may be witnessed in elegiac poems centuries apart, such as Ben
Jonson's "On My First Son" and Bishop's "One Art": a heightened
sense of the linguistic negotiation of loss together with an increasingly
resistant, intratextual consolation. Just as Jonson, in this expression of
grief for his son's death from plague, looks to the craft of writing for
comfort and deftly turns not outward (toward extratextual resources)
but inward (toward intratextual poetics) to achieve consolation—"his
best piece of poetry"[4]—Bishop, too, in her elegiac villanelle about losses
both personal and public, underscores her poem's inherent "art of losing" as a linguistic vehicle for grief's remedy—"(*Write it!*)."[5] This
heightened textuality of loss, in each poem, accordingly emphasizes the
intratextuality of elegiac resistance shaped as a form of and place for consolation, thereby underscoring the inherent irony in that rhetorical
proposition. Both writers thus conclude their engagements with this
new, modern work of mourning with strong qualifications for the role of
elegiac resistance: Jonson's ending couplet—"all his vows be such,/As
what he loves may never like too much" (48; 11–12)—projecting a classical distrust of hubris upon the poem's internalized text for grief;
Bishop's polyptoton—"like ... like disaster" (19)—foregrounding the

poem's deliberate artifice in a modernist strategy to enact and simultaneously contain the work's thematic and formal erosion under such internalized pressure from grief's inward articulation.[6]

Prior to the early modern era, English elegies and elegiac texts conventionally ground the telos of interpersonal expressions of grief and social practices of mourning upon a sacred locus of consolation that resides in an atemporal realm beyond the representational limits of literary art. Such a perspective bodied forth through a poetic work would uphold the doctrinal, Christian views that death is the will of God and that an immoderate outpouring of sorrow (especially in public) is tantamount to doubting God's divine purpose.[7] As the poets of "The Wanderer" (c. 940) and *The Pearl* (c. 1375) respectively emphasize, human suffering—though inevitable in this world of earthy temporality, change, and physical decay—conditions the possibility for the regenerate soul's eternal bliss, where "all stability resides"[8] in "Jerusalem new and royally dight,/As from the heavens descended."[9] In these and other poetic utterances of grief and mourning from the tenth through the fifteenth centuries, elegiac resistance underscores the finite mutability of this world and, by way of contrast, the infinite rewards of heavenly peace.[10] Resistance to consolation thus articulates, in early English elegiac works, a crisis of signification at the limit of the mourner's grief and the poem's discourse that yields to higher, extratextual principles. This traditional placement of consolation and an accordingly limited role of elegiac resistance persists for the scope of English elegiac poetry through much of the sixteenth century as well, but begins to shift somewhere in the early seventeenth century, thereby marking an epistemological break between the Renaissance and the early modern historical imagination.[11]

I argue that the elegy's historical and discursive realities change in at least four interrelated ways during the seventeenth century, each new characteristic bearing witness to transformations, on a cultural level, of the subject's greater autonomy as an "individual" within ecclesiastical, domestic, and civil spheres of discourse.[12] These four changes address: a heightened psychological experience of grief and the mourning process; intratextual elegiac resistance; the linguistic constitution of subjectivity and gender; and the placement of consolation within the context of human temporality. Together these new factors signal, I believe, the true emergence of the modern poetic elegy. While elegiac resistance (since the works of Bion and Moschus, Theocritus and Virgil) has always been integral to the genre's rhetorical structure, the increasingly linguistic and temporal nature of that resistance engaged as an intratextual, antithetical form of consolation occurs as a direct consequence of secularizing forces in early modern culture.

This chapter examines Jonson's elegiac verse and, in particular, "Eupheme" (1640)—his longest original poem and perhaps his best defense of poetry—within these contexts of cultural and literary transformation in seventeenth-century England by focusing, first of all, upon new developments in burial practices and mourning customs. A comparative study of burial rites first prescribed by *The Book of Common Prayer* (1549–59) and later overturned by *The Directory for Public Worship* (1645) illustrates the conflicting sacred and secular forces driving the growing anxiety of early modern individuals about their own subjectivity, gender, and authority to make public their private sorrows. A subsequent analysis of a related cultural shift from a rigorous to a more compassionate rhetoric of consolation in the late sixteenth and early seventeenth centuries—exemplified respectively by Thomas Becon's *The Sicke mannes Salue* (1560) and Jeremy Taylor's *The Rule and Exercises of Holy Dying* (1651)—underscores, within that context of increasing freedom for an individual's grief expression, an inherent gendering of mourning practices within the social discourse that generally required women to contain their grief within the private sphere of their own spiritual self-reckonings, and permitted men greater degrees of public agency for their works of mourning. The chapter then investigates, within and against that scope of contesting mourning customs, the ways in which various English elegies and elegiac poems from the seventeenth century—including Katherine Philips' "On the death of my first and dearest childe, Hector Philipps" (1667); and John Milton's "On Time" (1645) and "How Soon Hath Time" (1645)—increasingly exhibit those modern generic characteristics noted above (i.e., psychological grief, intratextual elegiac resistance, gendered subjectivity, and temporal consolation).

Jonson's "Eupheme," I will argue, demonstrates neither a purely Tacitean concern with historical contingencies, nor a purely stoic anti-historicist retreat into aesthetics, but enacts, through juxtapositions of temporal forms within a linguistic structure of occasion, a critique of monumental history. His elegy for Venetia Digby builds a timely monument to her timeless characteristics that manifest themselves in forms of lived human action that counter poetic representation. Jonson infuses elegiac resistance with gendered temporality, praising the feminine, eternal virtue of Digby's mind—"a thing that cannot sit" (238; 8)—through his text's deliberate, internal deconstruction. "Eupheme" thematically and literally breaks apart, each site of topical and formal erasure signifying the poet's masculine command of intratextual, elegiac resistance and iconoclastic historiography: "in her fall,/I sum up mine own breaking, and wish all" (241; 25–26). Jonson's elegy for the patron he affectionately called his "muse" thus offers a deft commentary upon the artistic impulse to monumentalize the past and thereby rejoins early modern debates concerning the role of funerary monuments in the representation of personal and public history.

The Tragical Act: Contexts for Grief and Mourning

Never did the English nation behold so much black worn as there was at her funeral. It was then but put on to try if it were fit, for the great day of mourning was set down in the book of Heaven to be held afterwards. That was but the dumb show: the tragical act hath been playing ever since.

—Thomas Dekker, *The Wonderfull yeare*, 1603

The seventeenth century in England was an era of unprecedented deaths and changing ideas about private grief expression and public practices of burial and mourning that were magnified, in 1603, by Queen Elizabeth's elaborate funeral and the first major epidemic of the plague. As Thomas Dekker reflects, the Queen's funeral, though momentous, "was but the dumb show."[13] Between 1592 and 1665 Londoners suffered through six plague outbreaks: that beginning in 1603 lasting for eight years; that beginning in 1636, twelve.[14] The plague, however, was merely one contributing factor in the nation's larger scope of tragedy. For the average person, life during these times was indeed not far off from the extreme condition of "Warre" that Thomas Hobbes theorizes in *Leviathan* (1651): "no Society; and which is worst of all, continuall feare, and danger of violent death; And the life of man, solitary, poore, nasty, brutish, and short."[15] John Graunt, author of *Natural and Political Observations* (1662), the first published statistical analysis of death in England, estimated that, during the first half of the century, "about thirty six *per centum* of all quick conceptions, died before six years old" (30).

The cultural codes for private grief expression and public mourning rites undergo a major transformation during the seventeenth century due to the decreasing role of the Church in the regulation of death and burial and the concomitant augmentation of State control. An attendant "anxiety over death" emerges due to a cluster of significant factors implicated in the early modern subject's new civil autonomy: an ideological distinction—rather than a theologically based notion of continuity—between the living and the dead; the prohibition of internments in church graveyards and consequent use of public graveyards; an intellectual emphasis upon the soul's difference (and separation at time of death) from the body; general superstitions about physical decay that led to the widespread coffining of corpses and gave rise to the embalmer's profession; and a growing desire for commemorations of worldly experience that, in turn, generated an increase in funeral sermons and the erection of tombs.[16] While the origins of this administrative shift in England toward greater state regulation of religious practices can be traced back to the mid-sixteenth century with the dissemination, within *The Book of Common Prayer*, of *An Act for the Uniformity of Common Prayer and Divine Service* (1549–59), the most drastic change in the nation's ideology of death, grief, burial and mourning customs occurs eighty-six years later with the publication of *The Directory for Public Worship* (1645), which outlines a civil service for the burial of the dead that stresses the individual's—not the priest's—authority to conduct the ceremony "decently and with order."[17] Mortality, which had hitherto been absolutely central to the orthodoxy of the Church, thus became pivotal as well in the constitution of a national ethos during the seventeenth century (Graunt 77–79). The subject's experience of death was no longer a purely personal and religious concern; it was now a civil matter.

Through most of the sixteenth century death and burial, grief and mourning were communal and ecclesiastical affairs (Gittings 7–17). Deaths typically occurred in the home, and communities were bound together through interpersonal relationship and mutual involvement with local churches. Death and life were held to be indivisible because the Church established a continuum between both poles of human experience—a tenet that Thomas Becon invokes, for example, near the conclusion of his dialogue, *The Sicke mannes Salue* (1560). Here Philemon consoles Epaphroditus, the sick man, that he will, upon departing this world, "straight-ways go" unto the joys of Heaven "and for evermore enjoy them."[18] *The Sicke mannes Salue* was "one of the most popular religious tracts of the sixteenth and early seventeenth centuries,"[19] going through nineteen separate editions between 1560 and 1632, and was probably composed before 1553, during the apex of the most rigorous stoicism concerning grief expression and mourning customs. For Becon, therefore, neither the individual's inner struggle with grief nor their emotional need to mourn warranted significant reflection.

Becon accordingly never discusses the subject of "grief" (as such) in *The Sicke mannes Salue* despite the fact that the idea of "grief" as signifying "mental pain, distress, or sorrow ... caused by loss or trouble" had been in English-language use since about 1350.[20] Likewise, "mourn"—"to feel sorrow, grief, or regret"—had been in use since c. 888; "mourning"—"feeling or expression of sorrow"—since c. 1250.[21] Becon abruptly dismisses mourning, noting, for example, that "mourning gowns, commonly used at funerals [are] not meet to be worn for those faithful who have entered the kingdom of God" (4; 120, 639). Becon's stoicism resonates with other "rigorist" writings in the *ars moriendi* tradition by theologians such as Hugh Latimer, Thomas Cartwright, and William Sclater (Pigman 32–36). For this rigorist attitude, the height of which G. W. Pigman locates during the reign of Edward VI (1547–53), consolation must ultimately rest with God, not with the individual's earthly needs, and thereby reaffirm the central role of the Church in the containment and proper channeling of strong emotions associated with loss. Excessive outpourings of sorrow for the death of a faithful Christian were tantamount to blasphemy, a principle that Jonson affirms in his brief poem "Of Death" from *Epigrams* (1616): "He that fears death, or mourns it, in the just,/Shows of the resurrection little trust" (45). From Plato to Cicero to Erasmus and well into the seventeenth century, the standard view was that all grief perishes with time and any prolonged venting of anguish or public observance of mourning was shameful and could be taken as a sign of effeminate weakness, mental distress, and amorality.[22]

Even for rigorists, though, the individual's need for compassion was difficult to ignore completely. The moderation of grief and duration of mourning therefore became among the most widely debated topics as theologians began to formulate a more sympathetic approach to consolation that would complement the changing needs of the subject's increasing domestic, ecclesiastical, and civil liberties. This new rhetoric of "compassionate" consolation begins to emerge after the death of Edward VI, perhaps as early as 1583 when, in a sermon, John Jewel defends the "natural affection" of grief: "The father if he feele not the deathe of his sonne: or, the sonne if he feele not the death of his Father, and haue not a deepe feeling of it, he is vnnatural."[23] Other theologians advocating compassionate consolation include Zacharie Boyd and James Cole, whose *Of Death a True Description* (1629), according to Pigman, advocates "mourning as a process that must run its course" and affirms that grief is "a necessary and helpful part of the process" (38). Later in the century Jeremy Taylor would invoke a similar view in *The Rule and Exercises of Holy Dying* (1651):

> Weep bitterly and make great moan, and use lamentation as he is worthy, and that a day or two, lest thou be evil spoken of; and then comfort thyself for thy heaviness. But take no grief to heart; for there is no turning again: thou shalt not do him good, but hurt thyself.[24]

Within this span of nearly seventy years, as the ideology of compassionate consolation began to take shape, there was little agreement about the proper duration for either the private expression of grief or the public observance of mourning. Although Taylor, in 1651, suggests "a day or two," Cole, in 1629, supports much longer periods of mourning: thirty days of lamentation for Moses; seventy for Jacob (Pigman 37–38). By the end of the Stuart era, according to David Cressy, "it was not thought improper to observe formal mourning for a year, though full compliance with this evolving etiquette was rare."[25]

Lawrence Stone, Philippe Aries, and Sara van den Berg also link an advance in compassionate consolation with the rise of individualism and an attendant need to assuage new subjective anxieties about death and the afterlife, which gather in response to the decreasing presence of the Church and the expanding role of government in the regulation of death and burial.[26] However, Ralph Houlbrooke and Anne Laurence hesitate to posit a paradigmatic improvement of the English emotional climate during the seventeenth century. Houlbrooke associates increased compassion in funeral sermons with the abolition of the doctrine of Purgatory, though not necessarily with a consequential diminishment of the individual's anxiety about death and bereavement.[27] Laurence charts a pervasive feeling of abruptness and resignation in expressions of grief that does not simply indicate a lack of affection, but rather "a more conscious process of withdrawal by the living person from the dying or the dead" necessitated in part by the popular belief that prolonged outpourings of grief could lead to fatal illness (Houlbrooke 74–75).

Juliana Schiesari has theorized the emergence, during the Renaissance, of "homo melancholicus," arguing that "melancholia ... became an elite 'illness' that afflicted *men* precisely as the *sign* of their exceptionality, as the inscription of genius within them."[28] Social discourses of grief and mourning were also strongly inflected by gender distinctions. For both men and women, though, grief expression was only permissible within culturally prescribed limits. If immoderate grief and mourning by a man could signify effeminacy, irrationality, and blasphemy, then similar outpourings of emotion exhibited by a woman might also signify not only irrationality and blasphemy, but licentiousness as well due to, on the one hand, the cultural mandates of silence, chastity, and obedience for virtuous, Christian women and, on the other, the gendering of the private sphere as feminine; the public, masculine.[29] These roles and values could be exaggerated, complicated, and even reversed, however, depending upon the gender of the mourner and the mourned as well as the occasion and audience for the individual's remediation of grief. Just as a melancholy disposition could convey masculine, artistic genius, profound grief and elegiac resistance could also be shaped into vehicles for historical reflection—Aemilia Lanyer's "The Description of Cooke-ham" (1611)—or political protest—An Collins' "A Song composed in time of the Civill Warr" (1653)—as well as for private emotional catharsis and inadvertent literary achievement—Henry King's "The Exequy" (1657). Despite the prevalent social and theological taboos concerning unrestricted grief expression, many men and women of the seventeenth century found numerous ways to transform their utterances of private anguish into public works of mourning. The manners in which those cultural restrictions impinge upon elegies and elegiac texts reveal the importance of elegiac resistance, gender, and temporality as tropes for social agency in an early modern poetics of loss.

In Strictest Measure Even: Intratextuality and Historicity

What bulky Heaps of doleful Rhymes I see!
Sure all the world runs mad with Elegy;
Lords, Ladies, Knights, Priests, Souldiers, Squires, Physicians,
Beaux, Lawyers, Merchants, Prentices, Musicians,
Play'rs, Footmen, Pedants, Scribes of all Conditions.

—Anonymous, 1695

By the end of the seventeenth century, as the anonymous elegist intones with gentle irony,[30] the market for elegiac poetry had reached new heights. Within this era of unprecedented losses of life due primarily to disease and warfare, the poetic elegy bears witness to the individual's heightened difficulty to achieve unqualified consolation in an increasingly secular society. For poets, the genre's trope of elegiac resistance consequently plays a key role in the poetics of loss. Whereas in earlier elegies and elegiac works from the Middle Ages and Renaissance, as noted above, the text's resistance to consolation signified a limit to poetic discourse and the concomitant submission of the mourner to extratextual, higher powers of the spirit and God's will, in the early modern period elegiac resistance increasingly comes to signify the poem's intratextual construction of loss, the mourning process, the gendering of grief and the forms of and places for consolation within the realm of human time. This new temporality, however, does not emerge uniformly during the century, but follows a persistent, albeit meandering, path of development.

While grief pertains to the individual's personal (and internalized) experience, mourning concerns social practice—that is, the externalized, public manifestation of emotional and psychological forces that remain largely hidden within those who struggle with loss.[31] Because the poetic elegy combines three fundamental modes of expression integral to both grief and mourning—lamentation, praise, and consolation—the genre is therefore uniquely poised to negotiate tensions between private and public spheres of discourse. An elegy serves as a vehicle for the transformation of loss into gain, absence into presence, sorrow into solace, and also—by logical extension—of the past into the wished-for present and/or future. The genre thus is inherently implicated in the philosophy of time. Prior to the early modern era, the English elegy articulates a place for sorrow in the realm of earthly temporality and particularity; for solace, in that of heavenly atemporality and universality. As Zacharie Boyd writes in *The Last Battell of the Soule in Death* (1628), "Nowe that which *Time* can doe to a *Pagane*, let Grace doe it to a Christian,"[32] implying that since grief perishes with time, grace, for a Christian, extinguishes anguish and engenders true rest from earthly contingency. In the seventeenth century, however, the poetic elegy begins to situate consolation within temporal contexts, offering intratextual resistance as a form of and place for both solace and the poem's contribution to historical discourse. The elegy thus comes to illustrate the individual's most inward apprehension not only of their own spiritual self-reckoning, but of his or her historical imagination; the genre itself thereby takes on a heightened chronotopic significance and reveals—more intimately than a cultural-material genealogy of horology, chronometry, and chronography—an early modern poetics of temporality particular to the aesthetics of literary discourse.[33]

Katherine Philips' elegy "On the death of my first and dearest childe, Hector Philipps" (1667) offers one of the most striking illustrations of the genre's early modern intratextuality. Like "The Wanderer" and *The Pearl*, Philips' poem also voices grief within and against the grain of elegiac resistance. Philips' stronger qualification of solace, however, turns such resistance inward upon the text's remediation of sorrow. In her elegy for Hector, who lived less than six weeks, Philips attempts to accommodate her distress to the genre's conventions in the third stanza: "Tears are my Muse, and sorrow all my Art,/So piercing groans must be thy Elogy."[34] Yet the text turns from this point toward the registers of pure lament, or the dirge, as Philips continues to doubt unqualified consolation. The elegy's concluding stanzas articulate both the poet's renunciation of the "unconcerned World" (15) and her utter abandonment to (and growing self-consciousness of) the poem's linguistic construction of loss and elegiac resistance, finally offering the work's "gasping numbers" (19) as a qualified intratextual resolution for Philips' (and her elegy's) crises of expression and signification.

Kate Lilley asserts that early modern English women's elegies are "unusually mobile" and disrupt "the putative divisions between high and low culture, literary and non-literary ... private and public, occasional and non-occasional writing."[35] However, the transition from private to public speech was often intractable for women writers not only because the public realm was culturally constructed as a male domain and the private as female, but because reading, writing, and publishing were subversive acts for women and were commonly troped as signs of disease, madness, and promiscuity.[36] An immoderate expression of grief by a woman either in speech or print would therefore require either the erasure or elision of her subjectivity. Whereas Philips concludes her poem for Hector with a consolatory gift—"The last of thy unhappy Mothers Verse" (20)—that turns upon the proposed negation of her own identity as a writer, An Collins, who figures herself in verse as a Bride of Christ, employs the poetic elegy in a devotional practice of self-abnegation in the service of Christian morality. In the majority of elegies in her only known volume, *Divine Songs and Meditacions* (1653), Collins articulates devotion and dissent, praise and social protest through the conversion of physical and spiritual strife into redemptive knowledge both for herself and her imagined readers.[37]

The elegy's early modern characteristics, though, follow an uneven path of emergence, as illustrated by Milton's "On Time" and elegiac sonnet "How Soon Hath Time." Although both works first appeared in the 1645 edition of Milton's poems, "On Time" was perhaps composed as late as 1637; "How Soon Hath Time," in 1632. "On Time" achieves the more conventional formulation of atemporal consolation by celebrating the loss of physical, earthly "mortal dross"[38] and the spiritual gain of the soul's blissful "individual kiss" (12). The elegy accordingly places solace within a timeless realm where, "Attired with stars, we shall for ever sit,/Triumphing over Death, and Chance, and thee O Time" (21–22). "How Soon Hath Time," though written five years before "On Time," tenuously accommodates the timely realm of human action to the timelessness of God's providence and thereby offers, I believe, one of the best examples of an early-seventeenth-century elegiac poem poised on the cusp of new secular ideas about time, human history, and historical interpretation.

Within time's "strictest measure even" (10), the poet's spiritual fulfillment "shall be still" (10)—revealing at once, as Milton's apt use of "still" implies, both the temporality and atemporality of the poet's elegiac resistance. Thus his "inward ripeness" will nevertheless remain (*still*) within time and will also be timelessly at rest (*still*) within God's suspension of time. Time thus leads the poet, in both of these senses, to God's providential reckoning: "Toward which time leads me, and the will of heaven" (12). Time's measure is God's eternal "As ever" (14).

Milton's subtle qualifications—*yet, or, however, if, as*—throughout the sestet further emphasize this paradox of elegiac resistance posited as a form of and place for consolation. According to the tally of grace, as the sonnet's last two lines assert, the poet's use of earthly time will manifest a heavenly measure: "All is, if I have grace to use it so,/As ever in my great task-master's eye" (13–14). Milton's final and ironic image of God as a great "task-master," I believe, underscores again the sonnet's balanced combination of virtuous human acts, which unfold within time, and divine acts, which comprehend time. The poem's consolation therefore imbricates the temporal present (*all is*) within the atemporal eternal (*as ever*) through the text's *strictest measure even*—that is, the work's trope for both sacred and secular historicity achieved through the sonnet's elegiac resistance.

As the seventeenth-century English subject increasingly became the nexus of cultural and discursive transformations from theocentric to more secular ideologies of private grief expression and social mourning rites, the poetic elegy reflected the individual's growing sense of new distinctions (rather than continuities) between death and life, body and soul, time and eternity. The early modern elegy thus not only contributed significantly to the nation's civil refashioning of death and burial, grief and mourning—what Graunt defined as "observations" upon mortality "both Political, and Natural" (6)—but also to the emergence of the individual's historical imagination.

May Every Line Be You: Praising Presence in Jonson's "Eupheme"

> I call you muse; now make it true:
> Henceforth may every line be you;
> That all may say, that see the frame,
> This is no picture, but the same.
> —Ben Jonson, "Eupheme," 1640

Due primarily to the strong historiographic motives in his plays *Sejanus* (1603) and *Catiline* (1611), critics of Jonson's nondramatic verse generally frame their interpretations of his works' engagement with historical discourse in one of two ways. Either the poems demonstrate a historicism consonant with an early modern English revival of Tacitus (associated with the Essex circle);[39] or Jonson's poems embody an antihistoricism that resonates with the aesthetics of classical stoicism.[40] While these two interpretive perspectives may appear to be mutually exclusive, they reveal, I believe, a paradox at the very heart of Jonson's poetics: "Newness of sense, antiquity of voice!" (*Underwoods* "XIV,"

149; 60). In other words, Jonson's nondramatic verse consistently addresses both the timely and the timeless. His elegies and elegiac poems, I wish to argue, articulate neither a purely Tacitean concern with historical contingencies, nor a purely stoic antihistoricist withdrawal from public discourse, but often embody, through their subtle juxtapositions of temporal forms within linguistic structures of occasion, critiques of the impulse to monumentalize the past. The elegy and elegiac mode thus provide Jonson with a means of accommodating epitaphic brevity and timeliness to a meditation upon the timelessness of human factors—the soul, virtue, the mind, love, or friendship, for example—that most truly manifest themselves in living forms of action, which destabilize and evade the literary text's horizon of signification. Elegiac resistance therefore plays a key role in Jonson's works of mourning by inscribing an intratextual limit to representation against, through, and within which the poem concomitantly breaks on thematic and formal levels.

Jonson's elegies and elegiac poems all generally affirm the standard, doctrinal view that immoderate expressions of grief for a Christian who has justly died signify blasphemy. For example: "Of Death,"as noted above, delivers an admonition that those who either fear or mourn death "in the just" (45; 1) lack confidence in the resurrection; "To Heaven" concludes with an apology for the poet's expression of anguish for physical and spiritual tribulations ("Yet dare I not complain, or wish for death/With holy Paul, lest it be thought the breath/Of discontent; or that these prayers be/For weariness of life, not love of thee" [119; 23–26]); and "To K[ing] Charles and Q[ueen] Mary, for the Loss of Their First-Born" sternly advises that "Who dares deny, that all first fruits are due/To God, denies the God-head to be true" (206; 1–2). Despite such consistent stoic refrains, though, the majority of Jonson's poems that negotiate grief enact different practices of mourning for men than for women, thus conveying a strongly gendered poetics and politics of loss that inflects each text's articulation of and placement for solace. When the one mourned is a man (or male child), Jonson situates the work's consolation within the masculine-gendered public sphere—as in "To Sir Robert Wroth" and "On My First Son"—thus bestowing upon his subject a pattern for social agency that may move others to act virtuously within the realm of human affairs. When mourning a woman's (or female child's) death, Jonson grounds the elegiac poem's consolation either within the feminine-gendered domestic sphere—as in "To the World"—or in Heaven—as in "On My First Daughter"—thus displacing his subject from the "manly" (and timely) arena of social discourse while praising her virtue (and timeless) "female glory!" (*Miscellaneous Poems* "XXIX," 276; 8), though not entirely denying her some influence upon the realm of worldly action.

In "Eupheme" Jonson praises this feminine principle of timeless virtue, desiring to install a just representation of Venetia Digby's ineffable spirit within the poem's intratextual place of dwelling: "I call you muse; now make it true:/Henceforth may every line be you" (238; 21–22). Lady Digby's gendered temporality complements the changeless omniscience of History invoked in "The Mind of the Frontispiece to a Book": "By which as proper titles she is known/Time's witness, herald of antiquity,/The light of truth, and life of memory" (161; 16–18). As both mourner and historiographer in "Eupheme," Jonson creates a work of grief expression that celebrates the timelessness of Digby's characteristics—especially her intelligence and soul, both of which transcend artistic representation—through his elegy's crafted thematic and formal destabilization. Jonson thus tropes intratextual elegiac resistance as a means to praise the atemporality of his subject's feminine virtue and restrain his outpouring of grief while also maintaining masculine control over his poem's embodiment of iconoclastic historiography.

"Eupheme" engages with these principles of elegiac resistance, gender, and temporality most vividly through the work's treatment of the *ut pictura poesis* theme. In section 4, "The Mind," Jonson challenges a painter—possibly Anthony Van Dyck[41]—to create a faithful portrait of Venetia's intelligence and spirit, but quickly denounces the relevance of visual art because, as Jonson holds, only the poet may "draw a thing that cannot sit" (238; 8) and thereby apprehend, within a structure of linguistic dwelling, a form of lived action that paradoxically transgresses both literary and historical discourses. Once inscribed within the elegy's "bounds of beauty" (239; 51), this conceit of Digby's active virtue poses a formidable challenge to the poem's architecture:

> In thee, fair mansion, let it rest,
> Yet know, with what thou art possessed,
> Thou entertaining in thy breast,
> But such a mind, mak'st God thy guest.
>
> (240; 69–72)

The qualities of Lady Digby's mind and soul manifest themselves through the actions of her life; Jonson's elegy offers a tribute to those lived experiences. Yet the full significance of those forms of action— "that flame" (238; 15)—transgresses both language and temporality, slowly eroding the text's timely monument, breaking apart the poet's vehicle and intention:

> My wounded mind cannot sustain this stroke,
> It rages, runs, flies, stands, and would provoke
> The world to ruin with it; in her fall,
> I sum up mine own breaking, and wish all.
>
> (241; 23–26)

In "Eupheme" Jonson thus critiques, through the poem's thematic intratextual elegiac resistance, his own desire to create a monument to Lady Venetia Digby, and thereby offers a vision of poetic history neither purely contingent nor stoically aesthetic, but constitutively figural. On a formal level "Eupheme" also dramatizes that iconoclasm through the elegy's fragmentary and lost components—portions of sections two ("The song of her descent"), four ("The mind"), and ten ("Her inscription, or crown")—which enact the work's inward-turning of grief expression and restraint, structural composition and decomposition.[42] Through such thematic and formal gestures of intratextual elegiac resistance, Jonson ultimately accomplishes what the painter cannot: a tribute to his patron's timeless and singular characteristics that may only be apprehended within and against forms of timely action. Here, as in many of Jonson's elegies, the poet's monument to loss constitutes a form of praise through the movement of presence.

These rhetorical characteristics place Jonson's "Eupheme," thus posited as a vehicle for historical discourse, within an early modern tradition of iconoclastic historiography, exemplified by texts such as William Camden's *Remaines of a Greater Worke* (1605) and John Weever's *Ancient Funerall Monuments* (1631). During the late sixteenth and early seventeenth centuries, as Joshua Scodel observes, "the erection of magnificent tombs for the ostentatious display of lineage and rank became a veritable craze among the English nobility and gentry, who not only raised monuments to their next of kin but also built or rebuilt tombs for their illustrious (though sometimes imaginary) ancestors."[43] Weever, for example, criticizes such vainglorious exhibitions, arguing that "sepulchres should bee made according to the qualitie and degree of the person deceased, that by the Tombe every one might be discerned of what ranke he was living."[44] Jonson's elegy for Venetia Digby affirms this perspective, offering an iconoclastic critique of monumental history grounded in the premise that only poetry can justly commemorate the forms of lived human action that evade other

artistic media. On this point it is intriguing to note that both Jonson
and his stepfather were, for a time, bricklayers. During the late sixteenth century in England, bricklayers, rather than sculptors, custom-
arily designed and built tombs and funeral monuments.[45] Jonson's
elegiac resistance in this case, as in his quarrel with painting in
"Eupheme," shapes his own expression of grief according to a context
for action both personal and public.

PART VII

ELEGIES AND RITES OF PASSAGE—THEN AND NOW

CHAPTER 15

FOR TOMMY: COMMENCEMENT ADDRESS, JUNE 1976

HARRY BERGER, JR.

You're all gathered here to celebrate an occasion, and since I think the celebration is premature, I'm going to talk about something else: about a worm, a word, and four encounters. The worm I have in mind belongs to the American painter Albert Ryder; the word is "celebrate," but not the way you mean it; the four encounters are mine—with Ryder, Plato, Robert Frost, and my son Tommy. Three of them might be called encounters of meaning. The fourth is an encounter of fact. But first to the worm and the word. The worm I have in mind is only an inchworm, so there's no need to recoil unless you're squeamish. I found it in one of Albert Ryder's letters: "Have you ever," he wrote, "seen an inchworm crawl up a leaf or twig, and then clinging to the very end, revolve in the air, feeling for something to reach something? That's like me. I am trying to find something out there beyond the place on which I have a footing." So much for the worm. I'm not ready to talk about it yet, but I'd like to let it hang there and revolve in your minds while I go on to the word.

When I was trying to decide how I could help you celebrate this occasion, I looked in the dictionary for guidance but didn't find anything listed under "celebrate" that I was prepared to do. I'm not here to perform a religious ceremony. I'm not in the mood to praise or extol. I haven't got anything to announce publicly or proclaim. And though I'm perfectly willing at some point to observe this occasion with appropriate respect, festivity, rejoicing, and merrymaking, especially merrymaking, the time is not yet. Since my English dictionary failed me, I went back into the past, scholar that I am, pulled out my worn Latin dictionary, slit the pages, and located what I was looking for among the meanings assigned to the word *celebrare*. One sense of *celebrare* is to visit frequently; to go away and come back, go away and come back, go away and come back. To me this suggests that celebrating is what you do the second or third time around, but not the first. To celebrate is to revisit. You have to go away from whatever-it-is for long enough and deep enough to find out, on revisiting, whether it was worth a celebration. These youngsters behind me haven't even graduated yet. It's too soon to tell whether there's anything to celebrate in their suddenly brief college experience. We have to let their slender lives matriculate away a little. And so I propose to ignore them from now on and consider a more suitable subject of celebration. I propose to celebrate myself. Not because there's anything to praise or proclaim or even set off a religious observance over. But simply because I've made fifty-one rolls around the sun with this planet. That alone makes me a likely prospect for revisitation. And so, as the worm revolves mysteriously in your minds, I want to cancel a certain number of those earth-rolls and take you back to a younger time.

Some fifteen years ago, in 1960 and 1961, I happened to be working on three projects, none of them related to any of the others. The first was the revision of an essay about a book of poems—one of the poems had been about Albert Ryder, and this was how he and his worm first came to my attention. The second was the job of re-thinking an old set of notes on Robert Frost for a course in modern poetry. The third was preparing for a course in ancient literary theory, part of which dealt with some dialogues by Plato. It was somebody else's course I was taking over, the syllabus was set, I didn't know much about Plato at the time, and so I fought my way through the dialogues and read a few standard Plato textbooks, and ended up feeling that I knew even less than when I started. It was all over my head, and very dry. Plato's imaginary discussions between Socrates and other old Greeks never got anywhere, and though they seemed interminable they ended too soon, before any answers were given or any conclusions were reached. I badly needed answers, since I was going into a class and I thought that's what students thought teachers were for. And I wondered how I was going to keep Plato from inflicting on my students the same torture he contrived for me. That year I failed, and the Plato part of the course added up to a heavy dose of sedation. So I went home after the last class and began reading the dialogues again. I thought I'd find out where Plato went wrong, and give him another chance.

I don't want you to think that this constitutes my encounter with Plato. The encounter only began that summer, when I came across a simple observation in a book about Plato, which was that if you boiled Socratic method down, it consisted "in asking a speaker to repeat himself and explain what he had meant . . . with the underlying assumption that there was something unsatisfactory about the statement, and it had better be rephrased." That seemed at first to be a perfect description of what I—a latterday Socrates—was doing to Plato: asking him to explain himself. And he did: he repeated himself word for word, he didn't say anything new or different, he gave no answers and came to no conclusions. I wondered why he was so famous, and I let him go and turned to more rewarding work—which, at the time, was the revision of my essay on the book of poems.

That was when the fateful convergence took place between my life and Ryder's inchworm. The image, and the poem about Ryder, haunted me—I didn't know why—and so I went back into Ryder's life looking for something—I didn't know what. He lived from 1847 to 1917, and spent the last half of his life in New York City, where I spent the earliest years of mine. Much of the visual data for his otherwordly landscapes or dreamscapes came from his walks through the city and its parks, from nocturnal ferry rides across the Hudson, and nightlong strolls along the waterfront. Ryder's biographer writes that "he cared nothing for money, social prestige, or even the ordinary comforts of living. He never married, he lived in disorder, dressed shabbily and ate poorly. He existed only for his art." Though he visited Europe several times, he remained relatively impervious to that past, never truly revisited the old masters. In New York he lived for fifteen years in two rooms where the wallpaper "hung in long streamers from the ceiling"; and since he didn't throw anything away the rooms were a clutter of "furniture, trunks, boxes, old newspapers and magazines, canvases, frames, painting materials, dirty clothes, food, unwashed dishes, milk bottles, ashes." "I never see all this," Ryder said, "unless someone comes to see me." What he saw, what he looked at, was something more cloistered, less cluttered, and much grander: "I have two windows in my workshop that look out on an old garden whose great trees thrust their green-laden branches over the casement sills, filtering a network of light and shadow on the bare boards of my floor. Beyond the low roof tops of neighboring houses sweeps the eternal firmament with its ever-changing panorama of mystery and beauty. I would not exchange these two windows for a palace with less a vision than this old garden with its whispering leafage."

I thought it poignant—and I still do—that it was only deep within such a retreat, and only as an inchworm, that Ryder could imagine himself trying to find something out there beyond the place on which he had a footing. There was a kind of courage, of bravery, mixed into his reticence. And there was patience. Ryder was fussy about his paintings; he was constantly re-touching and revising them, and he was often reluctant to let them go even after they had been bought. To me, his art is a little narrow in its range, and a little repetitive in theme and style. He didn't take many risks. He clung to his bachelor's poverty and his green shade to the very end. Nevertheless he reached out to me; he insisted, gently but firmly, that I make something of his inchworm, make more of it than he did, and not let it fall away.

My initial response to him that summer was that the Ryder in me was asking too little of himself, too much of me. Wasn't it too late to start a genuine dialogue between us? After all, he spent his first life cherishing his innocence and keeping himself pure of contacts, free of involvement with, or commitment to, other people. But as I was shutting the door on him, a phrase from the sentence on Socratic method crossed my mind: "the underlying assumption that there was something unsatisfactory about the statement, and it had better be rephrased." And that suddenly threw a new light on Ryder: I saw a man blessed or cursed from the beginning with a single pure and perfect vision—and not even a vision, but a blur, a half-glimpsed shimmer of something—some "panorama of mystery and beauty"—so extraordinary that it took his life away. His paintings were all one painting—all efforts to catch some remnant of the vision and make some statement about it. He spent his days feeling for something to reach something, always rephrasing, and always unsatisfied. The something out there was an overwhelming question in search of a final answer. But it was too deep within his mind, it sank deeper with his every refusal to open himself to life, and it buried itself under his cluttering and cloistering years, under the peeling wallpaper and the garden wall.

By default, Ryder taught me one meaning of celebration as revisiting, and one meaning of what it was to revise. Just as the Socratic rephrasing is more than re-saying, so revising is more than rewriting. The noun form of revising is re-vision: second sight. It was second sight that Ryder longed for, reached for, and missed. He held himself pure and tense, for the moment when that first vision would revisit him and disclose itself in full, when the seed planted in the garden would burst into flower in the branches above the inchworm. But—and this is what I discovered in the summer of 1960—that isn't the way to go about it. When I took my impressions of Ryder back to Plato, the contrast showed me something in the dialogues I hadn't seen before. I saw that Socrates wanted to make his fellow citizens let go of themselves, drop their guard against life and other people, take chances with each other, trust each other, and not flinch from conflict or criticism. For him, second sight and second thoughts were better than the first ones only if they were the product of a particular act of self-criticism: second thoughts become revisions when you discover and acknowledge there was something wrong or missing in your first thoughts—when you're willing to risk the drop in self-esteem connected with the admission that you didn't know something you thought you knew, and when, on that basis, you're willing to revisit and revise not only your thoughts but also yourself. One reason the dialogues are inconclusive is that Socrates seldom succeeds in getting very far with this project. The people he talks to resist his assault on their self-esteem and self-deception. A little like Ryder, they're afraid to go away from themselves, let themselves go, risk losses.

They're afraid of what Robert Frost, in "Birches," calls the weariness of considerations. *Consideration* is a fine word: it suggests attentive thought; looking at or worrying about problems; taking things into account; having regard for other people; and also, payments, remunerations for services—all the normal involvements of life that demand concern or commitment. No one knew more than Frost about this weariness, about the cost of the investment in other lives, the losses that love could bring. Moving from Ryder to Frost that summer, fifteen years ago, brought me from the edge of a sheltered life to the center of a turbulent one. It was a difficult life, and Frost was a difficult man, to himself as well as others. Part of him was continually tempted to hide in the garden and build the wall higher, like Albert Ryder. But another part was forever being drawn beyond himself—and not like a cautious inchworm, but with a reckless and self-squandering curiosity. He opened himself as Ryder never did because he had more faith in serendipity. "The impressions most useful to my purpose," he once wrote, "seem always those I was unaware of and so made no note of at the time when taken. . . . We are always hurling experience ahead of us to pave the future with against the day when we may want to strike a line of purpose across it." His poems and letters reveal the enormous richness and variety of those useful impressions. But they also reveal how many of them were grounded in his failures, and in his losses.

For example, he wrote a poem called "Iris by Night," in which the speaker remembers a walk he and his friend once took on a misty evening. The weather was strange, and it was climaxed by a weird miracle of nature: a rainbow that didn't move with and away from them as they went, but gathered its many-colored ends together in a ring and encircled the two friends. The poem would be little more than a casual impression, a versified memoir of an experience that was very odd meteorologically but not otherwise significant—it would be that, except for a single line: "I alone of us have lived to tell." This fact—the friend's death—changes everything. The poem becomes an effort to recapture a moment of a relationship that has ended, and more than that, an effort to revise the natural miracle in retrospect by making it symbolize a human miracle. Here are its final lines: "we stood in it [the rainbow] softly circled round/From all division time or foe can bring/In a relation of elected friends." The friendship as well as the past event, the dead friend as well as the friendship, are miraculously alive within the speaker's consciousness. But his second sight and second thoughts draw their power from the loss that intervened between them and the first impression.

Thinking about this poem reminded me of something in Plato that I hadn't fully considered. Each of the inconclusive dialogues I had taught covers one session with Socrates—in dramatic terms—and most of them can be imagined to last for an hour or so. Socrates didn't get very far with his partners in dialogue not only because they were too self-cloistering but also because Plato didn't expect even Socrates to change people's lives, effect conversions, in the course of a single conversation. That the dialogues are conspicuously abortive reminds us that dialogue in the true sense of the word isn't something you can finish off at a sitting, like a good dinner. It may take a lifetime, and it may take more. It may or it may not be face-to-face. Plato's works reveal by implication that the only true partner-in-dialogue Socrates had was Plato. Plato's dialogues constitute that true dialogue, and most of them were probably composed after Socrates was dead. My dialogue with Plato has been going on for some fifteen years now, and I'm just beginning to see where he really went wrong.

For me in the early '60s, there was, in these three encounters with Ryder, Plato, and Frost—encounters of meaning, as I've called them—a kind of positive message. I saw the dialogues and the poems as acts of recovery that celebrate friendship, and, in so doing, triumph over time and death. But the triumph is muted by the cost: What else but death can prove the indestructibility of friendship, or the resiliency of mind and love? I don't think Frost and Plato believed in immortality any more than I do. What they believed in was the power of mind, love, and art to perform the miracle through which alone other moments, other selves, are circled round from all division time or foe can bring. "The most exciting moment in nature," Frost once said, "is not progress, advance, but expansion and contraction, the opening and shutting of the eye, the hand, the heart, the mind. . . . We throw our arms wide with a gesture of religion to the universe; we close them around a person. We explore and adventure for a while and then draw in to consolidate our gains," and also to revisit and revise our losses.

The words I'm using today about Frost are for the most part words I wrote in 1960 and revised for a talk I gave a few years later. If I were writing them today for the first time, they wouldn't be the same. It was a little too easy for me then to moon over encounters of the mind while staying like Ryder in the garden. I think I'm less inclined now to work up pseudoprofound statements about overcoming death. And this is because of my fourth encounter, the encounter of fact, the encounter with my son. I haven't come across many people with his peculiar combination of Ryder's timidity and Frost's turbulent spirit: easily hurt, quick to anger, a little wild and reckless; hurling experience ahead of him to pave the future, with a bravery, sometimes bravado, sustained always at a cost. Tommy missed being seventeen by three weeks. He was killed on an icy road the night of January 16, 1965. His ashes still sit on a mortuary shelf in New Haven, Connecticut. When he visits my dreams he's never older than eleven or twelve, and this is probably because the years up to then were good, good for both of us, but in his last two years we gave each other hard times. About a week before the end we had a fine talk, and I suspect we both knew things would get better, given a little time.

It's taken me eleven years to think about this along with the other things I usually think about, like Plato, Ryder, and Frost, and I never expected to speak about it, much less speak in public. In the weeks after it happened, I found myself bemoaning the jaggedness of the break, everything irrevocably unfinished, and I kept wanting to find ways to make repairs, to force some conclusions from it. And a few months later, when I had to go back and finish something I was working on—it was still Plato—I thought it helped me see more deeply into the true Platonic pathos, which is that dialogue transpires always too late and always out of phase. But then it occurred to me that that wasn't where it really was. Where it really is, is that for Tommy everything finished. People kept telling me about the tragedy of my loss. But from the day after he died I had to keep telling myself another thing, saying it over and over: it happened to him, not to me. I lost him, but he lost everything. And that's what has stayed with me. That's the fact. I've drawn no lessons from it, no messages, no saving wisdom. It's laughable to speak of the mind's ability to triumph over death, to sustain the dead self in another self, and so forth. My literary wisdom doesn't apply. I can revisit the fact, but I'm not going to revise it. I have let go.

When I decided to give this talk, I knew I wanted to talk about this, but I didn't know why. It seemed totally inappropriate for the occasion. Yet as I thought about it, it came to seem less inappropriate; and at the same time I realized that there must be something wrong with the occasion—or with my sense of the occasion—if this is inappropriate to it. A few nights after Tommy died some of my friends came over, and two of them were musicians, and the three of us played jazz together, and it was good to do. It was, as they say, "joyous." And when I think of Tommy it makes me more joyous now to be standing here with good friends and with those students whom I've come to know well, and who mean much to me, and with whom I've wanted to share this encounter, and also to share one small thought that came to me as I was writing this. My encounter of fact has shown me the limits of my three encounters of meaning. Real death marks the limits of literary death, of dialogue, of revision, of celebration. Silence is its best rhetoric. Yet I go on talking about it because I don't believe the absolute limit of the fact has made the other encounters worthless. It's cut them down some, and taken their measure.

But I can still say something on their behalf. What I've learned from Plato, Ryder, and Frost is the necessity not only of revisiting and revising but also of having something to revisit; the value of having learned to let go and throw experience forward; the importance of working for—of hoping to find—something out there beyond the place on which I have a footing. In the early '60s Ryder, Plato, and Frost gave me a framework, a method, a way of looking that helped me water my academic garden. When they made contact with what remains the most real experience of my life they wanted me to reach for something that lay beyond their grasp of meaning. By their failure, they proved its reality for me, its profound meaninglessness, transcending thought. But I couldn't have come to that revelation unless I had pushed Ryder, Plato, and Frost to their limits and falsified or disconfirmed their claims to comprehend or overcome death. In failing, in guiding me beyond themselves, they became more than aids to academic gardening and literary interpretation. What I've discovered the last few days, thinking back on that period, is that they work for life if not for death. And I've also discovered that a basic pattern, something like a circadian rhythm, was moving me long before I met them, and that my inchworm mind reaching out only found its double in what it learned from Ryder, Plato, and Frost. The inchworm keeps revolving backward as the planet spins me forward, looking for something to stay by. I revisit and revise, hoping it will all come together, all fall into place, but knowing it never will. There's always something unsatisfactory that needs to be rephrased; always a question that doesn't want an answer; always a fact that resists meaning; always the confusing lights of a vision in a relationship glimpsed, desired, and lost. Revisiting is what I do, what I profess. I think, or at least hope, it's at the heart of what we do as teachers and students—and you who are graduating may find out whether it is or not later, but not now. For me, at any rate—and I can say it now—revisiting is an act of celebration. It's an act of education. It's the act of love.

16. AFTERWORD:

ONLY A RITE

DAVID LEE MILLER

*Only a rite, an endlessly repeated act, can commemorate this not
very memorable encounter—for no one can say what the death of a
child is, except the father* qua *father, that is to say, no conscious
being.*

—Jacques Lacan, *Four Fundamental Concepts*

On April 24, 1998, officials of Fayette county in central Kentucky
exhumed an urn buried in Lot 508 at the Lexington Cemetery. The urn,
according to published reports, "contained only potting soil."[1] But the
mystery surrounding this event does not concern a missing body—at least,
not the sort of body that can be subject to autopsy. The urn-burial in
question had been arranged the previous November by a North Carolina
physician, Dr. Hollis Tidmore. For ten years, friends and coworkers had
grieved with Dr. Tidmore over the loss of a family he never had. Late in
1997, as his "web of lies" began to unravel, Tidmore had the urn hastily
buried. His fraud was exposed, but newspaper accounts of the investigation suggest that something else remains to be unearthed:

> It seemed so real to so many people. Dr. Hollis Tidmore had lost his
> wife and son in a car accident, and years later he was still grieving, dis-
> traught, and lonely.
> The Charlotte surgeon talked about it often. Just a mention of that
> day—Aug. 21, 1987—could bring him to tears.
> Friends cried along with him, hoping he would heal someday.
> He marked the anniversary of the wreck each year by placing flowers in
> his church during Sunday services, recalls the Rev. Charles Page, his friend
> and former pastor at First Baptist Church. And every time, the doctor
> cried.

But the sad story was a fiction.

Tidmore never had a wife or son. There was no wreck. And the urn he buried in a Lexington cemetery contained only soil.

Somewhere in the absurdities of this imposture resides a kind of truth— the one that made an imaginary father's loss seem "so real to so many people." There was (to borrow Harry Berger's phrase) no "encounter of fact," only the utter redundancy of burying earth. Yet the emptiness at the heart of this sad story makes it an unusually pure "encounter of meaning." The grief, the sympathy of friends, the ritualized commemoration during religious services, the consolations of mourning and the sense of community in sorrow, all these were merely symbolic, deprived of their anchor in the literal truth. Yet in spite of the doctor's bad faith they were also real, and so, in some sense, was his loss. The sad story was false; but the true story is also sad. Surely Hollis Tidmore was himself the wreck for which he wept.

The essays in this collection, together with the growing body of work, both theoretical and historical, that they cite and elaborate, reflect a surge of critical fascination with the sad stories we tell ourselves about grief and mourning. The connection between grief and gender may not be intuitively obvious, but there is no question that the present critical preoccupation with loss, mourning, and elegy owes a great deal to gender theory. Freud's work, from the essay "Mourning and Melancholia" (1917) through *Beyond the Pleasure Principle* (1919) to *The Ego and the Id* (1921), laid down a track, retraced in the speculations of Judith Butler and others, that leads from the process of mourning to the formation of gender. In these works Freud projected an erotics of identity formation, a vision of sexual selfhood as resulting from the interplay between longing and identification in the child's mournful response to the incest taboo. It seems reasonable to suppose that grief in adults would call up the old mechanisms to repair new damage, rebuilding the self in the wake of a devastating blow. The reconstruction of gender identity— opening it to history, and hence to revision—would have to be part of this process, for sudden and profound loss shatters us to our foundations, wrenching us back to that archaic depth of being on which the sense of sexual selfhood first took shape. Death renews the first loss; gender is what we became in response to that loss; mourning resumes that becoming, and in doing so opens us painfully to a future not yet engendered.

The connection between grief and gender also marks a point of convergence between the two most influential critical practices of our time, psychoanalysis and historicism. As a primary stage of socialization, gender-formation is ground zero for the construction of the social self; if mourning calls upon us to repeat the assumption of gender, it also calls us to rebuild our ties to the world around us, reweaving the filaments of collective identity. Such a point of vulnerability and renewal must inevitably draw to itself the ideological forces and resources of its time and place, for it provides the human raw material on which they work. Literature and criticism alike belong to this process.

Literature and criticism belong to the process of renewal, but they also resist it. Elegy *imitates* grief and mourning, and its mimesis must begin by recreating the sense of loss. To the extent that this loss engages our fantasies and emotions, it will also enlist our sympathy for the motives of resistance. The elegy must create this resistance powerfully in order to overcome it convincingly: signs and ceremonies of mourning may bind us together socially, yet beneath that solidarity we feel the tug of a more inarticulate sympathy for the loss we cannot share, the stubborn clinging of the bereaved to the one who is deceased. This must be one reason critical studies of the elegiac tradition, such as Jahan Ramazani's *Poetry of Mourning,* lay such emphasis on resistance: consolation has to be authenticated by our faith in the uniqueness of each loss—in what Berger calls "its profound meaninglessness, transcending thought." Breaking more than a decade's silence about the death of his son, Berger still declines to find meaning in it. "Real death," he insists, "marks the limits of literary death, of dialogue, of revision, of celebration. Silence is its best rhetoric."

W. Scott Howard, in his essay for this collection, keys on the resistance to consolation as a way of writing the literary history of the form. Tracing in seventeenth-century texts what he calls "the true emergence of the modern poetic elegy," he revises an argument taken over from Ramanzani, who distinguishes modern from traditional elegy because the modern poet (in Howard's words) "resists consolation, thereby performing oppositional cultural work through the elegy's critique of the social conventions that govern private grief expression and public mourning practice." I suspect that unearned consolations are already slipping back into this account through the very language of "oppositional cultural work," which projects the elegiac poet as a wish-fulfilling image of the cultural critic. But critics do identify with the poets they study, and for this reason criticism itself can be a highly specialized form of mourning.

This is the burden of Harry Berger's "For Tommy: Commencement Address," a beautiful oration on the poetics of loss and consolation that embodies in its own carefully crafted form all the generic modulations Howard distinguishes in the elegiac tradition since the seventeenth century. Berger's "critique of the social conventions" is at once playful and serious, established immediately in the mock-antagonism with which he admonishes his audience that their celebration is premature. His resistance to consolation lodges itself in the distinction between encounters of meaning and of fact. We realize this distinction in loss, for there are no encounters of fact except in purely negative form. Every living encounter mingles fact and meaning inseparably—as when a teenage son confronts his father in a relationship bedeviled by misunderstanding because it is fraught and overfraught with contradictory meanings. Separation occurs through the irrevocable subtraction of death, which leaves us to choose between meaning and the silence into which that lost other has fallen. Berger confronts this choice at the turning point of his elegy, and accepts it with moving simplicity: "It happened to him, not to me. I lost him, but he lost everything. And that's what has stayed with me. That's the fact." This is the moment of separation, the moment of letting go.

The distinction between fact and meaning registers this deeper separation. Freud famously speculated that melancholy involves "a loss of a more ideal kind," observing with epigrammatic clarity that the patient "knows *whom* he has lost but not *what* he has lost in him."[2] The essays in this collection repeatedly find in the aftermath of separation a labor of interpretation that sorts through the meanings of loss and invests it with new significance: thus Martin Luther, in Patricia Phillipy's essay, sees "political and social losses figured in or attendant upon" his daughter's death; women in Anglo-Saxon texts after the Norman Invasion, as Patricia Ingham shows, "bear the grief for a culture in transition." Even resistance to the consolations of meaning takes on significance when, as Phillippy demonstrates, it serves to distinguish maternal grief from the public performance of masculine restraint. Meanings are themselves forms and objects of desire, ideal ties that bind us on the one hand to those we have lost and on the other hand to the persons, communities, and ideals around us.

Loss sets in motion an essentially textual process because it opens these meanings, the forms and objects of our deepest emotional investments, to revision. Grief resists speech so intensely because silence is the only response that can preserve our absolute fidelity to the one we have lost in all his (and its) uniqueness. To put loss into words is already to symbolize it, to renegotiate its meanings, to revise it—and, with it, ourselves. Anne Prescott reminds us that Marguerite de Navarre, writing in the wake of her brother's and her mother's deaths, "has, at least to some degree, taken the liberty . . . to remake her now helpless relatives if not out-and-out Lutherans then more Erasmian, more Evangelical, more like Marguerite." There is a kind of terrible freedom in this return to language—including, as the extreme example of Dr. Tidmore reminds us, the freedom to refashion ourselves through lies. In his fantasy of mourning, Hollis Tidmore became a husband, a father, and an object of pity. In her fantasy, Marguerite makes her brother more like herself and herself more like him, adopting "the person of a male lover" to explore the significance of her loss.

This freedom to revise ourselves and remake others in the aftermath of grief is real, but not absolute. Marshall Grossman invokes the psychoanalytic model of transference as a way of understanding the rhetorical structures through which mourning negotiates ideal losses and reconfigures the emotions they release. Transference counterbalances the awful freedom that we purchase at the cost of our dearest loves; its tropes suspend a thread of continuity across the radical discontinuity of separation. Between the absolute severance of death and the persistence of love borne across death by the rhetorical structures of the transference, we locate one possibility for what Berger calls "celebration," at once a separation and a return.

Among the defining features of the modern elegy as Howard describes it are "a heightened sense of the linguistic negotiation of loss" and "the placement of consolation within the context of human temporality." Berger's oration fuses these elements deftly, taking death into itself formally through the motifs of separation and timing, which it then carefully manages in order to create a sense of closure and decorum. First the speaker sets himself apart from his audience by declaring their celebration premature. Then, against the prematurity of their expectations, he opposes deliberate gestures of delay. He mentions the "encounter of fact" almost at once, but postpones any explanation in favor of "the worm and the word." The worm, too, is introduced only to be deferred: "I'm not ready to talk about it yet." And so is the word: the speaker will celebrate, he will rejoice and make merry with his listeners, but "not yet." First he must insist on separation: on his own isolation from the students behind him and the parents in front of him; on the distinctness of his four encounters, each introduced only to be suspended, held apart in the mind until he is ready for them all to come together; and on the separateness of events in time that allows for celebration in its root sense, as a revisiting of what is past.

All these separations are artfully overcome in the oration as the absolute rift between Harry and Tommy is, simply, accepted. "I have let go," says the speaker. In letting go he has taken the risk that Ryder avoided and that Socrates' companions resisted: "they're afraid to go away from themselves, let themselves go, risk losses." But without the risk of discontinuity, even in its extreme form as the shattering experience of a loved person's death, we cannot open ourselves to history or change, and so we cannot celebrate. Only after he lets go in this way can the speaker move to his peroration. Only then can he rediscover the decorum of the occasion, the propriety of mingling elegy with commencement, and, in doing so, rejoin the audience from which he has held himself aloof: "When I think of Tommy," he can say, "it makes me more joyous now to be standing here with good friends and with those students whom I've come to know well, and who mean much to me, and with whom I've wanted to share this encounter." At this moment, the "encounter of fact" yields, as it must, not to mere "encounters of meaning," but to what he calls the act of education and love, the living moment in which meaning and fact, like self and other, are not only separate, but also inseparable.

NOTES

INTRODUCTION

1. Edmund Spenser, *Works of Edmund Spenser: A Variorum Edition*, ed. Edwin Greenlaw et al., vol. 3 (1932–57; reprint, Baltimore: Johns Hopkins University Press, 1966), III.xi. 8, 13, 27.
2. Maurice Charney, "Marlowe's *Edward II* as Model for Shakespeare's *Richard II*," *Research Opportunities in Renaissance Drama* 33 (1994): 39.
3. *King Richard II*, ed. Peter Ure, The Arden Shakespeare (1956; reprint, London: Routledge, 1989), III.ii.145, 155–56, 178–79.
4. *The Winter's Tale*, ed. J. H. D. Pafford, The Arden Shakespeare (1963; reprint, London: Routledge, 1984), II.i.108–12 and III.ii.239.
5. Carol Zisowitz Stearns and Peter N. Sterns, *Anger: The Struggle for Emotional Control in America's History* (Chicago: University of Chicago Press, 1986), p. 22, as quoted by Gwynne Kennedy in *Just Anger: Representing Women's Anger in Early Modern England* (Carbondale: Southern Illinois University Press, 2000), p. 2.
6. *The Compact Edition of the Oxford English Dictionary*, s.v. "mourn" and s.v. "grief." Although early modern men and women certainly experienced emotions of grief, sadness, melancholy, joy, or anger, they tended to refer to these states of mind as "passions" or "affections": Michael C. Schoenfeldt, *Bodies and Selves in Early Modern England: Physiology and Inwardness in Spenser, Shakespeare, Herbert, and Milton* (Cambridge: Cambridge University Press, 1999), p. 16.
7. In his landmark study, *Grief and English Renaissance Elegy* (Cambridge: Cambridge University Press, 1985), p. 6, G. W. Pigman III distinguishes "grief" as an emotion from "mourning" as a process.
8. In *The Gendering of Melancholia: Feminism, Psychoanalysis, and the Symbolics of Loss in Renaissance Literature* (Ithaca, NY: Cornell University Press, 1992), p. 5, Juliana Schiesari provides this useful gloss upon Freud's definitions of mourning and melancholy in his famous essay in *The Standard Edition of the Complete Psychological Works of Sigmund Freud*, trans. James and Alix Strachey, 24 vols.(London: Hogarth, 1953–74), 14: 243–58.
9. *The Riverside Shakespeare*, ed. Blakemore Evans et al. (Boston: Houghton Mifflin, 1974), I.i.1.
10. See, for example, Julie Ellison's study of sensibility in the Anglo-American political tradition, in which she notes that "we do not possess a detailed

history of masculine emotion": *Cato's Tears: The Making of Anglo-American Emotion* (Chicago: University of Chicago Press, 1999), p. 19.

11. Those who have discussed early modern emotions include Gail Kern Paster on shame in *The Body Embarrassed: Drama and the Disciplines of Shame in Early Modern England* (Ithaca, NY: Cornell University Press, 1993); Schiesari, *The Gendering of Melancholia;* Lynn Enterline, *The Tears of Narcissus: Melancholia and Masculinity in Early Modern Writing* (Stanford, CA: Stanford University Press, 1995); and Kennedy, *Just Anger.*

Examples of recent works on the subject of mourning and grief in the Renaissance are Heather Dubrow, *Shakespeare and Domestic Loss: Forms of Deprivation, Mourning, and Recuperation* (Cambridge: Cambridge University Press, 1999); *Speaking Grief in English Literary Culture, Shakespeare to Marvell,* ed. Margo Swiss and David Kent (Duquesne University Press, 2002), and a collection entitled *Imagining Death in Spenser and Milton,* edited by Elizabeth J. Bellamy, Patrick Cheney, and Michael Schoenfeldt (Palgrave Macmillan 2003). Examples of social historians who have recently written on early modern grief, though without a particular focus on gender, are Ralph Houlbrooke, *Death, Religion, and the Family in England, 1480–1750* (Oxford: Oxford University Press, 2000) and David Cressy, *Birth, Marriage, and Death* (Oxford: Oxford University Press, 1997).

12. "Introduction: Emotion, Discourse, and the Politics of Everyday Life" in *Language and the Politics of Emotion,* eds. Lila Abu-Lughod and Catherine A. Lutz (Cambridge: Cambridge University Press, 1990), p. 7.

13. "Love and Knowledge: Emotion in Feminist Epistemology" in *Gender/Body/Knowledge: Feminist Reconstructions of Being and Knowing,* ed. Alison M. Jaggar (New Brunswick, NJ: Rutgers University Press, 1989), p. 159.

14. The use of the term "agency" throughout this volume is in keeping with Paul Smith's definition of "agent" as a form of subjectivity that provides the possibility of resisting "ideological pressure": *Discerning the Subject* (Minneapolis: University of Minnesota Press, 1988), p. xxxv.

15. See "Did Women Have a Renaissance?," in *Women, History, and Theory: The Essays of Joan Kelly,* ed. Joan Kelly (Chicago: University of Chicago Press, 1984), pp. 24–25.

16. Kelly, "Did Women Have a Renaissance?," pp. 35 and 38.

17. Jean Calvin, *The Institutes of Christian Religion,* trans. Thomas Norton (London, 1562), III, viii, 9, as quoted in "The Two Faces of Humanism: Stoicism and Augustinianism in Renaissance Thought" in William J. Bouwsma, *A Usable Past: Essays in European Cultural History* (Berkeley: University of California Press, 1990), pp. 47 and 48.

18. Louis L. Martz, "Donne and Herbert: Vehement Grief and Silent Tears," *John Donne Journal* 7 (1988): 33–34.

19. Thomas Laqueur, *Making Sex: Body and Gender from the Greeks to Freud* (Cambridge, MA: Harvard University Press, 1990). For a useful overview of Galen's influence on Renaissance understandings of male and female bod-

ies, see Bruce R. Smith, *Shakespeare and Masculinity* (Oxford: Oxford University Press, 2000), p. 15.

20. For a discussion of figures like Olivia in Shakespeare's *Twelfth Night* as "leaky vessels" see Paster, *The Body Embarrassed*, pp. 32–33.

21. Levinus Lemnius, *The Secret Miracles of Nature* (London, 1658), pp. 273–74, as quoted in Schoenfeldt, *Bodies and Selves in Early Modern England*, p. 36.

22. See Joan Wallach Scott, *Gender and the Politics of History* (New York: Columbia University Press, 1988), p. 32.

23. Judith Butler, *Bodies That Matter: On the Discursive Limits of "Sex"* (New York: Routledge, 1993), p. 7.

24. Mary Ellen Lamb, "Engendering the Narrative Act: Old Wives' Tales in *The Winter's Tale*, *Macbeth*, and *The Tempest*," *Criticism* 40 (1998): 529.

25. See Walter J. Ong, "Latin Language Study as a Renaissance Puberty Rite," *Studies in Philology* 55 (1959):105–6.

26. I would like to thank Patricia Phillippy, author of *Women, Death and Literature in Post-Reformation England* (Cambridge University Press, 2002), for reading and commenting on the Introduction. I am also grateful to my father, Carl G. Vaught, Distinguished Professor of Philosophy at Baylor University, for his kind and thoughtful comments on the Introduction as well.

27. I wish to thank Katharine Goodland for sharing this insight during our conversation following her delivery of a paper entitled " 'Speak what we feel, not what we ought to say': Performing Grief in Shakespeare's *King Lear*" at the Renaissance Society of America in Tempe, Arizona, in April 2002.

CHAPTER 1

1. Thanks to Mehnaz Choudhury for her good counsel and able assistance in the research preliminary to writing this essay. I am drawing this distinction between female authorship and female voice from Anne L. Klinck, "Lyric Voice and the Feminine in Some Ancient and Mediaeval *Frauenlieder*," *Florilegium* 13 (1994): 13–36. The question of anonymity, gender, and authorship has been brilliantly treated by Marilynn Desmond, "The Voice of Exile: Feminist Literary History and the Anonymous Anglo-Saxon Elegy," *Critical Inquiry* 16 (1990): 572–90. For bibliographies on the issue, see Desmond.

2. Implicitly a proponent of Anglo-American (as distinct from French) feminism, Olsen critiques the uses of cultural theories (like those of Claude Levi-Strauss, but also undoubtedly Jacques Lacan), which she sees as promoting, rather than merely describing, patriarchal cultural forms. Her definitions are taken from Gayle Green and Coppélia Kahn, "Feminist Scholarship and the Social Construction of Women," in *Making a Difference: Feminist Literary Criticism*, ed. Gayle Greene and Coppélia Kahn (London: Methuen, 1986), pp. 1–2, as cited on p. 68. Olsen's primary targets are feminist medievalists Gillian Overing and Elaine Tuttle Hansen. See Alexandra Hennessey Olsen,

"Old English Women, Old English Men: A Reconsideration of 'Minor' Characters," in *Old English Shorter Poems: Basic Readings*, ed. Katherine O'Brien O'Keeffe (New York: Garland, 1994), pp. 31–64.

3. Helen T. Bennett, "Exile and the Semiosis of Gender in Old English Elegies," in Britton J. Harwood and Gillian R. Overing, eds., *Class and Gender in Early English Literature* (Bloomington: Indiana University Press, 1994), pp. 43–58, p. 53. Bennett's work, indebted to Gillian R. Overing, follows some of the cultural theories (Lacanian for one) that Olsen wishes to repudiate. She deploys Kristevan notions of the semiotic, building upon Lacanian notions of women as fantasy, as "lack," in conjunction with a Peircean approach that (usefully) turns attention to the modern reader.

4. Bennett, p. 45.

5. Thus, and despite an obvious commitment to female agency, Bennett nonetheless concludes that within certain hierarchical frames (the likes of which she has earlier used to define Anglo-Saxon culture) "woman . . . is still something of a social or semiotic outcast—or exile" (54).

6. Female power, she argues, can be recognized only in "non-hierarchical" readings, specifically those performed by modern feminists. The question remains unclear as to whether Bennett tells a progressivist feminist history, in which modern scholarly feminism can recuperate a female semiotics unintelligible to early English culture. That is, while I appreciate the turn to "modern readers" that Bennett makes in her essay's final paragraphs, her feminist praxis seems to maintain the opposition of loss and agency as a fact of history. I return to the importance of this question for the politics of history in my conclusion.

7. Louise Fradenburg has argued that while both men and women mourn throughout medieval literature, losses suffered by men are often depicted as romantically tragic, while females come to be seen to bear loss in unproductive ways. The elegy tradition, for instance, tends to celebrate male mourning as productive for the inauguration of a literary career. This gendered assignment continues in some psychoanalytic treatments of melancholia. For feminist alternatives see Juliana Schiesari, *The Gendering of Melancholia: Feminism, Psychoanalysis, and the Symbolics of Loss in Renaissance Literature* (Ithaca, NY: Cornell University Press, 1992). I address Fradenburg's work more explicitly below.

8. On literary representations of queenship, see Jane Chance, *Woman as Hero in Old English Literature* (Syracuse, NY: Syracuse University Press, 1986) and Helen Damico and Alexander Hennessey Olsen's collection *New Readings on Women in Old English Literature* (Bloomington: Indiana University Press, 1990); and Michael Enright's "The Lady with the Mead-cup: Ritual Group Cohesion and Hierarchy in the German Warband" (*Fruh mittelalterliche Studien*, 1988: 170–230). For historical accounts, Pauline Stafford's work is particularly helpful, especially "The King's Wife in Wessex 800–1066," *Past and Present 91* (May 1981): 3–27, and *Queens, Concubines and Dowagers: The King's Wife in the Early Middle Ages* (Oxford: Oxford University Press, 1985) and *Unification and Conquest: A Political and Social*

History of England in the Tenth and Eleventh Centuries (London: Edward Arnold, 1989). While specifically referring to Continental models, Jo Ann McNamara and Suzanne Wemple's work is likewise helpful. See "The Power of Woman Through the Family in Medieval Europe: 500–1100," in Erler and Kowaleski, eds., *Women and Power in the Middle Ages* (Athens: University of Georgia Press, 1988). See also Janet Nelson's *Politics and Ritual in Early Medieval Europe* (London: Hambledon Press, 1986).

9. Queen Emma's marital history represents a particularly complex sequence of foreign alliance building in that she, as Norman, first apparently unites Norman and English interests in her marriage to Æthelred, and later constructs herself as "uniter of English and Dane" despite her Norman, foreign origin (Stafford, *Unification* 76). I find Emma a particular example of the power and danger of exogamous marriages, since she is both herself foreign and the means by which a foreign ruler (Canute) becomes legitimated. For analyses of Emma's queenship, see Alistair Campbell, ed., *Encomium Emmae Reginae* (London: Royal Historical Society, 1949); and Miles Campbell, "Queen Emma and Ælgifu of Northhampton: Canute the Great's Women," *Medieval Scandinavia* 4 (1971): 66–79. I am also indebted to Carol Pasternack's "Anxieties of Female Governance/Reading Social Formations in Prose and Poetry" (unpublished manuscript).

10. Connections between women and loss may, however, have more to do with the foreignness of queens than with their power as females. It may not be so much that a *woman* has special, relational access to persuasive intimacies with a sovereign, but that a *foreigner* and former enemy of the state has such intimate, and kin-based, access. Exemplary of the complexities of the association of queens with relational and domestic power we find in the insistence, within ninth-century Wessex, on referring to the female consort only as the king's wife and not as the queen. Asser, in his *Life of King Alfred*, describes the position of Judith, the daughter of Charles the Bald, who marries the king of the West Saxons: "[T]he West Saxons do not allow a queen to sit beside the king, nor indeed do they allow her to be called a queen, but rather king's wife" (Asser 71). The doubleness of this injunction seems to attempt to separate relational power from political power: the queen may not publicly position herself in physical proximity to her consort, presumably so as to avoid any perception that she wields political influence over his decisions, and she may not be referred to by a title that suggests political power in its own right. The title "king's wife," rather than "queen," certainly emphasizes domestic relationality rather than political agency. Perhaps the careful distinction of titles was designed to signify exactly that the king's domestic relations were well ordered. His sovereignty triumphed even in his own household.

The context of this assertion, however, is a description of a drastic change in West Saxon practice. Charles the Bald, the Frankish king, attempted to ensure his daughter's position by having her designated "queen" in a religious ceremony that occurred before Judith ever set foot on the English shore (Stafford, "The King's Wife" 56; Nelson 343; Asser 71). Judith's position enacts a change in practice. As foreign bride she has access to a certain kind of power from her cognate relations, power that, in this instance, results in a change in the practice of royal domestic relations with political ramifications. Asser's description implies a conflict, or at least a tension, between the cultural categories of "queen" and "king's wife," and suggests that the confluence of foreignness, domestic relationality, and political power may constitute one of the problematics of early Medieval queenship. For Asser's account, see Simon Keynes and Michael Lapidge, eds., *Alfred the Great: Asser's Life of King Alfred and Other Contemporary Sources* (London: Penguin, 1988). For an analysis of the implications of sovereign power and relationality, see Pierre Bourdieu, *Outline of A Theory of Practice*, trans. Richard Nice (Cambridge: Cambridge University Press, 1977); and Louise O. Fradenburg, *City, Marriage, Tournament: Arts of Rule in Late Medieval Scotland* (Madison: University of Wisconsin Press, 1992). For anthropological analyses of marriage exchange, see Claude Levi-Strauss, *Elementary Structures of Kinship*, trans. James H. Bell and J. R. von Sturmer (Boston: Beacon Press, 1969); and, for a feminist revision, Gayle Rubin, "The Traffic in Women: Notes on the Political Economy of Sex" in *Toward an Anthropology of Women*, ed. Rayna R. Reiter (New York: Monthly Review Press, 1975). For my related analysis of the assignment of risk with peaceweaving queenship (viewed in the context of the concerns of ms Cotton Vitellius A XV), see "Containing Foreign Queens: The Domestic Cosmology of Beowulf and Judith" in Rosmarie Morewedge, ed., *Roles for Women in the Middle Ages: A Reassessment* (Binghamton, NY: Medieval and Renaissance Texts and Studies, forthcoming).

11. The text for *Beowulf* is taken from Frederik Klaeber's third edition, *Beowulf and the Fight at Finnsburg* (Lexington, MA: D. C. Heath, 1950). The translations are my own.

12. The words are taken from Mary Dockrey-Miller's "*Beowulf's* Tears of Fatherhood," *Exemplaria* 10, 1 (1998): 1–28. See also Clare Lees, "Men and Beowulf" in *Medieval Masculinities: Regarding Men in the Middle Ages*, Clare Lees, ed., (Minneapolis: University of Minnesota Press, 1994), pp. 129–48.

13. It may well be that Wealtheow's foreignness is part of the motivation for her protection of the bonds of kin that she shares with Hrothgar. In any case, she is here depicted as loyal to exogamous alliance through her care for her sons' inheritance. Just as the historical queen Emma, a Norman woman, eventually came to represent English (rather than Norman) interests vis-à-vis the Danes, Wealtheow here protects the lineage of the Scyldings, a people originally foreign to her.

14. Michael Enright, "The Lady with the Mead-cup: Ritual Group Cohesion and Hierarchy in the German Warband" (*Fruh mittelalterliche Studien*, 1988: 170–230), p. 173.

15. Maurice Bloch, "Death, Women, Power," in *Death and the Regeneration of Life*, ed. Maurice Bloch and Jonathan Parry (Cambridge: Cambridge University Press, 1982), pp. 217–218. For an analysis of the implications of theorizations of loss for a reading of late Middle English Arthurian

Romance as a "national fantasy," see my *Sovereign Fantasies: Arthurian Romance and the Making of Britain* (Philadelphia: University of Pennsylvania Press, 2001).

16. See chapter five, "Dangerous Liaisons," in *Sovereign Fantasies*, especially pp. 137–57.

17. I am reminded of this connection by Martin Green's use of this passage in an essay concerning *The Wife's Lament:* "Time, Memory, and Elegy in *The Wife's Lament*" in *The Old English Elegies*, ed. Martin Green (Rutherford, NJ: Fairleigh Dickinson University Press, 1983), pp. 123–32. Green cites the passage on p. 123. Green's larger analysis (that Beowulf's treatment of time and death are "objective and comprehensive" [124] while the Wife's Lament depicts a subjective "absolute passivity and hopelessness" [129]) remains invested in the cultural oppositions that I am interested in critiquing.

18. Green, p. 130.

19. Marijane Osborne, "The Text and Context of *Wulf and Eadwacer*," ed. Martin Green, *The Old English Elegies*, pp. 174–89. Dolores Warwick Frese has offered a similar interpretation.

20. The texts for *Wulf and Eadwacer* and *The Wife's Lament* are taken from *The Exeter Book*, ed. Israel Gollancz (London: Early English Text Society, 1895), vols. 1 & 2.

21. See the notes to "The Wife's Lament" in Mitchell and Robinson, *A Guide to Old English*, 5th ed. (London: Blackwell, 1992), p. 265, n.2.

22. William Johnson, Jr., "The Wife's Lament as Death-Song," in Martin Green, ed. *The Old English Elegies*, pp. 69–81, p. 69.

23. "Women's Songs, Women's Language," in Helen Damico and Alexandra Hennessey Olsen, ed., *New Readings on Women in Old English Literature* (Bloomington: Indiana University Press, 1990), pp. 193–203, p. 201.

24. "Speech as Action in *The Wife's Lament*," ed. Katherine O'Brien O'Keeffe, *Old English Shorter Poems, Basic Readings* (New York: Garland, 1994), pp. 335–56, p. 337.

25. Barrie Ruth Straus, p. 350.

26. Wendy Larson, "Exile, Confession, Vision: Discourses of Subjectivity in Anglo-Saxon and Middle English Literature," Ph.D. Dissertation, University of Wisconsin, Madison, 1995, p. 40.

27. Unlike *The Wanderer*, which, according to James Doubleday, structurally follows a "healing process" from "venting grief" to Christian devotion, *The Wife's Lament* is said to offer no such transcendence, no consoling belief in futurity. James Doubleday, "The Three Faculties of the Soul in *The Wanderer*," *Neophilologus* 53 (1969): 189–93.

28. For an analysis of the ways in which women's responsibility for death is used to facilitate a simultaneous experience of cultural continuity and the transition to new technologies, see Klaus Theweleit's "The Politics of Orpheus: Between Women, Hades, Political Power and the Media," *New German Critique* 36 (1985): 133–56.

29. Freud emphasizes the impoverishment of the mourner's world; Lacanian and Kristevan theories note how language acts as a substitution for the lost

object. The definitive work on the problematics of this notion for a cultural analysis of gender and grief is Louise Fradenburg's " 'Voice Memorial': Loss and Reparation in Chaucer's Poetry," *Exemplaria* 2.1 (1990): 169–202. Fradenburg analyzes the gendered nature of fact that "language may indeed be imagined as transcending loss by the substitution of representation: the signifier replaces the signified; in place of the dead lover, the lovely elegy," a view that links linguistic mastery—the ability to articulate—with mastery *over, transcendence* of loss (184). My work is everywhere indebted to Fradenburg's brilliant analysis of this structure.

30. Criseyde's words can be found in *Troilus and Criseyde*, Book II, ll. 782–84. The text is from *The Riverside Chaucer*, ed. Larry Benson (Boston: Houghton Mifflin, 1987).

31. " 'Voice Memorial': Loss and Reparation in Chaucer's Poetry," *Exemplaria* 2.1 (1990): 169–202, 196, note 15. For a reading of Criseyde, and the "problem" of her survival (including a critique of Kristeva's *Black Sun*), see also Fradenburg, " 'Oure owen wo to drynke': Loss, Gender, and Chivalry in *Troilus and Criseyde*," in R. A. Shoaf and Catherine Cox, eds., *Chaucer's Troilus and Criseyde, "Subgit to alle Poesye"*: *Essays in Criticism* (Binghamton, NY: Medieval and Renaissance Texts and Studies, 1992), pp. 88–106.

CHAPTER 2

1. Susan Leigh Fry, *Burial in Medieval Ireland: A Review of the Written Sources* (Dublin: Four Courts Press, 1999).

2. Quoted from Albrecht Schöne, ed., *Das Zeitalter des Barock. Texte und Zeugnisse*. Die deutsche Literatur. Texte und Zeugnisse (Munich: Beck, 1988), p. 270; cf. Blake Lee Spahr, "Andreas Gryphius," *German Baroque Writers, 1580–1660* in *Dictionary of Literary Biography*, 164 (Detroit-Washington, D.C.-London: Gale Research, 1996), pp. 131–44.

3. Dewi Rees, *Death and Bereavement: The Psychological, Religious and Cultural Interfaces* (London: Whurr Publishers, 1997).

4. Colin Murray Parkes, Pittu Laungani, and Bill Young, eds. *Death and Bereavement Across Cultures* (New York: Routledge, 1997), 12f.; see also Austin H. Kutscher, *Death and Bereavement* (Springfield, IL: C. C. Thomas, 1969).

5. Robert J. Ursano and James E. McCarroll, "Exposure to Traumatic Death: The Nature of the Stressor," in *Individual and Community Responses to Trauma and Disaster: The Structure of Human Chaos*, ed. R. J. Ursano et al. (Cambridge: Cambridge University Press, 1994), pp. 46–71.

6. Richard Schulz, *The Psychology of Death, Dying, and Bereavement* (Reading, MA, Menlo Park, CA: Addison-Wesley Publishing, 1978), p. 137.

7. Quoted from Schulz, p. 137f.

8. C. Murray Parkes, *Bereavement: Studies of Grief in Adult Life* (New York: International Universities Press, 1972); Susan Letzler Cole, *The Absent One: Mourning Ritual, Tragedy, and the Performance of Ambivalence* (University Park: Pennsylvania State University Press, 1985).

9. James E. Lindemann, "Symptomatology and Management of Acute Grief," *American Journal of Psychiatry* 101 (1944): 141–48.

10. Ira O. Glick, Robert Stuart Weiss, and Colin Murray Parkes, *The First Year of Bereavement* (New York: Wiley, 1974).

11. Geoffrey Gorer, *Death, Grief and Mourning in Contemporary Britain* (London: Cresset, 1965).

12. Robert. Fulton, "Death, Grief, and Social Recuperation," *Omega: Journal of Death and Dying* 1 (1970): 23–28, here 27.

13. John S. Stephenson, *Death, Grief, and Mourning: Individual and Social Realities* (New York: The Free Press; London: Collier Macmillan, 1985), p. 129.

14. Fernand Braudel, "Histoire et sciences sociales: la longue duré" *Annales, E.S.C.* 13 (1958): 725–53.

15. Steven Bassett, ed., *Death in Towns: Urban Responses to the Dying and the Dead, 100–1600* (New York: Leicester University Press, 1992); Arno Borst, Gerhart von Graevenitz et al. *Tod im Mittelalter.* Kontanzer Bibliothek, 20 (Constance: Universitätsverlag, 1993); Colin Platt, *King Death: The Black Death and Its Aftermath in Late-Medieval England* (Toronto: The University of Toronto Press, 1996).

16. Cf. Markus J. Wenninger, ed., *Du guoter tôt. Sterben im Mittelalter—Ideal und Realität. Akten der Akademie Friesach "Stadt und Kultur im Mittelalter" Friesach (Kärnten), 19–23. September 1994.* Schriftenreihe der Akademie Friesach, 3 (Klagenfurt: Wieser Verlag, 1998).

17. Ulrike Lehmann-Langholz, *Kleiderkritik in mittelalterlicher Dichtung.* Europäische Hochschulschriften. Reihe I. Deutsche Sprache und Literatur, 885 (New York: Lang, 1985), pp. 116–20.

18. Urban Küsters, "Klagefiguren. Vom höfischen Umgang mit der Trauer," Gert Kaiser, ed. *An den Grenzen höfischer Figur. Anfechtungen der Lebensordnung in der deutschen Erzähldichtung des hohen Mittelalters.* Forschungen zur Geschichte der älteren deutschen Literatur, 12 (Munich: Fink, 1991), pp. 9–75; ibid., "Freude, Leid und Glück. Mittelalter." *Europäische Mentalitätsgeschichte. Hauptthemen in Einzeldarstellungen*, ed. Peter Dinzelbacher (Stuttgart: Kröner, 1993), pp. 307–17.

19. Peter von Moos, *Consolatio. Studien zur mittellateinischen Trostliteratur und zum Problem der christlichen Trauer.* Münstersche Mittelalter-Schriften, 3, 1–4 (Munich: Fink, 1971/72).

20. Peter Dinzelbacher, "Gefühl und Gesellschaft im Mittelalter. Vorschläge zu einer emotionsgeschichtlichen Darstellung des hochmittelalterlichen Umbruchs," *Höfische Literatur, Hofgesellschaft, Höfische Lebensformen um 1200*, ed. Gert Kaiser and Jan-Dirk Müller, *Studia Humaniora* 6 (Düsseldorf: Droste, 1986), pp. 213–41, here 225.

21. Cf. Wenninger, ed., 1998.

22. Cf. Joachim Bumke, *Die vier Fassungen der "Nibelungenklage". Untersuchungen zur Überlieferungsgeschichte und Textkritik der höfischen Epik im 13. Jahrhundert.* Quellen und Forschungen zur Literatur- und Kulturgeschichte, 8 (242) (New York: de Gruyter, 1996).

23. Küsters, 1991, 73–75; cf. also Alois M. Haas, *Todesbilder im Mittelalter. Fakten und Hinweise in der deutschen Literatur* (Darmstadt: Wissenschaftliche Buchgesellschaft, 1989).

24. *The Lament of the Nibelungen (Div Chlage)*, trans. and with an introduction by Winder McConnell. Translations from Medieval Literature (Columbia, SC: Camden House, 1994), p. xiii.

25. Daniel Leviton, ed., *Horrendous Death and Health: Toward Action.* Series in Death Education, Aging, and Health Care (Washington: Hemisphere Publishing, 1991).

26. Elisabeth Lienert, "Intertextualität in der Heldendichtung. Zu Nibelungenlied und 'Klage'," *Neue Wege der Mittelalter-Philologie: Landshuter Kolloquium 1996.* Wolfram-Studien XV (Berlin: Schmidt, 1998), pp. 276–98.

27. John Leach, *Survival Psychology* (London: Macmillan Press, 1994), 50f.

28. Angelika Günzburger, *Studien zur Nibelungenklage. Forschungsbericht— Bauform der Klage—Personendarstellung.* Europäische Hochschulschriften. Reihe 1. Deutsche Sprache und Literatur, 685 (New York: Lang, 1983), pp. 176–83; Küsters, 1991, 30.

29. *Diu Klage, mittelhochdeutsch—neuhochdeutsch. Einleitung, Übersetzung, Kommentar und Anmerkungen* von Albrecht Classen. Göppinger Arbeiten zur Germanistik, 647 (Göppingen: Kümmerle, 1997), xxi f.

30. Gerd Althoff, *Spielregeln der Politik im Mittelalter. Kommunikation in Frieden und Fehde* (Darmstadt: Primus Verlag, 1997), pp. 258–81.

31. Rees, 1997, 119f.; cf. also George L. Engel, "Is Grief a Disease Process? A Challenge for Medical Research," *Psychosomatic Medicine* 23 (1961): 18–22.

32. Albrecht Classen, "Medieval Manuscript Evidence Versus Modern (Mis)Interpretation: *Diu Klage*," *The International Fiction Review* 24, 1 & 2 (1997): 1–11.

33. Albrecht Classen, "Der 'Ackermann aus Böhmen'—Ein literarisches Zeugnis aus einer Schwellenzeit: Mittelalterliches Streitgespräch oder Dokument des deutschen Frühhumanismus," *Zeitschrift für deutsche Philologie* 110 (1991): 348–73.

34. Jelko Peters, *Mittelalterliche Literatur in der Schule lesen. Eine Studie zur Theorie und Praxis der Interpretation des Ackermanns aus Böhmen im literarischen Diskurs.* LernSprache Deutsch 5, 1–2 (Vienna: Edition Praesens, 1997).

35. Johannes von Tepl. *Der ackerman*, ed. Willy Krogmann. Sec. ed. Deutsche Klassiker des Mittelalters. Neue Folge, 1 (Wiesbaden: Brockhaus, 1964); for an English translation, see Johannes von Saaz, *The Plowman from Bohemia. In the Original Early New High German and in English.* Trans. Alexander and Elizabeth Henderson. Introduction by Reinhold Schneider (New York: Frederick Ungar, 1966).

36. Leach 1994, 49f.

37. Janet Coleman, *Ancient and Medieval Memories: Studies in the Reconstruction of the Past* (Cambridge: Cambridge University Press, 1992),

pp. 578–83; for a thorough discussion of the cultural-historical aspects of Johannes' *Plowman*, see Christian Kiening, *Schwierige Modernität. Der "Ackermann" des Johannes von Tepl und die Ambiguität historischen Wandels.* Münchener Texte und Untersuchungen zur deutschen Literatur des Mittelalters, 113 (Tübingen: Niemeyer, 1998).

38. Walter Haug, "Der Ackermann und der Tod," *Das Gespräch*, ed. Karlheinz Stierle and Rainer Warning. Poetik und Hermeneutik, 11 (Munich: Fink, 1984), pp. 281–86.

39. Gerhard Hahn, *Der Ackermann aus Böhmen des Johannes von Tepl*. Erträge der Forschung, 215 (Darmstadt: Wissenschaftliche Buchgesellschaft, 1984), p. 14.

40. Mary Carruthers, *The Book of Memory: A Study of Memory in Medieval Culture.* Cambridge Studies in Medieval Literature, 10 (Cambridge: University of Cambridge, 1990); see also Werner Röcke, "Die Faszination der Traurigkeit. Inszenierung und Reglementierung von Trauer und Melancholie in der Literatur des Spätmittelalters." *Emotionalität. Zur Geschichte der Gefühle*, ed. Claudia Benthien, Anne Fleig and Ingrid Kasten (Cologne: Böhlau, 2000), pp. 100–118.

41. Heinrich Wittenwiler *"Der Ring," herausgegeben, übersetzt und kommentiert von* Bernhard Sowinski. Helfant Texte, T 9 (Stuttgart: helfant edition, 1988).

42. Lutz, Conrad Eckart. *Spiritualis fornicatio : Heinrich Wittenwiler, seine Welt und sein "Ring."* Konstanzer Geschichts und Rechtsquellen; 32. Sigmaringen: J. Thorbecke Verlag, 1990; Albrecht Classen, "Wort und Gemeinschaft: Sprachliche Apokalypse in Heinrich Wittenwilers *Ring*," *Jahrbuch der Oswald von Wolkenstein Gesellschaft* 8 (1994/95): 141–57.

43. Sebastian Brant, *The Ship of Fools*, trans. Edwin Hermann Zeydel (New York: Dover, 1962).

Chapter 3

1. Pierre Macherey, *A Theory of Literary Production* (London: Routledge and Kegan Paul, 1978), esp. pp. 154–55.

2. To rework Kathleen Woodward's observation, "the parameters of grief are circumscribed by the perimeters of state terror": "Freud and Barthes: Theorizing Mourning, Sustaining Grief," *Discourse* 13.1 (1990–91): 92–110, 104.

3. Mary F. Wack, "Lovesickness in *Troilus*," *Pacific Coast Philology* 19 (1984): 55–61, 55.

4. Mary F. Wack, *Lovesickness in the Middle Ages: The Viaticum and its Commentaries* (Philadelphia: University of Pennsylvania Press, 1990), p. 73.

5. Julia Schiesari, *The Gendering of Melancholia: Feminism, Psychoanalysis, and the Symbolics of Loss in Renaissance Literature* (Ithaca, NY: Cornell University Press, 1992), pp. 6–7; x: "Melancholia has appeared to these male thinkers [Aristotle, Ficino, Tasso, Burton] as the disease of great men if not the secret of their inspiration."

6. Jacques Ferrand, *Treatise on Lovesickness*, trans. and ed. Donald A. Beecher and Massimo Ciavolella (Syracuse, NY: Syracuse University Press, 1990). See, especially, chapter 2: "Love Melancholy as a Medical Idea in the Ancient World."

7. Ferrand, p. 154.

8. Ferrand, p. 6.

9. Ferrand (154) "singles out the young courtiers who are seen every day in states of rapt devotion as epitomizing the disease of love melancholy." In his medical opinion, there is no doubt of "a causal relationship between erotic mental disorders and a recognized set of social values and behavioral codes," i.e., the "rites of aristocratic courtship" or *amor courtois* (154 and 155).

10. Ferrand, p. 154.

11. In fact, by the time of his 1623 treatise on the subject, Ferrand, already "seeking to control impossible erotic desire through therapy," was "join[ing] in the general movement toward a social regulation of love" (155).

12. Of particular relevance is the work done by Mary Wack, as well as Carol Falvo Heffernan, *The Melancholy Muse: Chaucer, Shakespeare, and Early Medicine* (Pittsburgh: Duquesne University Press, 1995). See also, Michael R. McVaugh's introduction to Arnald of Villanova's *De amore heroico* in which he discusses Gerald of Berry's commentary on the *Viaticum* (c. 1237), a widely circulating small encyclopedia for travelers, containing a chapter on the disease of Lovesickness.

13. The *Franklin's Tale* ("penaunce"—glossed as "distress, suffering.")

14. *The Riverside Chaucer*, ed. Larry D. Benson, 3rd ed. (Boston: Houghton Mifflin, 1987), lines 738–41; all subsequent citations of Chaucer are to this edition.

15. See Nina Manasan Greenberg, "Dorigen as Enigma: The Production of Meaning and the *Franklin's Tale*," *The Chaucer Review* 33, No. 4 (1999): 329–49, 340.

16. The emphasis upon "trouthe" has evoked scores of critical essays about its ideological ambiguities. My only comment here is to note that at this point in the tale, the term "trouthe" floats almost abandonedly between several language systems: the ethical language system (*veracity*), the pragmatic language system (*an established principle*), the mercantile language system (the *substance* of the contract), back to the ethical (her *trust*), and back again to the pragmatic (the *precision* applied to the terms of Dorigen's fulfilling her contract with Aurelius, as against merely the *verisimilitude* permitted to Aurelius' claim of having fulfilled the contract). Fluid semantic boundaries are, of course, an attractive playground for any poet; however, Chaucer's greater concern is, I think, to expose the way that distinct meanings of a word are both seriously corrupted and playfully challenged.

17. Nina Manasan Greenberg, p. 337.

18. G. L. Kittredge, "Chaucer's Discussion of Marriage," *Modern Philology* 9 (1912): 435–67, especially 460–62; Gertrude M. White, "The Franklin's Tale: Chaucer or the Critics," *PMLA* 89 (1974): 454–62, 456: "Arveragus

has chosen the spirit over the letter; the new covenant of love and truth over possession and the law"; Diane Speed, "Character and Circumstance in *The Franklin's Tale*," *Sydney Studies in English* 15 (1989–90): 3–30, 24–25; Bernard F. Huppé, *A Reading of the Canterbury Tales*, rev. ed. (New York: Albany State University of New York Press, 1967), p. 173, insists that only the clerk/magician is indisputably generous. David Seaman, " 'As thynketh yow': Conflicting Evidence and the Interpretation of *The Franklin's Tale*," *Medievalia et Humanistica*, New Series, no. 17 (1991): 41–58, 55–56, argues that a "case [for 'mooste fre'] can be made for each of the principle characters" including Dorigen and the clerk/magician, depending upon their, the pilgrims', and the readers' interpretative processes.

19. Schiesari, p. 168. See especially pp. 161–170.
20. Line 1113: "sursanure"—wound healed only on the surface.
21. So, too, 1527–28: "I se his grete gentillesse/To yow, *and eek* I se wel youre distresse."
22. *The Riverside Chaucer*, explanatory notes to the *Franklin's Tale*, ll.1355–1456.
23. Robert G. Benson, *Medieval Body Language: A Study of the Use of Gesture in Chaucer's Poetry, Anglistica* 21 (Copenhagen: Rosenkilde & Bagger, 1980), 54: "... the gestures in saints' lives and romances are symbolic indicators of states of being rather than psychological manifestations or dramatic devices...." "The ideals [of love, beauty, or conduct] are expounded, the doctrines of love as religion, or courtly behavior or Christian morality, call for conventional gestures, gestures which subordinate individual peculiarities to the general codes of either religion or Love," p. 43. See also, pp. 60–66.
24. Leslie Abend Callahan, "The Widow's Tears: The Pedagogy of Grief in Medieval France and the Image of the Grieving Widow," in *Constructions of Widowhood and Virginity in the Middle Ages*, ed. Cindy L. Carlson and Angela Jane Weisl (New York: Palgrave Macmillan, 1999), pp. 245–63, especially 245–49.
25. G. W. Pigman III, *Grief and English Renaissance Elegy* (Cambridge: Cambridge University Press, 1989), p. 129, n. 5. I have chosen to follow both Freud and John Bowlby, whom Pigman cites: "Freud includes in his definition of mourning losses of abstractions which have taken the place of the person," and Bowlby "uses 'mourning' to cover a variety of reactions to loss . . . and argues that infant and childhood separation from the mothering figure is a form of mourning." Pigman cites *The Standard Edition of the Complete Psychological Works of Sigmund Freud*, vol. 14 (London, 1957), p. 243, and John Bowlby, *Loss, Sadness and Depression* (New York: Basic Books, 1969–80), pp. 16, 9–14, respectively.
26. Callahan, p. 246.
27. Ambrose of Milan, "De viduis," *Patrilogia Latina* (hereafter *PL*) 16:258. Translated as "The Treatise of St. Ambrose, Bishop of Milan, Concerning Widows," in *Select Library of Nicene and Post-Nicene Fathers*, 2nd series, vol. 10 (Wheaton, IL: Christian Classics Ethereal Library, 1961), p. 397.

Cited in Leslie Abend Callahan, note 8. For Jerome's "Letter to Furia," see Callahan, p. 247.

28. Julia Schiesari, pp. 163–64, citing Petrarch's letter from Benjamin G. Kohl and Ronald G. Witt, eds., with Elizabeth B. Welles, *The Earthly Republic: Italian Humanists on Government and Society* (Philadelphia: University of Pennsylvania Press, 1978), pp. 35–78.

29. See also Margaret Hallissey, *Clean Maids, True Wives, Steadfast Widows: Chaucer's Women and Medieval Codes of Conduct* (Westport, CT: Greenwood Press, 1993), chapt. 9, " 'Wel at ese': Widowhood," pp. 135–61.

30. David Seaman's ascription of psychological depth to Dorigen's character is an interesting reading of the passage where she speaks fearfully about the rocks lining Brittany's coast. I wish that I could more wholly agree with him that the effect of our learning of those fears "through her own lengthy discussion of them" is to "encourage the reader to empathize with her situation in human terms" (45). However, early on, the narrator has blocked our empathy by characterizing her grief as arbitrary and as extreme. He continues: her mourning, he says, is a *type* of mourning: she mourns as noble wives do when it pleases them (818). Then he represents her mourning as "dark fantasy." By the time that she reflects upon the danger of the rocks, he has ascribed to her character such a prodigality of grief that psychological depth is fairly much precluded.

31. Nina Manasan Greenberg, p. 336. See also David Seaman's discussion of the various value systems implicit in religious, legal, and courtly love's oaths, thus illuminating the ways in which the tale supports not just one answer but several (46–50).

32. Legitimizing men's grief: first, through men's claims upon women—sanctioned by the courtly love dynamic—and, second, through the religious exchange of vows of "trouthe" and love, with their canonical and civil law implications concerning husbands' exclusive sexual rights to their wives.

33. Mary Bowman, " 'Half As She Were Mad,': Dorigen in the Male World of the *Franklin's Tale*," *Chaucer Review* 27, No. 3 (1993): 239–51.

34. Mary Bowman, p. 248.

35. *The Riverside Chaucer*, explanatory notes, the *Franklin's Tale*, 1355–1456: "Critics generally complain about the passage's inordinate length, rhetorical excesses, apparent disorganization, and display of learning for its own sake."

36. Jane H. Hill, "Weeping as a Meta-signal in a Mexicano Woman's Narrative" in *Journal of Folklore Research* 27, Nos. 1/2 (1990): 29–49, 43, n.9.

37. *The Riverside Chaucer*, explanatory notes, the *Clerk's Tale*, 880, cites as the tale's source "Petrarch's Latin story *De obedientia ac fide uxoria mythologia* (A Fable of Wifely Obedience and Faithfulness)"—a translation of the last story of Boccaccio's *Decameron*. "Petrarch first wrote his version in 1373 and placed it as the last letter of his final work, the *Epistolae seniles* (17.3)."

38. J. Burke Severs, *The Literary Relationship of Chaucer's "Clerk's Tale"* (New Haven, CT: Yale University Press, 1942), pp. 231–34; 231.

39. *The Riverside Chaucer*, explanatory notes, the *Clerk's Tale*, 880, notes that "Chaucer made extensive use of one of the French translations of Petrarch." See Severs, pp. 190–211.

40. Severs, p. 231.

41. As I've noted elsewhere ("The *Clerk's Tale:* Interrogating Virtue through Violence," in *Violence in the Middle Ages*, ed. D. Theirry [at press, University of Toronto]), Walter states that he tested Griselda to see how resolute her faithfulness was. However, Chaucer introduces a judgment voiced by the Clerk: "Nedelees, God woot, he thoghte hire for/t'affraye" (454–55), and "But as for me, I seye that yvele it sit/To assaye a wyf whan that it is no nede, and putten hire in angwyssh and in drede" (460–62).

42. "The *Clerk's Tale:* Interrogating Virtue through Violence," in *Violence in the Middle Ages*, ed. D. Theirry (at press, University of Toronto).

43. David Raybin, 81, points to Dorigen's rising to a "higher moral level" at the end when "She kindly pardons Arveragus' failure to defend her body, showing no anger, 1553." Yet, as I see it, the lines reflect very little moral resolution. The lines, 1551–55, read: "Arveragus and Dorigen his wyf/In sovereyn blisse leden forth hir lyf./Nevere eft ne was ther angre hem bitwene./He cherisseth hire as though she were a queene,/And she was to hym trewe for everemoore." Unfortunately, since she was not angry with him in the first place—and indeed sees herself at fault—the line suggests a dismaying irony, namely, that *he* was not ever angry again. In the second place, since she thanked Aurelius "upon hir knees al bare," her abject position assumes that she sees herself as *owing* gratitude to Aurelius. And, third, when she tells her husband of Aurelius' releasing her from her promise, the next line reads, And you can be certain that "he was so weel apayd." "Apayd" surely intends to echo Aurelius' "releasing" Dorigen from "every serement and every bond" (1533–34), reminding us that in their masculine economy Dorigen's body was a commodity, and reminding us, too, of the deficiencies in the gender-specific construct of "fraunchise" and "gentillesse."

44. Kathleen Woodward, "Grief-Work in Contemporary American Cultural Criticism," *Discourse* 15.2 (1992–93): 94–112. See also, Eric Santner, *Stranded Objects: Mourning, Memory, and Film in Postwar Germany* (Ithaca, NY: Cornell University Press, 1990), pp. 25–30, and 126–27.

Chapter 4

1. An early version of one segment of this chapter, " 'The Saracen Uncrystynde' in Malory's *Le Morte Arthur*," was delivered to the MLA, Session 740, December 1998; an early version of another segment was delivered as "Depression, Anxiety, and Knighthood: The Case of Malory's Sir Palomydes," to the 35rd International Medieval Congress, Kalamazoo, MI (May 2000).

2. Mark Strand, "A Poet's Alphabet," *The Weather of Words: Poetic Invention* (New York: Alfred A. Knopf, 2000), pp. 4–5. I thank my student Melissa Baland for this reference.

3. *La Chanson de Roland,* ed. Gerald J. Brault (University Park: Pennsylvania State University Press, 1984), ll. 2929–32.

4. *La Chanson de Roland,* ed. Brault, ll. 3720–23.

5. Homer, *The Iliad,* trans. Richard Lattimore (Chicago: University of Chicago Press, 1951), 18.22.

6. Homer, *The Iliad,* 19.213–14.

7. *The Riverside Chaucer,* ed. Larry D. Benson (Boston: Houghton Mifflin, 1987), "Knight's Tale," ll. 896–902.

8. Sir Thomas Malory, *The Works of Sir Thomas Malory,* ed. Eugène Vinaver, rev. P. J. C. Field, 3rd ed. (Oxford: Clarendon Press, 1990), 2.866. All subsequent citations will be to this edition of Malory and will be given parenthetically in the text.

9. This is found in an interpolation separating two Tristan–Palamédes challenges in a fourteenth-century variant, MS BN 757. Malory most probably worked from several texts of the French Prose *Tristan.* See Eilert Löseth, *Le roman en prose de Tristan, le roman de Palamède, et la compilation de Rusticien de Pise: analyse critique d'après les Manuscrits de Paris* (Émile Bouillon: Paris, 1890).

10. This is a keen moment of literary reflexivity, since this episode suggests that the "great book" is the whole of the Prose *Tristan* itself.

11. Löseth, *Le roman en prose de Tristan,* p. 302: "[I]l plaignait surtout la mort de Tristan, qu'il trouvait sans pareil et supérieur à Galaas, comme il préférait Palamède à Lancelot, pour quelle raison, car l'histoire du saint Graal ne dit pas que Lancelot soit moins digne d'éloge que Palamède." For a useful summary in English of the Prose *Tristan* and insights into Malory's Palomydes, see the unpublished dissertation of Nina H. Dulin-Mallory, "A Grete Sygnyfycasion: Malory's Palomides" (Auburn University, 1995).

12. Vida D. Scudder, *Le Morte Darthur of Sir Thomas Malory & its Sources* (New York: E.P. Dutton & Co, 1917), p. 229.

13. So titled by Vinaver.

14. The most useful contemporary studies of literary Saracens can be found in Jacqueline de Weever, *Sheba's Daughters: Whitening and Demonizing the Saracen Woman in Medieval French Epic* (New York: Garland, 1998), and John Darrah, *Paganism in Arthurian Romance* (Cambridge, UK: The Boydell Press, 1997). In "The Literary Role of the Saracens in the French Epic," *PMLA* 55 (1940): 628–59, W.W. Comfort argues that, by the twelfth century, Saracens had become simply the conventional, quite civilized enemies of Christendom.

15. The *OED* and *MED* tell us that the etymology of Saracen is uncertain, but the Oxford *Dictionary of the Christian Church* suggests it is a late antique name for nomadic people of Syro-Arabian desert, and later any non-Christian heathen. Saracens were commonly thought to derive from the Agareni (Hagarenes, descendents of Sarah). The term may derive etymologically from the Arabic *sharqi,* meaning eastern, oriental, sunrise. In any case, it first appears in the fourth century. For a full historical survey, see

John V. Tolan, *Saracens: Islam in the Medieval European Imagination* (New York: Columbia University Press, 2002).

16. Michel Foucault, *Folie et déraison. Histoire de la folie à l'âge classique* (Paris: Plon, 1961), pp. iv–v.

17. Darrah, *Paganism and Arthurian Romance*, especially pp. 246–47.

18. In Malory, however, Saracen is inevitably connected to Sarras, the city to which the Grail leads the three successful Grail knights, and of which Galahad becomes mayor for a year before being received into God's hands. Vinaver points out (*Works*, commentary 3.908.18) that Malory omits any geographical information about Sarras, suggesting "perhaps intentionally, that it is within the boundaries of Arthur's kingdom."

19. "It is clear that the hegemonic impulse thematized in the chivalric quest was a fact of culture and that its failure in the political realm . . . in no way invalidated its hold in other areas, as Edward Said has convincingly shown. Politically, the West may have had to grudgingly accept the existence of the Islamic otherness, but in the realm of knowledge it acknowledged no such possibility," Michel de Certeau, *Heterologies: Discourse on the Other,* trans. Brian Massumi (Minneapolis: University of Minnesota Press, 1986), p. xiii.

20. The Questing Beast may refer to "a peculiar barking uttered by dogs when in sight of game," as suggested by the OED; Malory tells us most inexplicitly that it is a "full wonderfull beste and a gret significasion" (2.717); see Dulin-Mallory, "A Grete Sygnyfycasion: Malory's Palomides" and Helmut Nickel, "What was the Questing Beast?" *Arthuriana* (forthcoming).

21. Fratricide is a prominent motif of the text: the brothers Balin and Balan kill each other; Gareth and Gawain barely avoid fratricide.

22. Even though both Sir Tristram and Sir Palomydes become knights of the Round Table in Malory, they are adamantly outsiders to Arthurian culture. They are men without countries, and therefore they lack the political medium through which adventure becomes most meaningful.

23. For ideas of worship in the "Tale of Sir Tristram," see Dhira Mahoney, "Malory's 'Tale of Sir Tristram': Source and Setting Reconsidered," *Medievalia et Humanistica* n.s. 9 (1979): 175–98.

24. As Mahoney says, "Malory's Palomydes is Tristram's rival as much in worship as in love, and, furthermore, a disciple as much as a rival" (189).

25. For readings that highlight the complex roles of Sir Palomydes, see particularly Robert Merrill, *Sir Thomas Malory and the Cultural Crisis of the Late Middle Ages*, American University Studies, Series 4, vol. 39 (New York: Peter Lang, 1986) and Andrew Lynch, *Malory's Book of Arms* (Cambridge, UK: D.S. Brewer, 1997).

26. Malory strips and condenses the "courtly colouring" of his source. Even Sir Palomydes questions its ennobling power in his famous " 'A, fayre lady, why love I the?' " speech, in which the knight calls himself " 'but a fool' " for being a lover. See Vinaver, *Works* (3.1488–89.592.4–14).

27. Malory emphasizes this triangulation and rivalry from each perspective. Sir Palomydes' desire for Isolde prompts her to love Tramtryst/Tristram, and "induced him to fall in love with her," Vinaver, *Works* (3.1458.385.6–8).

Chapter 5

1. In striking contrast to the interpretation offered here, an early reading describes the same subject as "very busy writing." See Wilhelm Bode, *Sandro Botticelli,* trans. F. Renfield and F. L. Rudston Brown (London: Methuen, 1925), p. 125. On this painting, see also Ronald W. Lightbown, *Sandro Botticelli,* vol. 2 (Berkeley and Los Angeles: University of California Press, 1978), pp. 85–86.

2. Dated to 1480, this fresco was painted as a pendant to Ghirlandaio's *Saint Jerome in His Study,* also in the church of the Ognissanti in Florence. Giorgio Vasari, *Lives of the Artists,* trans. George Bull, vol. 1 (London: Penguin, 1987), p. 225, describes this early version of Augustine as being "very favourably received, for Botticelli succeeded in expressing in the head of the saint that air of profound meditation and subtle perception characteristic of men of wisdom who ponder continuously on difficult and elevated matters."

3. See Laurie Schneider Adams, *Italian Renaissance Art* (Boulder, CO: Westview Press, 2001), pp. 234–37.

4. On the popularity of the cult of Monica in fifteenth-century Italy, see Clarissa W. Atkinson, " 'Your Servant, My Mother:' the Figure of St. Monica in the Ideology of Christian Motherhood," in *Immaculate and Powerful: The Female in Sacred Image and Social Reality,* ed. Constance H. Buchanan and Margaret R. Miles (Boston: Beacon Press, 1985), pp. 139–72, especially 147–52; Kate Lowe, "Nuns and Choice: Artistic Decision-Making in Medicean Florence," in *With and Without the Medici: Studies in Tuscan Art and Patronage 1434–1530,* ed. Eckart Marchand and Alison Wright (London: Ashgate, 1998), pp. 129–53, especially 138–41, which addresses the patronage patterns of the Augustinian convent of Santa Monaca in Florence; and Catherine Lawless, " 'Widowhood was the time of her greatest perfection': Ideals of Widowhood and Sanctity in Florentine Art," in *Widowhood and Visual Culture in Early Modern Europe,* ed. Allison Levy (Aldershot: Ashgate Publishing Company, 2003), pp. 19–38.

5. Augustine, *Confessions,* trans. Henry Chadwick (Oxford: Oxford University Press, 1991), pp. 174–75; italics mine. The following excerpts from the Latin text are taken from Augustine, *Confessionum* (Leipzig: Teubner, 1898), pp. 87–88:

> Premebam oculos eius, et confluebat in praecordia mea maestitudo ingens et transfluebat in lacrimas, ibidemque oculi mei violento animi imperio resorbebant fontem suum usque ad siccitatem, et in tali luctamine valde male mihi erat. tum vero, ubi efflavit extremum, puer Adeodatus exclamavit in planctu atque ab omnibus nobis cohercitus tacuit. hoc modo etiam meum quiddam puerile, quod labebatur in fletus, iuvenali voce, voce cordis, cohercebatur et tacebat. neque enim decere arbitrabamur funus illud questibus lacrimosis gemitibusque celebrare . . . ego in auribus tuis, ubi eorum nullus audiebat, increpabam mollitiam affectus mei et constringebam fluxum maeroris, cedebatque mihi paululum: rursusque impetu suo ferebatur non usque ad erup-

tionem lacrimarum nec usque ad vultus mutationem. . . . Cum ecce corpus elatum est, imus, redimus sine lacrimis. nam neque in eis precibus, quas tibi fudimus, cum offerretur pro ea sacrificium pretii nostri iam iuxta sepulchrum posito cadavere, priusquam deponeretur, sicut illic fieri solet, nec in eis ergo precibus flevi.

6. Augustine, 1991, pp. 49–51. The following excerpts from the Latin text are taken from Augustine, 1898, pp. 49–50:

cum pro me fleret ad te mea mater, fidelis tua, amplius quam flent matres corporea funera . . . exaudisti eam nec despexisti lacrimas eius, cum profluentes rigarent terram sub oculis eius in omni loco orationis eius . . . cum tamen illa vidua casta, pia et sobria, quales amas, iam quidem spe alacrior, sed fletu et gemitu non segnior, non desineret horis omnibus orationum suarum de me plangere ad te.

See also, Nancy A. Jones, "By Woman's Tears Redeemed: Female Lament in St. Augustine's *Confessions* and the Correspondence of Abelard and Heloise," in *Sex and Gender in Medieval and Renaissance Texts. The Latin Tradition,* ed. Barbara Gold, Paul Allen Miller, and Charles Platter (Albany: State University of New York Press, 1997), pp.15–39.

7. On the fresco cycle, see Diane Cole Ahl, *Benozzo Gozzoli* (New Haven and London: Yale University Press, 1996), pp. 121–41.

8. The miniature, which was probably commissioned after 1430, is attributed to the Master of the Osservanza, whose name derives from a triptych in the church of the Osservanza outside of Siena; active in the second quarter of the fifteenth century, this painter probably worked with Sassetta. See Keith Christiansen, Laurence B. Kanter, and Carl Brandon Strehlke, *Painting in Renaissance Siena, 1420–1500* (New York: The Metropolitan Museum of Art and Abrams, 1988), pp. 99–102.

9. See, especially, Juliana Schiesari, *The Gendering of Melancholia: Feminism, Psychoanalysis, and the Symbolics of Loss in Renaissance Literature* (Ithaca, NY: Cornell University Press, 1992) and Sharon Strocchia, *Death and Ritual in Renaissance Florence* (Baltimore: The Johns Hopkins University Press, 1992). See also the following publications by Strocchia: "Gender and the Rites of Honour in Italian Renaissance Cities," in *Gender and Society in Renaissance Italy,* ed. Judith C. Brown and Robert Davis (London and New York: Longman, 1998), pp. 39–60; "Funerals and the Politics of Gender in Early Renaissance Florence," in *Refiguring Woman: Perspectives on Gender and the Italian Renaissance,* ed. Marilyn Migiel and Juliana Schiesari (Ithaca, NY: Cornell University Press, 1991), pp. 155–68; "Remembering the Family: Women, Kin, and Commemorative Masses in Renaissance Florence," *Renaissance Quarterly* 42 (1989): 635–54; and "Death Rites and the Ritual Family in Renaissance Florence," in *Life and Death in Fifteenth-Century Florence,* ed. Marcel Tetel, Ronald G. Witt, and Rona Goffen (Durham, NC: Duke University Press, 1989), pp. 120–45. On the relationship between Augustine and Petrarch, see, especially, Carol Everhart

Quillen, *Rereading the Renaissance: Petrarch, Augustine, and the Language of Humanism* (Ann Arbor: The University of Michigan Press, 1998).

10. Francesco Petrarch, *Letters of Old Age; Rerum senilium libri I-XVIII*, trans. Aldo Bernardo, Saul Levin, and Reta A. Bernardo, vol. 2 (Baltimore and London: The Johns Hopkins University Press, 1992), pp. 521–52, citation at 552.

   For the Italian text, see Francesco Petrarca, *Lettere Senili*, ed. Giuseppe Fracassetti, vol. 2 (Florence, 1892), pp. 333–81; citation at 380–81:

   > Ma che chiedi dunque? dirai tu. Eccomi al punto. Si cava di casa il morto, e una caterva di donne si getta sulla strada empiendo le piazze e le vie di mesti ululati, di clamori, di grida, che a chi ne ignori la causa farebbe sospettare o esser quelle maniache, o venuta la città in man del nemico. Quando il funebre corteo tocca la soglia della chiesa si raddoppia il frastuono, e mentre dentro si cantano I salmi, o a voce bassa e in silenzio l'anima del defunto con divote preci a Dio si accomanda, percosse dai femminili ululati orrendamente rimbombano la volte, e sembran tremarne commossi gli altari dei santi. E tutto questo perchè? Perchè un que nacque a morire è morto. Questa è la costumanza, che contraria ad ogni legge di decenza civile e di buon ordinamento della città, siccome indegna del tuo saggio governo io ti consiglio, e se fa d'uopo, ti prego che tu corregga. Comanda che nessuna donna esca di casa per codiare il corrotto. Se dolce ai miseri è il pianto, piangan pur quanto vogliono, ma dentro le domestiche pareti, e non turbino co'loro schiamazzi la pubblica quiete.

   For the Latin text, see Francesco Petrarca, *Rerum senilium liber XIV. Ad magnificum Franciscum de Carraria Padue dominum. Epistola I. Qualis esse debeat qui rem publicam regit*, ed. V. Ussani (Padua, 1922), pp. 1–47, especially 47:

   > Quid peto igitur dicam. Effertur funus, matrone cateruatim prodeunt in publicum uicosque et plateas altis complent inconditisque clamoribus, ut siquis rei nescius interueniat, facile possit aut illas in furorem uersas aut urbem captam ab hostibus suspicari. Inde, ubi ad templi fores est peruentum, geminatur fragor horrisonus et, ubi Cristo laudes cani siue pro defuncti anima deuote preces uel submissa uoce uel in silentio fundi debent, illic meste reboant querele et femineis ululatibus altaria sacra pulsantur, quia scilicet mortuus sit mortalis. Hunc morem, quia graui et nobili contrarium politie tuoque regimine indignum, censeo ut emendes, non tantum consulo, sed, si licet, obsecro. Iube ne qua prorsus hanc ob causam pedem domo fleat, faciem publicam non contristet.

11. As cited by Mosche Barasch, *Gestures of Despair in Medieval and Early Renaissance Art* (New York: New York University Press, 1976), pp. 88. The original text, which appears in Ludwig Rockinger, *Briefsteller und Formelbucher des elften bis vierzehnten Jahrhunderts*, vol. 1 (Munich, 1863), pp. 141–3, reads as follows: " 'In Tuscio fit excoriacio vultuum, pannorum scissio, et evulsio capilorum.' "

12. Diane Owen Hughes, "Mourning Rites, Memory, and Civilization in Premodern Italy," in *Riti e Rituali nelle Società Medievali*, ed. Jacques

Chiffoleau, Lauro Martines, and Agostino Paravicini Bagliani (Spoleto, 1994), pp. 23–38, especially 25–6.

13. Ibid., p. 31.
14. Ibid.
15. Strocchia, 1992, p. 11.
16. Writing from a psychoanalytic perspective, Schiesari, 1992, pp. 163–64, asks of this politicized restaging:

> Were these women's ritualized expressions of grief really disorder? How could they be disorder when mourning was part precisely of a symbolic order? I think what we need to see is that in the transition from a feminized symbolic (or one at least in which women had a more central role) to a masculinist symbolic, the "disorder of women" becomes part of an ideological apparatus that would empower men to hegemonize the public sphere, hence to phallicize the symbolic.

17. Hughes, 1994, p. 34.
18. Patrick Geary, *Phantoms of Remembrance; Memory and Oblivion at the End of the First Millenium* (Princeton, NJ: Princeton University Press, 1994), p. 177.
19. As cited by Ronald G. Witt, *Hercules at the Crossroads: The Life, Works, and Thought of Coluccio Salutati* (Durham, NC: Duke University Press, 1983), pp. 313–16, especially 313. The passage is taken from a letter written by Salutati to Jacopo Manni on June 15, 1396: " 'siccavi lacrimas, finivi fletus et gratias Deo referens, sic me, ipso donante, composui, quod damnum sentiens, dolori prorsus insensibilis factus sum.' " For the complete text of this and three more letters written by Salutati describing Piera's death and his emotional state during and after her funeral, see *Epistolario di Coluccio Salutati*, ed. Francesco Novati, vol. 3 (Rome, 1891–1911), pp. 126–28 and 133–42, especially 138. See also Strocchia, 1992, pp. 116–17, who contextualizes Salutati's manner of mourning within the new humanist tradition.
20. See, especially, John McManamon, *Funeral Oratory and the Cultural Ideals of Italian Humanism* (Chapel Hill: University of North Carolina Press, 1989).
21. Edward Muir, *Ritual in Early Modern Europe* (Cambridge and New York: Cambridge University Press, 1997), p. 5.
22. Strocchia, 1992, p. 106.
23. Ibid.; according to Strocchia, "the first third of the fifteenth century represented a critical passage from a relatively mobile society to a more elitist, stratified one, a passage that was enacted and dramatized in death rites."
24. Gordon Griffiths, James Hankins, and David Thompson, trans. and ed., *The Humanism of Leonardo Bruni: Selected Texts* (Binghamton, NY: Medieval and Renaissance Texts and Studies in conjunction with the Renaissance Society of America, 1987), pp. 337–39; italics mine.
25. Ibid.; see also Pier Giorgio Ricci, "Una consolatoria inedita del Marsuppini," *Rinascità* 3 (1940): 363–433; and Alison M. Brown, "The Humanist Portrait of Cosimo de' Medici, Pater Patriae," *Journal of the Warburg and Courtauld Institutes* 24 (1961): 186–221, especially 190.

26. On these orations, see Strocchia, 1992, pp. 146; and McManamon, 1989, pp. 113–14 and 249–92 for a finding-list. See also, Constance Jordan, "Feminism and the Humanists: The Case of Sir Thomas Elyot's *Defense of Good Women,*" *Renaissance Quarterly* 36 (1983): 181–201; Margaret L. King, "Book-Lined Cells: Women and Humanism in the Early Italian Renaissance," in *Beyond Their Sex: Learned Women of the European Past,* ed. Patricia Labalme (New York and London: New York University Press, 1984), pp. 66–90; and Paul Oskar Kristeller, "Learned Women of Early Modern Italy: Humanists and University Scholars," in Labalme, 1994, pp. 91–116.

27. Anonymous on Elisabetta Malatesta, as cited by McManamon, 1989, p. 226, n. 79:

> Quid illum dicendi usum et orationem? Testis es tu, illustrissime princeps, vosque conscripti patres, qui saepe cum in senatu rogati venissetis, suavissimam vocem, gravissimas sententias maxima semper cum admiratione audivistis.

28. Giannantonio Campano on Battista Sforza, as cited by McManamon, 1989, p. 226, n. 80:

> Audita est a Pio secundo pontifice maximo tanta cum attentione aut stupore potius ut excusaverit se ille, parem adhibere orationem non posse, et dolere atque angi quod tantum miraculum eloquentiae publicae et freqnenti [*sic*] collegio non admisisset, facturum id fuisse affirmavit, si vel dimidium sperasset ex femina, nec minore admiratione prosecutus est familiarem eius sermonem, castigatum et modicum, gravitatis simul et prudentiae plenum ut saepe repetierit hanc unam esse quae recte sciret et multum et parum loqui sensisseque nunc dicendi vim in femina quantam nunquam antea percepisset in viro, et inique actum esse cum feminis quibus passim erepta esset occasio dandi litteris operam cum in earum aliqua tantum natura cumulasset ingenii.

29. McManamon, 1989, p. 81.

30. Bruni's estimation of who constituted an orator's audience is published in Lorenzo Mehus, ed., *Leonardi Bruni Arretini. Epistolarum libri VIII,* vol. 2 (Florence, 1741), pp. 62–63 and is cited by McManamon, 1989, p. 165, n. 8:

> Ego autem non maiora ista puto quam nunc sint Evangelia Missarumque solemnia latine ac litterate in audientium turba pronuntiari. Intelligunt enim homines licet illitterati sint, nec tamen ipsi ita locuntur, nec illo modo loqui scirent, licet intelligant, propterea quod longe facilius est intelligere alienum sermonem, quam proferre. . . . Sed multo magis ad eos qui in rei publicae gubernatione versabantur et quorum intererat quid populus decerneret, orator loquebatur. Praestantes igitur homines oratorem latine litterateque contionantem praeclare intelligebant; pistores vero et lanistae et huiusmodi turba sic intelligebant oratoris verba ut nunc intelligunt Missarum solemnia.

31. The English translation is mine; the original Latin reads as follows: "POSTQUAM LEONARDUS E VITA MIGRAVIT HISTORIA LUGET ELOQUENTIA

MUTA EST FERTURQUE MUSAS TUM GRAECAS TUM LATINAS LACRIMAS TENERE NON POTUISSE."

32. McManamon, "Continuity and Change in the Ideals of Humanism: The Evidence from Florentine Funeral Oratory," in Tetel, Witt, and Goffen, 1989, pp. 68–9.

33. See Nancy J. Vickers, "Widowed Words; Dante, Petrarch, and the Metaphors of Mourning," in *Discourses of Authority in Medieval and Renaissance Literature*, ed. K. Brownlee and W. Stephens (Hanover, NH: Published for Dartmouth College by University Press of New England, 1989), pp. 97–108.

34. See, especially, Muir, 1997, p. 5:

> In practice it is often tricky to determine whether a specific performance is modeling or mirroring. Rituals tend to blur these two processes, which is perhaps the very source of the creative tension in rituals, the tension between a conservative mirroring of what is and the utopian modeling of what might be. Rituals are inherently ambiguous in their function and meaning.

35. See, especially, Strocchia, 1998, p. 42:

> Rituals marked important sites for the creation of gender identity. Ritual activities provided the stage settings for women and men to carry out socially appropriate behaviors. . . . In the process, rituals posited a set of gender expectations that were complicated by the realities of everyday life, for ritual practices embodying definitions of masculinity and femininity were alive to other variables.

36. Augustine, 1991, p. 176. The following excerpts from the Latin text are taken from Augustine, 1898, p. 189:

> ut eram in lecto meo solus . . . et libuit flere in conspectu tuo de illa et pro illa, de me et pro me. et dimisi lacrimas, quas continebam, ut effluerent quantum vellent, substernens eas cordi meo: et requievit in eis, quoniam ibi erant aures tuae, non cuiusquam hominis superbe interpretantis ploratum meum. et nunc, domine, confiteor tibi in litteris. legat qui volet et interpretetur, ut volet, et si peccatum invenerit, flevisse me matrem exigua parte horae, matrem oculis meis interim mortuam, quae me multos annos fleverat, ut oculis tuis viverem, non inrideat, sed potius, si est grandi caritate, pro peccatis meis fleat ipse ad te.

37. See Ahl, 1996, p. 125, for the suggestion that these are portraits of Fra Domenico and his superior.

CHAPTER 6

1. I cite from Robert Durling's landmark edition with English translation of *Petrarch's Lyric Poems: The Rime sparse and Other Lyrics* (Cambridge, MA: Harvard University Press, 1976), pp. 194–95.

2. Gaspara Stampa, *Selected Poems,* ed. and trans. Laura Anna Stortoni and Mary Practice Lillie (New York: Italica Press, 1994), pp. 122–23; translation modified.

3. Erinna 4 in *Sappho's Lyre: Archaic Lyric and Women Poets of Ancient Greece*, trans. Diane J. Rayor (Berkeley: University of California Press, 1991), p. 123.
4. Louise Labé, Elegy III in *Oeuvres*, ed. Charles Boy (1887; reprint, Paris: Slatkine, 1968), pp. 84–88; English translation by Edith R. Farrell in *Louise Labé's Complete Works*, ed. Edith R. Farrell (Troy, NY: Whitson Publishing Company, 1986), pp. 91–93.
5. Mary Kelly, *Post-Partum Document* (London: Routledge and Kegan Paul, 1985), p. xvi; cited in Emily Apter, *Feminizing the Fetish: Psychoanalysis and Narrative Obsession in Turn-of-the-Century France* (Ithaca, NY: Cornell University Press, 1991), pp. 113–14.
6. Apter, pp. 114–15.

Chapter 7

1. On François, see R. L. Knecht, *Renaissance Warrior and Patron: The Reign of Francis I* (Cambridge: Cambridge University Press, 1994). Marguerite's influence, still perceptible in 1544 when little Elizabeth Tudor translated her *Miroir de l'âme pécheresse*, had declined and, after her brother's death, effectively ceased. The standard biography is Pierre Jourda, *Marguerite d'Angoulême, Duchesse d'Alençon, Reine de Navarre (1492–1549): Etude biographique et littéraire*, 2 vols. (Paris, 1930; Geneva: Slatkine, 1978).
2. The standard edition is *Les Prisons*, ed. Simone Glasson (Geneva: Droz, 1978); no one knows how much was written before François died, but the lines on his death probably postdate the account in the *Oraison funèbre* of Pierre Du Châtel (May, 1547). Composed at the monastery of Tusson, the poem exists in two manuscripts and was first printed in *Les dernières poésies*, ed. Abel Lefranc (Paris: Colin, 1896). The edition by Claire Lynch Wade (New York: Peter Lang, 1989) has a clever English translation, although the introduction has errors (e.g., crediting d'Aubigné's *Tragiques* to Du Bartas) and ignores Glasson. I modernize *Amye* and *Amy* as *Amie* and *Ami:* "Amy" just doesn't look male in English.
3. Paula Sommers, *Celestial Ladders: Readings in Marguerite de Navarre's Poetry of Spiritual Ascent* (Geneva: Droz, 1989), p. 84; each section, she observes, is marked by an address to "Amie." Sommers points out that the narrator's "independence, initiative, and aggressiveness," although associated with maleness, "confer no spiritual advantages" (109).
4. L. 177. The tower's phallic quality—the lover is in a large vertical structure, not in a garden or chamber—cannot have escaped Marguerite.
5. In ll. 2603–6, the lover learns, e.g., that Ovid's Acteon allegorizes Christ: the deer's horns are Jesus' crown of thorns, and he dies surrounded by dogs (cf. Jesus' quotation of Psalm 22; the dogs appear in verse 16). On Marguerite's allegorical poetics, see Carol Thysell, *The Pleasure of Discernment: Marguerite de Navarre as Theologian* (Oxford: Oxford University Press, 2000), pp. 109–16. I agree that her Platonism is inflected by the Christian (and Jewish) belief that God descends when we cannot, unaided, ascend.

6. For Porete, God and soul merge into a "Loingpres," but for Marguerite they make a "Loing Pres"; see Thyssel, pp. 22–24, citing Robert D. Cottrell's *Grammar of Silence: A Reading of Marguerite de Navarre's Poetry* (Washington: Catholic University of America Press, 1986).

7. So says Olivier Zegna Rata, "La Preuve par la mort: les récits de morts dans *Les Prisons* de Marguerite de Navarre," *Revue d'histoire littéraire de la France* 92 (1992): 163–77. Rata ignores gender. Cottrell, *Grammar*, calls the death scenes *exempla* (304ff). Yes; and yet the *Heptaméron* treats *exempla* with some skepticism. One wonders what its more ironic *dévisants* might say about these dying admissions; even these *récits*, if hardly in this context, might be subject to debate.

8. Glasson notes, p. 35, that Evangelical faith welcomed deathbed admissions of sin because knowledge of sin precludes pride; such admission, she says on p. 41, shows a final detachment from edification and moral values. See also Robert D. Cottrell, "Spirit, Body, and Flesh in the *Heptaméron*," in Dora Polachek, ed., *Spirit, Body, and Flesh in Marguerite de Navarre's Heptaméron* (Amherst: Hestia, 1993), pp. 23–37; Cottrell notes that for Marguerite the "flesh" is sinful, but the body itself is merely human. (Religion, Marguerite might remind promoters of "family values," is not the same as behaving oneself.)

9. Gary Ferguson, *Mirroring Belief: Marguerite de Navarre's Devotional Poetry* (Edinburgh: Edinburgh University Press, 1992), p. 46.

10. This is often said in scholarship on the *Heptaméron*. Marguerite's charity does not extend to the regular clergy, roundly condemned for hypocrisy, superstition, and sexual misconduct.

11. *Poésies du roi François Ier, de Louise de Savoie Duchesse d'Angoulême, de Marguerite, reine de Navarre, et Correspondance intime du roi avec Diane de Poitiers et plusieurs autres dames de la cour*, ed. M. Aimé Champollion-Figeac (Geneva: Slatkine, 1970). The four deaths make a quaternity, or perhaps a double set of mother-son dyads with Marguerite somewhere near both—a double role in the formation of *two* linked "trinities." For Cottrell (*Grammar* p. 310), the deaths impose a "Pythagorean tetrad, the symbol of created matter," on "the triadic configurations so deliberately stressed throughout much of the work."

12. Recent treatments of posthumous rumors have focused on Marguerite's adoration and ignored François' less hyperbolic expressions.

13. François Ier, *Oeuvres poétiques*, ed. J. E. Kane (Geneva: Slatkine, 1984), p. 6.

14. Edgar Wind, *Pagan Mysteries of the Renaissance* (New York, 1958); Raymond Waddington, "The Bisexual Portrait of Francis I: Fontainebleau, Castiglione, and the Tone of Courtly Mythology," in Jean Brink et al., ed., *Playing With Gender: A Renaissance Pursuit* (Urbana: University of Illinois Press, 1991), pp. 99–132; and Barbara Hochstetler Meyer, "Marguerite de Navarre and the Androgynous Portrait of François Ier," *Renaissance Quarterly* 48 (1995): 287–325. Mayer quotes some loving lines by Marguerite, although none by François, which may explain her reference on p. 309 to "unrequited love." The king is cooler—male reticence? an iden-

tity less bound up with the more powerful sibling?—but he could be affectionate. Meyer, too, rejects any thought of actual incest. On François, Marguerite, death, and love see also Collette H. Winn, "L'Expérience de la mort dans *La Navire*," in *Love and Death in the Renaissance*, eds. Kenneth Bartlett, Konrad Eisenbichler, and Janice Liedl (Ottawa: Dovehouse, 1991), pp. 199–219; in *Navire* the dead François, says Winn, treats death as the pair's recoveries ("retrouvailles"), a sort of "union amoureuse" (209) that recalls their life together in the world below.

15. Leah Middlebrook, " 'Tout mon office': Body Politics and Family Dynamics in the Verse and Epîtres of Marguerite de Navarre," *Renaissance Quarterly* 54 (2001): 1108–41; surprising errors, though, can spoil her clever claims, and she underestimates Marguerite's public role. Middlebrook does not comment on the Evangelical-minded letter that Marguerite sent her brother with the gift of a "David" (an implicit instruction?) or the king's more traditionally Catholic reply (an implicit rebuke?) that accompanied his return gift of a "Saint Katherine" (Champollion-Figeac, pp. 63–72), traditionally an aid to childbirth. François offers Marguerite's baby an almost paternal welcome: come, sweet child, however little we sinners deserve you, and I will hold you in my arms.

16. Cf. Julia Kristeva, *Black Sun: Depression and Melancholia*, trans. Leon S. Roudiez (New York: Columbia University Press, 1989), p. 45, who notes the presence in female mourning/depression of "the fantasy of a phallic mother." Marguerite's "phallic mother" was no fantasy, however, and the narrator of *Prisons* praises her strength. A "denial of the father's function," as Kristeva puts it, was easier for Marguerite in that her actual father had died when she was a baby. For a related but distinct view see Lynn Enterline's provocative (if sometimes cryptic) *Tears of Narcissus: Melancholia and Masculinity in Early Modern Writing* (Stanford, CA: Stanford University Press, 1995). Does cross-gendering offer escape from narcissism? With a sex change, Narcissus might learn Echo's trick of ventriloquizing, and Echo might take a look in the pool. She would see nothing, of course, but for Marguerite discovering one's "rien" is a grace.

17. Susan Snyder, "Guilty Sisters: Marguerite de Navarre, Elizabeth of England, and the *Miroir de l'âme pécheresse*," *Renaissance Quarterly* 50 (1997): 443–58, finds some ambivalence in Marguerite's love for François. On Mary Sidney, see Margaret P. Hannay, *Philips's Phoenix* (Oxford: Oxford University Press, 1990). Elizabeth Harris Sagaser's conference paper, "Elegiac Intimacy: Pembroke's 'To the Angell spirit of the most excellent Sir Philip Sidney,' " suggests that Mary Sidney's mourning for her brother entailed gestures toward both merged identity (including collaboration in the "world of words") and maternal loss, the poem being a paradoxical mix of humility and assertiveness. What Sagaser says fits well with Mary Moore's " 'This Coupled Work': Mary Sidney's 'To the Angell Spirit,' " presented at the 2002 RSA conference. Jennifer Vaught reminds me of the likewise complex dynamics in Viola's love for and temporary replacement of her brother in Shakespeare's *Twelfth Night*.

18. What Sylvie L. F. Richards says of male voices in the *Heptaméron* and how they enable Marguerite's comments on the gender system is relevant: "The separation of the authoritative voice into composite parts allows for a narration with a fractured time frame"; see her "Politically Correct in the Feminine Voice," in Jonathan Hart, ed., *Imagining Culture: Essays in Early Modern History and Literature* (New York: Garland, 2001), 121–32.

19. Sheri Wolfe Valentine, "Personal Ties: Book I of Marguerite de Navarre's *Les Prisons*" (http:/tell.fll.purdue.edu/RLA-Archive/1991/French-html/ Valentine, SheriWolfe.htm), hears anger in the narrator's disabused remarks on love and marriage. The poem "contains evidence enough of bitterness long held back, at last allowed expression"; no wonder, she adds, that it was not printed. She does not discuss the deaths but does suggest that the narrator's gender helps Marguerite's make use of her Neoplatonism, for in that tradition the aspiring soul is that of a man (indeed; yet the souls themselves can be female).

20. Ferguson, *Mirroring Belief,* pp. 118–19, notes that when visiting her captive brother, Marguerite had taken communion for him when he was too ill to do so.

21. Cottrell, *Grammar,* however, says that Ami comes to see diachrony itself as an illusion (292).

22. The unkind might also note the relevance of Kristeva's claim that depressive speech is "repetitive, monotonous" (43); Marguerite's *Prisons* is brilliantly conceived but does tend to expatiate where other poets might move on. For Marguerite, furthermore, as for many mystics, silence is less a failure of language than its triumph, the emptiness within the laurel wreath.

23. How speech relates to hiatus in *Les Prisons,* and to the split self that speaks in the voice of the other, is an interesting question. On rupture between human speech and God's Word, between language and Being, see Jan Miernowski, "La Parole entre l'Etre et le Néant: 'Les Prisons' de Marguerite de Navarre aux limites de la poésie exégétique," *French Forum* 16 (1991): 261–84. Marguerite's narrator is one response to the dilemma Miernowski notes: "La créature ne peut parler de sa propre voix" (the creature cannot speak in its own voice), for speech presupposes being, and being is from God. By ventriloquizing a male voice in so intimate a poem (a voice unlike the fictions in the *Heptaméron* or the persons in her drama), Marguerite separates her voice from herself, dis-*owns* it.

24. Cottrell says, p. 249, that "The seeming reversal of roles in *Les Prisons* is an illusion that disappears if we examine the functions that Marguerite assigns Amy and Amye within the text." Amie is not a Beatrice, he adds, because Ami has the authority, which as usual is male.

25. Although he never mentions Marguerite, the Lacanian arguments of Bruce Thomas Boehrer's *Monarchy and Incest in Renaissance England: Literature, Culture, Kinship, and Kingship* (Philadelphia: University of Pennsylvania Press, 1992) are suggestive.

26. On Marguerite's Platonism see, e.g., George Mallary Masters, "Marguerite de Navarre's "Prisons," *Renaissance Papers* (1973): 11–21.

27. For a complaint to this effect (and the problem it causes in studying Renaissance magic), see D. P. Walker, "Ficino's *Spiritus* and Music," in *Music, Spirit and Language in the Renaissance,* ed. Penelope Gouk (London: Variorum Reprints, 1985), pp. 146–50.

28. G. M. Masters exploits Jungian theory in "La Libération des prisons structurées: Les Prisons de Marguerite de Navarre," in *International Colloquium Celebrating the 500th Anniversary of the Birth of Marguerite de Navarre,* ed. Régine Reynolds-Cornell (Birmingham: Summa, 1995), pp. 111–22. For more on the Androgyne and the union of Rien and Tout, see Matthew Morris, "Diotima Liberata," pp. 53–61 in the same volume.

Chapter 8

1. *Midsummer Night's Dream,* V.i.52–55. Cited from *The Riverside Shakespeare,* ed. G. Blakemore Evans (Boston: Houghton Mifflin, 1974).

2. At least, not until Aesculapius has pieced together the broken Hippolytus so he can be restored to a more sheltered private life as Virbius, as he relates his story in Ovid's concluding book (15.491 ff), to comfort the grieving Egeria.

3. Furthermore, Lysander's prior commitment to Helena, together with Aegeus' preference for him, makes his love for Hermia seem doubly capricious. Shakespeare has kept the interchangeability of the two lovers but larded it with the stuff of comedy.

4. She recalls England's Cynthia, whose reluctance to see her nobles marry is continuing to frustrate them and incite them to secret marriages; but we are constantly being given conflicting information as to whether this story of the night unfolds in the darkness of a waning moon or the brightness of a full one. "A calendar, a calendar! Look in the almanac. Find out moonshine, find out moonshine" (III.i.53–4).

5. William Oram, in Oram et al., eds., *The Yale Edition of the Shorter Poems of Edmund Spenser* (New Haven and London: Yale University Press, 1984), p. 487.

6. A detailed comparison of the two poems is provided by (among others) D. Harris and N. L. Steffen, "The Other Side of the Garden: An Interpretative Comparison of Chaucer's *Book of the Duchess* and Spenser's *Daphnaïda*," *Journal of Medieval and Renaissance Studies* 8 (1978): 17–36. See also Dennis Kay, *Melodious Tears: The English Funeral Elegy from Spenser to Milton* (Oxford: Clarendon Press, 1990), especially pp. 47–66.

7. Cf. D.W. Robertson's review of scholarship on the poem in B. Rowland, ed., *A Companion to Chaucer Studies,* rev. ed. (New York: Oxford University Press, 1979), pp. 403–13. See also J. I. Wimsatt, *Chaucer and the French Love Poets: The Literary Background of the Book of the Duchess* (Chapel Hill: University of North Carolina Press, 1968); R. B. Burlin, *Chaucerian Fiction* (Princeton, NJ: Princeton University Press, 1977), pp. 69–74.

8. Useful general studies are those of A. S. Miskimin, *The Renaissance Chaucer* (New Haven, CT and London: Yale University Press, 1975) and A. K. Hieatt,

Chaucer, Spenser, Milton: Mythopoeic Continuities and Transformations (Montreal: McGill-Queen's University Press, 1975).

9. See the explanatory notes by Colin Wilcockson in L. D. Benson, ed., *The Riverside Chaucer*, 3rd ed. (Boston: Houghton Mifflin, 1987). All quotations from Chaucer are taken from this edition.

10. *Ovid*, vol 2., *Metamorphoses: Books IX–XV*, trans. F. J. Miller (1916; reprint, Cambridge, MA and London: Harvard University Press, 1984). All future references to Ovid are from this edition.

10. The mysterious Eclympasteyr may be a corruption via Froissart of Ovid's Icelos and Phobetor, other sons of Sleep, with a possible play on his inclining posterior; Wilcockson, *loc.cit.*.

11. Quotations from *The Faerie Queene* follow the Longman edition of A.C. Hamilton, 2nd ed. (Harlow and London: Pearson Education, 2001), text edited by Shohachi Fukuda, Hiroshi Yamashita, and Toshiyuki Suzuki. For fuller commentary on this passage, cf. Donald Cheney, *Spenser's Image of Nature* (New Haven, CT and London: Yale University Press, 1966), pp. 29ff.

12. The fact that Alcyone is a daughter of Aeolus, god of the winds, seems to implicate her further in her husband's fate, as if (like Theseus above) Ceyx had wed the storm that would destroy him. Apollodorus, I.vii.4, says that Ceyx and Alcyone were punished for their pride, having considered themselves such a perfect match that they called each other Zeus and Hera.

13. Quotations from *Daphnaïda* follow the edition by Richard A. McCabe, *The Shorter Poems* (New York: Penguin, 1999). McCabe observes (642), that Spenser's adoption of a rhyme royal variant lacking the concluding couplet of each stanza reinforces the brooding and unresolved tone of the work.

14. William Oram, "*Daphnaïda* and Spenser's Later Poetry," *Spenser Studies* 2 (1981): 141–58. McCabe suggests (*ed. cit.*, 643–4) that in giving Gorges the name of Ovid's Alcyone, Spenser's transference of a feminine name to his male protagonist may be intended to suggest the emasculating effects of excessive grief—a common Renaissance topos. . . . "Alcyon later compares himself to Ceres (463) and Philomela (475)."

15. See especially H. E. Sandison, "Arthur Gorges, Spenser's Alcyon and Ralegh's Friend," *PMLA* 43 (1928): 645–74, and her later edition of Gorges' *Poems* (Oxford: Clarendon University Press, 1953). From the apparent allusion in "March" of *The Shepheardes Calender* to Leicester's secret marriage to Lettice Knowles ("Tho shall we sporten in delight,/And learne with Lettice to wexe light," 19–20), to the identification of Timias and Amoret with the Ralegh-Throckmorton marriage, Spenser goes out of his way to allude to transgressive marriages. If he knew of Apollodorus' view of the Ceyx-Alcyone marriage as a similar instance of *lèse-majesté*, he might well have decided to pull out every stop in celebrating Alcyon's love and its loss at the hands of a "satyre."

16. Cf. Annabel Patterson, "Re-opening the Green Cabinet: Clément Marot and Edmund Spenser," *English Literary Renaissance* 16 (1986): 44–70.

17. The formal structure of the poem, in seven sections of seven seven-line stanzas, has in itself been taken as an elegiac containment of grief, whether or not the speaker understands it as such. Dennis Kay, *Melodious Tears: The English Funeral Elegy from Spenser to Milton* (Oxford: Oxford University Press, 1990); Maren-Sofie Røstvig, *The Hidden Sense and Other Essays* (Oslo: Inneholder, 1963).

18. Applied to Cyparissus, who "pynd away" to become a cypress after the death of his pet deer, *F.Q.*, I.vi.17.

19. As Sandison documents in great detail, Ambrosia was also cherished as an heiress who could have made her father's fortune if she had not died before he could marry her off. Some sense of the contested monetary worth of Douglas and her offspring may have added a further resonance to this passage.

20. Even more oddly, perhaps, Spenser compares himself to Orpheus at the opening of *Epithalamion:* "So Orpheus did for his owne bride,/So I vnto my selfe alone will sing . . ." Ovid (*Met.* 10.1–10) tells that Orpheus' attempt to summon Hymen in song was the beginning of his troubles: the torch sputtered, and then the bride was bitten by the serpent. The anxieties of *Epithalamion* seem to echo the gloom expressed by Alcyon and Colin.

21. Robert M. Durling, ed., *Petrarch's Lyric Poems* (Cambridge, MA and London: Harvard University Press, 1976), p. 311: "Quel rossigniuol che sì soave piagne/forse suoi figli o sua cara consorte. . . ."

22. Especially, it might be suggested, at a time when the Protestant and Catholic Reformations were making artistic images a contested arena—and, by questioning the existence of Purgatory, doing the same with ghostly visions.

23. Apollodorus has them changed into two different species, but Ovid is naturally silent on this detail.

24. An earlier version of some of the ideas developed in this essay appears in my "Spenser's Fortieth Birthday and Related Fictions," *Spenser Studies* 4 (1984): 9–12.

CHAPTER 9

1. This developmental trajectory of the male, first sketched by Nancy Chodorow in *The Reproduction of Mothering: Psychoanalysis and the Sociology of Gender* (Berkeley: University of California Press, 1978), has generated a large field of feminist analyses of Renaissance culture. Coppélia Kahn gives a lucid summary in "The Hand That Rocks the Cradle: Recent Gender Theories and Their Implications," in *The (M)other Tongue: Essays in Feminist Psychoanalytic Interpretation,* ed. Shirley Nelson Garner, Claire Kahane, and Madelon Sprengnether (Ithaca, NY: Cornell University Press, 1985), pp. 72–88. For the Renaissance, see, e.g., Kahn, *Man's Estate: Masculine Identity in Shakespeare* (Berkeley: University of California Press, 1980); Janet Adelman, *Suffocating Mothers: Fantasies of Maternal Origin in Shakespeare, "Hamlet" to "The Tempest"* (Berkeley: University of California Press, 1992); Barbara Bono, " 'The Chief Knot of All the Discourse': The Maternal Subtext Tying Sidney's *Arcadia* to Shakespeare's *King Lear,*" in

Gloriana's Face: Women, Public and Private, in the English Renaissance, ed. S. P. Cerasano and Marion Wynne-Davies (Detroit: Wayne State University Press, 1992), pp. 105–28; Gail Kern Paster, *The Body Embarrassed: Drama and the Disciplines of Shame in Early Modern England* (Ithaca, NY: Cornell University Press, 1993).

2. Interview called "On the Maternal Order," in Luce Irigaray, *Je, Te, Nous: Toward a Culture of Difference,* trans. Alison Martin (New York and London: Routledge, 1993), pp. 37–44, at 42.

3. Irigaray, "Divine Women" (1984), in *Sexes and Genealogies,* trans. Gillian Gill (New York: Columbia University Press, 1993), pp. 53–72, at 66.

4. Irigaray, *Speculum of the Other Woman* (1974) trans. Gillian Gill (Ithaca, NY: Cornell University Press, 1985), pp. 244–48.

5. Irigaray, *The Forgetting of Air in Martin Heidegger* (1983), trans. Mary Beth Mader (Austin: University of Texas Press, 1999), pp. 42–43.

6. Irigaray, "Place, Interval: A Reading of Aristotle, *Physics* IV," in *An Ethics of Sexual Difference* (1974), trans. Carolyn Burke and Gillian Gill (Ithaca, NY: Cornell University Press, 1993), pp. 34–55, at 49. See also Eve Tavor Bannet, "There Have to Be At Least Two," *Diacritics* 23, 1 (Spring 1993): 84–98, at 89–90.

7. Freud, "Female Sexuality" (1931) in *The Standard Edition of the Complete Psychological Works of Sigmund Freud,* ed. and trans. James Strachey et al. (London: Hogarth, 1953–74) vol. XXI, p. 225. Irigaray suggests the hope of release from these burdensome and haunting types, could we acknowledge and mourn birth:

> That mouth cavity of the child, like any desire, becomes a bottomless pit if the time spent in utero is a taboo issue and if no attempt is made to interpret and come to terms with the losses and the scars involved in our separation from that primary home and that first nurse. The child [of psychoanalysis] demands that the breast offer him everything.
>
> The everything that he once received in his mother's womb: life, home, both the home of his own body and of the mother's body that he inhabits, food, air, warmth, movement, etc. This everything is displaced into oral avidity because there is no way to place it in its space, its time. . . . The wound we can never heal, never cure, opens up when the umbilical cord is severed. . . . [but] the cord, already, has been cut and . . . all that is needed is to take cognizance of that fact. (*Sexes* 16)

8. Here I extend a point made by Kenneth Gross at a conference on Spenser held at Pembroke College, Cambridge, in July 2001, in a paper called "Green Thoughts in a Green Shade." See also Lauren Silberman on the ways that the Garden episode reflects critically on the representation of ideals, in her *Transforming Desire: Erotic Knowledge in Books III and IV of "The Faerie Queene"* (Berkeley: University of California Press, 1995), pp. 40–48. She argues that "the Gardens of Adonis rework Plato's theory of learning as recollection by emphasizing the dimension of fecundity excluded in the Platonic scheme" (41), an insight I extend later in this essay.

9. I borrow this term and freely adapt it from Hannah Arendt, e.g. in "Labor, Work, Action" in *Amor Mundi: Explorations in the Faith and Thought of Hannah Arendt*, ed. James W. Bernauer (Dordrecht and Boston: Martinus Nijhoff, 1987), pp. 29–42, or in *The Life of the Mind*, v. 2: *Willing* (New York and London: Harcourt Brace Jovanovich, 1978).

10. Just before the account of Belphoebe and Amoret's conception, the narrator tells us that at Belphoebe's nativity the heavens "all the gifts of grace and chastitee/On her... poured forth of plenteous horne/.../And all the *Graces* rockt her cradle being borne" (III.vi.2). The next stanza opens, "Her berth was of the wombe of Morning dew,/And her conception of the ioyous Prime," with an allusion to Psalm 110, "Thy birthes dew is the dew that doth from wombe of morning fall" (here cited, following Hamilton's edition, from the *Book of Common Prayer*). See Hamilton's full notes to III.vi.2–3; David Lee Miller, *The Poem's Two Bodies: The Poetics of the 1590 "Faerie Queene"* (Princeton, NJ: Princeton University Press, 1988), pp. 235–37.

11. *The Faerie Queene* is cited from A. C. Hamilton's edition (New York: Longman, 1977). Parenthetical references give book, canto, and stanza numbers.

   Spenser often displaces elements of his narrative from an expected locus to an unexpected one. The House of Alma in Book II, for instance, is allegorically structured like a body—perhaps a female body, presided over by a lady named Alma—but famously excludes anatomical sexual markers; the female sexual body missing there is represented in a different tonal register in the Garden of Adonis. See also note 15 below.

12. MacCaffrey, *Spenser's Allegory: The Anatomy of Imagination* (Princeton, NJ: Princeton University Press, 1976), p. 262.

13. Upton notes that "Goddesses and heroines often bring forth their children without pain; so Latona brought forth Diana, so Danae brought forth Perseus." *Variorum*, loc. cit. III.vi.27. But Chrysogonee's birthing in her sleep, without awareness, presents us with a greater anomaly and a bigger problem.

14. See Krier, *Gazing on Secret Sights: Spenser, Classical Imitation, and the Decorums of Vision* (Ithaca, NY: Cornell University Press, 1990), p. 141.

15. As Spenserians well know, Spenserian romance and its forebears by Malory and medieval writers displace to rhetorical set pieces and objects of the landscape emotions and psychic process not vouchsafed to their characters, thereby permitting the reader a gathering of affect and consciousness; furthermore in their mysterious events and unaccountable actions they imply parental figures who hold the characters even when they themselves cannot understand their experiences. Another way to get at the waywardness of romance is offered by Gordon Teskey in " 'As a stranger give it welcome': Courtesy and Thinking," presented at the Cambridge conference on Spenser in July 2001; he argues that romance introduces disorder or noise into thought, forces the structures of thought to become open and exploratory.

16. Quitslund makes this suggestion in "Mourning," 25: "The 'secret' state in which Adonis lies, protected in Venus' 'gloomy groue of mirtle trees' (43.3) and '*Lapped* in flowres and pretious spycery' (46.5, italics added), strongly suggests the living death of mummification." He and others also summon the parallel iconographic depiction of the Circean temptress Acrasia with Verdant, "Whose sleepie head she *in her lap* did soft dispose" (II.xii.76). But Verdant is not dead, and I think that both "lapped" and "in her lap" suggests infancy at least as much as they suggest death. They also suggest infantilization of a youth, but this does not preclude a more literal infancy as well.

17. Apollodorus tells of Aphrodite's wrath against Adonis' mother—in his *Library* named Smyrna—for not honoring her, and the goddess' punishment of inciting Smyrna's lust for her own father; later, after she's been transformed into a tree, "the tree split open and the baby named Adonis was born. Because of his beauty, Aphrodite secreted him away in a chest, keeping it from the gods, and left him with Persephone. But when Persephone got a glimpse of Adonis, she refused to return him. When the matter was brought to Zeus for arbitration, he divided the year into three parts and decreed that Adonis would spend one third of the year by himself, one third with Persephone, and the rest with Aphrodite. But Adonis added his own portion to Aphrodite's." Apollodorus, *The Library of Greek Mythology*, trans. Keith Aldrich (Lawrence, KS: Coronado Press, 1975), III.183–5 (pp.82–3). Aldrich tells us in a note that the smyrna "is an Arabian balsam, producing an especially sweet myrrh" (147). So being lapped in precious spicery would also have been, for Adonis, the nature of his life before birth, gestating within the tree. Marcel Detienne, *The Gardens of Adonis: Spices in Greek Mythology*, originally published in 1972, trans. Janet Lloyd (Princeton, NJ: Princeton University Press, 1994), is most useful in tracing many aspects of myth, cult, and botany with which Adonis is linked.

18. Jon Quitslund, "The Work of Mourning in Spenser's Garden of Adonis," *Renaissance Papers* (1997): 23–31, at 25. I am much indebted to this essay, now reworked in Quitslund's *Spenser's Supreme Fiction: Platonic Natural Philosophy and The Faerie Queene* (Toronto: University of Toronto Press, 2001), pp. 211–26. On Sidney as Amintas and his relationship to Adonis, see suggestions at least as early as Spenser's eighteenth-century readers and editors forward, in the Variorum *Works of Edmund Spenser*, ed. Edwin Greenlaw, Charles Osgood, and Frederick Padelford (Baltimore: Johns Hopkins University Press, 1934), *The Faerie Queene* Book III, pp. 259–60. But then I think that Sidney/Amintas (Adonis) is himself synecdochic for the many early deaths, in the 1580s, of boys and young men in the linked families of the Sidneys, the Russells, and the Dudleys; see Quitslund, "Spenser and the Patronesses of the *Fowre Hymnes*: 'Ornaments of All True Love and Beauty,'" in *Silent But for the Word: Tudor Women as Patrons, Translators, and Writers of Religious Works* (Kent, OH: Kent State University Press, 1985), pp.184–202. For a replete survey of the links between flowers and Adonis, see Nohrnberg, *Analogy*, pp. 513–14.

Hamilton reminds us that the broken fourth line was added in the 1609 edition; the 1590 edition had an 8-line stanza of complete lines. "There may be a witty point: the poet's verse is cut short even as lover's lives have been cut short" (*loc. cit.* III.vi.45).

19. There are now many accounts and analyses of maternal ambivalence; see for example the essays in *Representations of Motherhood,* ed. Donna Bassin, Margaret Honey, and Meryle Mahrer Kaplan (New Haven, CT: Yale University Press, 1994); Rozsika Parker, *Mother Love/Mother Hate: The Power of Maternal Ambivalence* (New York: Basic Books, 1995).

20. Elizabeth J. Bellamy, *Translations of Power: Narcissism and the Unconscious in Epic History* (Ithaca, NY: Cornell University Press, 1992), p. 198.

21. I am indebted to Jon Quitslund's unpublished translation of and commentary on this poem, and cite from his translation.

22. Quitslund, draft of essay published as "Questionable Evidence in the *Letters* of 1580 between Gabriel Harvey and Edmund Spenser," in *Spenser's Life and the Subject of Biography,* ed. Judith H. Anderson, Donald Cheney, and David A. Richardson (Amherst: University of Massachusetts Press, 1996), pp. 81–98. This essay incorporates many of Quitslund's ideas on "Ad Ornatissimum virum," and is another essay to which I am much indebted. See, *Spenser's Supreme Fiction,* pp. 35–48.

23. For surveys of interpretive activity on the boar, see Hamilton's edition, notes to III.vi.48 (p. 364) and Nohrnberg, *Analogy,* p. 560. Upton's suggestion can be found in the *Variorum,* loc. cit.

24. Silberman usefully addresses the issue of reader identification with Venus and/or Adonis, and takes "the problem of individual identification with models" as part of Spenser's "exploration of the larger question of philosophical idealism" in the canto (*Transforming Desire,* 40–41). The uterine nature of the cave is not in doubt; it is just one of many maternal "enigmatic spaces of feminine enclosure," as Bellamy calls them in her survey of such spaces in Book III (*Translations of Power,* 199–200). See also Dorothy Stephens' extended treatment of enclosed spaces of feminine intimacy in *Limits of Eroticism;* Philippa Berry, "Woman and Space According to Kristeva and Irigaray," in *Shadow of Spirit: Postmodernism and Religion,* ed. Berry and Andrew Wernick (New York and London: Routledge, 1992), pp. 250–64.

CHAPTER 10

1. Reference to Shakespeare is to the 2nd Riverside edition, ed. G. Blakemore Evans et al. (Boston: Houghton Mifflin, 1997). Reference to *The Faerie Queene* will be to A. C. Hamilton's edition (London: Longman, 1977). I have discussed the Spenserian allusions in *Richard III* in *Biographical Truth: The Representation of Historical Persons in Tudor-Stuart Writing* (New Haven, CT: Yale University Press, 1984), pp. 118–20.

2. See Hamilton, ed., p. 360, notes.

3. Frederick Copleston, *A History of Philosophy* (1950; rpt. Garden City, NY: Doubleday, 1962), v2:91. Cf. Edmund Spenser, *The Faerie Queene*, p. 360, note on stanza 30. For numerous additional examples of the seminal reasons in Renaissance thought, see James Nohrnberg, *The Analogy of "The Faerie Queene"* (Princeton, NJ: Princeton University Press, 1976), pp. 537–54, and John Erskine Hankins, *Source and Meaning in Spenser's Allegory: A Study of "The Faerie Queene"* (Oxford: Clarendon, 1971), pp. 234–86.

4. *Inventions: Writing, Textuality, and Understanding in Literary History* (New Haven, CT: Yale University Press, 1982), pp. 55–56.

5. *A New Variorum Edition of Shakespeare: The Poems*, ed. Hyder Edward Rollins (Philadelphia: J. B. Lippincott, 1938): 390–405, here 400.

6. "Venus and Adonis: Shakespeare's Critique of Spenser," *The Journal of the Rutgers University Library* 39 (1977): 44–60, here 52.

7. "Actaeon at the Hinder Gate: The Stag Party in Spenser's Gardens of Adonis," in *Desire in the Renaissance: Psychoanalysis and Literature*, ed. Valeria Finucci and Regina Schwartz (Princeton, NJ: Princeton University Press, 1994), pp. 91–119.

8. Williams, "The Coming of Age in Shakespeare's Adonis," *Modern Language Review* 78 (1983): 769–76, here 770, 775.

9. Cf. Lauren Silberman, "Singing Unsung Heroines: Androgynous Discourse in Book 3 of *The Faerie Queene*," in *Rewriting the Renaissance: The Discourses of Sexual Difference in Early Modern Europe*, ed. Margaret W. Ferguson, Maureen Quilligan, and Nancy J. Vickers (Chicago: University of Chicago Press, 1986), pp. 259–71, here 271. On sexuality and passion in the Garden, see also Katherine Eggert, "Spenser's Ravishment: Rape and Rapture in *The Faerie Queene*," *Representations* 70 (2000): 1–26.

10. See Peter S. Hawkins, "From Mythography to Myth-making: Spenser and the *Magna Mater Cybele*," *Sixteenth-Century Journal* 12 (1981): 51–64, here 57, 59; also my essay "The 'couert vele': Chaucer, Spenser, and Venus," in *English Literary Renaissance* 24 (1994): 638–59, here 653–54.

11. According to the Vulgate reading of Genesis 2:7, "Adam's fall infected the substance of which he was made, the *limus terrae*, or slime of the earth"; John Erskine Hankins, *Source and Meaning in Spenser's Allegory*, p. 137.

12. See also Eggert's discussion of "rapture" (in opposition to gynephobia) in the Garden, p. 9.

13. See my "Arthur, Argante, and the Ideal Vision: An Exercise in Speculation and Parody," in *The Passing of Arthur: New Essays in Arthurian Tradition*, ed. Christopher Baswell and William Sharpe (New York: Garland, 1988), pp. 193–206, here 194–95.

14. "Love as Trompe-L'oeil: Taxonomies of Desire in *Venus and Adonis*," in *Venus and Adonis: Critical Essays*, ed. Philip C. Kolin (New York: Garland, 1997), p. 281.

15. *Captive Victors: Shakespeare's Narrative Poems and Sonnets* (Ithaca, NY: Cornell University Press, 1987), p. 537.

Chapter 11

1. Thomas Heywood, *An Apology for Actors* (1612), I, B4r; Thomas Nashe, *Pierce Penilesse his Supplication to the Divell*, in *The Works of Thomas Nashe*, ed. Ronald B. McKerrow, vol. 1 (London: A. H. Bullen, 1904), p. 212.

2. Linda Bamber, *Comic Women, Tragic Men: A Study of Gender and Genre in Shakespeare* (Stanford, CA: Stanford University Press, 1982), p. 163; Jean Howard and Phyllis Rackin, *Engendering a Nation: A Feminist Account of Shakespeare's English Histories* (London and New York: Routledge, 1997), p. 101.

3. Anthony Munday, et al., *Sir Thomas More*, ed. Vittorio Gabrieli and Giorgio Melchiori (Manchester: Manchester University Press, 1990), 4.4.55–58.

4. Stephen Gosson, *Plays Confuted in Five Actions*, in E. K. Chambers, *The Elizabethan Stage*, vol. 3 (Oxford: Clarendon Press, 1923), p. 215.

5. Howard and Rackin, *Engendering a Nation*, p. 101. Alexander Leggatt points out that, while "[o]ur habitual division of Shakespeare's plays into comedies, histories, and tragedies, each play fitting one category, is largely based on the Folio of 1623," in fact, title-page evidence suggests that in Shakespeare's time the lines could be drawn differently and were not so absolute. The Quarto texts of *Richard III* and *Richard II* identify them as tragedies. The play we know as *3 Henry VI* was first published as "*The true tragedy of Richard Duke of Yorke, and the death of good King Henrie the Sixth*. . ." Alexander Leggatt, "The Death of John Talbot," *Shakespeare's English Histories: A Quest for Form and Genre*, ed. John W. Velz (Binghamton, NY: Medieval and Renaissance Texts and Studies, 1996), p. 11.

6. "Although antitheatrical invective typically attacked all theatrical perform-ance as effeminating, the English history play offered a significant excep-tion": Howard and Rackin, *Engendering a Nation*, p. 101.

7. The order in which the plays were composed has been the subject of con-siderable debate. For the purposes of this paper, however, I am interested only in the order in which the story is meant to unfold. Even if *Part I* was, as Edward Burns describes it in his recent Arden edition, a "prequel" writ-ten after the two plays now known as *Part II* and *Part III*, it was still clearly designed to function as the first part of a three-part series—in fact, it would be more clearly intended as a first part than if it had been written to be an independent play, with the sequels added later. See Burns, introduction to *Henry VI, Part I*, Arden Shakespeare (London: Thomson Learning, 2000), p. 4–5.

8. All references to *Part I* are to the Arden edition by Edward Burns.

9. On the gendering of wounded bodies as feminine, see Gail Kern Paster, *The Body Embarrassed: Drama and the Disciplines of Shame in Early Modern England* (Ithaca, NY: Cornell University Press, 1993), pp. 64–112.

10. All references to *Part II* are to the Arden edition by Ronald Knowles (Walton-on-Thames, Surrey: Thomas Nelson, 1999).

11. All references to *Part III* are to the Arden edition by Andrew S. Cairncross (London: Methuen, 1964).

12. See, for instance, *Part I* 3.1.107–122.

13. Margaret, who has played a leading role in the plot against Gloucester, seems dumbfounded: "What," she demands, "will your highness leave the parliament?" (*Part II* 3.1.197).

14. Knowles, *II Henry VI*, p. 244, ff.

15. The word derives from the same root as "gender," and implies a falling away from one's own sort or kind.

16. Most commentators on this scene suggest that Cade's dismissal of Saye "for pleading so well" is an extension of the class conflict over education that has been developed throughout the scene. But Cade is resisting, not only Saye's educated speech, but the softening effect that speech has on him.

17. While I agree with the many recent critics who see Shakespeare here as making "theatrical capital . . . by staging the cultural fantasy of the monstrous Amazonian woman" (Howard and Rackin, *Engendering a Nation*, p. 94), it should be clear that this is not all that is going on, since Margaret shares the stage, and the horrors, with Clifford during York's death and elsewhere.

18. Thomas Nashe, *Pierce Penilesse*, p. 212. On the probable identity of the scene Nashe describes with *I Henry VI*, see Burns, *I Henry VI*, p. 4 ff. Burns suggests that Nashe's numbers might even be underestimated (9).

19. Unlike Heywood, Nashe never says that the history play would inspire heroic action from its audience, but only that it inspired tears. Howard and Rackin, who use Nashe's quotation as support for their argument that the history play was viewed as a "masculine" genre, deal with the question of the audience's tears by distinguishing sharply between "historical" and "theatrical" representation in the Nashe passage. Because Nashe speaks of "the Tragedian that represents his [Talbot's] person," Howard and Rackin argue that "[t]he present actor who elicits the spectators' feminine tears suddenly displaces the historical character who constitutes the object of masculine emulation." They thus distinguish between the play "[c]onceived as historical drama," which "features the objects of representation" (i.e., the historical characters), and the play "[c]onceived as tragedy," which "features the theatrical power of the actor" (*Engendering a Nation*, p. 113). It seems more accurate, however, to acknowledge that the *Henry VI* plays function as both history and tragedy simultaneously; the one does not exclude the other (see Leggatt, "The Death of John Talbot," pp. 1–30). It is also misleading to maintain, as Howard and Rackin do, a distinction between "historical" and "theatrical" representation, the one "masculine" and the other "feminine," in the histories. While a figure like Joan of Arc is certainly both female and theatrical, an intensely masculine figure like Talbot is also intensely theatrical—as Nashe's passage surely makes clear.

20. Burns, *Henry VI, Part I*, pp. 2–3. On Alleyn's fame and wealth, see Andrew Gurr, *The Shakespearean Stage, 1574–1642*, 2nd ed. (Cambridge: Cambridge University Press, 1980), pp. 88–89. Alleyn's investments and his position as Philip Henslowe's son-in-law certainly contributed to his finan-

cial success, but it is clear that his popularity as an actor was also an important factor.

Chapter 12

1. *Hamlet.* IV.iii.52–56. All quotations of *Hamlet* are from *Hamlet,* ed. Harold Jenkins, The Arden Shakespeare (London: Thomas Nelson and Sons, 1997).
2. T. S. Eliot. "The Love Song of J. Alfred Prufrock," cited from *The Norton Anthology of Poetry,* 4th ed., ed. Margaret Ferguson, Mary Jo Salter, and Jon Stallworthy (New York: Norton, 1996).
3. Jacques Lacan, "Desire and the Question of Desire in *Hamlet,*" trans. James Hulbert, in *Literature and Psychoanalysis: The Question of Reading, Otherwise,* ed. Shoshana Felman (Baltimore, MD: Johns Hopkins University Press, 1982), p. 40.
4. The term *cross-coupler* (for chiasmus) is Puttenham's; see *The Arte of Englishe Poesie, 1589* (facsimile ed.) Kent, OH: Kent State University Press, 1970), p. 216, but see also, Joel Fineman, *Shakespeare's Perjured Eye: The Invention of Poetic Subjectivity in the Sonnets* (Berkeley: University of California Press, 1986), especially pp. 37–39, 71–74.
5. The usual proof texts for the prohibition against marrying a brother's widow, Lev.18:16, "Thou shalt not uncouer the nakednesse of thy brothers wife: it is thy brothers nakednesse," and Lev. 20:21, "And if a man shall take his brothers wife, it is an vncleane thing: hee hath vncouered his brothers nakednesse, they shall be childlesse" (KJV, facsimile ed. [Oxford: 1911]) clearly ground the incest as an encroachment on the brother's intimacy. To *uncover* one's brother's wife is to *see* his nakedness. The homoerotic implications are best understood in terms of the creative tension in Shakespeare's writing between a "poetics of the same" and a "poetics of difference," explored by Fineman in *Shakespeare's Perjured Eye.* Given that Elizabeth's legitimacy rested to some extent on the incestuous nature and consequent nullity of her father's marriage to his brother's widow, Catherine, the issue may have had renewed currency as her reign drew to a close with the succession unresolved. On the politics of the incest prohibition in early modern England, see Bruce Thomas Boehrer, *Monarchy and Incest in Renaissance England: Literature, Culture, Kinship, and Kingship* (Philadelphia: University of Pennsylvania Press, 1992).
6. I am indebted to David L. Miller for this point.
7. *I Henry IV,* V.iv. 65 cited from *The Riverside Shakespeare,* ed. G. Blakemore Evans, et al. (Boston: Houghton Mifflin, 1974). On fratricidal rivalry in Shakespeare, see Joel Fineman, "Fratricide and Cuckoldry: Shakespeare's Doubles," *Psychoanalytic Review* 64 (1977): 409–53. In *Shakespeare's Perjured Eye,* Fineman finds a rhetorical relationship between the theme of fratricide in the plays and the (literary) homoeroticism of the sonnets.
8. Joel Fineman, "The Sound of O in *Othello:* The Real of the Tragedy of Desire," *The Subjectivity Effect in Western Literary Tradition: Essays Toward*

the Release of Shakespeare's Will (Cambridge: Massachusetts Institute of Technology Press, 1991), pp.158–59; see also, *Shakespeare's Perjured Eye*, p. 299 and passim.

9. Cf. the third appearance of the ghost in *Hamlet*, when it appears in Gertrude's closet, telling Hamlet it has come "but to whet/Thy almost blunted purpose" (III.iv.111).

10. *Macbeth*, V.i.215–37, cited from *The Norton Shakespeare*, ed. Stephen Greenblatt, et al. (New York: Norton, 1999). On the relation of grief to male violence, see Gordon Braden, *Renaissance Tragedy and the Senecan Tradition: Anger's Privilege* (New Haven, CT: Yale University Press, 1985).

11. Jenkins follows F1 and so reads *scullion*. But Q2's *stallyon* has the merit of continuing and regendering the simile of the whore or drab who unpacks her heart with words, whereas *scullion* introduces a class notion otherwise not reflected in the passage. See OED: Stallion, 2b: "A man of lascivious life; in 17th and 18th-c., a woman's hired paramour," and 3a. "A courtesan. *Obs.*" The Q2 reading may also shed light on Hamlet's remark to Ophelia before the play-within-the-play in III.ii. "But by'r lady a must build churches then, or else sholl a suffer not thinking on, with the hobby-horse, whose epitaph is 'For O, for O, the hobby-horse is forgot" (130–33). Jenkins' curiously demure "longer note" on the hobby-horse begins "the *hobby-horse* is well described by Nares as consisting of 'the figure of a horse fastened round the waist of a man, his own legs going through the body of the horse, and enabling him to walk, but concealed by a long foot cloth; while false legs appeared where those of the man should be, at the sides of the horse.' The Puritan disapproval of his lewd antics sometimes led the hobby–horse to be omitted from the Games." Jenkins stops short of mentioning the obvious sexual innuendo of Hamlet's "epitaph," "For O, for O, the hobby-horse is forgot," which completes a bout of *double-entendre* that includes the exchange: "*Ham.* Do you think I meant country matters? *Oph:* I think nothing, my lord. *Ham.* That's a fair thought to lie between maids' legs" (III.ii.110–33). See also *OED* Hobby-Horse, n: 4. "A stick with a horse's head which children bestride as a toy horse." The phallic imagery of the hobby-horse between the legs is patent, as is Hamlet's conviction that his mother's sexuality forgets his father: forgets the phallic hobby-horse for O.

12. For a succinct and useful account of the development of the theories of transference, see the entry for *Transference* in J. Laplanche and J.-B. Pontalis, *The Language of Psychoanalysis*, trans. Donald Nicholson-Smith (New York: Norton, 1973).

13. *The Interpretation of Dreams* in *The Standard Edition of the Complete Psychological Works of Sigmund Freud*, trans. James and Alix Strachey, 24 vols. (London: Hogarth, 1953–73), 5, p. 562. This edition is hereafter cited as *SE*.

14. It is perhaps worth noting, however, that in the accounts of Saxo and Belleforest, the prince, who is a minor when his father dies and his uncle ascends the throne, survives to reign after his uncle's death. These source texts continue the story through the prince's reign to his death, at about the

age of Shakespeare's Hamlet. The design of the play thus collapses the trau-
matized youth and the man he becomes. There are obvious dramatic reasons for this redesign, but the effect, inadvertent or otherwise, is to animate
the child in the man, which helps explain why people (and theatrical direc-
tors) tend to think of Hamlet as younger than the thirty years the play
explicitly assigns him.

15. "The Dynamics of Transference" in *SE* 12, pp. 97–108.

16. "Remembering, Repeating and Working-Through" in *SE* 12, pp.145–156.
On transference and repetition, see also *Beyond the Pleasure Principle*, in *SE*
18, pp.18–23. The process of binding emotion through unconscious repetition underlies the classic readings by Freud and Jones of *Hamlet* as a reenactment of unresolved oedipal passions. In *The Interpretation of Dreams*,
Freud remarks that "Hamlet is capable of doing anything—except take
vengeance on the man who did away with his father and took that father's
place with his mother, the man who shows him the repressed wishes of his
own childhood realized. Thus the loathing which should drive him on to
revenge is replaced by self-reproaches, by scruples of conscience, which
remind him that he himself is literally no better than the sinner whom he is
to punish" (*SE* 4, p. 265). See also, *Introductory Lectures on Psychoanalysis*,
XXI: "But let us now turn from the direct observation of children to the
analytic examination of adults who have become neurotic. What help does
analysis give towards a further knowledge of the Oedipus Complex? . . .
Analysis . . . shows that each of these neurotics has himself been an Oedipus
or, what comes to the same thing, has, as a reaction to the complex, become
a Hamlet" (*SE* 16, p. 335). For a full-length Freudian reading of the play,
see Ernest Jones, *Hamlet and Oedipus* (London: Gollancz, 1949).

17. Aristotle, *Poetics*, Bk. 6, par 1; Milton, *Samson Agonistes*, line 1759, cited
from *John Milton: The Complete Poems*, ed. John Leonard (New York,
London: Penguin Books, 1998); see also, Jacques Lacan, "The Tragic
Dimension of Psychoanalytic Experience," in *The Seminar of Jacques Lacan,
Book VII: The Ethics of Psychoanalysis 1959–1960*, ed. Jacques-Alain Miller,
trans. Dennis Porter (New York: Norton, 1992), pp. 289–325.

18. Jacques Lacan, *The Four Fundamental Concepts of Psycho-Analysis*, ed.
Jacques-Alain Miller, trans. Alan Sheridan (New York: Norton, 1978),
pp. 244–60.

19. John Rajchman, *Truth and Eros: Foucault, Lacan, and The Question of Ethics*
(New York and London: Routledge, 1991), p. 43. See also, Lacan, *Four
Fundamental Concepts of Psycho-Analysis*, p. 254: "[W]hat is there, behind
the love known as transference, is the affirmation of the link between the
desire of the analyst and the desire of the patient. . . . It is the patient's
desire, yes, but in its meeting with analyst's desire."

20. Lacan, *Four Fundamental Concepts of Psycho-Analysis*, pp. 247–53.

21. *After Oedipus: Shakespeare in Psychoanalysis* (Ithaca, NY: Cornell University
Press, 1993), p. 15 and note 4.

22. T. S. Eliot, "Hamlet" in *Selected Essays* (New York: Harcourt, Brace, 1950),
pp. 121–27.

23. Lacan, "Desire and the Question of Desire in *Hamlet*," p. 11.

24. *Pitch* is the Q2 reading. F1 reads *pith*, which is also reasonable, but see Jenkins' gloss on *pitch*: "height, especially 'the height to which a falcon soared, before she stooped upon her prey' (Nares). Cf. *R[ichard]2* I.i.109, 'How high a pitch his resolution soars!' The association of *pitch* with *resolution* confirms the more authoritative reading of Q2." Of course Hamlet also asserts that his madness is asymmetrical: when the wind blows from the right direction he can tell "a hawk from a handsaw."

25. I am, once again, indebted to David L. Miller, for pointing out that the senses of hunt and peddle ascribed to the word *hawk* derive from two separate but homophonic verbs. See *OED, hawk*, v.[1] 4: ". . . to hunt after to endeavor to catch or gain," which comes from the noun *hawk* for the bird of prey, and *hawk*, v.[2] "to carry about from place to place and offer for sale, to cry in the street" and derives from low German *hocken* "to take upon the back." See *OED, hawker*, n.[2]

26. Rajchman, pp. 14–27.

27. Lynn Enterline, *The Tears of Narcissus: Melancholia and Masculinity in Early Modern Writing* (Stanford, CA: Stanford University Press, 1995), p. 15.

28. On the distinction between the *ideal ego* (the narcissistic image on which the ego is first constructed) and the *ego ideal* (the introjected image to which the ego unsuccessfully aspires), see Jacques Lacan, "The Subversion of the Subject and the Dialectic of Desire in the Freudian Unconscious," *Ecrits: A Selection*, trans. Alan Sheridan (New York: Norton, 1977), p. 315.

CHAPTER 13

1. Vera Fortunati, *Lavinia Fontana of Bologna, 1552–1614* (Milan: Electa, 1998), p. 70. On the painting, see Angela Ghirardi, entry for Cat. 49, in *Lavinia Fontana, 1552–1614*, ed. Vera Fortunati (Milan: Electa, 1994), p. 190, and Angela Ghirardi, "Exempla per l'iconografia dell'Infanzia nel secondo Cinquecento padano," *Il Carrobbio* 21–22 (1993–4): 123–39.

2. Margaret Whinney, *Sculpture in Britain, 1530–1830* (London: Penguin Books, 1988), pp. 9 and 230, n. 30, attributes to the tomb of Philip and Edward Hoby, commissioned by Elizabeth Russell in 1556, the importation of this style into England. See also Adam White, "Classical Learning and the Early Stuart Renaissance," *Church Monuments* 1 (1985): 23, and Helen C. Gladstone, *Building an Identity: Two Noblewomen in England, 1566–1666*, diss. Open University, 1989, p. 260. While there is no way of knowing whether the newborn is a son or a daughter, the death of a male heir and the failure of succession that his death entailed may have been a more likely prompt to the memorial canvas than the relatively less "meaningful" death of a daughter.

3. As Ghirardi, "Exempla," p. 130, suggests, the image imitates " 'state portraits' reconceived according to a more careful sensitivity to the world of infancy."

4. Moshe Barasch, *Gestures of Despair in Medieval and Early Renaissance Art* (New York: New York University Press, 1976), pp. 23–33, surveys the classical and medieval history of this gesture in detail.

5. Dorothy Leigh, *The Mothers Blessing. Or, The Godly Counsaile of a Gentlewoman, Not Long Since Deceased, Left Behind for her Children.* (London: John Budge), p. 7. The first edition appeared in 1616. See also Elizabeth Grymeston, *Miscellanea, Meditations, Memoratives* (London: Felix Norton, 1604), A2, who explains, "there is no love so forcible as the love of an affectionate mother to her natural child."

6. Judith Butler, *Gender Trouble: Feminism and the Subversion of Identity* (New York and London: Routledge, 1990), p. 92.

7. See Wendy Wall, *The Imprint of Gender: Authorship and Publication in the English Renaissance* (Ithaca, NY: Cornell University Press, 1993), pp. 296–310, for the argument that the mother's legacy involves the dissolution of their authors as a condition of their publication. Neither Vere's nor Carey's poems were apparently written with publication in mind. For discussion of Vere's sonnets, see Ellen Moody, "Six Elegiac Poems, Possibly by Anne Cecil de Vere, Countess of Oxford," *English Literary Renaissance* 19 (1989): 152–70; Steven May, "The Countess of Oxford's Sonnets: A Caveat," *English Literary Notes* 29 (1992): 9–19; and Louise Schleiner, *Tudor and Stuart Women Writers* (Bloomington: Indiana University Press, 1994), pp. 85–93. Carey's elegies appear within her *Meditation*, written at the age of forty-five, probably with the private readership of her family and descendants in mind and not published until the twentieth century. See *Kissing the Rod: An Anthology of Seventeenth-Century Women's Verse*, ed. Germaine Greer, Susan Hastings, Jeslyn Medoff, and Melinda Sansone (London: Virago Press, 1988), pp. 158–61.

8. I borrow the phrase, and its implications, from Jahan Ramazani, *The Poetry of Mourning: The Modern Elegy from Hardy to Heaney* (Chicago: University of Chicago Press, 1994), pp. x–xi and 1–31.

9. Anne de Vere, "Foure Epytaphes, made by the Countes of Oxenford after the death of her young Sonne, the Lord Bulbeck," in John Soowthern, *Pandora* (1584) (facs. New York: Columbia University Press, 1938), C4v. All further citations are to this edition and appear parenthetically.

10. Samuel Clarke, *The Marrow of Ecclesiastical History, Consisting of Two Parts* (London: Robert White for William Roybould, 1654), p. 250.

11. Francis Petrarch, "How a Ruler Ought to Govern His State" [*Seniles* 14:1], in Benjamin G. Kohl and Ronald G. Witt, *The Earthly Republic: Italian Humanists on Government and Society* (Philadelphia: University of Pennsylvania Press, 1978), pp. 77–78. For discussion, see Sharon Strocchia, *Death and Ritual in Renaissance Florence* (Baltimore: Johns Hopkins University Press, 1992), pp. 17–19, and Juliana Schiesari, *The Gendering of Melancholia: Feminism, Psychoanalysis, and the Symbolics of Loss in*

Renaissance Literature (Ithaca, NY: Cornell University Press, 1992), 163–64.

12. Clarke, *Marrow*, p. 250.

13. For examples of mother's diaries in the period, see Alice Thornton, *The Autobiography of Mrs. Alice Thornton*, ed. Charles Jackson (Durham: Andrews & Company, 1875); Anne Clifford, *The Diaries of Anne Clifford*, ed. D. J. H. Clifford (Wolfeboro Falls, NH: Alan Sutton, 1990); and Elizabeth Egerton, *True Coppies of certain Loose Papers left by the Right Honorable Elizabeth, Countess of Bridgewater. Collected and Transcribed Together here since Her Death, Anno Domini 1663*, BL Egerton MS 607. For discussion, see Patricia Phillippy, *Sisters of Magdalene: Women, Death and Mourning in Post-Reformation England* (Cambridge: Cambridge University Press, 2002), especially chapter 5.

14. Ralph Josselin, *The Diary of Ralph Josselin, 1616–1683*, ed. Alan MacFarlane (Oxford: Oxford University Press, 1976), pp. 61 and 33. For similar diary accounts of paternal grief, see Henry Newcome, *The Autobiography of Henry Newcome, M. A.*, ed. Richard Parkinson (Manchester: Charles Simms and Co., 1852), 2:252–4, and John Evelyn, *The Diary of John Evelyn*, ed. E. S. de Beer (Oxford: Clarendon Press, 1955), 3:420–31.

15. Josselin, pp. 114–5.

16. Josselin's first entries in the diary occur at the beginning of his career, retrospectively treating the events of his life up to that point. See 1–12.

17. Anonymous, *Preparation to Deeth* (London: Thomas Petyte 1545), N5. See also Valerie Wayne, "Advice for women from mothers and patriarchs," in *Women and Literature in Britain, 1500–1700*, ed. Helen Wilcox (Cambridge: Cambridge University Press, 1996), pp. 60–62, for Erasmus' renewed emphasis on this dictum in his *Puerpera (The New Mother)* and the extensive influence of this colloquy on sixteenth- and seventeenth-century ideals of maternity.

18. See Pamela Hammons, "Despised Creatures: The Illusion of Maternal Self-Effacement in Seventeenth-Century Child Loss Poetry," *English Literary History* 66 (1999): 25–49, for a provocative discussion of mourning mothers' manipulations of the cultural requirement for their own self-erasure in publication and interrogations of the conventions that blame mothers for their children's deaths.

19. Philippe de Mornay, *Philip Mornay, Lord of Plessis his Teares for the Death of his Sonne. Unto his Wife Charlotte Baliste*, trans. John Healey (London: G. Eld, 1609). All further citations are to this edition and appear parenthetically. According to Mornay's biography, he first wrote the treatise in Latin and translated it himself into French "for the love of his wife" (Apour l'amour de sa femme"): see Charlotte d'Arbaleste de Mornay, *Histoire de la vie de Messire Phillippe de Mornay Seigneur du Plessis Marly, &c.* (Leyden: Bonaventure & Abraham Elsevier, 1647), p. 317. The original Latin edition is *Philippi Mornai Lachrimae* (Paris, 1606). Philippe de Mornay's *Discours de la vie et la mort* was translated into English by Mary Sidney Herbert in 1592. See *A Discourse of Life and Death and Marcus Antonius* (London: William Ponosby, 1592).

20. Madame de Mornay concludes her husband's biography with the announce-ment of her son's death: "Happy end for him [our son] . . . But for us the beginning of a sorrow which can only end in death, with no other consola-tion but what the feare and the grace of God can give us while we chew the bitter cud of our grief." See Lucy Crump, *A Huguenot Family in the XVI Century: The Memoirs of Philippe de Mornay, Sieur de Plessis Marly Written by his Wife* (London: George Routledge, 1926), pp. 284–85.

21. Charlotte d'Arbaleste de Mornay, *Histoire*, pp. 318–19 and 322. The biog-raphy was compiled by David de Licques after the manuscript of Madame de Mornay until 1606 and for the seventeen years following, until the death of Philippe, using information furnished by his secretaries. The work ends by recording the good death of Philippe himself (705–715).

22. Sigmund Freud, "Mourning and Melancholia," in *The Standard Edition of the Complete Psychological Works*, trans. and ed. James Strachey et al. (London: The Hogarth Press, 1974), 14: 253.

23. Moody, p. 161.

24. Celeste Schenck, "Feminism and Deconstruction: Re-Constructing the Elegy," *Tulsa Studies in Women's Literature* 5 (1986): 16–18. See also Kate Lilley, "True State Within: Women's Elegy 1640–1740," in *Women, Writing, History 1640–1740*, ed. Isobel Grundy and Susan Wiseman (Athens: University of Georgia Press, 1992), p. 90. Melissa F. Zeiger, *Beyond Consolation: Death, Sexuality, and the Changing Shapes of Elegy* (Ithaca, NY: Cornell University Press, 1997), p. 64, makes a similar claim for contemporary women's elegies: "For women, as opposed to men, an alliance and continuity with the dead, and hence a rejection of canonical poetic iden-tity and succession, dangerously reinstate the old Orphean associations of women with death, silence, darkness, and above all, the loss of the body."

25. The image of the maternal body as sepulchre occurs in Thomas Becon's *Sicke Mannes Salve*, in *Prayers and Other Pieces of Thomas Becon*, ed. John Ayre (Cambridge: Cambridge University Press, 1846), p. 93, as a marker of desperate (that is, pre-consolation) fear of death: "O that my mother had been my grave herself, that the birth might not have come out, but remained still in her!"

26. See Thomas Laqueur, *Making Sex: Body and Gender from the Greeks to Freud* (Cambridge, MA: Harvard University Press, 1990), especially pp. 43–52.

27. This unorthodox resurrection employs "a nostalgia for maternal rather than paternal origins," which Schenck (23) sees as characteristic of women's elegies.

28. On the *planctus Mariae*, see Sandro Sticca, *The Planctus Mariae in the Dramatic Tradition of the Middle Ages*, trans. Joseph R. Berrigan (Athens: University of Georgia Press, 1988).

29. Kim Walker, *Women Writers of the English Renaissance* (New York: Twayne, 1996), pp. 61–62.

30. Freud, "Mourning and Melancholia," p. 246.

31. As Nicholas Abraham and Maria Torok "Introjection-Incorporation: Mourning *or* Melancholia," in *Psychoanalysis in France*, ed. Serge Lebovici and Daniel Widlocher (New York: International University Press, 1980), p. 6, write of the process of incorporation peculiar to melancholia: "it is because the mouth cannot articulate certain words, cannot utter certain phrases—for reasons to be determined—that in fantasy one will take into the mouth the unspeakable, the thing itself. The empty mouth, calling in vain to be filled with introjective words, again becomes the mouth greedy for food over speech: unable to obtain nourishment from words exchanged with others, it will take within itself, in fantasy, all or part of a person, the only depository for that which is nameless."

32. Schleiner (92) identifies the source for this image in the Ovidian myth of Tityus, whose liver is perpetually eaten by a vulture as punishment for transgressing against the gods. Similarly, Vere's self-consumption is staged as a transgressive, resistant discursive and lamentational form.

33. Referring to Carey's poem, Jonathan Sawday, *The Body Emblazoned: Dissection and the Human Body in Renaissance Culture* (New York and London: Routledge, 1995), p. 227, asserts that, "Very occasionally, we can glimpse a woman struggling against this pervasive system, questioning the analogical discourses within which her own language (of necessity) was formed. But usually, the result was failure."

34. Mary Carey, "Upon the Sight of my abortive Birth," in *Kissing the Rod: An Anthology of Seventeenth-Century Women's Verse*, ed. Germaine Greer, Susan Hastings, Jeslyn Medoff, and Melinda Sansone (London: Virago Press, 1988), pp. 158–61, ll. 28–29. All further citations are to this edition and appear parenthetically. Carey wrote poems on the deaths of two other children as well: "Wretten by me att the same tyme; on the death of my 4th, & only Child, Robert Payler;" in Greer, et al., pp. 156–7, and "Wretten by me at the death of my 4th sonne and 5th Child Perigrene Payler:" in Greer, et al., 157–8. Her husband, George Payler, also wrote a poem on the death of his son Robert, which begins, "Dear wife, let's learne to get that Skill,/Of free Submission to God's holy Will." See Greer, et al., p. 157, and for discussion, see Hammons, pp. 27–8.

35. Josselin, p. 371.

36. Charlotte F. Otten, ed., *English Women's Voices, 1540–1700* (Miami: Florida International Press, 1992), p. 225, similarly argues that Carey's use of reproductive metaphors "establishes her female identity, and . . . brings her female experience into an area free from male mediation." I find Otten's view of Carey's autonomy optimistic, but agree that the use of female reproductive metaphors carry particular weight in the female-authored work. See also Donna J. Long, " 'It is a lovely bonne I make to thee': Mary Carey's 'abortive Birth' as Recuperative Religious Lyric," in *Discovering and Recovering the Seventeenth-Century Religious Lyric*, ed. Jeff Johnson and Eugene Cunnar (Pittsburgh: Duquesne University Press, 2001, pp. 248–72), for a view of Carey's "empowerment" through "recuperative" metaphors of birth and rebirth.

37. Long, " 'It is a lovely bonne,' " makes a similar point about the "maternal history" contained within the poem's title and its later references to Carey's experiences of childbirth and child-loss. An interesting modern parallel to Carey's emphasis on ocular experience is found in the film *Alfie*, dir. Lewis Gilbert (Paramount Pictures, 1965), when the title character's sight of the fetus of his child, whose abortion he has just procured, prompts a moral conversion from irresponsible womanizer to angst-ridden subject.

38. Gertrude Thimelby, "Upon a Command to Write on my Father," in *Tixall Poetry*, ed. Arthur Clifford (Edinburgh: James Ballantyne and Co., 1813), p. 92. On the poem, see Donna J. Long, " 'She Endeavoured to Relieve Her Owne Emotions': Gertrude Thimelby's Elegies," unpublished paper presented at Shakespeare Association of America, Cleveland, March, 1998, and Hammons, p. 32.

39. Grace, Lady Mildmay, *Autobiography*, in Randall Martin, ed., *Women Writers of Renaissance England* (London and New York: Longman, 1997), p. 225.

40. Thomas Tuke, *A Discourse of Death* (London: William Stansbie for George Norton 1613), pp. 46–7. For a fascinating discussion of shifting theological notions of infants' innocence in the Reformation and laypeople's efforts "to expand the period in which children were seen as innocent" through their changing interpretations of the "chrisom child," see Will Coster, "Tokens of Innocence: Infant Baptism and Burial in Early Modern England," in *The Place of the Dead: Death and Remembrance in Late Medieval and Early Modern Europe*, ed. Bruce Gordon and Peter Marshall (Cambridge: Cambridge University Press, 2000), pp. 266–287. I see Carey's assertion of the innocence of her miscarried infant as an example of this effort. For a similar view, see Hammons, pp. 41–6.

41. Philip Stubbes, *A Chrystal Glasse for Christian Women* (London: Richard Jones, 1592) also presents a female speaker who condemns as cruel the notion that infants who die before baptism are damned (C1).

42. Helen Wilcox, "My Soule in Silence'? Devotional Representations of Renaissance Englishwomen," in *Representing Women in Renaissance England*, ed. Claude J. Summers and Ted-Larry Pebworth (Columbia: University of South Carolina Press, 1997), pp. 21–2.

43. Carey, "Wretten by me att the same tyme; on the death of my 4th, & only Child, Robert Payler," ll. 7–8.

44. Carey's "Wretten by me at the death of my 4th sonne and 5th Child Perigrene Payler" stages the same reciprocal relationship, again indicating the completeness of maternal sacrifice in its opening lines: "I thought my all was given before/but mercy ordred me one more" (ll. 1–2).

45. Thomas Goad, "Approbation," in Elizabeth Jocelin, *The Mothers Legacie to her Unborne Childe* (London: F.K for Robert Allot, 1635), A6v. On Jocelin's work and the other mother's legacies of the period, see Elaine V. Beilin, *Redeeming Eve: Women Writers of the English Renaissance* (Princeton, NJ: Princeton University Press, 1987), pp. 266–85, and Wayne.

46. Goad, A3.

47. Ibid, A4v.

48. Ibid.
49. Ibid, B1v.
50. Ibid, A9v.
51. Ibid, A9v-10.
52. Ibid, A9v.
53. For a valuable discussion of the prayer closet and its relationship to performances of subjectivity in the post-Reformation, see Richard Rambuss, *Closet Devotions* (Durham and London: Duke University Press, 1998), pp. 103–35.
54. Schenck, p. 23.

CHAPTER 14

1. Jahan Ramazani, *Poetry of Mourning* (Chicago: University of Chicago Press, 1994), pp. 1–31. All subsequent citations from and/or references to this work will be noted by in-text, parenthetical format.
2. W. Scott Howard, " 'The Brevities': Formal Mourning, Transgression & Postmodern American Elegies," in *The World in Time and Space*, ed. Edward Foster and Joseph Donahue (Jersey City: Talisman, 2002), pp. 122–46.
3. See respectively: Margaret Alexiou, *The Ritual Lament in Greek Tradition* (Cambridge: Cambridge University Press, 1974), p. 4–23; Sigmund Freud, "Mourning and Melancholia," trans. Joan Riviere, in *Collected Papers*, vol. 4 (London: Hogarth, 1934), pp. 152–70; and Melanie Klein, "Mourning and Its Relation to Manic-Depressive States," in *Love, Guilt and Reparation and Other Works, 1921–1945*, ed. Masud R. Khan (London: Hogarth, 1981), pp. 344–69.
4. Ben Jonson, "On My First Son," in *Ben Jonson: The Complete Poems*, ed. George Parfitt (London: Penguin, 1975), 48, l. 10. All subsequent citations from and/or references to Jonson's works will correspond with this edition, hereafter noted by in-text, parenthetical format respectively according to page and then line number(s).
5. Elizabeth Bishop, "One Art," in *Elizabeth Bishop: The Complete Poems, 1927–1979* (1979; reprint, New York: Farrar, Straus and Giroux, 1994), p. 178, l. 19. All subsequent citations from and/or references to Bishop's works will correspond with this edition, hereafter noted by in-text, parenthetical format according to line number(s).
6. I wish to thank my colleague, Ann Dobyns, for her insightful comments about the rhetoric of like "like" and there "there."
7. Anne Laurence, "Godly Grief," in *Death, Ritual, and Bereavement*, ed. Ralph Houlbrooke (London: Routledge, 1989), p. 75. All subsequent citations from and/or references to this work will be noted by in-text, parenthetical format.
8. "The Wanderer," trans. E. Talbot Donaldson, in *The Norton Anthology of English Literature*, ed. M. H. Abrams, 5th ed., vol. 1 (New York: Norton, 1986), p. 81.

9. *The Pearl*, trans. Sara deFord et al. (Northbrook: AHM, 1967), p. 83, ll. 987–88.

10. Martin Green, "Introduction," in *The Old English Elegies*, ed. Martin Green (Rutherford, NJ: Fairleigh Dickinson University Press, 1983), pp.16–17.

11. For studies in the English elegy, see especially: Peter Sacks, *The English Elegy* (Baltimore: Johns Hopkins University Press, 1985); and Dennis Kay, *Melodious Tears* (Oxford: Clarendon, 1990). For studies in the early modern "historical Renaissance," see: Donald R. Kelley and David Harris Sacks, eds., *The Historical Imagination in Early Modern Britain* (Cambridge: Cambridge University Press, 1997).

12. Here I employ Milton's taxonomy of the "three species of liberty" to outline the early modern subject's expanded private and public agency. See: "Pro Populo Anglicano Defensio Secunda," trans. George Burnett, in *John Milton: Selected Prose*, ed. C. A. Patrides (Columbia: University of Missouri Press, 1985), pp. 71–74.

13. Thomas Dekker, *The Wonderfull yeare* (London: 1603), p. 34.

14. John Graunt, *Natural and Political Observations made upon the Bills of Mortality*, ed. Walter F. Willcox (Baltimore: Johns Hopkins University Press, 1939), pp. 45–48. All subsequent citations from and/or references to this work will be noted by in-text, parenthetical format.

15. Thomas Hobbes, *Leviathan*, ed. C. B. Macpherson (1968; reprint, London: Penguin, 1985), p. 186.

16. Clare Gittings, *Death, Burial and the Individual in Early Modern England* (London: Croom Helm, 1984), p. 13. All subsequent citations from and/or references to this work will be noted by in-text, parenthetical format.

17. *Directory for Public Worship*, in *Religion and Society in Early Modern England*, ed. David Cressy and Lori Anne Ferrell (London: Routledge, 1996), p. 186.

18. Thomas Becon, *The Sicke mannes Salue*, in *Works of Thomas Becon*, ed. John Ayre, 4 vols. (Cambridge: Cambridge University Press, 1844), 4: 189–90. All subsequent citations from and/or references to Becon's works will correspond with this edition, hereafter noted by in-text, parenthetical format respectively according to volume and then page number(s).

19. G. W. Pigman III, *Grief and English Renaissance Elegy* (Cambridge: Cambridge University Press, 1985), p. 31. All subsequent citations from and/or references to this work will be noted by in-text, parenthetical format.

20. *The Compact Edition of the Oxford English Dictionary*, s. v. "grief."

21. *The Compact Edition of the Oxford English Dictionary*, s. v. "mourn"; "mourning."

22. Plato, *Republic*, X, pp. 603–8, trans. Paul Shorey, in *Plato: The Collected Dialogues*, ed. Edith Hamilton and Huntington Cairns (Princeton, NJ: Princeton University Press, 1961); Cicero, Marcus Tullius, *De amicitia*, X, ed. Charles E. Bennett (1897; reprint, Boston: B. H. Sanborn, 1910); and Desiderius Erasmus, *A treatise perswadynge a man patientlye to suffre the deth of his frende* (London, 1531).

23. John Jewel, *An Exposition vpon the two Epistles of the Apostle Sainct Paule to the Thessalonians* (London, 1583), p. 160.

24. Jeremy Taylor, *The Rule and Exercises of Holy Dying* (1651; reprint, London: William Pickering, 1847), p. 311.

25. David Cressy, *Birth, Marriage, and Death* (Oxford: Oxford University Press, 1997), p. 439.

26. Lawrence Stone, *The Family, Sex and Marriage in England 1500–1800* (New York: Harper & Row, 1977), p. 207; Philippe Aries, *The Hour of Our Death* (New York: Knopf, 1981), pp. 297–321; and Sara van den Berg, "The Passing of the Elizabethan Court," *The Ben Jonson Journal* 1 (1994): 31–61.

27. Ralph Houlbrooke, "Death, Church, and Family in England Between the Late Fifteenth and the Early Eighteenth Centuries," in *Death, Ritual, and Bereavement,* ed. Ralph Houlbrooke (London: Routledge, 1989), p. 36.

28. Juliana Schiesari, *The Gendering of Melancholia* (Ithaca, NY: Cornell University Press, 1992), p. 7.

29. Mary Prior, "Women and the Urban Economy," in *Women in English Society 1500–1800,* ed. Mary Prior (London: Methuen, 1985), pp. 93–117; Elaine Hobby, *Virtue of Necessity* (Ann Arbor: University of Michigan, 1989), pp. 1–25; Patricia Crawford, *Women and Religion in England 1500–1720* (London: Routledge, 1993), pp. 1–52; and Jacqueline Pearson, "Women Reading, Reading Women," *Women and Literature in Britain,* ed. Helen Wilcox (Cambridge: Cambridge University Press, 1996), pp. 80–99.

30. John W. Draper, *The Funeral Elegy and the Rise of English Romanticism* (1929; reprint, New York: Octagon, 1967), p. vii. All subsequent citations from and/or references to this work will be noted by in-text, parenthetical format.

31. Ralph Houlbrooke, "Introduction," in *Death, Ritual, and Bereavement,* ed. Ralph Houlbrooke (London: Routledge, 1989), p. 14.

32. Zacharie Boyd, *The Last Battell of the Soule in Death* (Edinburgh, 1628), p. 1237.

33. See: Stuart Sherman, *Telling Time* (Chicago: University of Chicago Press, 1996), pp. 1–28. Sherman's compelling thesis about chronometric innovation and the emergence of prose from 1660 to1785 exaggerates, I believe, the influence upon literary discourse of the invention of Christiaan Huygens' pendulum regulator. My goal here is to listen as closely as possible to the inherent rhythms within the elegy, which has always embodied a poetics of temporality apart from the time devised and measured by either modern clocks, sand glasses, or sun dials.

34. Katherine Philips, "On the death of my first and dearest childe, Hector Philipps," in *Kissing the Rod,* ed. Germaine Greer et al. (New York: Farrar Straus Giroux, 1989), pp. 196–97. All subsequent citations from and/or references to Philips' works will correspond with this edition, hereafter noted by in-text, parenthetical format according to line number(s).

35. Kate Lilley, "True state within: Women's elegy 1640–1740," in *Women, Writing, History 1640–1740,* ed. Isobel Grundy and Susan Wiseman (Athens: University of Georgia Press, 1992), p. 72.

36. Pearson, pp. 80–99.

37. See: W. Scott Howard, "An Collins & the Politics of Mourning," in *Speaking Grief in English Literary Culture*, ed. Margo Swiss and David Kent (Pittsburgh: Duquesne University Press, 2002), pp. 177–96.

38. John Milton, "On Time," in *Complete Shorter Poems*, ed. John Carey (London: Longman, 1971), p. 165, l. 6. All subsequent citations from and/or references to Milton's works will correspond with this edition, here-after noted by in-text, parenthetical format according to line number(s).

39. Don Wayne, *Penshurst: The Semiotics of Place and the Poetics of History* (Madison: University of Wisconsin Press, 1984), p. 32; Sara van den Berg, *The Action of Ben Jonson's Poetry* (Newark: University of Delaware Press, 1987), p. 59; and Robert C. Evans, *Habits of Mind* (Lewisburgh, PA: Bucknell University Press, 1995), p. 165.

40. Katharine Maus, *Ben Jonson and the Roman Frame of Mind* (Princeton, NJ: Princeton University Press, 1984), p. 36; Achsah Guibbory, *The Map of Time* (Urbana: University of Illinois Press, 1986), p. 106; and Joshua Scodel, *The English Poetic Epitaph* (Ithaca, NY: Cornell University Press, 1991), p. 39.

41. Clare Gittings, "Venetia's Death and Kenelm's Mourning," in *Death, Passion and Politics*, ed. Ann Sumner (London: Dulwich Picture Gallery, 1995), p. 66.

42. Herford and the Simpsons see imperfection and anachronism in these frag-mentary components to "Eupheme." My reading allows Jonson's elegy to stand "as is"—that is, in the form of the work's presentation to Sir Kenelm Digby in 1633. See C. H. Herford, Percy and Evelyn Simpson, eds., *Ben Jonson*, 11 vols. (Oxford: Clarendon, 1952), 11: 103.

43. Scodel, p. 16.

44. John Weever, *Ancient Funerall Monuments* (London, 1631), p. 10.

45. Scodel, p. 107.

AFTERWORD

1. All quotations are cited from the account of Blair Anthony Roberts of the Knight Ridder News Service, as published in the *Lexington Herald-Leader* (Monday, July 27, 1998), pp. B1 and B3.

2. Sigmund Freud, "Mourning and Melancholia," in *The Standard Edition of the Complete Works*, trans. James Strachey (London: Hogarth, 1955), 14: 245.

Contributors

Judith H. Anderson is Chancellor's professor of English at Indiana University. She is the author of *Words that Matter: Linguistic Perception in Renaissance English* (1996), *Biographical Truth: The Representation of Historical Persons in Tudor-Stuart Writing* (1984), and *The Growth of a Personal Voice: "Piers Plowman" and "The Faerie Queene"* (1976). She is co-editor of *Spenser's Life and the Subject of Biography* (1996) and *Piers Plowman: An Alliterative Verse Translation* (1990). She has also published numerous scholarly essays on Spenser, Shakespeare, and Donne. She is currently writing a book on metaphor, both linguistic and more broadly cultural, and co-editing a book on *Integrating Literature and Writing Instruction in First-Year English*.

Harry Berger, Jr. is professor emeritus of Literature and Art History at the University of California, Santa Cruz. He has published various books and articles on Spenser, Shakespeare, and Renaissance visual culture, including most recently *Making Trifles of Terrors: Redistributing Complicities in Shakespeare* (1997), *Fictions of the Pose: Rembrandt Against the Italian Renaissance* (2000), and *The Absence of Grace: Sprezzatura and Suspicion in Two Renaissance Courtesy Books* (2000). Other publications by him concern Plato and early modern painting.

M. C. Bodden is associate professor of English at Marquette University and has published articles on the evidence for the knowledge of Greek in Anglo-Saxon England, on violence in Chaucer's works, and on the eroticization of social and religious institutions, as well as literary constructs, in medieval culture. She has edited *The Old English Finding of the True Cross* (1987) and is completing a book entitled *Religious Language: Privileging Violence Toward Women*.

Donald Cheney is professor emeritus of English at the University of Massachusetts. He is author of *Spenser's Image of Nature: Wild Man and Shepherd in "The Faerie Queene"* (1967) and has published a number of scholarly essays on Spenser. He is co-editor and translator of *The Works of Elizabeth Jane Weston* (2000) and co-editor of *The Spenser Encyclopedia* (1990) and *Spenser's Life and the Subject of Biography* (1996).

Albrecht Classen is professor of German Studies at the University of Arizona and has published books and articles on medieval German and European literature. His recent monographs include studies on the German chapbook (1995), on late medieval German women's erotic love poetry (1999), and on the late medieval German songbook (2001). He has edited a number of collections, such as *Medieval German Voices in the 21st Century* (2000), *The Book and the Magic of Reading in the Middle Ages* (1998), and *Women as Protagonists and Poets in the German Middle Ages: Feminist Approaches to the Study of Middle High German Literature* (1991). He has been editor of *Tristania* since 1992 and co-editor of *Mediaevistik* since 1993.

Marshall Grossman is professor of English at the University of Maryland. He is author of *The Story of All Things: Writing the Self in Renaissance English Narrative Poetry* (1998) and *"Authors to Themselves": Milton and the Revelation of History* (1987), as well as numerous articles on Spenser, Shakespeare, Milton, Marvell, and literary theory, particularly psychoanalysis. He has also edited *Aemilia Lanyer: Gender, Genre and the Canon* (1998), and he is currently working on *The Seventeenth Century* volume in the Blackwell Guide to English Literature series.

W. Scott Howard is assistant professor of English at the University of Denver. He is currently completing a book, *Fantastic Surmise: Seventeenth-Century English Elegies, Elegiac Modes, and the Historical Imagination from Donne to Philips*, and has recently published essays on the politics of mourning, postmodern American elegies, landscapes of memorialization, and the poetics of history. He is also currently editing, with Sara van den Berg, *John Milton's Divorce Tracts*.

Patricia Clare Ingham is associate professor of English at Indiana University. She is author of *Sovereign Fantasies: Arthurian Romance and the Making of Britain* (2001) and co-editor with Michelle Warren of *Postcolonial Moves, Medieval through Modern* (2003). She has published articles on masculinities in medieval literature, and the implications of postcolonial analysis for medieval cultural studies.

Theresa M. Krier teaches at the University of Notre Dame. She is author of *Birth Passages: Maternity and Nostalgia, Antiquity to Shakespeare* (2001) and *Gazing on Secret Sights: Spenser, Classical Imitation, and the Decorums of Vision* (1990). She has edited *Refiguring Chaucer in the Renaissance* (1998) and has published a number of scholarly essays on Spenser, psychoanalysis, Shakespeare, Chaucer, and Ovid. She is currently editor of the *Spenser Review*.

Martha A. Kurtz has published articles on Shakespeare, Elizabethan history plays, and gender and is completing a book entitled *Laughter and Power in the Elizabethan History Play*. She organized and led the seminar "Laughter and Tears: Historicizing Emotion and Audience Response" at the Shakespeare Association of America 2000.

Allison M. Levy is assistant professor of Italian Renaissance Art History at Wheaton College in Massachusetts. She has published essays on early modern widows and portraiture and is editor of *Widowhood and Visual Culture in Early Modern Europe* (2003). She is currently completing a book entitled *Re-membering Masculinity: Widowed Bodies, Mourning, and Representation in Early Modern Italy*, which, drawing upon disability theory, offers a critical re-assessment of "Renaissance Man."

David Lee Miller is professor of English at the University of Kentucky. He is the author of *The Poem's Two Bodies: The Poetics of the 1590 "Faerie Queene"* (1988) and *Dreams of the Burning Child: Sacrificial Sons and the Father's Witness* (2003) on filial sacrifice and patriarchal masculinity. He has published essays on Spenser, Renaissance literature, and psychoanalysis and has edited *Approaches to Teaching Spenser's "Faerie Queene"* (1994), *The Production of English Renaissance Culture* (1994), and *After Strange Texts: The Role of Theory in the Study of Literature* (1985). He is one of four general editors for a new edition of Spenser in preparation for the Oxford English Text Series.

Patricia Phillippy is associate professor of English at Texas A&M University. She is author of *Women, Death and Literature in Post-Reformation England* (2002) and *Love's Remedies: Recantation and Renaissance Lyric Poetry* (1995). She has published various articles on early modern women writers, literature, and culture. Her most recent book, *Painting Women: Gender, Genre, and Subjectivity in Early Modern Europe*, is under contract at the Johns Hopkins University Press.

Anne Lake Prescott is professor of English at Barnard College. She is author of *Imagining Rabelais in Renaissance England* (1998) and *French Poets and the English Renaissance: Studies in Fame and Transformation* (1978). She has published numerous scholarly articles on the reception of French writers such as Marguerite de Navarre, Du Bellay, and Rabelais in England and on Spenser, Sidney, More, Shakespeare, and Donne. She is co-editor of *The Norton Edition of Edmund Spenser's Poetry* (1993), *Female and Male Voices* (2000), and *Approaches to Teaching Shorter Poetry of the Sixteenth Century* (2000). She is also co-editor of *Spenser Studies* and, with Betty Travitsky, series editor of texts by or about early modern Englishwomen for Ashgate Press.

Juliana Schiesari is professor of Comparative Literature, French and Italian at the University of California, Davis. She is author of *The Gendering of Melancholia: Feminism, Psychoanalysis and the Symbolics of Loss in Renaissance Literature* (1992). She has recently completed a new book *Beauties and Beasts: Pets, Desire and Bodies in the Renaissance and Afterwards*. She has also published essays on gender, psychoanalysis, and on animals and human culture. She is co-editor of *Refiguring Woman: Perspectives on Gender and the Italian Renaissance*.

Jennifer C. Vaught is assistant professor of English at the University of Louisiana at Lafayette. She has published articles on Spenser and Shakespeare and is currently completing a book about emotion and masculinity, entitled *Renaissance Men of Sensibility: Spenser, Shakespeare, and their Contemporaries*.

Bonnie Wheeler is associate professor of English at Southern Methodist University. She has published essays on the rhetorics of gender in the Middle Ages and on Malory and Chaucer. She is editor of a number of volumes, including *Becoming Male in the Middle Ages* with Jeffrey Jerome Cohen (1997), *Listening to Heloise: The Voice of a Twelfth-Century Woman* (2000), and *Eleanor of Aquitaine: Lord and Lady* (2003). She is the editor of the journal *Arthuriana*, Series Editor for *The New Middle Ages* (a book series on medieval cultural and gender studies from Palgrave Macmillan), and has published pedagogical essays on medieval studies.

INDEX

In this index scholarly works cited or mentioned briefly in the notes are not included, except in a few cases to facilitate bibliographical reference.